THE PHILC
ANIMAL

CW00740717

This volume is a collection of fourteen new essays by leading philosophers on issues concerning the nature, the existence, and our knowledge of animal minds. The nature of animal minds has been a topic of interest to philosophers since the origins of philosophy, and recent years have seen significant philosophical engagement with the subject. However, there is no volume that represents the current state of play in this important and growing field. The purpose of this volume is to highlight the state of the debate. The issues which are covered include whether and to what degree animals think in a language or in iconic structures, possess concepts, are conscious and self-aware, metacognize, attribute states of mind to others, and have emotions, as well as issues pertaining to our knowledge of mental states in animals and the scientific standards for attributing them.

ROBERT W. LURZ is Associate Professor in the Department of Philosophy, Brooklyn College of The City University of New York.

THE PHILOSOPHY OF
ANIMAL MINDS

EDITED BY
ROBERT W. LURZ

CAMBRIDGE
UNIVERSITY PRESS

CAMBRIDGE UNIVERSITY PRESS
Cambridge, New York, Melbourne, Madrid, Cape Town, Singapore, São Paulo, Delhi

Cambridge University Press
The Edinburgh Building, Cambridge CB2 8RU, UK

Published in the United States of America by Cambridge University Press, New York

www.cambridge.org
Information on this title: www.cambridge.org/9780521711814

First published 2009

Printed in the United Kingdom at the University Press, Cambridge

A catalogue record for this publication is available from the British Library

Library of Congress Cataloguing in Publication data
The Philosophy of animal minds / edited by Robert W. Lurz.
p.   cm.
Includes bibliographical references (p.   ) and index.
ISBN 978-0-521-88502-7 (hardback)
1. Animals (Philosophy)   2. Cognition in animals.   3. Philosophy of mind.
I. Lurz, Robert W., 1968–   II. Title.
B105.A55.P56   2009
113′.8 – dc22   2009014242

ISBN 978-0-521-88502-7 hardback
ISBN 978-0-521-71181-4 paperback

*For
Mary Jane, William and James
for their love and patience*

Contents

Contributors

COLIN ALLEN Professor of History and Philosophy of Science and Professor of Cognitive Science, Indiana University

JOSÉ LUIS BERMÚDEZ Professor of Philosophy, Washington University

ELISABETH CAMP Assistant Professor of Philosophy, University of Pennsylvania

PETER CARRUTHERS Professor of Philosophy, University of Maryland

DAVID DeGRAZIA Professor of Philosophy, George Washington University

SIMON FITZPATRICK Research Associate, AHRC Culture and the Mind Project, University of Sheffield

ROCCO J. GENNARO Professor of Philosophy, The University of Southern Indiana

GRANT GOODRICH Doctoral Student in the History and Philosophy of Science, Indiana University

DALE JAMIESON Professor of Environmental Studies and Philosophy Affiliated Professor of Law, New York University

ROBERT W. LURZ Associate Professor of Philosophy, Brooklyn College, City University of New York

ANDREW McANINCH Doctoral Student in Philosophy, Indiana University

JOËLLE PROUST Director of Research at CNRS, Institut Jean-Nicod

MICHAEL RESCORLA Assistant Professor of Philosophy, University of California, Santa Barbara

GEORGES REY Professor of Philosophy, University of Maryland

ROBERT C. ROBERTS Distinguished Professor of Ethics, Baylor University

ERIC SAIDEL Assistant Professor of Philosophy, George Washington University

ELLIOTT SOBER Hans Reichenbach Professor and William Vilas Research Professor, University of Wisconsin

MICHAEL TETZLAFF Visiting Instructor, University of Maryland

Acknowledgments

As with most projects, this one started out as a fairly rough idea that was eventually molded and shaped into a recognizable form by various people along the way. During its early stages, I was given invaluable advice about its direction and content by two anonymous referees, Colin Allen, Peter Carruthers, David Chalmers, Rocco Gennaro, and Uriah Kriegel. While in the thick of the editing process, I was helped immensely by the insightful comments and suggestions of Jonathan Adler, Daniel Campos, Emily Michael, Mathew Moore, and Saam Trivedi. The greatest help by far, however, was from the contributors, who met deadlines, actively communicated with each other and myself, effectively responded to (and graciously tolerated) my numerous questions and comments, and (despite all that) produced original work of the highest quality. I thank each and every one of you.

I wish also to thank Brooklyn College and my department for a much needed reduction in my teaching load during the spring semester. Finally, I wish to thank Gillian Dadd and Malcolm Todd for their helpful editorial guidance and, above all, Hilary Gaskin for her faith in and support for the volume from beginning to end.

The philosophy of animal minds: an introduction

Robert W. Lurz

I. INTRODUCTION

The minds of animals has been an abiding topic in philosophy since its earliest beginnings. Some may find this surprising. After all, a fairly common picture of the philosopher is someone (in a darkened study) ruminating on the nature of the human mind, or on the mind of God, or on some other abstruse idea, but certainly not on the minds of cats, dogs, and honeybees. As common as this picture may be, however, it does not paint an entirely accurate portrait. Philosophers have thought long and hard about the minds of animals and have held and defended significant and influential views on the topic. Moreover, in the past ten years or so there has been an unprecedented amount of interest among philosophers in animal minds, with numerous publications and conferences dedicated to the subject. The level of interest and publication has reached a critical mass and has sustained itself long enough that it is now appropriate to say that the *philosophy of animal minds* is a field in its own right. The purpose of this volume is to highlight the state of the art in the field by bringing together a collection of new and cutting-edge essays by the best and brightest philosophers.

Since the essays in this volume have been shaped by various lines in the rich history of philosophical thought on animal minds, I provide a brief (albeit, vastly incomplete) sketch of some of the most important and influential ideas and arguments in this history, as well as a road map to the volume itself.

2. HISTORICAL DEBATES

Historically the central issue in philosophy concerning animal minds was whether animals possessed thought and reason. Aristotle famously defined

Portions of this introduction are from Lurz (2008). I wish to thank the editors of the *Internet Encyclopedia of Philosophy* for their kind permission to reproduce the material here. I also wish to thank Peter Carruthers for his helpful comments on an earlier draft of this introduction.

I

human beings as rational animals thereby denying thought and reason to non-human animals (see *Nicomachean Ethics*, book 1, chap. 7 and *De Anima*, book 3, chap. 10).[1] His chief reason for doing so was his belief that animals, due largely to their failure to speak, were incapable of grasping genuinely abstract concepts and general propositions. For centuries afterward, Aristotle's denial of thought and reason to animals provoked numerous debates among philosophers. Some, such as Chrysippus, Augustine, Aquinas, Leibniz, and Kant largely argued in favor of the Aristotelian position, while others, such as Theophrastus, Porphyry, Galen, Gassendi, and Locke, largely argued against it.[2] The debate reached its fullest expression in the seventeenth and eighteenth centuries in the figures of René Descartes and David Hume.

Descartes went to the extreme of the Aristotelian position and notoriously denied all types of mentality – reason, thought, *and* consciousness – to animals. Animals, for Descartes, were nothing more than sophisticated biological machines. Descartes gave two general arguments in support of his "beast-machine" doctrine (1637/1988, chap. 5). The first rested upon his observation that animals appear incapable of transferring their skills in one domain (e.g., migration) to any other domain (e.g., locating new habitats). This failure to transfer or generalize, Descartes argued, proved that the intelligent-like behaviors of animals were due not to reason – that is, "a universal instrument which can be used in all kinds of situations" – but to naturally endowed instincts and reflexes.[3] Descartes's second reason rested upon the claim that animals lack speech. Like Aristotle, Descartes denied speech to animals, pointing to the fact that they never "use words or put together other signs, as we do in order to declare our thoughts to others."[4] The absence of speech, Descartes reasoned, could only be explained in terms of animals lacking what speech

---

[1] Aristotle acknowledged that animals possessed sensory perception, desires, memory, imagination, and even emotions. According to Sorabji (1993), Aristotle was able to ascribe emotions to animals, despite their lacking thought, by taking emotion in animals to be a kind of perception. See Roberts (chapter 12) for a recent perception-based account of emotions in animals.

[2] See Sorabji (1993) for an excellent account of the early history of the philosophical debate over animal thought and reason.

[3] It is consistent with the Cartesian position to allow various types of learning in animals (e.g., imprinting, song learning, associative learning, etc.) so long as they do not involve thought or consciousness. The fact that some kinds of associative learning have been demonstrated in the spinal chords of rats without brains strongly suggests that such forms of learning exist in animals (see Grau [2002]).

[4] Descartes was aware that animals produce various vocalizations but argued (much in the Aristotelian tradition) that their function was merely to express "passions," not thought. See McAninch, Goodrich, and Allen (chapter 7) for the latest on the modern debate over expressive versus referential theories of animal calls.

expressed – *thought*. From this, he went on to conclude that animals also lacked all forms of consciousness, since, for Descartes, thought was taken (in the unusually wide sense) as the very object of conscious awareness – it was, as he writes in the *Principles*, "everything which we are aware of as happening within us, in so far as we have awareness of it" (1644/1988, p. 162).

The chief problem for Descartes's position has always been to explain animal behavior without attributing mentality. As noted above, Descartes attempted to do this by appealing to mechanical reflexes and instincts in animals. But it seemed to a number of his contemporaries (as well as to a number of philosophers and scientists today) that this cannot be done for certain types of animal behaviors. As Arnauld famously replied to Descartes,

It seems incredible that it can come about, without the assistance of any soul [i.e., without any conscious awareness], that the light reflected from the body of a wolf onto the eyes of a sheep should move the minute fibers of the optic nerves, and that on reaching the brain this motion should spread the animal spirits throughout the nerves in the manner necessary to precipitate the sheep's flight. (Quoted in Descartes [1641/1984], p. 144.)

However, as we shall see later in this introduction and in a number of the essays in this volume, it is anything but obvious what (if any) types of behaviors in animals require an explanation in terms of thought, reason, or consciousness.

Equally as famous as Descartes's denial of mentality to animals was David Hume's (1739/1978) proclamation that "no truth appears to me more evident, than that beasts are endow'd with thought and reason as well as men" (p. 176). The type of thought that Hume had in mind here was belief, which he defined as a "lively idea" or "image" caused by (or associated with) a prior sensory experience (p. 94). Hume defined "reason" as a mere disposition or instinct to form associations among such ideas on the basis of past experience. He argued by analogy that since animals behave in ways that closely resemble the behaviors of human beings, which we know introspectively to be accompanied by the association of ideas, it is likely that animals too behave as a result of forming similar associations among ideas in their minds. This argument, Hume claimed, not only described the type of thought process that ordinary persons go through in ascribing thought and reason to animals, it provided an "incontestable" proof that animals possess thought and reason in the same manner as human beings. The only difference between the thought and reasoning of animals and humans, Hume held, was a matter of degree.[5]

There are two well-known problems with Hume's theory. First, although it may be true, as Hume held, that belief and reasoning in animals are constituted by lively images and their associations, many types of beliefs and reasoning in humans are not. We can, for example, form beliefs about all sorts of abstract matters (e.g., about numbers, complex relations, non-Euclidean spaces) of which it is impossible to form an image, as well as engage in many forms of non-associative reasoning. It is difficult, therefore, to understand how human belief and reasoning could be, as Hume held, just a difference in degree from animal belief and reasoning. The other problem with Hume's theory is that his analogical argument appears to lead to an objectionable form of anthropomorphism. After all, toy robotic dogs, computers, radios, heat-seeking missiles, and even animated circles and squares on a computer screen behave in ways that (at times) strike us as resembling the ways that we behave when we have associated ideas presented to our consciousness. But few would take such resemblances alone as incontestable proof that these objects too act as a result of associated ideas presented to their consciousness.

3. QUESTIONS AND APPROACHES IN THE PHILOSOPHY OF ANIMAL MINDS

From this very brief historical sketch, two distinct types of questions and approaches emerge which, as we shall see, carry through to the contemporary debates on animal minds and are used (in part) to organize the essays in this volume. Philosophical questions concerning animal minds generally come in two (non-exclusive) types: *metaphysical* and *epistemological*. Metaphysical questions are questions about what kinds of minds animals possess or could possess consistent with the facts about their behaviors, brains, environments, and histories. As we have seen, the focal metaphysical question in the history of the field has been whether animals could think and reason given that they cannot speak. Epistemological questions, on the other hand, are questions about our knowledge and understanding of animal minds. Such questions can be either normative or descriptive

---

[5] Hume went on to argue on similar analogical grounds that animals possess various types of emotions, such as pride, humility, love, and hatred (1739/1978, book II, part 1, sect. 12 and part 2, sect. 12). See Roberts (chapter 12) for an importantly different account of the existence and limits of emotions in animals.

in import. They can be about what *justifies* our attributions of mentality to animals, for example, or about how we *in fact* go about attributing mentality to animals – although the answers may be the same for both, as was seen in the case of Hume's analogical argument.

When considering these types of questions, philosophers tend to take a *top-down approach* (as exemplified by Aristotle and Descartes) or a *bottom-up approach* (as exemplified by Hume), or some combination of both. The top-down approach begins with reflection upon mentality in humans, with special emphasis on how such mentality is expressed and described in language. The approach takes the human mind as the paradigm and judges animals more likely to have minds the closer they approximate this paradigm. The bottom-up approach, on the other hand, begins with taking our intuitively plausible (or, in some versions, our scientifically informed) ascriptions of mentality to animals at face value and proceeds with designing a theory of animal minds, such as Hume's theory of ideas, that aims to explain the truth of such ascriptions.

Each of these approaches has its potential problems and distinctive virtues. What is yet to be seen is whether one of them, or some combination of both, can yield an account that can satisfactorily answer the various metaphysical and epistemological questions that define the field. With this in mind, let us turn to the contemporary philosophical debates over animal minds.

4. THE CONTEMPORARY DEBATE OVER ANIMAL THOUGHT AND REASON

There are three main types of arguments in contemporary philosophy for animal thought and reason: *the argument from intentional systems theory* (Dennett [1987]), *the argument from common-sense functionalism* (Carruthers [2004]; Fodor [1987]; Stich [1979]), and *the argument from science* (Allen and Bekoff [1997]; Bermúdez [2003a]).

The intentional systems theory consists of two general ideas. The first is that our ordinary mental-state concepts, such as our concepts *belief, desire,* and *perceiving,* are theoretical concepts whose identity and existence are determined by a common-sense theory or *folk psychology.* In many cases, we apply our folk psychology to animals to predict and make sense of their behaviors, and when we do, we view animals as *intentional systems* and take up what Dennett calls the *intentional stance* toward them. The second important idea of the intentional systems theory is its *instrumentalist* interpretation of folk psychology. On the instrumentalist interpretation, what it is for a creature to have mental states is simply for its behaviors to be richly and voluminously predicted by the principles of our folk psychology. Therefore, according to the intentional systems theory, the fact that much of animal behavior is successfully predicted from the intentional stance *makes* animals genuine thinkers and reasoners. The chief objection to this argument, similar to the one raised against Hume's analogical argument, is that is seems to lead to an objectionable form of anthropomorphism. One can, after all, effectively predict the behaviors of heat-seeking missiles and even the class of thermostats by taking up the intentional stance toward them.[6]

Common-sense functionalism, on the other hand, avoids this problem by taking a *realist* and *functionalist* interpretation of folk psychology. On this interpretation, for a subject to have mental states is for the subject to have in his brain a variety of discrete internal states that play the causal/functional roles and have the internal structures that our mental-state concepts describe. On this view, if Fido (for example) believes that the cat is up the tree, then he has in his brain an individual state, s, that plays the causal/functional role that beliefs play according to our folk psychology and has an internal structure similar to the "that"-clause that we use to specify its content (i.e., s has the structure Rxy, where "R" represents the two-place relation *up*, "x" represents *the cat*, and "y" represents *the tree*). Since the internal state s is seen as having an internal structure similar to the sentence "the cat is up the tree," common-sense functionalism is often taken to support the view that thinking (including animal thinking) involves a language of thought (Fodor [1975]). It is argued that since animal behavior is often successfully predicted and explained by our folk psychology, we have defeasible grounds for supposing that animals actually have such internal states in their heads. It has been questioned, however, whether our everyday ascriptions of thought to animals really do presuppose the existence of sentence-like representations in their heads (Stalnaker [1999]) or whether there is any empirical evidence that shows that animals have and process such representations as opposed to iconic (non-sentential) representations.[7]

---

[6] Some (e.g., Searle [1994]) would take this to be a *reductio* of the intentional systems theory, but not Dan Dennett and John McCarthy: both claim that a "thermostat is one of the simplest, most rudimentary, least interesting systems that should be included in the class of believers" (Dennett [1995], p. 114).

[7] For the latest on the instrumentalism versus realism debate regarding mental-state attributions to animals, see Jamieson (chapter 1), Saidel (chapter 2), Tetzlaff and Rey (chapter 4), and Sober (chapter 13); and for the latest on the sentential versus iconic debate regarding mental representations in animals, see Rescorla (chapter 3), Tetzlaff and Rey (chapter 4), Carruthers (chapter 5), and Camp (chapter 6).

In the past thirty years or so, due in large measure to the demise of radical behaviorism and the birth of cognitivism in psychology, as well as from the influential writings of Donald Griffin (1976, 2001) and Randy Gallistel (1990), scientists from various fields have found it increasingly useful to propose, test, and ultimately accept hypotheses about the causes of animal behavior in explicitly folk-psychological terms. According to the argument from science, since scientists are finding it useful to test and accept hypotheses about animal behavior in folk-psychological terms, we are justified in believing that animals have such states of mind. Not everyone, however, has found the argument from science convincing. The chief concern is whether explanations of animal behavior in folk-psychological terms are, as the argument assumes, scientifically respectable (see Wynne [2004]; Kennedy [1992]). It is sometimes argued that many (if not all) such attributions of mentality to animals violate a basic methodological tenet of the science of animal behavior called Lloyd Morgan's canon:

In no case may we interpret an action as the outcome of the exercise of a higher psychical faculty, if it can be interpreted as the outcome of the exercise of one which stands lower in the psychological scale. (Morgan [1894], p. 53)

Since animal behavior can always be explained in psychological or behavioral terms that do not appeal to our folk-psychological concepts, any scientific explanation of animal behavior in terms of such concepts is extravagant and scientifically unwarranted. It is also argued that scientific explanations of animal behavior are objective in that there is typically general agreement among researchers on what counts in favor of or against the explanation, which implies that, since the only generally agreed-upon indicators of consciousness are the verbal reports of subjects, explanations of animal behavior in terms of consciousness are unscientific (see Clayton *et al.* [2006], p. 206).[8]

No contemporary philosopher is better known for his criticism of thought and reason in animals than Donald Davidson. In a series of articles (1984b, 1985, 1997), Davidson put forward three interrelated arguments for his denial of thought and reason in animals. The first, known as the *intensionality test*, argues that our *de dicto* belief ascriptions to animals – that is, our belief ascriptions that aim to describe *how* the animal is thinking about some object in the world – are unwarranted, since without linguistic

---

[8] For the latest on the debate over the justification of Lloyd Morgan's canon (and other principles of simplicity) used by scientists, see Sober (chapter 13) and Fitzpatrick (chapter 14); for the latest on the debate over the ascription of consciousness to animals, see Gennaro (chapter 10), DeGrazia (chapter 11), and Roberts (chapter 12).

behavior to appeal to, there are always countless different ways of saying how the animal is thinking and no principled method of deciding among them. Davidson's second argument, the *argument from holism*, claims that we are also unwarranted in our *de re* belief ascriptions to animals – that is, our belief ascriptions that aim to identify the objects in the world the animal is thinking about independently of *how* it is thinking about them – since there are always countless different categories of objects about which the animal might be thinking and the only way to decide among them is to know what general background beliefs the animal holds, which, Davidson claims, is impossible without the animal being able to speak. Finally, Davidson's main argument is that if animals really did have beliefs, then they should be subject to surprises on those occasions when their beliefs turn out to be false; but being so surprised, Davidson maintains, involves being aware that one's former belief failed to fit the facts and thus requires having an idea of a world of objective facts. Davidson goes on to claim that the only way for a creature to come to have an idea of a world of objective facts is by comparing its own beliefs with those of others, which it cannot do, according to the intensionality test and the argument from holism, if it cannot interpret the speech of others – as animals, Davidson maintains, plainly cannot. The upshot is that only creatures capable of understanding speech can have beliefs.

Detractors of Davidson's arguments have tended to take one of three approaches. Some, such as Bermúdez (2003b), have sought to develop a theory of how to make principled *de dicto* ascriptions to animals; others, following Armstrong (1973), have sought to defend our *de re* ascriptions to animals by rejecting Davidson's radical holism; and still others, such as Carruthers (2008) and Tye (1997), have sought to undermine Davidson's main argument by challenging its pivotal claim that surprise involves beliefs about beliefs.[9]

5. THE CONTEMPORARY DEBATE OVER ANIMAL CONSCIOUSNESS

Two general approaches to consciousness – the *higher-order representational (HOR) approach* and the *first-order representational (FOR) approach* – have played an important role in the philosophical debate over the status of animal consciousness. The dominant HOR approach has been the *higher-order thought (HOT) theory* of consciousness, according to which a mental

---

[9] See Jamieson (chapter 1) for a critical commentary on Davidson's arguments, as well as Lurz (2008) for a general list of such critical commentary.

state is conscious just in case the subject has (or is disposed to have) the higher-order thought that he is in such a mental state (Carruthers [2000]; Rosenthal [1986]).[10] The question of animal consciousness on this theory becomes the question of whether animals are capable of such higher-order thoughts.

A common argument against higher-order thoughts in animals is that the possession of such thoughts, in virtue of the mental-state concepts they contain, entails certain linguistic or mindreading capabilities that animals appear to lack. Bermúdez (2003a, and chapter 8, this vol.), for example, argues that since animals are incapable of speaking and interpreting a public language, they cannot possess concepts of propositional attitudes (e.g., beliefs and desires) and, therefore, cannot have higher-order thoughts about their own or others' thoughts. On different grounds, Carruthers (2000) has argued that if animals really do possess mental-state concepts, then they ought to be able to apply these concepts to other animals for the purpose of anticipating and manipulating their behaviors – that is, they ought to be able to engage in *mindreading*. Carruthers goes on to argue, however, there are no incontestable empirical cases of mindreading in animals and some studies appear to show that not even the chimpanzee – the animal most likely to engage in mindreading – is capable of it (see, for example, Penn and Povinelli [2007b]; Povinelli [1996]). Both of these arguments, however, have been challenged recently. Lurz (2007) has raised a series of objections to Bermúdez's argument against propositional attitude mindreading in animals, and Gennaro (chapter 10) and DeGrazia (chapter 11) argue that a number of recent studies of animal mindreading and metacognition strongly indicate that apes, monkeys, and dolphins are capable of higher-order thoughts about their own minds and the minds of other animals.

In contrast to HOT theories of consciousness, FOR theories hold that mental states are conscious *not* because the subject is higher-order aware of having them but because the states themselves make the subject aware of the external environment (Dretske [1995]; Tye [1997]). Mental states that make subjects aware of the environment do so, according to FOR theories, in virtue of their having (or being poised to have) an effect on the subjects' belief-forming system. FOR theorists argue that many varieties of animals, from fish to bees to chimpanzees, form beliefs about their environment based upon their perceptional states and bodily sensations and, therefore, enjoy conscious perceptual states and bodily sensations.

---

[10] The alternative HOR approach is the *higher-order perception* (HOP) *theory* of consciousness, defended by Lycan (1996) and Armstrong (1997). See Lurz (2008) for a description of the HOP theory and its place in the philosophical debate over animal consciousness.

FOR theories are at their best, it has been argued, when explaining the consciousness of perceptual states and bodily sensations but have difficulty explaining the consciousness of beliefs and desires (Lurz [2004]). Some FOR theorists have responded by endorsing a HOT theory for conscious belief and desire and a FOR theory for perceptual and sensory states (see Tye [1997]; Dretske [2000], p. 188). However, such a hybrid view would appear to belie the FOR theory's claim to parsimony and antecedent plausibility regarding ascriptions of consciousness to many lower animals. For it seems rather reasonable to suppose that a perceptual state or bodily sensation would count as conscious only if it has an effect (or is poised to have an effect) on the subject's *conscious* belief-forming system.[11] But if that is so, then a creature will have conscious states on this hybrid view only if it is capable of forming higher-order thoughts about its own beliefs. Not only would such a view require higher-order thought for consciousness, as HOT theories do, it would be more demanding than HOT theories by requiring animals capable of conscious perceptual states and bodily sensations to have higher-order thoughts about their own *beliefs*. What appears to be needed here in order to save FOR theories from this problem is a non-higher-order account of conscious belief (see Lurz [2006] for a sketch of such an account).

6. THE ROADMAP TO THE VOLUME

The essays in this volume are organized around topics as well as whether their focus is metaphysical or epistemological. The first two essays by Jamieson (chapter 1) and Saidel (chapter 2) are on epistemic questions concerning our ascriptions of thought (e.g., belief and desire) to animals. Jamieson proposes to resolve a tension that he identifies as existing between the belief that animals think and the belief that what they think cannot be characterized. After rejecting various eliminativist and realist approaches, Jamieson concludes that interpretivism – the view, roughly, that whether and what animals think is deeply connected to whether we find it useful to attribute thoughts to them – offers the best resolution. Saidel, on the other hand, puts forward a realist argument for beliefs and desires in animals based on evolutionary and empirical considerations. He argues that since human beings satisfy the behavioral criterion for belief-desire attribution

---

[11] If scientists were to discover, for example, that the perceptual states involved in subliminal perception or blindsight actually caused subjects to form *unconscious* beliefs about their environment, none but the most committed FOR theorist would conclude from *this alone* that subliminal perception and blindsight were, after all, just cases of conscious perceptual awareness.

(i.e., goal-directed behavior), it is likely that many animals with which we share a close evolutionary past do too; he argues further that there are a number of scientific observations of goal-directed behaviors in monkeys, chimpanzees, and bonobos that are justifiably explained in terms of beliefs and desires.

The next three essays are on the topic of the representational basis of animal thinking and reasoning (particularly about environmental matters). The question – which has both metaphysical and epistemic dimensions – is whether animals think and reason by means of sentence-like representations in a language of thought or by means of iconic representations, such as cognitive maps. Rescorla (chapter 3) argues that even the most deductive-like reasoning in animals – such as the syllogistic reasoning famously depicted in the tale of Chrysippus' dog – can be sufficiently explained without recourse to sentential representations. Rescorla illustrates the viability of this position by providing an explanation of the behavior of Chrysippus' dog, as well as similar deductive-like behaviors in chimpanzees, in terms of Bayesian probability calculations over cognitive maps. Tetzlaff and Rey (chapter 4), on the other hand, argue that the mental representations of honeybees that underlie their navigational and communicational abilities are systematic and, therefore, are best understood as sentential representations in a language of thought. Carruthers (chapter 5) goes further and argues that not only do honeybees and invertebrates in general have compositionally structured mental representations, but their mental representations in some cases constitute genuine thoughts and concepts. Carruthers defends this position against the generality constraint on concept possession, showing that on its most plausible interpretation, the mental representations of invertebrates conform to it.

The next two essays by Camp (chapter 6) and McAninch, Goodrich, and Allen (chapter 7) continue the discussion on the representational and conceptual abilities of animals by examining some recent empirical data and theoretical arguments on the cognitive and emotive natures of vocal communication in monkeys. Camp examines a recent argument by Cheney and Seyfarth (2007) that the vocal communicative behaviors of baboons indicate that these monkeys think in a language of thought. Camp disagrees and argues that the communicative behavior of baboons can be explained in terms of their thinking in mental maps, diagrams, and other iconic representations. She argues further that one plausible difference between the baboon's representational system and a genuinely linguistic one is that in baboons, the syntactic structures by which representational constituents are composed themselves still have a dedicated semantic function, whereas in a recognizably linguistic system, the compositional relation is sufficiently abstract or general to permit the composition of a wide range of distinct representational constituents. McAninch, Goodrich, and Allen re-examine a longstanding debate in cognitive ethology over whether animal communicative vocalizations are merely expressive or referential. The authors advance the debate by arguing that a neo-expressivist theory of avowals and ethical claims, in which an utterance is understood to have both expressive and referential functions, offers a new and better account of the data on the cognitive and emotive elements of animal calls.

The next two essays, by José Luis Bermúdez (chapter 8) and Joëlle Proust (chapter 9), continue the debate over the representational basis of animal thought and thinking; however, their focus is on the question of what kinds of representational structures are necessary for thinking and reasoning about *mental states*, and whether animals are capable of thinking in such structures. Bermúdez draws an important distinction between *minimal mindreading* (i.e., the capacity to coordinate one's behavior with another subject's mental states) and two types of substantive mindreading – *perceptual mindreading* (i.e., the capacity to think and reason about the perceptual states of others) and *propositional attitude mindreading* (i.e., the capacity to think and reason about the propositional attitudes of others). He argues that since the latter type of mindreading requires the deployment of representational vehicles that are both propositional and accessible to consciousness, and arguably possible only through the possession of a public language, animals are incapable of propositional attitude mindreading – although they are capable of minimal mindreading and perceptual mindreading. Proust agrees with Bermúdez's conclusion that animals are incapable of mindreading (or metarepresenting) their own and others' propositional attitudes, but argues that they are, nevertheless, able to engage in *metacognition* (i.e., the ability to control and monitor one's own cognition). After reviewing some of the recent studies on metacognition in animals, Proust shows that the data can be plausibly accommodated by a non-propositional, feature-based representational format.

The next three essays, by Gennaro (chapter 10), DeGrazia (chapter 11), and Roberts (chapter 12), examine various questions pertaining to the existence and the nature of consciousness, self-awareness, and emotions in animals, as well as questions pertaining to our epistemic grounds for ascribing such states to animals. Gennaro defends the existence of consciousness in animals according to the higher-order thought (HOT) theory of consciousness. He argues that a number of recent studies in metacognition, episodic memory, and mindreading in animals persuasively show that many animals possess the kinds of higher-order thoughts required for consciousness according to the HOT theory. DeGrazia draws a useful distinction between different levels of self-awareness and argues that the cumulative force of various empirical findings on intentional behavior, episodic memory, imitation, mirror self-recognition, mindreading, and metacognition in animals shows that bodily self-awareness is quite widespread in the animal kingdom, and that social self-awareness and (even) introspective self-awareness are likely present in various higher species (e.g., monkeys, apes, and cetaceans). Roberts examines the existence and limits of animal emotions through the lens of his concern-based construal theory of emotion. According to this theory, emotions are a kind of perception that do not require thought and, therefore, are likely possessed by a wide range of animals. However, Roberts argues that emotions differ in sophistication according to a number of important dimensions, and that the level of sophistication of emotion in animals, as measured by these dimensions, is importantly lower compared with that of human beings.

The last two essays, by Sober (chapter 13) and Fitzpatrick (chapter 14), return the volume to a set of epistemological concerns – in this case, regarding the scientific knowledge and practice of investigating animal minds. As noted in section 4 above, appeals to Lloyd Morgan's canon (or the principle of conservatism or simplicity) are often used by scientists to justify or refute a particular hypothesis about animal behavior and cognition, and yet the content and justification of the principle has long been recognized as obscure. Sober uses model selection theory in statistics to clarify the content of the principle and provide it with a rational (albeit instrumental) basis, which he argues is consistent with a realist interpretation of beliefs and desire in animals. He goes on to show how, on model selection theory, a higher-order intentional model of animal behavior (as in Hare *et al.*'s [2000] experiment on chimpanzees) may turn out to be more parsimonious (and thereby more justified) than the competing lower-order intentional model of the behavior. Fitzpatrick examines the use of the principle of simplicity in the recent debate over mindreading versus behavior-reading in chimpanzees and argues that the principle's use in the debate is best understood on a deflationary model, according to which a simpler theory is justified over a complex one, not on grounds of simplicity per se, but on the various background theoretical considerations in play. Fitzpatrick goes on to show that, on the deflationary model, the simplicity arguments (by Tomasello and Call [2006]) that have been advanced in favor of the mindreading hypothesis and against the behavior-reading hypothesis (by

Povinelli and Vonk [2006]) are justified and suggest exciting new avenues of future empirical research.

The essays in this volume represent the current state of play in the field at its highest level. For this reason, I believe, the volume will be of value to both philosopher and scientific researcher alike. In addition, I am hopeful that the essays, by virtue of raising new and exciting ideas and reinvigorating important old debates, will come to serve as a welcome invitation and a useful springboard for future philosophical reflections on the nature, the existence, and our knowledge of animal minds.

CHAPTER I

What do animals think?

Dale Jamieson

I. INTRODUCTION

You may have noticed that the title of this essay is ambiguous. Asking what animals think could be part of an inquiry into animal public opinion, focusing perhaps on such questions as what apes think about the Endangered Species Act or whether frogs prefer Tom Waits to Leonard Cohen. Or if you read the right punctuation into the title you might see it as an exclamation of surprise: "What! Do animals think?" What I am actually concerned with in this essay is how we should think about specifying exactly what it is that a particular animal thinks on a particular occasion. Some would say that I am concerned with the problem of content as it applies to non-human animals.

The first response to the question of what animals think may be to say that they think thoughts. This is harmless, so long as we do not succumb to the temptation of reading psychology or ontology directly off of the language. However, it is downright harmful if, after assimilating thinking to having a thought, we go on to suppose that having a thought is the same as having a propositional attitude. At the outset, anyway, I want to leave open a wide range of possibilities including whether animal thinking implies having propositional attitudes; and if it does, the meaning, status, and nature of these propositional attitudes. For these reasons, unless I say otherwise, I will use expressions such as "thinking" and "having a thought" in neutral, common-sense ways, and I will take believing and desiring as examples of thinking, and beliefs and desires as examples of thoughts.

Why should we be interested in what animals think? I am interested in this question because of how it relates to other questions. In earlier work I have argued that a plausible theory of value is one which distinguishes

Thanks to Beatrice Longuenesse for her comments on an earlier draft, and especially Robert Lurz for his probing questions, not all of which I have been able to answer.

things of primary value from things of derivative value.[1] This is not a distinction in the degree or extent of value, but in the source of value. What is of primary value are those creatures who we take to be animate and sentient, and this includes many non-human as well as human animals.[2] We owe moral duties to such creatures, but exactly which moral duties depends on the creature's interests, and this in turn is associated with the character of the creature's psychological life. In order to know what our duties to animals are, it is not enough to know that they think, we must also know something about what they think.

An additional reason for being interested in what animals think is because it is unsatisfying to be told that we have good reasons for supposing that animals think even though we know very little about what they think. This is a little like being told that Sean is beautiful by someone who has never seen Sean. In both cases the claim could be both true and justified. There may be inductive reasons for the claim, a highly credible authority may testify that the claims are true, or the claims may follow from a well-confirmed scientific theory. Nevertheless in the normal case we expect there to be an association between the general or abstract claim, and more specific claims that bear on it directly. When this is not the case it is somewhat disconcerting.[3]

For both of these reasons my question is important. Many of the considerations I adduce are not new, but they have not often been systematically brought to bear on the question that I am asking. Moreover, I believe that some of the most important lessons of the philosophy of mind of the second half of the last century have faded, and that there is some point in being reminded of them. As we shall see, answering my question turns out to be surprisingly difficult, and may lead us to question some conventional views about what we are doing when we attribute thoughts to human as well as non-human animals.

Before beginning in earnest, I want to clarify the language that I will be using and confess to some simplifications. I will sometimes use "humans and animals" to mark the same distinction as that between human and non-human animals. I will also assume, unless I note otherwise, that humans are language-users and non-humans are not.

---

[1] Jamieson (2002), Essay 14.
[2] There are of course important questions here about the role of justification and correctness in these "takings," some of which I discuss in Jamieson (2002), Essay 4.
[3] While there are analogies between these two cases there are also disanalogies. It is natural to suppose that Sean's beauty supervenes on properties that are in principle observable, while the claim that animals think is a generalization from particular instances of animal thinking.

2. THE PROBLEM

The fundamental problem we face is that most people are committed to the following pair of propositions:

(1) Many animals think.
(2) Exactly what animals think on particular occasions cannot reliably be characterized.

There are many reasons that figure in the widespread endorsement of (1). For many or most cases, when it comes to anticipating, explaining, and modifying their behavior, supposing that animals think works about as well as supposing that humans think (it seems equally natural to attribute to Grete the dog and Riki the infant the desire to play – perhaps with each other). Many animals behave in ways that are similar to humans, and there is also remarkable physiological and neurological similarity and continuity between us and at least many of them. It would be surprising, perhaps even the biological equivalent of the Immaculate Conception, if we were nature's only minded creatures. A further consideration comes from evolutionary theory. Some influential accounts of the evolution of mind appeal to the sorts of environmental and social problems that our ancestors would have faced relating to the pressures of group living and the need to engage in cooperative hunting and foraging.[4] Since the ancestors of many other animals faced similar problems in similar environments, it is plausible to suppose that the same evolutionary forces that selected minded human ancestors selected minded ancestors of other closely related animals as well. Finally, attributing mental states to animals is generally part of an outlook that recognizes them as morally significant. While most people are not animal rights activists, they do think it matters morally how animals are treated, and a commitment to (1) coheres with this commitment. While these considerations may or may not, singly or together, with or without further commitments, constitute a full justification for (1), they are certainly important in explaining why the commitment to (1) is so ubiquitous.[5]

The ground of our belief in (2) is less obvious, but it is brought out clearly in the following passage from Stich (1983/1989).

Suppose . . . that Fido is in hot pursuit of a squirrel . . . A moment later we see Fido craning his neck and barking excitedly at the foot of an oak tree . . . To

[4] I have in mind the work of Alison Jolly and Nicholas Humphrey. Their early papers are reprinted in Byrne and Whiten (1988).
[5] In Jamieson (2002, Essay 4), I express skepticism about whether our commitment to the view that some animals are minded requires justification at all.

explain Fido's behavior, it would be perfectly natural to say he believes that the squirrel is up in the oak tree. But suppose now that some skeptic challenges our claim by focusing our attention on the differences separating Fido's belief from ours. "Does Fido really believe it is a squirrel up in the oak tree? Are there not indefinitely many logically possible creatures which are not squirrels but which Fido would treat indistinguishably from the way he treats real squirrels? Indeed, does he believe . . . that the thing in the tree is an *animal*? Would it not be quite the same to Fido if he had been chasing some bit of squirrel-shaped and squirrel-smelling machinery . . . ? The concept of animal is tied to the distinction between living and nonliving, as well as to the distinction between animals and plants. But Fido has little grasp of these distinctions. How can you say that he believes it is a squirrel if he doesn't even know that squirrels are animals?" (pp. 104–105)

It is these sorts of considerations that lead to our endorsement of (2).[6] If we lose confidence in supposing that Fido believes that the squirrel is up in the oak tree, then there are going to be many cases in which we should lose confidence in supposing that we can reliably characterize what an animal thinks. What is true in this case generalizes to other cases.

It is of course logically consistent to hold both (1) and (2), but for reasons that I have already discussed it is uncomfortable to do so. For it is natural to wonder why you would hold (1) if you hold (2). Suppose, for example, that I go on about how Grete is a highly sophisticated thinker, but when you ask what it is that she thinks, I reply that I haven't the faintest idea. It is certainly reasonable for you, in light of my response, to wonder why I have such confidence in Grete's cognitive powers. The problem that we face is not to evade some supposed inconsistency between (1) and (2), but rather to resolve the unease that arises from the conjunction of our confident commitment to the view that animals think and our apparent ignorance about what it is that they think.

3. SOME RESPONSES

In this section I discuss in turn four families of responses to our problem: eliminativism, wet eliminativism, the brute content view, and interpretivism. While none of these views can be rejected out of hand, I explain why I am most attracted to some version of interpretivism.

---

[6] Davidson (1985) adduces similar considerations. However, we should be cautious in over-generalizing. If we were to follow Geach, Kripke, and Ziff in supposing that proper names are purely referential devices, then these considerations would not count against Fido having such beliefs as *this is Paula*, when in the presence of his guardian.

3.1. Eliminativism (reject (1))

Eliminativism, which rejects the claim that animals think, comes in more or less sophisticated versions. The most sophisticated version is Davidson's; the least sophisticated version is the verificationism with which his view is sometimes confused.[7] We'll begin with verificationism.

The verificationist argument asserts that the truth of (2) is grounds for giving up (1). Roughly, if we cannot know what animals think, then we cannot know that they think. The argument can be reconstructed as a *reductio ad absurdum* in the following way.

(i) Many animals think.

(ii) Thinking entails thinking something in particular.

(iii) Exactly what animals think cannot reliably be characterized.

(iv) We cannot verify the truth of (i).

(v) We should only believe what we can verify.

(vi) We should not believe (i).

(i) is the claim that is under consideration. (ii) might be regarded as analytic. (iii) is supported by the sort of considerations adduced by Stich and quoted in section 2. (iv) might be thought to follow from (iii), based on some such principle as "no verification without reliable specification." (v) is the statement of the verification principle, and (vi) draws the conclusion from (iv) and (v).

It should be clear that this argument is only as good as the verification principle and the principle that licenses the inference from (iii) to (iv). These principles are implausible because they prove too much: they imply that we should not believe some truths which we surely should believe.

Consider, for example, the following case, which appears to be analogous to (1) and (2):

(3) Black holes exist.

(4) Exactly what black holes are like cannot reliably be characterized.

(4) may well be true, but this does not seem to require us to give up (3). We may believe that black holes exist because we know something about the causal roles that they play (e.g., that their gravitational force affects neighboring bodies), even if we can say little about them in other respects.

---

[7] For Davidson's view see his (1984a), Essay 11; (1985); and (2005), Essays 1 and 9. In the text I discuss a weak version of verificationism, which holds that we should only believe what we can verify, rather than a strong version such as the one espoused by the logical positivists, which holds (roughly) that what cannot be verified is meaningless. I discuss the weak version because it is more likely to be thought plausible.

It may be replied that knowing the causal roles that black holes play constitutes reliably characterizing them, but this is not plausible. I may know that it was Kelly who broke up my marriage, but if I know nothing else about Kelly (even Kelly's gender), then surely I have not reliably characterized Kelly when I say that Kelley is the person (?) who broke up my marriage, even though I certainly know that Kelly exists.[8]

But suppose that we were to agree that in specifying Kelly's causal role (at least with respect to my marriage) I have reliably characterized Kelly, and thus Kelly's existence has been verified. If we were to say this, then it seems just as plausible to say that animal thinking is also verified since it seems plausible to say that on particular occasions we know the causal role of what an animal thinks in producing the animal's behavior (think, for example, of Fido). If knowing something's causal role is sufficient for reliably characterizing it, then we can reliably characterize what an animal thinks on many particular occasions, and thus, on this view, we are entitled to say that animals think.

Whichever way we go on the question of whether knowing something's causal role is sufficient for reliably characterizing the thing in question has unwelcome consequences for the eliminativist. For the eliminativist claims that (2) (with some further assumptions) is sufficient for rejecting (1), but my arguments show that either (2) fails to be sufficient for rejecting (1), or many other important beliefs will have to be rejected as well.

There is of course more to say. For example, an eliminativist could attempt to sever the analogy between (3) and (4), and (1) and (2), perhaps because the logic of the sentences is not analogous or because thoughts are not like physical objects. However, given that verificationism is generally down on its luck, I will put these possible rejoinders aside and move on to other views that might be thought to be more plausible.

Davidson's version of eliminativism is more sophisticated. While his arguments can be reconstructed in a number of different ways, this gets to the heart of what he is asserting:

(i) In order to think, a creature must have a full range of propositional attitudes.

(ii) Having a full range of propositional attitudes rests on having language.

---

[8] Some may reject the analogy between Kelly and black holes because Kelly is an individual and black holes are kinds. While I don't believe that this dissimilarity matters in this case, I think the same sort of intuitions that I am attempting to mobilize here arise with respect to other examples which involve kinds (e.g., I doubt that we would say that we can reliably characterize a kind of artifact about which we only know that it is a kind and that it triggered an explosion in human cultural evolution).

(iii) Animals do not have language.

(iv) Therefore, animals do not have a full range of propositional attitudes.

(v) Therefore animals do not think.

The intuitive core of Davidson's argument is that ascribing a single belief to something requires ascribing "endless" further beliefs to it (as we saw in the Fido case), and having "endless" further beliefs requires such a sophisticated ability to make discriminations that only language is complex enough to do the trick.

Premise (i), which expresses Davidson's commitment to holism, is controversial, but I will not challenge it here. Instead I will focus on premise (ii).

On the face of it, (ii) is not very plausible. It does not seem difficult to imagine languageless creatures who have propositional attitudes. Nevertheless, Davidson argues that this is wrong. Languageless creatures do not have propositional attitudes because (a) language is required for a belief to have content and identity; and (b) one must be able to have beliefs about beliefs in order to have any beliefs at all, and having beliefs about beliefs requires language.

There are at least two reasons why the first argument (a) for supposing that (ii) is correct seems implausible. First, while it may be plausible to suppose that having a representational system is necessary for a belief to have content and identity, it is not obvious that the representational system must constitute a language. Davidson has arguments that are supposed to show that only a language has the associative and expressive power required for having propositional attitudes, but again these are controversial. Moreover, even if it is true that propositional attitudes require a representational system with the associative and expressive power of a language, why must this be a language that is deployed publicly and interactively rather than occurring simply as a language of thought?[9] It would be consistent with this view to suppose that many animals have languages of thought that play a role in determining the content of their thinking, but that these thoughts are not expressed publicly in language. Finally, and more controversially, even if we suppose that language is required for an organism to have propositional attitudes, why must it be the organism rather than the organism's interpreter who is the language-user? On this view (related to the interpretivism that I will discuss in section 3.4), propositional attitudes can be thought of as co-creations between the organisms

---

[9] This is basically Fodor's view in (1975), though he also rejects most of Davidson's other arguments as well. This view will be discussed further in section 3.3.

to whom they are attributed and the language-users who attribute them.

Davidson's second argument (b) for supposing that having propositional attitudes rests on having a language is also implausible. This argument supposes that one must be able to have beliefs about beliefs in order to have any beliefs at all, and that having beliefs about beliefs requires language.

Davidson's idea is that if I believe that P, then I would be surprised to discover that not P. If I am surprised to discover that not P, then I come to believe that my original belief was false. This involves having the second-order belief that my first-order belief was false, which involves having the concept of belief.

One can question almost every claim and step in the argument. On the face of it, it seems implausible to suppose that having a first-order belief requires having a second-order belief, and that having such a second-order belief is required for surprise. Animals often behave in ways that are described both by ordinary people and scientists as surprised, and this doesn't seem to require second-order beliefs.[10] It is easy to imagine Grete expressing surprise that the bone which she previously buried in some particular place is not there when she returns to dig it up. She expresses her surprise through barking, running in circles, general agitation, looking up at her guardian, and so forth. While it seems plausible to say in such a case that Grete is surprised that her bone is not there, this attribution does not seem to make essential reference to Grete forming a second-order belief that her first-order belief about the location of the bone was false. Attributing surprise to Grete in this case seems to make reference only to her behavior, expectations, and state of the world.

Even if we supposed that first-order beliefs do require second-order beliefs, it would seem that some animals satisfy this criterion. Although I cannot pursue this point here, it has been persuasively argued that deception, play, and self-recognition (attributed to various apes, monkeys, canids, and cetaceans) all involve second-order beliefs.[11]

In order for Davidson's view to be convincing, it must be shown that several options that on their face seem plausible are not really options at all. Most of us would want to distinguish the following: Grete having a belief that we don't know how to interpret, Grete having a belief about bones that is different from our belief about bones, and Grete and us sharing a belief

---

[10] See, e.g., Tinkelpaugh (1928).
[11] See, e.g., Allen and Bekoff (1997), Tomasello *et al.* (2003), and Whiten and Byrne (1997).

about bones. However, if Davidson is right, these distinctions collapse: they are not viable, at least as ordinarily understood.[12]

Eliminativism is a view that is implausible on the face of it, and embracing it requires accepting implausible philosophical doctrines such as verificationism, or arguments that are very difficult to defend. It is not surprising that, except for some hold-outs, eliminativism has been in retreat since the seventeenth century.

3.2. Wet Eliminativism (weaken (1))

A second approach is to embrace a weaker form of eliminativism. Rather than rejecting (1) outright, this view accepts (1) in some weaker form while rejecting it in another stronger form. As Stich concludes in an earlier article (1979, p. 28): "Do animals have beliefs? To paraphrase my young son: 'A little bit they do. And a little bit they don't.'"

The idea here is that something belief-like goes on with many animals and that is why we find it natural to say that they have beliefs: they behave in a goal-directed way, they discriminate between various stimuli, and so on. But the fact that these apparent beliefs cannot be reliably characterized indicates that they are not beliefs in the same sense in which humans have beliefs. Hence animals "a little bit" have beliefs and "a little bit" do not, and animal thinking is "a little bit" eliminated and "a little bit" not.

Wet eliminativism seems ambiguous between two general views. On one of these views, having a belief comes in degrees. Humans and other animals both have beliefs, but humans have beliefs to a greater extent than other animals. On the second general view it is only humans that have beliefs. Animals have states that are similar to beliefs in some respects, but they are not beliefs at all.

The first of these two general views of wet eliminativism is itself ambiguous between two readings: is it the *having* of beliefs that comes in degrees, or is it the *beliefs* that are matters of degree? The first of these readings borders on the unintelligible. Suppose that we are untroubled about saying that both Grete and I believe that Paula is at the door. It would then be strange to suppose that while Grete and I have a belief in common, I have it to a greater extent than she does. Of course, I may hold the belief more strongly than Grete does (or vice versa); there is no mystery about degrees

---

[12] The discussion of Davidson reprises and revises some material in Bekoff and Jamieson (1991). Indeed, many of the core ideas of this essay were first mooted there and in Jamieson (2002, Essay 6).

of belief in this sense.[13] We may even assign a metric (perhaps related to the probability calculus) and say that my degree of belief is .9 while Grete's is .8. However, it doesn't follow from our having different degrees of belief in this sense that our *having* of the belief we have comes in degrees. On the second reading of this view it is the belief (rather than the having) that comes in degrees. On this reading both Grete and I have the belief that Paula is at the door in the same sense, but my belief is more of a belief than Grete's belief. While it may seem plausible to suppose that Grete's belief that Paula is at the door is in some ways different from my belief that Paula is at the door, it is not easy to see how such differences would be mapped onto a scale such that my belief is more of a belief than Grete's belief. In any case it seems strange to say that while Grete and I share a belief, my belief is more of a belief than her belief.

The second general view that a wet eliminativist may hold is that although animals do not have beliefs, they have states that are similar to beliefs in some respects. While this view may be plausible it cries out for development. The challenge is first to identify the respects in which animal states are similar to human beliefs, and then show why these are not sufficient for classifying the animal states as beliefs. Since this goes against the widely shared intuition that humans and animals have beliefs in the same sense (if not exactly the same beliefs), the wet eliminativist has a serious burden of proof to discharge in this case.

There is a third general view that a wet eliminativist could hold. On this view animals have states that are similar to the states that we have when we have beliefs, but whether or not a state counts as beliefs on a particular occasion depends on how similar it is to a belief state that we would be in on such an occasion. So, for example, it is true that Grete believes that Paula is at the door on a particular occasion on condition that Grete is in a state sufficiently similar to the state that I am in when I too believe that Paula is at the door. This view moves away from eliminativism by sometimes embracing (1), and on those occasions generally rejecting (2).

An obvious problem for this view is to provide a well-motivated account of what makes an animal state sufficiently similar to a human belief state on a particular occasion to count it as a belief. One response is to say that similarity on an occasion is determined by context. For example, if we're interested in explaining Grete's behavior, then we might say that our states are similar enough on this occasion for it to be true that Grete believes that Paula is at the door. If on the other hand the context is one in which we are interrogating Grete's entire "worldview," then on this occasion the

---

[13] See Jeffrey (1985).

similarities would not be sufficient for it to be true to say that Grete has this belief (or presumably, any beliefs at all).

Something has gone badly wrong. Context may be powerful enough to affect how to specify a belief correctly (as we will see in section 3.4), but it is not powerful enough to transform a non-belief state into a belief, or a non-believer into a believer (and presumably back again). Either Grete's state is a belief or it is not and either she is a believer or she is not, whatever wooly (or non-wooly) questions I may be asking. What has gone wrong is supposing that attributing beliefs to animals is really a disguised way of comparing their states to ours. It is not. Suppose that we weren't around, either because we had never evolved, or because we had decided to take a permanent vacation from the planet. What, then, would we say about Grete's states?[14] Whether an organism has beliefs depends on the organism and its environment, not on the relations between its states and ours.

In this discussion of wet eliminativism, I have followed Stich in focusing on belief as an instance of thought. To some extent our intuitions are affected if we focus on thinking rather than thought, and on specific forms of thinking rather than thinking in general. For example, it may seem more plausible to suppose that thinking comes in degrees rather than that specific forms of thinking (such as believing or desiring) come in degrees. Humans think to a greater extent than animals, it might be supposed, because humans engage in more types of thought (including higher-order thought) than other animals. However, even if this is plausible it would not imply that with respect to a particular form of thinking that is shared by humans and other animals (e.g., believing or desiring) humans have this form of thinking to a greater extent than other animals, much less that it would be the only form of thinking worthy of the name. Thus, this view is consistent with the full-throated endorsement of (1). Nor would this view, even if true, help to explain why (2) seems false with respect to humans but true with respect to animals. However intuitive wet eliminativism may appear, it seems to do little to resolve the tension between (1) and (2).

3.3. The brute content view (weaken (2))

The brute content view resolves the tension between (1) and (2) by weakening (2), and claiming that in principle if not in practice we can reliably characterize what animals think on particular occasions. On this view there

---

[14] Of course, answers can be given, and philosophers being what they are, counterfactuals loom. When the question of whether a Springer Spaniel believes that Paula is at the door is supposed to turn on heavy-duty metaphysics, you know that something has really gone badly wrong.

is some fact of the matter about exactly what animals think on particular occasions, though empirical circumstances or general difficulties about knowledge of other minds may stand in the way of our knowing exactly what it is. Such considerations may help to explain why many people find (2) plausible. However, despite difficulties that may arise in practice, in principle we can reliably characterize what animals think.

One version of the brute content view is the brain-writing view.[15] On this view there is a "language of thought" or some other system of mental representation encoded in the nervous systems of all those creatures (human and non-human) who have thoughts.[16] There are different theories about how nervous systems encode representations and about the exact structure of the system of mental representation that the nervous system instantiates. What these views share is the idea that an animal's brain is (metaphorically speaking) a text. If we cannot on a particular occasion reliably characterize what an animal thinks it is only because we cannot (yet) read the text. The information is there, in the animal's brain, and in principle can be reliably characterized.

A second version of the brute content view is one that I shall call Fregean.[17] Like the brain-writing view this view holds that there is some fact of the matter about what an animal is thinking on a particular occasion that can, in principle, be reliably characterized. Unlike the brain-writing view, which holds that what an animal thinks can in principle be read off from the animal's brain, the Fregean view holds that what an animal thinks can only be approached through the animal's mind. While both views could be materialist in their ultimate ontologies, their proximate ontologies are different, as are their views about how we can come to know what an organism is thinking.

Returning to Stich's example of Fido helps us to see what these views have in common, how they are different, and how they attempt to resolve the tension between (1) and (2). When we last checked in, Stich was puzzled about what exactly Fido believed when, after chasing a squirrel up an oak tree, he sat at the foot of the tree barking. After posing some apparently unanswerable questions, Stich's puzzlement turned to skepticism about whether there was any fact of the matter about what exactly Fido believed. The mistake enters, according to the brute content view, when puzzlement

---

[15] This term is drawn from Dennett (1975). I am greatly indebted to his discussion there and elsewhere.

[16] The term "language of thought," as well as the brain-writing view itself, was brought to prominence by Fodor (1975).

[17] This may be an unhappy name for this view. I call it thus because it can be seen as a version of a view in which sense determines reference.

turns to skepticism. There is some fact of the matter about what Fido believes, even if Stich on this occasion does not know what it is. On the brain-writing view, the belief is constituted by mental representations in Fido's brain that in principle could be read off if we were smart enough to do so and had the proper equipment. According to the Fregean view, our ignorance may be more immediately intractable (new, shinier equipment will not help), but nevertheless there is some fact of the matter about what Fido believes that is present in Fido's mind, which we can discover in much the same way in which we discover what is present in the minds of humans. Since introspection is the epistemological gold standard for such views, in practice it may be difficult for us to know what Fido is thinking, but in practice it may also be difficult for us to know what our boss is thinking on a particular occasion. However, in principle in both cases the contents of thought can be reliably characterized, using roughly the same means. Thus the relation between (1) and (2) seems to be basically the same in both humans and other animals.[18]

There are several reasons why people find brute content views plausible. First, standard realist views in most domains hold that there can be a robust distinction between what is the case and what we are currently in a position to know. And whatever discomfort there may be between holding (1) and (2), if we have good general reasons for supposing that animals think, then the fact that in practice our access may be poor on particular occasions is no reason to give up our belief that they think, especially if we have reason to think that in principle their thought can be reliably characterized. Second, many people seem to accept a particular model of our knowledge of other minds that may help to explain the residual differences between our knowledge of other human minds as opposed to our knowledge of animal minds. On this model people tell us what they think, while we infer the thoughts of animals and other languageless creatures. The fact that we can make these inferences about animals is grounds for weakening (2), even though we are better at grasping the content of human minds than we are with animal minds.[19] Finally, in our own case we have a strong intuition that part of what it is for us to be minded is that we can determine the

---

[18] Of course, the striking difference between humans and other animals that may be thought to bear on our knowledge of what they are thinking is that humans are language-users and other animals are not. Different brute-content theorists attach different degrees of importance and kinds of significance to this difference. I discuss this further in the next paragraph and in section 3.4. See also Jamieson (2002), Essay 4.

[19] Animals discriminate among stimuli, and it is plausible to suppose that this provides a basis for at least some rough and ready content attribution. For work in this tradition, see Allen and Bekoff (1997) and other papers by Colin Allen.

contents of our own thoughts at least on some occasions, and it seems plausible to many people that if we can do this maybe Fido can do it too.

Consider an example. Suppose that I tell you that I am thinking of a number between 1 and 20 and I ask you to guess what the number is. You don't reject the question out of hand on the grounds that I can't actually perform the task of thinking of such a number. We both think that I can determine the content of my thought in such a way that I can think of a number and you can be right or wrong when you guess which number it is. In this case there seems to be some brute content about what I am thinking. Either I am thinking of, say, 15 or I am not. If this is true for me about numbers, why can't Fido's thinking about a bone be like this as well? Of course, Fido does not think *what a yummy bone!* in English (or Latin for that matter), but the intuition here is that there is something that Fido is thinking, and insofar as he is a good phenomenologist he knows what it is while we are only guessing.

It is difficult to argue against this view definitively for several reasons. First, it would require proving a negative existential (i.e., that this sort of thinking is not going on in Fido's mind) and this is notoriously difficult to do. Second, this view is an expression of deep-seated Cartesian intuitions that, for whatever reason, never seem to go away. Finally, it is just plain difficult to deny that the sort of thinking described in the "choose a number" game actually goes on. But this apparent fact raises as many questions as it answers. How characteristic is this form of thinking? What is its relationship to other forms of thought? Are there other explanations (or descriptions) available for what is going on in this game? In what follows I will present some reasons for supposing that the brute content view is implausible, at least in comparison to the view that I will sketch in the next section, but I admit that nothing I say forces one to come down on one side of the question or the other. But then, that is hardly unusual in philosophical argument.

There are various technical problems in formulating brute content views, but for many people the greatest obstacle to accepting them concerns the way in which they construe knowledge of our own minds and the minds of others. On the brain-writing version, the best way in principle to find out what someone is thinking is to look at the state of their nervous system. On the Fregean view, the best way in principle to find out what someone is thinking is to have access to what they introspect. On both views behavior provides, at best, derivative information that may support inferences regarding the representational state that the person is tokening or the mental state that the person is in. But this is hard to accept.

Imagine that someone is in the presence of a dog. The person is grimacing, recoiling, and trembling. His blood pressure, respiration, and pulse are all elevated.[20] It is difficult to imagine that we would give up our claim that the person was afraid of the dog simply on the basis of his denial, or even for that matter on the basis of a brain scan that proposed to show that what was inscribed in the person's brain was that he liked the dog and wanted to pet her. In this case the relation between the behavior and the mental state seems as least as intimate as the relation between the mental state and the first-person report, or the mental state and the brain scan. What this brings out is how Cartesian both versions of the brute content view are in placing thought in the mind or in the brain. Indeed, on the Fregean view, the mind has many of the usual Cartesian properties (such as transparency). It is thus not surprising that such views have difficulty in acknowledging that our actual attributions of mental states are responsive to a wide range of considerations.

There are some broader philosophical concerns that one may have with brute content views. Such views seem to rely on some idea of intrinsic representation, which is far from easy to characterize and make plausible.[21] Presumably such representations are either irreducible or somehow derive from non-representational sources. While there is lively philosophical discussion about these alternatives, it is worth pointing out that our characteristic experiences are of representational systems such as language in which rather than being intrinsic, representations are interpreter-relative (e.g., rather than being intrinsic the meaning of "chair" is relative to interpreters: thus English-speakers normally use it to refer to chairs and French-speakers to flesh).[22] Indeed, in our discussion of fear in the previous paragraph we were getting close to discussing the broader question of whether content attribution is interpreter-relative. While I cannot hope to settle the issue here, these remarks may set the stage for discussing what we might call an interpretivist approach to our question.

3.4. *Interpretivism (reject (2))*

Interpretivism begins from a view about why we are interested in knowing what a human or animal is thinking on a particular occasion. The

---

[20] Not all of these responses may count as behaviors, but what they have in common is that they are not the sort of data that the brute content view takes as bearing directly (as opposed to inferentially) on being in a particular psychological state.

[21] For some skepticism about such views see Dennett (1990) and Clark (2005).

[22] The same is also true (of course) with sounds. Thus the sound associated with "dude" in English is normally used to refer to dudes by English-speakers and milk by Nepali-speakers. I owe these examples to Raquelle Stiefler and Anne Rademacher.

interpretivist's answer, in varying degrees of complexity and sophistication, is that we're interested in making others intelligible and in living with them productively. If this is what we're up to, then all sorts of things will bear on our attributions: background knowledge, appreciation of context, specific information about the human or animal, familiarity with his or her way of life, and general knowledge about the relation between mental states and behavior. On this view attributions may be true or false, but the truth-makers will be connected to some idea of success. In short, content attributions are one way among others of making ourselves and others intelligible; they aren't just about corresponding to what's in the mind or brain, they have important pragmatic dimensions as well.

The core of interpretivism is the idea that there is a deep connection between what an organism thinks and what thoughts an interpreter would attribute to the organism. This characterization is both vague and rough, and there are many complications that I will put aside here, including these: What is the nature of the "deep connection"? Is it only organisms that can think? What are the relevant characteristics of the interpreter? What are the standards of correctness that apply to the interpreter's attributions?

Three features of interpretivism are especially important for our purposes. The first is the contrast between interpretivism and the brute content view. Rather than content being written in the brain or dancing before the mind's eye, it is the product of an interaction between an organism and an interpreter. Second, while much of our thinking about the mind privileges the first-person point of view, interpretivism privileges other points of view. It is from the second- or third-person perspective that we answer questions about what an animal is thinking on a particular occasion.[23] Finally, interpretivism resolves the tension between (1) and (2) in a way that is so simple that it will strike some people as a cheat. Since our reliably characterizing what an animal thinks on an occasion is "deeply connected" with supposing that it is minded, accepting (1) implies rejecting (2) (on at least most plausible interpretations).

It is worth distinguishing two different strands of interpretivism, although I will not go into detail about them.[24] Dennett's interpretivism is an expression of empiricist skepticism about "inner" entities such as content and qualia. He admits to beginning with a "tactical" choice, declaring his "starting point to be the objective, materialistic, third-person world

---

[23] I have been helped here by discussions with Mihailis Diamantis.

[24] See Byrne (1998) and Child (1994) for good discussions of interpretivism (though, unfortunately, they do not agree on the name of the view, much less on how best to characterize it). For the views of the godfather of interpretivism, see Quine (1960).

of the physical sciences." He doesn't claim to refute those who take the first-person perspective as the starting point, simply saying that "we beg the question against each other." Nevertheless Dennett does not think his choice is arbitrary: "we can see more and better if we start here."[25] Davidson on the other hand is a transcendental philosopher. He sees some sort of a priori connection between the content of a thinker's thoughts and an interpreter's attributions. His interpreter is not Dennett's happy-go-lucky guy in thrall to science, but rather what Davidson calls a "fully informed" interpreter.[26] While Dennett's interpreter is scientific and in principle willing to give up folk psychology at the end of neuroscience, Davidson thinks there are embedded norms and anomalies in our understandings of ourselves and others that are resistant to scientific reduction.

Here, my interest in interpretivism is in how it resolves the tension between (1) and (2) rather than in the details of any particular account. For an interpretivist, the question of whether an animal thinks is deeply connected to the question of whether we can attribute thoughts to the animal on particular occasions. An interpretivist thinks we can. The question is how.

Ideally, we would know all of the discriminations an animal would make on all possible stimuli. We would also know whether variances in response were due to discriminations on stimuli, or changes in state through time or circumstance. Of course, we could never know all of this and even if we did, there would still be indeterminacy about what particular state to attribute to the animal. For example, Grete's behavior of walking to the door can variously be explained by mutually adjusting beliefs and desires. If we fix a desire, for example that Grete wants to urinate, then we can specify a belief (e.g., that on the other side of the door is a place in which it is appropriate for her to urinate) that will make the behavior intelligible. But if we fix a different desire (for example that Grete wants to play with Jethro), then we will have to adjust Grete's beliefs accordingly in order to explain the behavior. This story about the interactions between contents and attitudes ramifies. While not anything goes, attributions answer to various pragmatic concerns, including those involving other attributions, and not only to what is known about the organism's body, behavior, and

---

[25] Dennett (1987), pp. 5–6.

[26] Davidson (1983/1986), p. 325. It may seem surprising to enlist Davidson on the side of those who endorse (1), especially in light of the discussion of his eliminativist views in section 3.1. Philosophers often have inconsistent strands in their thought, or fail to follow where their ideas lead. I agree with Jeffrey (1985) that Davidson fails to draw the correct conclusions about animal thought from his interpretivist view. For further discussion, see also Jamieson (2002), Essay 6.

the world. The indeterminacy is regimented on the basis of our purposes, interests, and other attributions, but it will not all go away. We can never wring out all the indeterminacies in explanation and attribution. Other attributions would be possible, and there would remain questions that we would not be able to answer. A crucial experiment about what Grete wants or believes would never eliminate all competing explanations. A decisive moment is, to some extent, in the mind of the beholder. In short, attributions are not uniquely determined.

We can see what this comes to by returning to Stich's Fido. Does Fido believe that the squirrel is up in the oak tree? Sure. That's a good enough answer for most purposes. Of course, more questions can be asked, and in some cases answers can be given but in others they cannot. Attributions can be more or less finely honed and precisely shaped, but for most purposes the answer that I gave at the outset (and Stich came to doubt) is good enough.

This may not satisfy everyone, but I think we should just get used to it. I don't think there is much difference in asking this question about Fido and asking it about a person who has chased the squirrel up the oak tree. Does this person believe that the squirrel is up in the oak tree? Sure. Why wouldn't he? There are many questions that we could ask about this person's beliefs and the answers would be different depending on whether he is a Druid, a creationist, an arbologist, or just an ordinary guy who likes to chase squirrels (?!). There will also be questions without answers. But this may take us back to language. You might say the difference between the man and Fido is that we can ask the man whether he believes that the squirrel is up in the oak tree and he can tell us. Assuming he is not linguistically or audiologically impaired, yes he can tell us. Of course, the man may, like Fido, just look at us quizzically when we ask the question. Or he may instead utter some words. Whatever he does, whether it involves words or not, is just more behavior requiring further interpretation, subject to the same sorts of indeterminacies I have already discussed.

What many may find most disturbing about interpretivism is that the first-person point of view seems to drop out. Have we left behind the idea that there is something that it is like to be Fido? What can an interpretivist say about the "choose a number" game?

The first-person point of view need not fall away. We interpret ourselves as well as others. What was I thinking when I agreed to go to Manitoba in February? Do I really care about Sean as much as it seems? Why do I always find myself behaving this way around Kelly? What may fall away is the sort of first-person privilege that some philosophers seem to think we have. It may be replaced by a view in which we see ourselves as corrigible, self-interpreting creatures who sometimes know the minds of others better than we know our own, and sometimes are known better by others than we know ourselves. We may come to see ourselves as relentless story-tellers, constructing and reconstructing narratives in a constant attempt to make sense of ourselves and others, in a world in which our lives are thoroughly enmeshed with the material and social realities that govern our existence.

Whatever is true about Fido, he is not a relentless story-teller, constantly engaged in the project of trying to make sense of himself. What, if anything, follows from this? Less than one might think. Perhaps, Fido's first-person privilege is even thinner than yours or mine (should he or anyone else care). What certainly would not follow is that there is nothing that it is like to be Fido, or that Fido lacks a tendency towards coherence in action and belief. Indeed, a rich literature in animal behavior shows how many creatures revise their behavior in light of experience and novel circumstances.[27]

But what can an interpretivist say about the really hard case, the "choose a number" game? There are two ways an interpretivist might approach what is going on here.

One way would be to weaken interpretivism and allow that there are some thoughts that are not subject to the interpretivist account as I have developed it. The trick, on this approach, is to quarantine these thoughts; try to show that rather than being central cases of thinking, they are in fact derivative: nothing more than some aimless spinning on the part of creatures who for a few moments have some respite from the struggle for survival and have nothing better to do. It would not be surprising, after all, if some kinds of thoughts are endemic to particular creatures. Perhaps creatures with language can have thoughts that languageless creatures cannot, just as creatures with sonar may be able to have thoughts that creatures without sonar cannot. The "choose a number" game is closed to rats and infants just as the NBA is off-limits to those under six foot six. However, this should not lead us to think that some special importance attaches to either. Just as we may play the "choose a number" game when we have nothing better to do (or when we are doing philosophy), so humpback whales may privately entertain the songs that they might like to sing. What would be a mistake is to take these peculiarities as central to thinking, or even perhaps as central to the thinking of the creatures who have them. On this view some idea of a "subjective" perspective may persist, but the idea that it has much freedom in fixing content or is at all paradigmatic of

---

[27] For references, and a defense of this claim, see Hurley (2003).

thinking may fade. We may come to see endemic phenomenology as rare and indeterminate, at least with respect to a wide range of attributions.

The second approach is perhaps more elegant but even less plausible. This approach imagines a time in which the first-person point of view has disappeared. People continue to self-report, but they no longer see such information as substantially different in kind from other reports about the world. Once our intuitions about the "choose a number" game are exposed to the clarifying solvent of advanced neuroscience and philosophy, they begin to cloud, and then disappear.

Interpretivism in any version is not a view that is immediately plausible to everyone.[28] However, it is a way of resolving the tension between (1) and (2), and there is a case for it being more plausible than the other alternatives that we have canvassed. In the end, philosophical consistency always does seem to exact a price.

4. CONCLUDING REMARKS: CONTENT REVISITED

In this essay I have identified a tension in our thinking about animal minds and reviewed some ways of trying to resolve it. If we are tempted by interpretivism, or find none of the approaches plausible, then perhaps we should rethink, not just the problem with which we began, but the very way in which we have come to portray the mind in philosophical discourse.

For the most part I have avoided the word "content" in this essay, yet in the philosopher's sense of the term it is the problem of content that I have been addressing. But what exactly is the problem of content? What is content anyway? The idea of content is a metaphor that infuses the way in which philosophers think about mind and language. Like all metaphors, it drags along its own presuppositions and associations like uninvited houseguests. In my opinion, we have not done enough to subject this metaphor to scrutiny, and, as it might be said, the unexamined metaphor is not worth deploying. One thing we can say for sure is that whatever mental content is like, it is not like the contents of a can of tomatoes. So with that remark I end – along with the advice that if you don't like any of the answers to my question that are on offer, perhaps you should find some new metaphors.[29]

---

[28] Though I do think that it comports well with at least some emerging scientific views of the mind – see, e.g., Edelman and Tononi (2001).

[29] The only person I know who has written about the metaphorical nature of the problem of content is Eric Schwitzgebel. His observations are available on the web at http://www.faculty.ucr.edu/~eschwitz/SchwitzPapers/Containers010228.pdf.

CHAPTER 2

Attributing mental representations to animals
Eric Saidel

I. INTRODUCTION

We quite naturally attribute mental representations in order to explain
actions. The cat is scratching at the door because he wants to come in the
house and believes that scratching at the door will get him into the house.
The dog is following me because she wants some of my food and believes
that by following me she can get some of my food. Some of our attributions
of mental representations are without doubt fanciful (does my car really
not like to start on cold mornings?), but some of these attributions are
accurate. For example, some, if perhaps not all, of the actions of adult
human beings are properly explained by their desires and their beliefs
about how to achieve those desires. What about the behavior of (non-
human) animals? Are belief-desire explanations the right explanations of
their actions? I argue that some (non-human) animal behavior is properly so
explained, and thus that some animals truly have beliefs and desires. There
are two strands of evidence which separately support this conclusion. First,
behavior that is appropriately explained in terms of mental states such as
beliefs and desires is behavior directed at a goal relative to which the agent
is able to *learn*; and since human behavior meets this criterion, I argue,
we should expect, on evolutionary grounds, that some animal behavior
meets this criterion as well. Second, I show that a number of different
scientific observations of animal behavior strongly support the hypothesis
that animals engage in goal-directed behavior, behavior that is organized
around a goal with respect to which they are able to learn and, hence,
behavior that is justifiably explained in terms of their having beliefs and
desires.

A version of this essay was presented to the faculty of the philosophy department at George Washington
University. I am indebted to them, especially to David DeGrazia and Tad Zawidzki, for their helpful
comments. I am also indebted to Robert Lurz for his detailed comments on a draft of this essay.

2. THE IMPLICATIONS OF CAUSAL REALISM

When an organism behaves in a way that is caused and structured by its goals, we naturally say of the organism that it *wants* to achieve such and such a goal and that it *believes* that the way it is behaving will enable it to achieve that goal. In this essay I assume a realist position regarding belief-desire explanation: belief-desire explanations, if accurate, entail that the organism whose behavior is so explained genuinely has beliefs and desires which are causally responsible for the behavior in question. The question I pursue here is whether some animal behavior is properly so explained, that is, do (some) animals have beliefs and desires, and is (some of) their behavior caused by these mental states?

The assumption with which I begin – that belief-desire explanations are causal explanations which commit us to the claim that there are beliefs and desires – leads to three theses: that beliefs and desires are representations, that beliefs and desires are distinct, and that those organisms that have beliefs and desires are able to act in what I call a "goal-directed" manner.

2.1. Representationalism

To attribute beliefs to an organism is to attribute to it internal states which vary with perceived qualities of the world. Beliefs are at minimum representations, internal states that aim to depict the way the world is. That is, in believing, one believes that the world is a particular way; one represents the world as being that way. If a dog believes that you are his master, then the dog has an internal state which represents you as being his master. For the purposes of this essay, I speak of desires as if they are representations as well – internal states that depict the world as the agent would have it be; however, as some who are committed to the reality of folk-psychological explanation are not committed to the claim that desires are representations, I remain agnostic as to their true nature.[1]

Thus, to ask whether animals have beliefs and desires is to ask if they represent their goals and means to achieve those goals. An animal that has beliefs and desires and that acts on those beliefs and desires represents both the way the world is and the way it would have the world be, and both of these representations contribute to the animal's actions, to its bringing about the satisfaction of its desires.

---

[1] See, for example, Dretske (1988).

2.2. Distinctness

If, whenever I saw a piece of cake, I ate it, no matter what my state of hunger (or the presence or absence of any other relevant desires) might be, then my desires would play no role in bringing about my eating of the cake. Similarly, if I always engage in eating behavior, whether there is a cake present or not, then my eating behavior on this occasion, in the presence of cake, is not properly explained by citing my belief that cake is present. Belief-desire explanation requires a causal contribution from both beliefs and desires. Moreover, implicit to the idea of belief-desire explanation is that we can project from a particular explanation citing particular beliefs and desires to future behaviors also caused by those beliefs and desires. If the proper explanation for my cake-eating behavior involves my belief that cake is present, then, as long as nothing has changed, if I believe you want cake, then absent countervailing desires I will offer you cake, something I would not do if I did not believe cake was present. This ability to project from an explanation of one behavior to other behaviors requires that the beliefs and desires must be distinct, that individual beliefs and desires are able to enter causal transactions without each other.

Of course, we might reject the idea that belief-desire explanations should be projectable. Causal realism about belief-desire explanation does not entail that the properties cited in such explanations are capable of entering into causal transactions other than those cited in a particular explanation. Nonetheless, the commitment to distinct representations should be maintained. Having both beliefs and desires is an advantage – even if a particular belief is not able to enter into causal transactions with any but a particular desire – because they are sensitive to distinct states of the world. Beliefs trigger actions based on what is the case, whereas desires trigger action based on what the agent would have be the case. These two triggers together are more valuable than either might be alone, as would be the case were they not represented distinctly. A bee that forages for pollen here and now because it has distinct representations of the presence of pollen here and the need for pollen now will be better off than a bee that forages based only on the presence of pollen or based only on the need for pollen.

To ask whether animals have beliefs and desires is to ask if they have distinct representations of their goals and the means to achieve those goals.

2.3. Goal-directed behavior

An organism whose behavior is caused by, and thus appropriately explained by, its beliefs and desires has distinct representations of its goals and means to achieve those goals. These distinct representations allow it to behave in a goal-directed, rather than merely goal-oriented, fashion, in the sense I describe below. That means that evidence that an organism's behavior is goal-directed, rather than merely goal-oriented, is evidence that the organism's behavior is caused by its distinct representations, that it has beliefs and desires.

Goal-directed behavior is behavior directed toward achieving a goal, whereas goal-oriented behavior is behavior oriented, say by evolution, so that if it is performed in the right environment, it will lead to a goal. A representation of the goal does not play a role in causing goal-oriented behavior.[2] For example, heliotropic flowers that turn their heads to follow the sun do so because chemicals (the growth hormone auxin) react to the sun's rays (specifically to light of the shorter, blue wavelengths) by moving from the light and causing greater growth on the side of the plant away from the light and thus tilting the head of the plant toward the sun.[3] The goal of following the sun is not represented by the plant, nor does the plant even represent the position of the sun in the sky. Instead, evolution has structured the plant in such a way as to guarantee that the plant will follow the sun across the sky. Such movement is goal-oriented: it is oriented by evolution to achieve a particular goal, but that goal plays no role in the present movement of the plant.[4] Similarly, when the greylag goose engages in its stereotypical egg-retrieval behavior – it will use its bill to roll errant eggs back to its nest, but it will continue to move its bill as if rolling an egg even if the egg is no longer in place – the individual goals of the goose play no role in causing this behavior. Instead it performs this behavior as a result of the way evolution has structured it to behave, as a consequence of many generations of selection in which those geese who performed this behavior in a stereotypical fashion produced more viable offspring than their conspecifics. One might put this point in intentional terms (which are not intended literally!): evolution has the goal of producing as many viable greylag goose offspring as it can and so it orients the goose in such a

---

[2] See Saidel (1998).   [3] See Galen (1999).

[4] See Galen (1999) for a sample of the simple sorts of experiments that demonstrate this conclusion. The experiments she cites include blocking light of particular wavelengths, removing the heads of plants, and blocking parts of the flower stem from the sun by applying liquid paper!

way as to ensure that the goose engages in behavior that has the result that this goal is met.

Goal-directed behavior, on the other hand, is behavior which is caused in part by (a representation of) the goal. When an organism's behavior is goal-directed, then the organism does what it is doing in order to achieve a goal it has. When a rat navigates a maze to reach the food at the end, it seems to be engaged in goal-directed behavior. When a chimpanzee places a nut just so on a stone and pounds it with a stick, opening the nut and releasing the meat inside, it seems to be engaged in goal-directed behavior. When an organism behaves in a goal-directed fashion it is able to overcome obstacles that might otherwise prevent it from reaching its goal. When the organism's behavior is goal-oriented, it can only overcome those obstacles that evolution has foreseen and accounted for. The question this essay asks – does animal behavior ever provide evidence that it is caused by the animal's beliefs and desires? – can be answered by answering the question suggested here: does animal behavior provide evidence that it is goal-directed rather than goal-oriented?

Even an organism which represents its environment would be unable to engage in goal-directed behavior if its representations of its goals and the means to achieve those goals were not distinct. If evolution had so structured the organism that it lacked distinct representations of its goals and the means to achieve those goals, then the organism would not be able to abandon a particular behavior – a means to a goal – while retaining the goal. Having distinct representations allows an organism to abandon one behavior and adopt another while still retaining the goal that the previous behavior was aimed at achieving, and toward which the new behavior is now directed. Having distinct representations of goals and means to achieve them is thus a prerequisite for behaving in a goal-directed fashion.

2.4. Learning

This means that those animals which engage in goal-directed behavior, those animals which represent their goals and the means to achieve those goals distinctly, are capable of a type of learning that other animals are incapable of. Specifically, they have the ability to form new associations of goals and the means to achieve those goals.

Not all learning is evidence of distinctly represented goals and means to achieve those goals. Some learning does not implicate representation, of means or of goals, at all. For example, swamp sparrows[5] learn their species-specific song as a consequence of hearing the song (or a variation of it) at a particular moment in their development. They are merely filling in gaps in an evolutionarily pre-programmed behavioral pattern. This learning is functionally similar to that of the goose which imprints on whatever large moving object happens to be at hand when it is an infant. No representation of the goal of learning the song is implicated. Nor does their learning exhibit the ability to overcome obstacles that is characteristic of goal-directed behavior.

Similarly, conditioned learning fails to implicate representations. When the pigeon learns to peck at a particular spot or at a particular time in order to achieve food, it is merely altering where or when it pecks for food. It is not learning a new means to get food. This inability to adopt a new means to achieve an (old) end is nicely illustrated in a pair of articles by Keller and Marian Breland (1951, 1961). In their first article they practically crow in anticipation of all the various tasks they can use conditioning to train animals to perform. But within a decade they found that their training methodology was limited. If the reward was food, then they could only train their animals – including such "intelligent" creatures as pigs – to behave in ways that they were equipped by evolution to behave in order to receive that reward. Thus, for example, pigs could learn to associate rooting behavior with food, but for the goal of food, they could not learn to perform a behavior that did not involve rooting. In the plainest example of this, the Brelands attempted to condition pigs to not root in order to receive food. The pigs would starve instead. They would become hungry and as a consequence of their hunger they would root, and so they would not receive food.

The learning that counts as evidence of the presence of representations is learning that cannot be explained by conditioning or by a filling in of behaviors in evolutionarily pre-established patterns. These sorts of learning are stereotypic responses to the organism's environment. The organism's adoption of novel behavior is narrowly structured by its environment to take advantage of certain regularities in that environment (e.g., the songbird will be in an environment which includes other songbirds of the same species, the pigeon will be in an environment in which pecking will prove useful in obtaining food and in which certain sources of food will regularly yield food). We will have evidence of mental representations in animals when we have evidence of animals which are able to respond to

---

[5] See, for example, Marler (1989).

their environment plastically, for example by adopting a wholly novel way of getting food.

I started by asking what would count as evidence that (non-human) animals have, as causes of their behavior, beliefs and desires. I have argued that we're looking for evidence of distinct representation of an animal's goals and the means to achieve those goals, and that one source of evidence for this is in an animal's ability to learn to adopt new means to achieve a goal, or to adapt old behaviors as means to achieve new goals. This sort of evidence can be top-down – that is, evidence that comes as the result of theoretical considerations – or bottom-up: that is, evidence that comes as a result of examining changes in animal behavior. In section 3 I give a top-down argument, and in section 4 I discuss evidence that provides bottom-up support for the thesis that some animals do learn in the requisite manner and are thus likely to have distinct representations of their goals and means to achieve those goals, that they have desires and beliefs which help them satisfy these desires.

3. THE EVOLUTION OF DISTINCT REPRESENTATIONS OF MEANS AND ENDS

I make two assumptions for the purposes of the argument presented in this section. First, I assume that human beings are able to act on distinct representations of their goals and means to achieve those goals. One might think of the conclusion I reach as being conditional: if human beings have distinct representations, then considerations of evolution give us good reason to think that some animals do too. Second, I assume that this trait – the ability to represent one's goals and means to achieve those goals distinctly – is present in the human phenotype because of the advantages in fitness that have accrued to those of our ancestors who had this trait in virtue of their having it. That is, the trait is present because of the advantages that it caused, rather than advantages with which it was concomitant.[6] The fact of the matter is, of course, beyond the reach of discovery; nonetheless, this seems a plausible assumption.

There are three basic evolutionary goals each organism has: to feed, to avoid predators, and to reproduce. When the members of a species are able to satisfy these goals, the species will flourish; when they fail to satisfy

---

[6] That is, I assume that the ability to represent one's goals and the means to achieve those goals distinctly was itself "selected for" and is not present as a consequence of "selection of" some other trait, in the language introduced by Sober (1984).

these goals, the species will die out. Merely being able to satisfy these goals is good, but being able to overcome obstacles to satisfying these goals is even better. One way that evolution can equip organisms to overcome obstacles to their evolutionary goals is by recognizing those obstacles ahead of time and programming the organisms with strategies for overcoming those obstacles.[7]

An example of behavior that is able to overcome the individual's obstacles, but which may be accounted for by evolutionary programming rather than as a consequence of representing one's goals and recruiting new means to achieve those goals, is the piping plover's various strategies used to keep predators away from its eggs.[8] These include camouflaging its nest, peeping loudly while walking near an intruder (apparently in order to distract the intruder from the nest), flying slowly and conspicuously near the intruder (also apparently in order to distract the intruder from the nest), brooding on a false nest (where there are no eggs), and leading the intruder away from the nest by walking as if its wing were broken. Whatever the true explanation of the plover's behavior may be – perhaps its behavior is truly caused by distinct representations the plover has of its goals and different means it might use to achieve those goals – one way that evolution may have equipped the plover to respond to intruders was to give it various non-plastic responses to possible predators, each triggered by, say, the plover's sense of the distance the intruder is from the nest.[9] Then we can imagine that evolution has equipped the plover with the following conditionals: "If the intruder is distant from the nest, brood a false nest

---

[7] I use intentional idioms hesitantly. Evolution doesn't plan anything; it is not an intelligent agent. When I use an intentional idiom it is merely shorthand for a much longer account of what might actually have happened. For instance, in the example discussed in the text, the more accurate explanation for the plover's behavior doesn't involve any pre-cognition of the possible threats to its eggs, but instead involves selection for the ancestors of the current generation of plovers as a consequence of their having more offspring than their conspecifics because they (the ancestors) were likely to, for example, brood on a false nest in response to a nearby predator. The greater relative survival of the eggs of the false-brooder as compared with its conspecifics which did not false-brood, coupled with the heritability of this behavior, ensured the presence of false-brooding in future generations.

[8] See Ristau (1996).

[9] I wish to be careful here: I do not mean to suggest that I am giving the correct explanation for the plover's behavior, or even that I am in the business of giving that explanation. I am merely using the variety of responses available to the plover – responses that seem to be both various and limited – as an example of how evolution might equip an organism to surmount obstacles in the path of achieving its evolutionary goals. If plovers are programmed by evolution to have these responses, then I imagine that the triggers for their behavior are more complex than the distance the intruder is from the nest. The triggers most likely also include the size of the intruder, whether the intruder is able to fly, the age of the eggs, the orientation of the intruder, and the speed of the intruder, to name just a few possible cues to which the plover might be sensitive.

away from the actual nest"; "If the intruder is closer to the nest, fly slowly near the intruder to distract it from the nest"; "If the intruder is even closer to the nest, lead the intruder away from the nest with a broken wing display."

Such behavior is only successful when the obstacles the organism typically faces are included in its behavioral programming. If a predator navigates by the smell of the eggs (suppose that the calcium in plover eggs gives off a particular aroma to which this predator is sensitive) and not by visual cues such as spotting the nest or an easy prey, then the predator will not be distracted by any of the plover's various displays and it will eat the eggs. In such a circumstance, the successful animal will be the one that can respond to the challenge presented by this predator. It will have to recognize that the predator is not distracted by the displays it customarily uses to distract predators, and then it will have to recruit a new behavior to defend its nest. That is, the successful animal will have to generate a new representation of its environment, jettison the old representations that are linked to its goal of protecting its nest, and link that old goal to a new behavior aimed at achieving that goal.

Perhaps there are no such predators in the plovers' environment, or perhaps such predators are rare enough that it is not worth the evolutionary cost to develop resources to deal with them. Or perhaps the plovers haven't had the right mutations which might lead to selection for the resources needed to respond to their environment in quite so plastic a fashion. Whatever the case may be for the plovers, there are animals whose evolutionary environment was so variable that those who were able to represent their goals and their means to achieve those goals distinctly were better fit than those who relied on evolutionarily selected strategies for success: human beings. Did this trait evolve after the hominid and primate lines split or before?

It will come as no surprise that my answer to this question is that the trait evolved before the split. The evidence needed to demonstrate the presence of distinct representations of goals and means to achieve those goals is variation in behavior that cannot be explained by the interaction of a few simple conditionals. Chimpanzee feeding behavior is suggestive in this regard. The chimpanzee population occupies several different niches, each with different sources of food. For example, some chimpanzees live in the relatively austere region of Sierra Leone in West Africa in which they have found the fatty fruit of the Kapok tree to be an important resource. Some of these chimpanzees have found that using sticks to cover their feet makes accessing the fruit on the thorny trees to be a less painful experience.[10] Chimpanzees in other regions eat nuts, which requires that they learn how to crack open the nuts in order to reach the meat. Some chimpanzees "fish" for termites by stripping leaves from sticks of a certain size, inserting the sticks into the termite mounds and then carefully maneuvering the sticks to withdraw them with the termites still attached (care is needed so that the termites aren't brushed off the stick in the process of removing it from the mound). As Matsuzawa and Yamakoshi (1996) report, chimpanzee feeding behavior is both varied and determined by their environment. They describe two communities, the Bossou and the Nimba, which live approximately 10 kilometers from each other, separated by 3–4 kilometers of savannah. The Nimba crack and eat the fruit of the *Carapa Procera* tree, the Bossou eat the leaves, flowers, and gum on the trunk, but not the nut in the fruit; Bossou use twigs to dip for Safari ants (they strip the twig of leaves), but the Nimba do not dip for Safari ants although they are available (and neither group fishes for termites); the Bossou use leaves for drinking water, but the Nimba do not. This is just a sample of the variations found in chimpanzee feeding behavior between different groups. This variation is too great – especially between populations that are so close to each other that genetic intermingling seems likely – for it to be explained by a series of evolutionarily (and thus genetically) determined conditionals; instead, their feeding behavior is more closely structured by the food that is available in their current environment and the trial and error that comes with associating new representations with old goals, with adopting new means to achieve those old goals.

Of course, while this variation in chimpanzee habitat and the consequent variation in chimpanzee feeding behavior suggests that the chimpanzee feeding behavior is a result of their representations of their goals and means to achieve those goals, it is only suggestive of this conclusion. Perhaps there is some other way that evolution has equipped these animals to achieve their goal of attaining food in diverse environments. Suppose this is the case. Then we are left with a puzzle: both humans and chimpanzees are able to adapt their behavior to meet their goals in various environments. According to this supposition, chimpanzees do so without distinct representations of their goals and means to achieve their goals. Humans, on the other hand, do distinctly represent their goals and means to achieve their goals. What was the engine driving the selection of this trait in human beings? It could not have been the advantage in fitness an organism gains by being able

---

[10] See Alp (1997). I discuss this behavior further in section 4.

to respond appropriately in various environments; the ancestral condition already provided this advantage.

Absent any satisfactory solution to this puzzle, that both humans and chimpanzees have the ability to achieve their goals despite variations in their environments suggests the same traits support this ability in both species, namely that chimpanzees and human beings both represent distinctly their goals and their means to achieve those goals.

It should be noted that a possible solution to this puzzle is selection for language use. According to this proposal, primitive language use somehow led to primitive use of representations, which then better enabled language use, and so, through selection for minds better able to use language, there was also the development of distinct representations of goals and means to achieve those goals.[11] If this is right, then chimpanzees – a species in which there was no selection for language use – are able to adapt their behavior to meet their goals in different environments without distinct representations of their goals and means to achieve those goals, whereas human beings do have distinct representations as a consequence of selection for language use. Discussing this proposal fully would take me too far afield here, but it is worth noting that it merely shifts the argument from one about evidence for the presence in animals of distinct representations of goals and means to achieve those goals to one about evidence for primitive language use in animals. For key to this proposal is that there was no selection for primitive language use in animals. If we think that primitive language use led to the ability to represent one's goals and means to achieve those goals distinctly, and we also think that some animals have primitive language use, then this proposal merely describes how distinct representations might have evolved, but it doesn't place that evolution before the hominid/primate split. What we need is evidence that some animals have (or lack) the ability to represent their goals and means to achieve those goals distinctly.[12]

4. GOAL-DIRECTED BEHAVIOR IN ANIMALS

In section 2.4, I argued that evidence that an animal's behavior is caused by its beliefs and desires is provided by the animal's ability to recruit new

---

[11] I am indebted to Tad Zawidzki for raising this objection.

[12] See Allen and Saidel (1998) for an argument that primitive elements of language can be found in animals. It is worth noting as well that this proposed solution to the puzzle violates the assumption I made at the beginning of this section, that the trait of having distinct representations of one's goals and means to achieve those goals was itself directly selected for. Of course, if the solution works, then the assumption is incorrect.

means to achieve old goals. This learning is evidence that the animal has separate representations of its goals and the means by which it might achieve those goals. In this section I present five examples of animals adopting new behaviors, one involving monkeys, the others involving chimpanzees and bonobos.[13] All but the last of these examples feature wild animals observed in their natural habitat (although the first involves some interaction with humans). I argue that these are demonstrations of the kind of learning that is relevant here, thus that at least this behavior was caused by these animals' beliefs and desires.

(1) A notorious[14] example is that of the sweet-potato-washing macaques of Koshima Island, Japan. These macaques were provided with sweet potatoes (for food) by their caretakers. The potatoes were deposited in the sand, which resulted in their being covered with sand. Most of the macaques would brush the sand off the sweet potatoes before eating. However, in 1953, Imo, an 18-month-old female, began bringing her food to a stream to wash it before eating it. Soon (about a month later) one of Imo's playmates (fellow juveniles) started washing sweet potatoes, followed (within two more months) by Imo's mother and another playmate. Eventually – within a decade – sweet-potato-washing became common in the troop.

Sweet-potato-washing was not the only novel behavior Imo intro-duced to her troop.[15] The macaques were also provided with wheat, which also became sandy and thus, we can assume, unpleasant to eat. Imo learned to carry the wheat to the water and drop it in. The heavier sand fell to the bottom while the lighter wheat floated on the surface. She then retrieved and ate the wheat. This placer-mining behavior also spread through the troop, albeit more slowly than did the potato washing.

(2) Rosalind Alp (1997) reports observations of chimpanzees in Tenkere, Sierra Leone, West Africa using sticks as quasi-shoes. The range these chimpanzees occupy is poor in food resources, which means that the fat-rich fruit of the *Ceiba pentanda* (Kapok) tree is a valuable source of nutrients. However, feeding on the fruit has to be very painful, as

---

[13] There are many suggestive examples I do not discuss here, including, in addition to primates, animals in other families.

[14] There has been considerable debate about the best explanation of the sweet-potato-washing behavior exhibited by the Koshima macaques. For a small sample, see the discussion below.

[15] Was the behavior truly novel? Does Imo truly deserve credit for introducing this behavior? Was Imo a cognitively gifted individual who single-handedly changed the behavioral patterns (and perhaps the evolution) of her troop? I discuss these and related issues below. I argue that the answer to these questions doesn't matter for my purposes.

the branches of the tree are covered with thorns. Alp reports observing several individuals removing bare branches, gripping them between their greater and lesser toes, and using the branches to protect their feet as they perched on the tree, feeding on the fruit. These individuals would continue to hold the branch with their toes as they stood and reached for more fruit, even as the foot was no longer resting on the tree, positioning the branch under the foot again as they returned to squatting and eating. Alp also observed individuals placing a similar branch for use as a seating platform.

Unlike the washing behavior of the macaques, the use of a branch as a protective tool did not spread through the population (at least not as of the time of Alp's report), nor was it common for the individuals who did use it: for example, one individual used a "stepping-stick" for only about ten minutes of several hours during which Alp observed him feeding in the Kapok tree.

(3) As noted in Section 3, evidence of chimpanzee nut-cracking behavior is widespread. Christophe Boesch (1991) observed chimpanzees learning to crack nuts. Nut-cracking involves placing a nut on an appropriate (usually stone) surface – the anvil – and then hitting it with another stone or a branch – the hammer. Boesch notes that although chimpanzees generally carry their hammers with them, mothers with 3-year-old infants will often leave their hammers behind, by their anvils, while they forage and their infant also remains near the anvil. This carries some risk: other chimpanzees may steal the hammer, or the infant may use and damage or refuse to return the hammer, forcing the mother to find a new hammer. Boesch also observed mothers placing nuts on the anvil for their young, as well as a mother stopping her child from trying to open a nut haphazardly placed on the anvil until she had cleared the anvil off and replaced the nut carefully.

Boesch's most striking observation was of an apparent instance of teaching:

On 18 February 1987, Ricci's daughter, 5 year old Nina, tried to open nuts with the only available hammer, which was of an irregular shape. As she struggled unsuccessfully with this tool, alternately changing her posture, hammer grip and the position of the nut, Ricci was resting. Eventually, after 8 min of this struggle, Ricci joined her and Nina immediately gave her the hammer. Then, with Nina sitting in front of her, Ricci, in a very deliberate manner, slowly rotated the hammer into the best position with which to pound the nut effectively. As if to emphasize the meaning of this movement, it took her a full minute to perform this simple rotation. With Nina watching her, she then proceeded to use the hammer to crack 10 nuts (of which Nina received six entire kernels and a portion of the other four). Then Ricci left and Nina resumed cracking. Now, by adopting the same hammer grip as her mother, she succeeded in opening four nuts in 15 min. Although she had difficulties and regularly changed her posture (18 times), she always maintained the hammer in the same position as did her mother. (Boesch [1991], p. 532)

(4) Tetsuro Matsuzawa (1994) reports two cases of tool construction, one of which involves using a tool to create a tool. In the first, chimpanzees broke either their hammer or their anvil during nut-cracking and then chose one of the pieces to use as a new hammer. One might think that this is merely a case of replacing a broken hammer with an available stone tool, but on some of these occasions, the original hammer did not break: the anvil broke and the chimpanzee recognized one of the resulting pieces as a better hammer than the one s/he had been using.

   Matsuzawa also observed three separate chimpanzees using a stone wedge to prop up the anvil, thus making the surface of the anvil more level and the anvil more stable.

(5) Finally, Susan Savage-Rumbaugh, Nicholas Toth, and Kathy Schick (2006) report that they were able to teach Kanzi, a domesticated bonobo who has learned some sign language, how to knap stone. Knapping stone is the process whereby our Stone Age ancestors (Homo sapiens) would strike one stone on another in order to create arrowheads and spear points. Toth demonstrated knapping for Kanzi, and they motivated Kanzi by providing him with a box with grapes inside. Kanzi had to knap stone to manufacture a tool which he could then use to open the box to fetch his reward. He was able to do so.

In each of these examples the animals take an old goal and adopt a new means to achieve that goal. Several aspects of the newly adopted behaviors are worth noting. First, even though the goals all involved acquiring food, of these behaviors – washing food, placing a stick under one's feet, cracking nuts this way rather than that way, replacing a hammer, propping an anvil, and knapping stone – only cracking nuts is part of the typical behavioral repertoire associated with feeding. Remember the puzzle Breland and Breland (1961) encountered: when the reward was food, they were unable to condition their subjects to perform behaviors not typically associated with acquiring food in order to receive the reward. Even if, as some commentators have observed, some of these novel behaviors are not completely novel to these animals, they are now performing these behaviors in order to achieve goals toward which they were not originally directed. That means that even if the means to achieve the goal is not new, the animals are creating new means–ends pairings.

As I remark above, the exploits of the Koshima Island macaques are notorious. Many commentators are incredulous, doubting that this behavior is genuine as described. For just one example, consider Galef (1996), who suggests that the behavior of the Koshima macaques might be the result of rewards from their caretakers, that those who wash their sweet potatoes might be fed first. (But see de Waal [2004] for an opposing view.) Even if this is so now, it wasn't the case then: Imo did not learn to wash her food as a consequence of conditioning. Conditioning works by reinforcing the association of a behavior with a stimulus. The association of the behavior and stimulus cannot be reinforced if it does not already exist. Thus conditioning cannot explain the novel behavior that Imo initiated; at best it might explain Imo's continued potato-washing.

This response to Galef's challenge illustrates my general response to challenges of this sort. I think these challenges miss the true significance of the newly adopted behaviors in protesting that these behaviors are not wildly significant. Imo may not have been a macaque Leonardo, inventing strategies generations ahead of her peers; it is significant enough that she initiated a new behavior, that she learned a new association of a behavior and a goal. Mithen (1996), for example, worries about the chimpanzee creation of tools, such as sticks used to fish for termites, that their tools are not as complex as those humans create, that the movements used to create them are the same as movements used to perform other behaviors, that each tool is used for just one task rather than being adaptable for use in achieving other goals, and that chimpanzee tool-learning behavior is laborious, rather than intuitive.[16] Of course, he is correct about each of these observations, but despite this, in creating and in learning how to create tools, those chimpanzees are forming new representations of ends and means to achieve those ends. This is only possible if they have beliefs about their environment and desires toward the achievement of which their behavior is directed.

One might object that these examples of learning are simply instances of "monkey see, monkey do" imitation. Perhaps primates are wired by evolution to copy behaviors of those around them, and so instead of adopting a new behavior as a means to achieve a goal, implicating the separate representation of the behavior and the goal, these are examples

---

[16] Mithen's conclusion is that chimpanzees lack what he calls "technical intelligence," which human beings have. Perhaps he is right about this, but this is beside the point here.

of primates merely mindlessly copying the behavior they observe. Several details of these examples make this interpretation unlikely.

(1) The other members of Imo's troop did not imitate her immediately. In fact, it took a month for even one other macaque to wash sweet potatoes, several months for others to join in, and years for the entire troop to adopt the behavior. Moreover, when Imo initiated another novel behavior, the troop took even longer to adopt the behavior. If this were simply an example of behavior being mimicked, we would expect other members of the troop to copy the behavior, even if they did not adopt the behavior, much earlier.

(2) The first Tenkere chimpanzee to use a stepping-stick was not copying any behavior in doing so, and if other members of the group copied him, they did not do so in any obvious fashion. He used the stick in front of others, who continued to feed with their feet unprotected.

(3) Nina did copy her mother's grip on the hammer, but, as Boesch notes, she did not copy other aspects of her mother's behavior; she had difficulties cracking the nuts even after her mother showed her the proper grip, difficulties which led to her changing her posture several times as she cracked nuts. Imitation this is, but it is goal-directed imitation, not rote copying.

(4) Propping the anvil is, like creating a stepping-stick and washing sweet potatoes, a novel behavior that could not have arisen as a consequence of copying. Each of these behaviors is also unlikely to come about as result of chance.

I think the conclusion here is clear. These are examples in which the animals are able to retain a goal while adopting a new method of achieving that goal. This means that they represented the goal and the means to achieve that goal distinctly. I think that we can truly say of these animals that they wanted to achieve their goals and that they had beliefs about how to do so.

5. CONCLUDING REMARKS

I have focused my attention on the goals toward which behavior is directed without saying much about representations of the means to achieve these goals. One might naturally wonder if the learning that I am highlighting might not be possible without representations of one's means to achieve one's goals at all. If an animal has a representation of a goal which is not tied to a particular behavior, could it not maintain that goal while adopting new behaviors aimed at achieving the goal without representing the behaviors? This seems right: much of what we do, we apparently do without representing our activity. For example, we reach with our hands just so to grab a glass, and if the glass is too large or too small, we alter our grip without thinking about it. Perhaps the learning I describe above is similarly an unrepresented adjustment.

In fact, the learning I have described could not be this sort of unrepresented adjustment. Hammering open nuts is not a slight adjustment from termite-fishing (or whatever means of foraging the ancestors of nut-cracking chimpanzees used). Nor could it be a conditioned response to a novel environment. As discussed above, conditioning reinforces pre-existing behaviors, but we don't see evidence of nut-cracking behavior in those chimpanzees that don't crack nuts: the behavior is not there to be reinforced. Moreover, were conditioning the explanation for the kind of learning cited in section 4, then we would expect more random behaviors prior to conditioning, and there is no evidence of that. The Tenkere chimpanzees who fashioned "stepping-sticks" were not randomly behaving only to stop when their behavior was reinforced (by pain-free eating). If anything, their behavior was exactly the opposite of this: they ate (with pain), they stopped eating, fashioned a "stepping-stick," and then commenced eating again. Then they abandoned the "stepping-stick" *despite the reinforcement that supported its use*. These examples of learning are illustrations of problem-solving behavior involving representation of solutions, of means to achieve goals, rather than mindless actions that happen to hit upon means to achieve goals.

The story doesn't end here. Human mental representations are often described as "propositional attitudes." They can be manipulated in ways that resemble a language. Can the same be said for animal mental representations? Humans don't merely believe and desire; we also hope, fear, anticipate, and engage in a variety of mental attitudes so complex that they can only be described by complex German words (e.g., "schadenfreude"). Is the same true for animals? Human mental states exhibit opacity. Do animals'? These are questions for further study. For now, I have argued that we see in some animal behavior evidence that the animals are behaving in a goal-directed fashion, and that therefore they are making use of representations of means to achieve their ends and representations of their ends in order to satisfy their goals. This means that we are right to attribute to these animals beliefs and desires in order to explain this behavior.

CHAPTER 3

Chrysippus' dog as a case study in non-linguistic cognition

Michael Rescorla

1. INTRODUCTION: LANGUAGE AND THOUGHT

Do non-linguistic creatures think? Debate over this question tends to calcify into two extreme doctrines. The first, espoused by Descartes, regards language as necessary for cognition. Modern proponents include Brandom (1994, pp. 145–157), Davidson (1984a, pp. 155–170), McDowell (1996), and Sellars (1963, pp. 177–189). Cartesians may grant that ascribing cognitive activity to non-linguistic creatures is instrumentally useful, but they regard such ascriptions as strictly speaking false. The second extreme doctrine, espoused by Gassendi, Hume, and Locke, maintains that linguistic and non-linguistic cognition are fundamentally the same. Modern proponents include Fodor (2003), Peacocke (1997), Stalnaker (1984), and many others. Proponents may grant that non-linguistic creatures entertain a narrower range of thoughts than us, but they deny any principled difference in kind.[1]

An intermediate position holds that non-linguistic creatures display cognitive activity of a fundamentally different kind than human thought. Hobbes and Leibniz favored this intermediate position. Modern advocates include Bermúdez (2003a), Carruthers (2002, 2004), Dummett (1993, pp. 147–149), Malcolm (1972), and Putnam (1992, pp. 28–30). Proponents may grant that our lower-level cognition resembles the mental activity of languageless creatures, but they insist that we *also* manifest higher-level cognition unavailable to such creatures. The main challenge facing such a view is to describe non-linguistic cognitive processes that differ in a principled way from higher-level human thought.

I will try to meet this challenge by exploring a putative example of non-linguistic cognition. Tolman (1948) introduced the notion of *cognitive*

I am indebted to José Luis Bermúdez, Robert Lurz, and Jason Newman for helpful comments.
[1] M. Wilson (1995) offers an historical overview.

maps to explain how rats in a laboratory maze take detours and shortcuts to reach destinations. Although Tolman's analysis proved controversial, many psychologists have followed him in proposing that human and animal navigation exploits cognitive maps. These have representational content: they represent the world as being a certain way, so we can evaluate them as veridical or non-veridical. Moreover, they are involved in rational mental processes that update them based on perception and exploit them during locomotion. Thus, cognitive maps are genuinely cognitive. Yet they differ from higher-level human thought in two crucial ways: they do not have logical form, and they do not figure in deductive inference.

To illustrate the explanatory potential of cognitive maps, I will deploy them against a venerable philosophical argument for languageless thought and reasoning. Sextus Empiricus, who credits the argument to Chrysippus, presents it as follows:

[Chrysippus] declares that the dog makes use of the fifth complex indemonstrable syllogism when, on arriving at a spot where three ways meet . . ., after smelling at the two roads by which the quarry did not pass, he rushes off at once by the third without stopping to smell. For, says the old writer, the dog implicitly reasons thus: "The animal went either by this road, or by that, or by the other: but it did not go by this or that, therefore he went the other way."[2]

Many commentators, including Aquinas, Gassendi, Jevons, Montaigne, and even King James I of England, have argued on this basis that non-linguistic creatures execute logical reasoning. More recently, Glock (2000) and Horgan and Tienson (1996, p. 93) concur.

Despite millennia of discussion, opponents of non-linguistic deduction have not yet answered this argument satisfactorily. They have not shown how to explain the described phenomena without imputing logical reasoning to Chrysippus' dog. I seek to fill this gap. My proposed explanation, which draws heavily upon research from contemporary robotics, cites rational, non-deductive mental processes defined over cognitive maps. The explanation shows that we can accommodate Chrysippus' dog without assimilating animal minds to human minds. Yet it also militates against Cartesianism, because it invokes representational mental states and rational processes defined over those states. Thus, my treatment illustrates the explanatory resources of an intermediate position that countenances non-linguistic cognition while sharply distinguishing it from linguistic cognition.

---

[2] From *Outlines of Pyrrhonism*, I.69, as translated in Floridi (1997).

2. LOGICAL FORM AND COGNITIVE MAPS

I focus on two crucial features of human propositional attitudes: they have logical form, and they participate in deductive reasoning sensitive to that form. Both features have been recognized since Aristotle, but Frege profoundly enhanced our understanding of them. The Fregean tradition, culminating in Tarski's work, analyzes how truth-conditions of logically complex thoughts depend on semantic values of their parts. It thereby illuminates the semantically and inferentially relevant structure of human thought (Burge [2005], pp. 12–26). The paradigmatic structural elements are compositional mechanisms of the predicate calculus: truth-functional connectives, universal and existential quantifiers, and predication. Additional compositional devices, such as modal operators and generalized quantifiers, have also received compelling semantic analysis over the past century.

My question is whether non-linguistic animals enter into mental states with logical form, where "logical form" minimally includes the familiar compositional mechanisms of the predicate calculus. As already indicated, I will study a single putative case of non-logical cognition: spatial representation. The phrase "cognitive map" appears frequently in contemporary psychology and philosophy. As Bermúdez (1998, pp. 203–207) and Kitchin (1994) document, researchers associate it with diverse meanings. Gallistel (1990, p. 103) defines a cognitive map as "a record in the central nervous system of macroscopic geometric relations among surfaces in the environment used to plan movements through the environment." This definition remains neutral about the extent to which cognitive maps resemble ordinary concrete maps. I will employ a more literal usage: a cognitive map is a mental representation that represents geometric features of the physical environment and that employs the same basic representational mechanisms as a concrete map. On this usage, which seems close to that of O'Keefe and Nadel (1978, pp. 80–96, 389–391), cognitive and concrete maps share a common representational format. Specifically, they have comparable compositional structures. A fuller elucidation of my usage would require systematic discussion of the compositional mechanisms underlying concrete cartographic representation. Unfortunately, those mechanisms are not completely understood. Despite the efforts of such authors as Casati and Varzi (1999), Pratt (1993), and A. Sloman (1978), we have no canonical cartographic semantics analogous to Tarski's semantics for the predicate calculus. Nevertheless, my definition of "cognitive map" seems clear enough for present purposes.

I will assume that cognitive maps do not have logical form. This assumption follows from two premises: first, ordinary concrete maps do not have logical form; second, cognitive maps and concrete maps employ the same basic representational mechanisms. Regarding the first premise, most philosophers who address the matter agree that maps do not express negation, disjunction, the conditional, or the quantifiers (Fodor [1991], p. 295; Millikan [1993], p. 302; Pylyshyn [2003], pp. 424–425).[3] This verdict merits more extended defense than it typically receives, but it seems plausible enough for us to assume it here. Whether concrete maps can express conjunction strikes me as more debatable, but I will again assume a negative verdict. More debatable still is the thesis that concrete maps do not feature predication. One might propose that attaching a map symbol (such as a symbol denoting mountains) to a map coordinate amounts to predicating the corresponding property of the corresponding spatial location. Casati and Varzi (1999) develop a formal cartographic semantics designed to incorporate this proposal. If the proposal is correct, then maps feature rudimentary logical form akin to atomic sentences. I attack this proposal in Rescorla (in press b), arguing that maps do not feature predication, as construed within Fregean or Tarskian semantics.

However, suppose we were to concede that maps have predicative structure. A system of cartographic mental representations would still not support deductive reasoning. It would not allow familiar inference patterns like modus ponens, argument by cases, or universal instantiation. Not even the laws of identity would apply, since concrete maps do not feature an identity sign. Thus, even if we were to concede that cognitive maps have predicative structure, a principled distinction would separate mental processes defined over them from higher-level human cognition.

Given that cognitive maps do not participate in logical inference, can they figure in *any* rational mental processes? Philosophers often suggest that they cannot, on the grounds that rationality requires logically structured mental states (Devitt [2006], pp. 146–147; Pylyshyn [1986], pp. 195–196; Rey [1995], p. 203). If so, then mental activity defined solely over cartographic mental representations is not rational. Accordingly, many philosophers will resist calling the activity "cognitive."

To address these worries, I want to discuss an instructive case study: Chrysippus' dog. I will analyze this case study through a detailed description of rational mental activity defined over cognitive maps.

---

[3] Camp (2007) considers how one might enrich maps with semantic devices akin to negation, disjunction, the conditional, and the quantifiers. However, she seems to grant that these semantic devices go beyond ordinary cartographic representational mechanisms.

3. EXPLAINING THE PHENOMENA

Discussions of Chrysippus' dog typically choose among four strategies:
(1) Treat the dog as executing a deductive inference.
This strategy is probably the most popular. Fry (2002), who works within a cybernetic framework, develops it in fairly rigorous detail. Since logical reasoning presupposes logical structure, (1) requires us to ascribe logically structured mental states to the dog.
(2) Attribute logical reasoning to the dog, but construe the attribution instrumentally.
According to (2), the dog does not "really" execute deductive inference. When we impute logical reasoning to the dog, we are *interpreting* its behavior, not describing observer-independent states and processes. Ironically, Sorabji (1993, p. 26) suggests that Chrysippus himself advocated (2). Similarly, Dennett (1996, p. 115) suggests that our attribution of logical reasoning to Chrysippus' dog is just a matter of adopting the "intentional stance."
(3) Do not attribute logical reasoning to the dog. Instead, maintain that the dog records relevant sensory observations regarding the third path.
Plutarch favored (3): "it is perception itself, by means of track and spoor, which indicates the way the creature fled; [the dog] does not bother with disjunctive and copulative propositions" (1957, 969a–b). Samuel Coleridge adopted a similar analysis. More recently, Gärdenfors maintains that the dog "could have smelled the scent so clearly along the third path that it did not need to do any sniffing" (2003, p. 71).
(4) Grant that the dog records no additional relevant observations beyond those mentioned by Chrysippus. Explain the dog's behavior by citing observer-independent mental processes distinct from logical reasoning.
Proponents of (4) include Philo of Alexandria, Basil of Caesarea, and Ambrose. For instance, Ambrose (1961) cites not logical inference but rather "the training given by nature" (vi.4.23).[4]

Strategy (3) is inadequate. It denies what Chrysippus takes as a datum: that the dog forms no relevant observations of the third path. Setting aside whether Chrysippus himself saw a dog behave as he describes, many philosophers seem convinced that non-linguistic animals routinely exhibit similar behavior. To satisfy these philosophers, we must show that the behavior could result from a mental process other than logical reasoning.

---

[4] Floridi (1997) offers a useful overview of the extensive historical literature.

Strategy (2) is appealing only if we accept an instrumentalist or "interpretivist" approach to intentionality, like that espoused by Brandom, Davidson, or Dennett. I reject any such approach. From the realist perspective that I favor, creatures enter into representational mental states that depict the world as being a certain way, states whose representational contents do not result from interpretation by an observer. Cognitive psychology should isolate laws governing how representational mental states interact with one another, with perceptual inputs, and with behavioral outputs. As Fodor (1981, pp. 100–123) argues, there is no more reason to adopt an instrumentalist stance towards the theoretical posits of cognitive psychology than towards those of any other science. Thus, we should reject an instrumentalist treatment of Chrysippus' dog.

Strategy (4) is more promising than (2) and (3). The problem is that no one has developed it satisfactorily. Vague appeals to "nature" do not suffice. We must describe a psychological mechanism that differs in a principled way from logical reasoning, and we must show that the proposed mechanism generates the desired behavior.[5]

In my view, an adequate development of strategy (4) should satisfy three constraints. First, it should predict the desired behavior, rather than dismissing Chrysippus' description in the style of strategy (3). Second, it should support appropriate counterfactuals about how the dog would have behaved had circumstances been different. For instance, it should support the counterfactual: if the prey had traversed the second path, then the dog would have chosen that path rather than the third. Similarly, it should support the counterfactual: if the dog had sniffed the second and third paths without detecting the prey, then it would have chosen the first path without bothering to sniff. Finally, a good account should isolate a general cognitive mechanism that produces the dog's behavior and that is deployable in diverse circumstances. To take an absurd example, we should not posit an innate "hunting at a three-way fork in the road" cognitive module with the following property: if the dog pursues its prey to a three-way fork in the road, and if the dog detects no signs that the prey traversed two of the three forks, then the dog immediately proceeds down the third

---

[5] Bermúdez (2003a, pp. 140–149) denies that non-linguistic creatures execute logical reasoning, but he ascribes to them a more primitive mode of reasoning ("proto-logic") not involving standard logical connectives. Specifically, he isolates a proto-logic analog to the inference "p or q; not-p; therefore q." He does not apply his discussion of proto-logic to the case of Chrysippus' dog. However, one might try to elaborate (4) by citing Bermúdez's proto-logical analog to the disjunctive syllogism. My alternative approach should be seen as complementary to Bermúdez's. For criticism of Bermúdez, see Lurz (2007).

fork. This putative explanation is unsatisfying, because it cites an ad hoc mental module rather than a general mental capacity applicable in various environmental contexts.

Strategy (1) satisfies all three constraints. I will develop an approach that satisfies the constraints while eschewing logical form and logical inference. My proposal is that Chrysippus' dog performs a probabilistic inference over the space of cognitive maps.

4. BAYESIAN REASONING OVER COGNITIVE MAPS

Bayesian decision theory is a formal framework for modeling probabilistic reasoning and decision-making. It represents a subject's "degree of belief" in various hypotheses through a subjective probability distribution p. Mathematically precise rules dictate how to update p in light of new evidence and how to act based upon p and one's utilities. Given that p measures degree of belief, the question naturally arises: belief in what? It might seem that any adequate answer will cite sentences, propositions, or their ilk.[6] Accordingly, philosophers often present subjective probability distributions as defined over logically structured entities. But Bayesianism is more general than this. It presupposes only an hypothesis space satisfying certain closure constraints.[7] Elements of the hypothesis space must represent possible states of the world, but they need not have logical structure. In particular, they might be cognitive maps. Thus, we may posit a probability distribution defined not over logically structured representations but over cartographic mental representations.

To illustrate, I will present a Bayesian-cum-cartographic model of Chrysippus' dog. My treatment deploys ideas from probabilistic robotics. Indeed, one of my unofficial goals is to publicize this important field, which philosophers have largely ignored.

I assume that Chrysippus' dog (henceforth D) hunts its prey (henceforth X) by updating and consulting a probability distribution defined over the space of possible cognitive maps. When D reaches the crossroads, it recognizes three relevant possible states of the world, represented by

---

[6] I am indebted to José Luis Bermúdez for pressing this question.

[7] More precisely, the standard Kolmogorov axiomatization of probability defines a probability space as (Ω, A, p), where Ω is a non-empty set, A is a σ-algebra over Ω (i.e., a set of subsets of Ω that contains Ω and is closed under countable union and complementation in Ω), and p is a probability measure. It is consistent with this axiomatization to construe Ω as containing cognitive maps.

three cognitive maps, M_1, M_2, and M_3, that correspond respectively to the following three concrete maps:

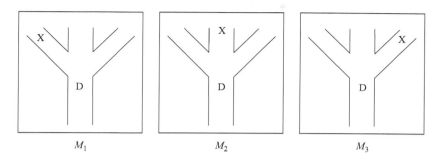

$$p(M_1) = p(M_2) = p(M_3) = 1/3.$$

M_1, M_2, and M_3 do not purport to represent distances accurately, but they purport to capture relations of location and connectedness. More technically: they purport to capture topological properties but not metric properties. In this regard, they resemble subway maps.[8] Since D initially lacks evidence regarding which path X chose, D's initial probability distribution treats all three maps on a par:

$$p(M_1) = p(M_2) = p(M_3) = 1/3.$$

The probabilities sum to 1, because M_1, M_2, and M_3 exhaust the space of possibilities.

From left to right, label the three branches 1, 2, 3. D can sniff each branch i, an observation with two possible outcomes: y_i, signifying that D detects some olfactory trace of X on branch i; and n_i, signifying that D detects no such olfactory trace. Since these are the only two possible options,

$$p(y_i) + p(n_i) = 1.$$

I assume that D assigns *conditional probabilities* $p(y_i|M_j)$: the probability of measurement y_i when D sniffs branch i, assuming that M_j is veridical. Since D's perceptual systems are fallible, $p(y_i|M_i)$ is less than 1: even if X chose branch i, D may not smell it. To be conservative, I assume the "prior likelihood"

$$p(y_i|M_i) = 2/3.$$

---

[8] Some writers restrict the phrase "cognitive map" to representations that represent metric structure. However, this usage is hardly universal. For instance, Gallistel's official definition, quoted in section 2, mentions "geometric relations" without privileging metric over topological properties.

Since $p(y_i) + p(n_i) = 1$, it follows that the chance of false negatives is

$$p(n_i|M_i) = 1/3.$$

There is also a slight chance of false positives, presumably less than that of false negatives. For $i \neq j$, I assume that

$$p(y_i|M_j) = 1/6,$$

and hence that

$$p(n_i|M_j) = 5/6.$$

As I explain below, one could vary these numbers considerably without altering the thrust of my analysis.

I divide D's activity into three stages. Stage one: D sniffs branch 1. Stage two: D sniffs branch 2. Stage three: D chooses branch 3 without sniffing. I now describe each stage in more detail.

Stage one
D sniffs branch 1, obtaining result n_1. How does this observation lead D to update p? Bayes' law, a fundamental result of probability theory, asserts that:

$$p(a|b) = \frac{p(b|a)p(a)}{p(b)}.$$

It is convenient to rewrite this formula as:

$$p(a|b) = \eta p(b|a)p(a),$$

where we regard η as a normalization constant ensuring that relevant probabilities sum to 1. In the cases that interest us, Bayes' law entails

$$p(M_i|n_1) = \eta p(n_1|M_i)p(M_i).$$

Intuitively: the probability of a given hypothesis, conditional on our evidence, is proportional to the prior probability of the hypothesis times the prior likelihood of our evidence conditional on the hypothesis. Substituting our assumed values for relevant probabilities, it is easy to show that

$$p(M_1|n_1) = 1/6$$
$$p(M_2|n_1) = 5/12$$
$$p(M_3|n_1) = 5/12.$$

Following standard Bayesian procedure, we assume that D "conditionalizes": as a result of observation n_1, D updates its probabilities so that the new probability assigned to M_i is $p(M_i|n_1)$. Thus, D redistributes probabilities over M_1, M_2, and M_3 to $1/6$, $5/12$, and $5/12$, respectively. This is intuitively plausible. Since D did not detect any sign of X down path 1, D lowers the probability it assigns to M_1. No evidence yet differentiates between M_2 and M_3, so D assigns them equal probability.

Stage two
D sniffs branch 2, obtaining result n_2. How does this observation lead D to update p? We employ a generalized form of Bayes' law:

$$p(a|b, c) = \beta p(b|a, c)p(a|c),$$

where $p(x|y, z)$ is the probability of x given that y and z obtain, and where β is a normalization constant ensuring that relevant probabilities sum to 1. Thus,

$$p(M_i|n_1, n_2) = \beta p(n_2|M_i, n_1)p(M_i|n_1).$$

Following typical practice in probabilistic robotics (Thrun *et al.* [2005], p. 33), we deploy the *Markov assumption*: given the current state of the world, past observations are irrelevant to predictions about future observations. More formally,

$$p(n_2|M_i, n_1) = p(n_2|M_i).$$

Under this assumption, it is easy to show that

$$p(M_1|n_1, n_2) = 2/9$$
$$p(M_2|n_1, n_2) = 2/9$$
$$p(M_3|n_1, n_2) = 5/9.$$

Assume that D conditionalizes once again. Then D assigns probabilities $2/9$, $2/9$, and $5/9$ to M_1, M_2, and M_3, respectively. This is intuitively plausible. D's two observations render M_3 most probable, and they do not differentiate between M_1 and M_2.

Stage three
So far, we have considered how D updates probabilities. We must now examine D's utilities. I assume that D has four available actions: remain at the fork of the road (whether performing further observations or merely abandoning the chase); or else traverse branches 1, 2, or 3, respectively. Call these actions H, x_1, x_2, and x_3. Action u and map M_i jointly determine a

new map, depicting what the world is like if it begins in the state depicted by M_i and then changes only in that D performs u. I denote this new map with "(M_i, u)." For instance, (M_1, H) is just M_1, while (M_1, x_2) is

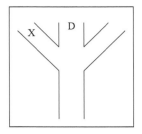

Note that, although I defined the metalinguistic term "(M_i, u)" by using the material conditional, the cognitive map denoted by this metalinguistic term does not itself have conditional structure, or logical form more generally. There are twelve maps (M_i, u), each associated with a *payoff* $C(M_i, u)$. The following chart summarizes one possible set of payoffs:

	M_1	M_2	M_3
H	0	0	0
x_1	1	−1	−1
x_2	−1	1	−1
x_3	−1	−1	1

Columns correspond to possible initial states of the world. Rows correspond to D's four possible actions. The entry in column M_i and row u is the payoff $C(M_i, u)$ if map (M_i, u) is veridical. Our chart reflects two assumptions: D prefers catching X to not catching X; and D prefers remaining immobile to wasting resources in failed pursuit of X.

The *expected payoff* $E(u)$ of action u is a weighted average of the possible payoffs resulting from u:

$$E(u) = \sum_{i=1,2,3} p((M_i, u)|u) \times C(M_i, u),$$

where $p((M_i, u)|u)$ is the conditional probability that map (M_i, u) is veridical given that D performs u. I assume that D's actions generate no additional uncertainty, so that $p((M_i, u)|u) = p(M_i)$. Thus,

$$E(u) = \sum_{i=1,2,3} p(M_i) \times C(M_i, u).$$

At stage one,

$$E(H) = 0, E(x_1) = E(x_2) = E(x_3) = -1/3.$$

At stage two,

$$E(H) = 0, E(x_1) = -2/3, E(x_2) = E(x_3) = -1/6.$$

At stage three,

$$E(H) = 0, E(x_1) = E(x_2) = -5/9, E(x_3) = 1/9.$$

Under the standard assumption that D performs the action with highest expected payoff, our analysis predicts that D performs H at stage one, H at stage two, and x_3 at stage three. This is the phenomenon we wished to explain.

5. A GENERAL THEORETICAL FRAMEWORK

Our Bayesian model of Chrysippus' dog satisfies the three criteria from section 3. First, it explains the desired phenomena. Second, it supports appropriate counterfactuals. For instance, if X had chosen path 2 rather than path 3, then at stage two D would have recorded observation y_2. It is easy to show that D would then have immediately chosen path 2. Third, our model depicts D's behavior as reflecting a more general capacity to perform Bayesian reasoning over cognitive maps.

That capacity extends far beyond the scenario described in section 4. Probabilistic robotics studies how robots equipped with the capacity to reason over cognitive maps can navigate through diverse physical environments (Thrun *et al.* [2005]). It offers computational models describing how perceptual input induces a rational robot to update its probability distribution over a space of possible maps. Recently, robots along these lines performed impressively in the DARPA Grand Challenge Race, sponsored by the United States Department of Defense. Of course, current robotics algorithms are far more sophisticated than the tinker-toy model from section 4. But the basic ingredients are the same: probability distributions over cognitive maps, Bayes' law, conditionalization, the Markov assumption, expected utility maximization, and so on. Thus, our simplistic model of Chrysippus' dog illustrates a flexible theoretical framework that has already enjoyed great practical success.

We could refine our model in various ways. For instance, we might consider maps that represent *metric* features of the environment, such as distances and angles. Or we might describe how D alters its heading as it sniffs different branches. Or we might describe D's actions not in terms of their environment-involving consequences (e.g., D *travels down the third path*) but in terms of more specific environment-independent motor commands. Or we might describe D as updating its probability distribution and its motor commands even after it begins moving down path 3. Or we might treat D's actions as introducing additional uncertainty, in which case we would abandon the assumption that $p((M_i, u)|u) = p(M_i)$. Contemporary robotics offers many ideas about how to effect these and other refinements. Although refinement might improve our analysis, it would not change the moral: we can build a robot that employs Bayesian reasoning over cognitive maps and that behaves as Chrysippus describes. The robot would also behave appropriately in counterfactual variants on Chrysippus' scenario.

6. COMPARING THE TWO EXPLANATORY STRATEGIES

How might proponents of strategy (1) react to my discussion so far? I consider three possible objections.

Objection: The model from section 4 is an instance of strategy (1), not an alternative to it. Even if we grant that the model assigns probabilities and utilities to non-logical representations, the assignments employ identities, such as "$p(M_1) = 1/3$" and "$C(M_1, H) = 0$," that have logical structure. Moreover, the proposed model treats D as performing mathematical calculations, which requires logical inference from mathematical axioms. Thus, section 4 implicitly posits deductive reasoning over logically structured mental states.

Reply: Identities such as "$p(M_3) = 1/3$" and "$C(M_1, H) = 0$" describe which probabilities and utilities D assigns to which maps. But D itself can assign probabilities and utilities without employing these identities. The "assignment" consists in suitable functional relations between cognitive maps and mental representations denoting numbers.[9] What is it for D to assign probability $1/3$ to M_1? It is for D to enter into a mental state bearing

---

[9] For empirical evidence that even fairly primitive animals such as rats represent and perform computations involving numbers, including non-integral rationals, see Gallistel (1990, pp. 317–383). Note also that much of the scientific literature on perception treats low-level visual processes as performing

appropriate functional relations to other mental states: the functional relations described in section 4. An assignment of probabilities or utilities to cognitive maps is a mental state that occupies a suitable role in probabilistic calculation. Nor does probabilistic calculation presuppose logical structure or logical inference. The literature offers numerous models of mathematical computation, such as Turing machines and register machines, that do not employ logical inference. These computational models demonstrate that mathematical calculation need not involve deducing theorems from axioms.

Objection: The map-like character of cognitive maps plays no essential role in section 4. The same probabilistic calculations would apply if p were defined over unstructured representations, rather than representations with internal structure akin to concrete maps. Since Bayesianism rather than cartographic structure does all the work, section 4 illustrates nothing about the explanatory potential of cognitive maps.

Reply: A model defined over unstructured representations fails to explain a crucial phenomenon: *systematicity*. As Fodor (1987, pp. 147–153) emphasizes, a basic empirical fact about cognition is that creatures able to instantiate certain contentful mental states are necessarily able to instantiate certain other contentful mental states. For instance, it seems plausible that any terrestrial animal able to entertain the possibility represented by M_1 could also entertain the possibilities represented by M_2 or M_3. Fodor argues that a cognitive model based on unstructured mental representations cannot explain these systematic interrelations among possible mental states. He argues that a satisfying explanation should treat contentful mental states as relations to structured mental representations. We explain systematicity by noting that a representation's parts can be recombined to form new representations. The model from section 4 implements this proposal, treating relevant mental states as relations to mental representations whose semantically relevant structure resembles that of ordinary concrete maps. As Braddon-Mitchell and Jackson (2007, p. 182) note, ordinary cartographic representation is systematic, so a system of cartographic mental representations would likewise be systematic. I conclude that section 4 is far more satisfying than a model that replaces cognitive maps with unstructured representation.[10]

sophisticated Bayesian computations (Knill and Richards [1996]). Thus, the fact that my Bayesian-cum-cartographic model attributes numerical computation to Chrysippus' dog should not seem at all problematic.

[10] Editor's note: See Tetzlaff and Rey (chapter 4) for the argument that the best account of the systematicity of honeybee mental representations is that they are sentential (i.e., non-cartographic) in format.

Objection: Section 4 relies on post hoc assumptions about D's mental states. It assumes that D has winnowed the space of possibilities to M_1, M_2, and M_3. It assumes that D has selected appropriate *prior probabilities* – $p(M_1)$, $p(M_2)$, and $p(M_3)$ – and *prior likelihoods* – $p(y_i|M_j)$ and $p(n_i|M_j)$. It assumes that D associates various payoffs with various outcomes. Altering these assumptions would block the proposed derivation of D's behavior or, even worse, generate an incorrect prediction. Since section 4 retroactively tailors its assumptions to the desired outcome, it yields a thoroughly vacuous account.

Reply: The key question is how my account compares to strategy (1). Presumably, proponents of (1) envisage something like the following explanation:

D tracks X to the fork in the road, so D believes that X chose one of the three paths. D observes no olfactory signs that X chose either path 1 or path 2, so it concludes that X chose neither path. By logical reasoning, D concludes that X chose path 3. Since D prefers catching X to not catching X, D chooses path 3.

This explanation assumes that D believes itself to be facing a three-pronged fork in the road. It assumes that D believes X could have traveled down any of the three paths. It assumes that D can record relevant olfactory observations, which D then takes at face value as veridical. Finally, it assumes that D prefers catching X to not catching X. Altering any of these assumptions would block the proposed explanation of D's behavior, or, even worse, yield an incorrect prediction. Our question is whether these assumptions are any less "post hoc" than those required by my treatment.

In many respects, the assumptions seem comparable. The main apparent difference is that my assumptions are more specific. I assign precise numerical probabilities and payoffs, and I exploit my numerical assumptions in an essential way. Let us consider the various assumptions in turn.

Prior probabilities: It is highly plausible that D initially assigns approximately equal probabilities to M_1, M_2, and M_3, since by stipulation D lacks any differentiating evidence. If desired, we could extend our model backwards in time, discussing how D generates an initial probability distribution over the space of possible maps. Mapping is a central research topic of probabilistic robotics, which offers a wealth of theories. Any such extended model should depict D as tending to assign roughly equal probabilities to M_1, M_2, and M_3 until it collects relevant differentiating evidence.

Prior likelihoods: My assumptions here are quite conservative. Specifically, the assumed high probability of false negatives – $p(n_i | M_i) = 1/3$ – shows that D can act appropriately even if it treats its own perceptual faculties as unreliable. Furthermore, we could vary my specific numerical assumptions considerably while generating the same predictions. Holding fixed the utilities and prior probabilities, and assuming that D treats the three paths symmetrically, we can easily show that any assignment of prior likelihoods yields the desired behavior if it satisfies these constraints:

$$p(n_i|M_i) > 0$$
$$p(n_i|M_i) < p(n_i|M_j)/2,$$

where $i \neq j$. In other words, we achieve our desired result if D allows some probability of false negatives and if that probability is not too outrageously large.

Payoffs: Once again, we can vary the specific numbers considerably while generating the same predicted behavior. Let $a = C(M_i, u_i)$. If $i \neq j$, let $b = -C(M_i, u_j)$. Let $C(M_i, H) = 0$. Holding fixed the prior probabilities and likelihoods, we can easily show that any values of a and b yield the desired behavior if

$$4b/5 < a < 7b/5.$$

This inequality imposes a non-trivial constraint upon possible models of D. The constraint is a virtue, not a defect. It yields a quantitative analysis of how D's payoffs and probabilities jointly determine action. For instance, if $a < 4b/5$, then the prospect of wasted resources outweighs the prospect of catching X, so D remains immobile even while realizing that X probably chose path 3. In contrast, the explanation based on strategy (1) given above appeals vaguely to a "preference" for catching X. It offers no guidance in comparing that preference with D's preference for conserving resources. Bayesian decision theory provides an appealing framework for conducting such comparisons, as illustrated by the above analysis.

Apparently, then, section 4 is no less a priori plausible than the proposal advanced for strategy (1). If so, then a satisfying treatment of Chrysippus' dog need not cite logical reasoning over logically structured mental states. We can instead cite Bayesian reasoning over cognitive maps.

7. ANIMAL COGNITION

Chrysippus' dog is scarcely more than a thought experiment. To what extent does my discussion bear on actual non-linguistic creatures? Do such creatures perform Bayesian reasoning over cognitive maps? Do they execute deductive inferences? These questions, which transgress the limits of a priori analysis, impel us to leave the armchair and engage with scientific psychology. Thought experiments are useful. They facilitate comparison of alternative theories in a relatively clean setting. But they must eventually yield to actual experiments featuring quantitative measures and proper controls.

In this spirit, let us first ask whether the approach sketched in sections 4–5 illuminates navigation. As already noted, many psychologists enthusiastically posit cognitive maps. Bayesian models are also popular within psychology, as applied to perception, word learning, and many other phenomena. A few researchers combine these two strands into cognitive models that posit probabilistic reasoning over cognitive maps. For instance, Balakrishnan et al. (1999) argue that such models help explain various experimental results. This approach seems likely to receive further empirical application as its success within robotics becomes better known among psychologists. Of course, the particular model from section 4 is highly simplified. An empirically credible model would feature many refinements, including those mentioned in section 5. But the basic strategy looks promising. For further discussion, see Rescorla (in press a).

What about logical reasoning? Many psychologists claim that non-linguistic creatures perform deductive inferences. Building on work of Premack and Premack (1994), Call and Carpenter (2001) presented a chimpanzee with two hollow tubes. As the chimpanzee watched, experimenters placed food inside one tube. A screen obscured which tube they selected. They then allowed the chimpanzee to search inside the tubes for the food. In 20–30 percent of the trials, a chimpanzee who discovered that one tube was empty immediately selected the second tube without searching inside it. Call (2004) concludes that the chimpanzee employed disjunctive syllogistic reasoning to determine which cup contained food. Erdőhegyi et al. (2007) report a similar but somewhat weaker result for dogs. In another series of experiments, Call (2004) presented apes with two opaque cups, only one of which contained food. He then shook the empty cup so that the ape could observe that no noise was produced. Three out of nine test subjects performed above chance in selecting the unshaken cup. Call (2004, 2006) argues that these subjects executed a disjunctive syllogism.

Each of the foregoing studies sought to disconfirm rival hypotheses through appropriate controls. For instance, Call (2004) employed controls to show that his apes were not just smelling the hidden food or detecting inadvertent cues about its location from experimenters. He performed additional experiments designed to show that the apes' behavior did not simply reflect a reinforcement history resulting in learned associations, such as an aversion to a noiseless shaken cup (Call [2006, 2007]).

Nevertheless, many psychologists remain unconvinced. According to Penn and Povinelli (2007a), proponents of non-linguistic logical inference mistakenly assume a rigid dichotomy between associationist and deductivist theories of mental activity: either learned associations exhaust a creature's mental activity, or else the creature performs logical inferences. This rigid dichotomy neglects the possibility of non-deductive mental processes vastly more sophisticated than associative learning. Penn and Povinelli caution that, even if we disconfirm an associationist explanation of some observed phenomena, we should not immediately embrace a deductivist conclusion.

My approach, articulated in sections 4–5, occupies Penn and Povinelli's desired middle ground. It is neither deductivist nor associationist. Rather than positing logical inferences or learned associations, it posits rational probabilistic inferences over contentful mental representations. This approach can explain many behavioral phenomena supposedly indicative of non-linguistic syllogistic reasoning. For instance, the results from Call and Carpenter (2001) and Erdőhegyi *et al.* (2007) recall Chrysippus' dog. We can readily explain those results through suitably altered versions of section 4's simplistic model. We treat the animal as updating a probability distribution over possible maps of its surroundings.

The results reported in Call (2004) are harder to accommodate, because they introduce a novel element: the relation between the cup's contents, the shaking of the cup, and the noise thereby produced. We might accommodate this novel element through prior likelihoods $p(n \mid M, s)$, where M is a map, s represents that a shaking of the cup occurs, and n represents that the ape's sensors detect noise. But this maneuver substantially alters the model from section 4, in which prior likelihoods are conditional only upon cognitive maps, not upon spatiotemporal events (such as a shaking of a cup). An adequate theory of how the ape arrives at a suitable prior likelihood $p(n \mid M, s)$ will go substantially beyond the models of map-learning and navigation currently employed within probabilistic robotics.

What additional representational and inferential resources beyond those posited in section 4 would an adequate theory require? According to Call, his results show that the ape represents and reasons about causal relations. Penn and Povinelli (2007a, pp. 109–110) disagree. But suppose we concede that Call is correct. In particular, suppose we concede that the prior likelihood $p(n \mid M, s)$ reflects the ape's grasp of causal relations among physical events. We do not thereby concede that the ape engages in anything resembling *logical* reasoning. There is no obvious reason why a systematic theory of causal representation and reasoning must invoke logically structured mental states.

For instance, consider the theory of *causal Bayes nets* (Pearle [2000]). A causal Bayes net is a directed acyclic graph. Each node is a variable whose values represent possible events or states of the world. A directed edge from one node to another represents direct causal influence of the former upon the latter. Every node is associated with a subjective probability distribution, conditional on the values of its parents. Causal influence and probabilistic dependence relate through the *causal Markov Condition*: a node is probabilistically independent of its nondescendants, conditional on its parents. Under the Markov assumption, conditional probability distributions for individual nodes determine a unique joint probability distribution defined over all the nodes.

This formalism yields an elegant framework for representing and reasoning about causal relations among events. Working within the framework, researchers have proposed various algorithms for inferring causal relations from observed correlations. Although the framework originated in statistics, computer science, and philosophy, several cognitive scientists have recently deployed it within empirical theories of causal reasoning in humans (Gopnik and Schulz [2007]) and non-humans (Blaisdell *et al.* [2006]). To my knowledge, no one has yet integrated cognitive maps and causal Bayes nets into a synthesized theory of map-learning, navigation, and causal reasoning. But I see no obvious bar to an integrated theory. Since neither element of the proposed synthesis requires logically structured representations or deductive inferences, I see no reason why the proposed synthesis would require those resources. Clearly, the topic deserves further investigation.

Although my discussion of causal reasoning may seem intolerably vague, I have offered more detail than psychologists who attribute logical reasoning to non-linguistic animals. As Penn and Povinelli note, such psychologists never provide or even gesture towards formal models. For instance, Call offers only vague folk-psychological talk about "causal-logical reasoning," without hinting how to convert such talk into actual psychological models. Thus, my proposal is no vaguer than Call's.

I submit that many experimental results supposedly indicative of non-linguistic deduction can be explained without citing logical reasoning or logically structured mental states. Admittedly, I have addressed only one strand in the relevant psychological literature. A more thorough discussion would survey the many other experimental results that purportedly reflect non-linguistic deduction.[11] Nevertheless, we can draw some pre-liminary conclusions. First, rational psychological processes defined over cartographic mental representations are possible. The relevant processes, grounded in Bayesian decision theory, differ markedly from deduction. Second, behavioral phenomena that superficially appear to involve logical reasoning may instead reflect non-deductive mental processes defined over non-logical mental representations. Hence, we must exercise caution when arguing through anecdotes, thought experiments, or scientific experiments that non-linguistic creatures' mental states have logical form. Whether non-linguistic cognition features logically structured mental states is an open question, to be settled through sustained engagement between philosophy and scientific psychology.

---

[11] For critical discussion of relevant psychological literature, see Allen (2006), Bermúdez (2003a, pp. 112–114), and Penn *et al.* (2008).

CHAPTER 4

Systematicity and intentional realism in honeybee navigation

Michael Tetzlaff and Georges Rey

I. INTRODUCTION

Do animals really have intentional states, or is intentional ascription merely a convenient instrument for predicting their behavior that involves no commitment to the reality of those states? One way to give substance to this question is to consider the recent debate between "classical" and "radical connectionist" approaches to cerebral architecture. According to the classical, realist theory of cognition, championed by Fodor (1975, 1987), cognitive processes consist of computations defined over causally efficacious, syntactically specified representations, for example sentences in a "language of thought," whose syntactic structure preserves the content of those representations compositionally: representations are either simple or complex, the complex ones being composed by concatenation of the simple ones in such a way that the semantic properties of the complex are a function of the semantic properties of the simple. The main rival to classicism is (non-implementational, or "radical," "distributed") connectionism, which proposes instead that cognitive processes are computations defined over syntactically simple, distributed representations, for which the constituency relation is certainly not concatenative, nor standardly compositional. Indeed, in contrast to classical machine architectures, connectionist architectures standardly do not make available to an organism recombinable representations that might be stored in memory and deployed at different times for different tasks. This air of unreality about internal representations can lend support to the aforementioned instrumentalism, as in Dennett (1987, 1991a).[1]

This essay is largely a distillation of Tetzlaff (2006).

[1] The lines are not always drawn quite so sharply; see, e.g., Horgan and Tienson (1996) and McLaughlin (1998) for discussion.

The main literature debating these issues (e.g., Fodor [1987], Fodor and Pylyshyn [1995], Marcus [2001], and Smolensky [1995]) has focused largely on human beings and the apparent *systematicity* of their thought. As we will understand it, systematicity may be characterized thus:

(SYS) *Ceteris Paribus*:
  x is sensitive to the content [p] iff x is sensitive to F[p],

the square brackets indicating the content of the expressions they enclose (see section 2.1), and "F[p]" any permissible, formal permutation of [p].[2] The most obvious case of syntactic structure is logical structure. Thus, someone understands [If Bill goes, then Ann or Jill stays] iff she understands, for example, [If Ann stays, then Jill or Bill goes]. An example closer to the bee examples we will discuss is: x understands [Ann is north of Bill] iff x understands [Bill is north of Ann]. Fodor (1987) argues that this condition is patently satisfied by normal, linguistically competent adults.

Fodor's discussion focused, however, largely on human linguistic competence.[3] This unfortunately confounded the discussion with issues about the systematicity of natural language, which, arguably, provides a special medium for peculiarly human thought (see Dennett [1991a]). We propose to control for this confound by considering the recent literature on honeybee navigation. After a brief discussion of some background issues (section 2), we will summarize some of the substantial research on honeybees' remarkable abilities to navigate and to convey information about various resources to other bees by means of their "waggle dance" (section 3). We will argue (section 3) that an examination of those abilities reveals that the processes underlying them are systematic, that this systematicity is best explained by presuming that honeybees implement some sort of classical language of thought (section 4), and that this explanation needs to be understood realistically (section 5).

---

[2] The formal permutations are, of course, of the natural language expressions that express the propositions. We assume that a law like (SYS) is intensional (with an "s"), relating properties consisting of these propositions, and thus sensitive to how those propositions are expressed, but that nothing in the present discussion depends upon working out the details of this (we will discuss other features of (SYS) in section 2.2).

[3] Fodor and Pylyshyn (1995) occasionally allude to non-linguistic cases, but do not develop them in detail.

2. BACKGROUND PHILOSOPHICAL ISSUES

2.1. Intentional content

Claims like:

(1) The bees learned that the feeder is 200m east of the hive

are common in the literature on bee and insect navigation generally. Taking such claims at face value, we will assume what they presuppose, that the relevant behavior of bees requires *intentional* explanation (i.e., explanation in terms of *some* sort of representations of "information" – e.g., regarding properties, objects, and locations[4] – that is at least indirectly indicated in English by "that . . ." clauses towards which organisms bear some or other "propositional attitude").[5] Following philosophical practice, we will refer to such "information" as *intentional content*, which we designate by enclosing expressions that express that content in square brackets (e.g., "cats snore" expresses the content [Cats snore]). We will avoid the more common rubric of "meaning" in view of its entanglement with issues of natural language and speech pragmatics; and when we do use the term "information" we intend it as synonymous with "intentional content," without its sometimes misleading association with the purely *physical* notion (roughly, negative entropy) that goes by the same name, and, so far as we can see, has little to do with the present discussion.[6] Other than claiming that intentional content is what representations are "representations of," we have no good definition or theory of it, and suspect no one else so far has either.[7]

Of course, a problem of enormous significance and difficulty for psychology in general is how to characterize *precisely* the intentional content of representations. We suspect that any expert on bee cognition would admit

---

[4] N.b., the objects or properties may or may not be real. We want to leave it an open question whether bees actually do succeed in representing actual objects in real space, a controversial issue between "internalists" and "externalists" about intentionality; see G. Evans (1982), Fodor (1987), and Rey (2008).

[5] We remain completely neutral about just what these attitudes might be (e.g., whether they are "beliefs" and "desires" or perhaps more technically defined attitudes, such as "cognize"). There is, of course, no presumption that the attitudes are the least bit *conscious*.

[6] Dretske (1981) and Fodor (1987) have tried to introduce notions that look to both the physical and the intentional notions, and it is certainly not implausible to suppose (what we think researchers routinely suppose, see Gallistel [1990]) that some intentional content is determined by some sort of "informational," covariation relation. However, precisely how to specify that relation is open to considerable controversy (see Loewer [1987]), and so we shall not presuppose such views here.

[7] *Pace* Quine (1960) and his followers, we do not see this as an occasion for despair. Plenty of notions have proved indispensable to science despite resisting clear definition for centuries – consider the notions of "limit" and "infinitesimal"!

that there is a sense in which (1) could be true, even though the precise content of the bees' representations would not be [the feeder is 200m east of the hive]. Bees, after all, probably do not entertain representations with the specific content [feeder] or [200m]. So how are we to understand content attributions such as those involved in such claims? We do not pretend to have any adequate answer to this question. Indeed, we think the answer can only be approached by considering in ever finer detail the work ascriptions of content will do in explaining phenomena like that of perception, reasoning, decision-making, and animal navigation, such as that of bees, along lines we pursue here.

It will help, however, to note a distinction between so-called "*de re*" and "*de dicto*" ways of reporting (or ascribing) intentional states. A dog might bark at the mailman, and, to a first approximation, that might be explained by saying that the dog thought the mailman was a threat. But this would not ordinarily be taken to imply that the dog really represented the mailman *as a mailman*, that the dog had the remotest concept or conception of the man as a carrier of *mail*. The dog was presumably just barking at the man who we, the ascribers, know to be the mailman. Such is a *de re* (or "of the thing") ascription, as opposed to a *de dicto* (or "in those very words") one, which *would* attempt to characterize the actual way the dog, itself, represented the man. But, of course, this latter is, at this stage of our knowledge, immensely difficult to determine. We will not attempt to determine such questions in the case of the bees, but will by and large restrict ourselves to what we take to be the *de re* ascriptions intended by the researchers in the area.[8] And, even then, our descriptions (as those of the researchers) must be taken tentatively, since even saying exactly what *actual thing* (if any) – a hive, a foraging site, the azimuth of the sun, optic flow, an angle number – a bee might be representing may not be easy to determine. For example, it is possible that bees do not represent their hive per se. Rather, they may represent only various parts or features of it, while lacking a representation of the entire structure. A proffered object or property may be a sub-instance of a larger category to which the bee is sensitive: perhaps it is not [hive], but maybe [oval solid]. It is even possible that the extensions of many or all bee mental-representational constituents do not include anything external to bees at all: they could turn out to be "lucky" (though not accidentally successful) hallucinators (cf. fn. 4).[9] One

---

[8] Consequently, we will not be committed to whether the relevant intentional content is "conceptual" or not.

[9] Issues of error of course raise the "disjunction" problem discussed by Kripke (1982) and Fodor (1987), which we mercifully will not address here. See Pietroski and Rey (1995) for a way of dealing with it consonant with the present discussion.

does the best one can. We do think, however, that our conclusions about systematicity will not turn on determining at this point precisely which of alternative *de re* or *de dicto* ascriptions are appropriate: we think bees' sensitivities are systematic whichever of them (within plausible bounds) is correct.

2.2. Features of (SYS)

A number of features of (SYS) bear emphasis:

(i) As a *ceteris paribus* law, it is open to apparent exceptions, especially those due to the interference of independently identifiable factors, such as distraction, fatigue, or worldly anomaly (perhaps it is too preposterous to think that Ann stays). We assume the issues here are typical of macro-scientific laws (cf. Pietroski and Rey [1995]), and afford a reply to the apparent exceptions raised by, e.g., Dennett (1991a) and Kaye (1995).

(ii) As a *law*, (SYS) presumably supports counterfactuals that are entailed by it. Thus, a system is not systematic if it just *happens* to be sensitive to F[p] iff it is sensitive to [p]. The proverbial primates randomly typing on a typewriter are not systematic simply because, in time, they will produce "F[p]" iff they produce "p." (This feature is relevant in considering defenses of connectionist rivals to classicism; see section 4 below, and Fodor and McLaughlin [1990].)

(iii) We do not address here the question of precisely how systematic honeybee cognition is *overall*. Perhaps some cognitive systems are modularized (see Fodor [1983]; Carruthers [2006]) and representations from one module cannot be permuted with representations from another. Or perhaps systematicity breaks down for bizarre possibilities: a dog might be able to represent [there is no water in the dish or people are in the room], but have trouble with [there are no people in the dish or water is in the room] (cf. Kaye [1995]). Our claim will be merely that there is *a significant domain* in which (SYS) is true for bees.

3. THE HONEYBEE DATA AND SYSTEMATICITY

In the next nine sections, we will describe some of the most relevant experiments and data for establishing the reality of classical representations in honeybees, and argue that they have systematically related navigational capacities.[10]

---

[10] For rich, recent reviews of the data on honeybee psychology, see Giurfa (2007) and Menzel and Giurfa (2006).

3.1. The waggle dance

Perhaps the best known and most remarkable fact about bees is their waggle dance, about which the following seems to be true (*modulo* the aforementioned difficulties of intentional ascription). Bees perform this dance in front of other bees upon returning to their hive after their foraging expeditions for various useful items (e.g., nectar, pollen, resin, water, and potential new nest sites). The dance encodes the relative location of their hive and a recent foraging site in terms of the distance and direction between them. The bees estimate distance flown primarily by monitoring optic flow, or image movement across the retina (Dacke and Srinivasan [2007]), and they estimate direction principally by means of their solar-compass mechanism (see section 3.3). Dances consist of multiple, straight waggle "runs," followed alternately by a clockwise or counterclockwise loop back to the start of the next run. The duration of the run corresponds to the distance to the site, and the angle of the run with respect to gravity corresponds to the site's direction relative to the current solar azimuth (the compass direction of the sun) (Dyer [2002]). For example, a vertical run indicates that the direction to the site is toward the current azimuth; a run 30° right of vertical indicates that the direction is 30° right of it. Recent experiments have shown that the information encoded in waggle dances is effectually transferred to the bees that respond to them (Riley *et al.* [2005]).

It is important to note the cognitive difficulty confronting a bee producing or decoding a dance. *Apis mellifora* foragers dance in darkness on the vertical surface of a hive comb. The dancer has to "translate" orientation with respect to solar cues, no longer available in darkness, into orientation with respect to gravity. Moreover, they are able to do this often hours or days later than their original foraging flight, correcting the dance to allow for the intervening changes in the solar azimuth (see Lindauer [1960]). The bees that respond to the dance have to decode this updated dance, determining where to fly. It is hard to underestimate the significance of these facts: they seem to require the bees to be able to integrate and access highly specific information about spatial relations, and translate it from one mode of presentation (dances oriented to gravity) to another (representations of the solar azimuth), with the former being carefully updated to keep track of the latter. On the face of it, it is hard to see how they could accomplish this without highly articulated representations of space and of various objects (a site, a hive, the sun) within it, representations that, moreover, would appear to have constituent structure, as we think the following facts about their abilities reveal.

3.2. Vector navigation

The ability to navigate by path integration is ubiquitous in animals from insects to humans (Gallistel [1990]). Path integration is the process by which an animal continually updates the current distance and direction from its present location to its departure point, solely by monitoring its angular and linear displacements. Such a process explains a wide number of phenomena observable in bees: their ability in featureless terrain to home directly toward the hive after performing a circuitous flight (Chittka *et al.* [1995]); their ability to retain a course over featureless terrain after having been blown off it by strong crosswinds; and their performing extensive search flights, periodically returning to the origin of the search flight, even in the absence of sensory cues marking its location (Reynolds *et al.* [2007]). It also explains how the waggle dances of foragers trained to follow a detour around a large obstacle nonetheless indicate the straight-line direction from the hive to the foraging site.

The extent to which honeybees rely on distance and direction information is clearly manifest in their performance of vector flights. Harmonic-radar experiments have shown that honeybees trained to a single established feeding station will navigate by relying on learned vector information, tending to disregard landscape cues (Riley *et al.* [2003]; although, as we will see, they do rely on these sometimes as well). After such training, honeybees captured at the feeder after filling their crops, and soon released at an unfamiliar location, will fly a vector that would have taken them from the feeder to the vicinity of the hive had they not been displaced. They will do so despite the presence of conspicuous landmarks not present along their trained route. The converse also holds: if the bees are captured when preparing to depart from the hive, then, once released at an unfamiliar location, they will fly a vector that otherwise would have taken them from the hive to the vicinity of the feeder.

A good example of vector integration is afforded by "shortcut" behavior, which Menzel *et al.* (2005) have observed bees exhibit between familiar locations other than the hive. Harmonic radar tracked the bees over the entire course of their flights. One group of bees was trained to a feeder situated 200m east of the hive. They were captured at the feeder after they filled their crops, and released at a distant location. They then performed a vector flight that otherwise would have led them to the hive. Having unexpectedly arrived somewhere other than the hive, and finding themselves lost, they began an extensive search. Eventually, the bees encountered a familiar landmark, the location of which, in relation to the hive, they had previously learned (presumably by path integration) while exploring the experimental area. Many of the bees then flew directly to the hive, even though they may not have previously flown directly to the hive from the relevant landmark. And many of the bees flew to the feeder instead by a completely novel route! Furthermore, no sensory cues were available to the bees that would have enabled them to locate the feeder from the location of the landmark on the basis of previous learning. Apparently, these bees recalled both the distance and direction to the hive from the familiar landmark, the distance and direction of the hive to the feeder, and integrated those memories in order to set their course.

3.3. The solar ephemeris

As we mentioned, honeybees compute direction by exploiting the solar azimuth, which they use as a reference point in order to set and hold a compass course. They are also able to use the sun-linked pattern of polarized light in blue sky to locate the azimuth when the sun is blocked from view. Because the sun moves in relation to the landscape, a bee's returning to a familiar site at different times of day requires its flying at different angles in relation to the azimuth, so it must be able to estimate how much the azimuth changes during the relevant time spans. This in turn requires the organism to be informed about the time of day (information provided by its circadian clock), and to have a record of the solar azimuth as a function of time of day. Such a record is called a solar ephemeris.

The solar ephemeris varies with time of year and latitude. Hence, although sensitivity to the solar azimuth seems to be innate (see Dyer and Dickinson [1994]), the current ephemeris for a particular locale must be learned. Complicating matters is the fact that the rate of change of the solar azimuth varies with time of day, and the fact that the solar ephemeris must be learned quickly, since a honeybee lives on average for only about ten days after it becomes a forager, making few exploratory flights before beginning to forage.

The solar ephemeris learning mechanism produces a record that allows bees to estimate fairly accurately the azimuth of the sun at times when they are not seeing it, due to heavy overcast, or have not ever seen it, due to controlled, limited exposure (Dyer and Dickinson [1994]). Perhaps most remarkably, their solar ephemeris allows bees to estimate the solar azimuth at night – and this is true not only for nocturnal, but also diurnal, foragers. Dyer (1985) observed the waggle dances of *Apis dorsata* after night flights to known foraging locations. Some of the recorded dances occurred about three hours after sunset, some before dawn, and both fairly accurately indicated the actual solar azimuth (the accuracy at night seems to be less good). Lindauer (1957) trained a colony of diurnal foragers to feed at a station to the south during the one-hour period after sunrise and to feed at a station to the east during the one-hour period before sunset, and then stimulated the bees to perform waggle dances at night. Apart from a few hours around midnight, the dances approximately indicated the solar azimuth.[11]

3.4. First systematicity hypothesis

We will now propose our first systematicity hypothesis. Crucially, the solar compass mechanism, which allows bees to represent hive-to-site solar bearings, also allows them to represent site-to-hive solar bearings. It provides them with a general capacity sufficient for the possession of numerous, more specific capacities, such that possession of that general capacity, together with one of the specific capacities, nomologically guarantees possession of the others. Thus, for any solar bearing α, bees have the capacity to represent the solar bearing from a particular familiar site to the hive, when that bearing is α iff they have the capacity to represent the solar bearing from the hive to that site, when that bearing is α; that is:

Ceteris paribus: A honeybee is sensitive to the content
    [the solar bearing of foraging site S from the hive is α]
  iff it is sensitive to the content
    [the solar bearing of the hive from foraging site S is α].

Our case for this hypothesis does not rely solely on the apparent nature of the honeybees' solar ephemeris. Thus, a feeder at a fixed distance from the hive could be slowly moved to a place 180° from its original one, the bees all the while updating their representations of the feeder's location (see section 3.6).

3.5. Landscape cues

Neither bees nor other animals rely on path integration alone. Small path integration errors accumulate, so it is quite useful to be able to compare and perhaps correct information provided by the current output of the path integrator with information about the previously learned locations of stable landmarks. It is also quite useful to be able to override default reliance on learned vector information (section 3.2). Instead of just flying off willy-nilly on the basis of where you think you are, it might pay to verify where you are first.

---

[11] For more on nocturnal dances, see Edrich (1981), von Frisch (1967), and Lindauer (1960).

In fact, when surreptitiously displaced and released, honeybees do not always fly the vector they otherwise would have flown, but instead rely on familiar landscape features in order to set their course. Menzel *et al.* (1998) introduced honeybees to an unfamiliar area and trained them to forage at two distant feeding stations: at one, *M*, southeast of the hive, only in the morning, and at the other, *A*, northeast of the hive, only in the afternoon (see diagram 1).

A (afternoon feeding station)

H (Hive)　　R (release site)

M (morning feeding station)

Diagram 1

R is a release-only site, east of the hive, situated between the feeding sites. Bees were captured either at the hive, *H*, after arrival from one of the feeders (hive-arriving bees), at the hive when preparing to depart to the time-appropriate feeder (hive-departing), upon arrival at one of the feeders, or while preparing to depart from one of the feeders. They were then displaced to one of the other sites, *A*, *M*, or *R*, where they were released. Bees of every group that were captured in the afternoon and released at *M* were able to fly toward the hive upon release. The hive-arriving bees and hive-departing bees captured in the morning and released at *A* also flew toward the hive upon release. These bees seem to have been able both to recognize their location of release and to recall the appropriate homeward direction: instead of flying along the vector they otherwise would have flown, they relied on familiar landscape features in order to set their course. This is particularly significant in considering the richness of the representational system the bees must use, since it must perforce be one that is capable of integrating the aforementioned representations of direction and distance with arbitrary information about things or properties at various locations at various times.

3.6. *Conflicting information about the same place*

These results of Menzel *et al.* (1998) illustrate another important feature of bee navigation, the ability to refer to the same place and resolve conflicting information about it.[12] This is not an ability that a creature comes by automatically by merely having two representations that as a matter of

---

[12] This ability is also manifest in the way bees update their information about the location of a familiar site in relation to local landmarks (see Wei *et al.* [2002]).

fact refer to the same place. After all, they might represent hive-1 as a certain point in a vector integration and hive-2 as something to the left of a tree, and not represent hive-1 as identical to hive-2, even when it is. However, as we are about to argue, it would be difficult to explain the actual navigational abilities of bees if we could not assume that they are able to integrate information about the same place *as the same place*, resolving conflicts that might arise in that information.

Menzel *et al.*'s results suggest that the displaced bees represented the two foraging sites and the hive in the same way in which they represented them during previous foraging excursions after they had filled their crops. Neither their having just flown to the foraging site nor their having fed there (or fed at all) was necessary in order for them to call up the appropriate homeward bearing. Likewise, when released at previously unvisited Site *R*, both hive-departing bees and hive-arriving bees were able to adopt the novel *R*-to-*H* flight-path, regardless of time of day. As Menzel and colleagues argue, these novel-shortcut bees seemed to recall both site-to-hive directions and "averaged" them to obtain the novel *R*-to-*H* direction (see Tetzlaff [2006] for discussion). Thus, those bees must have represented the hive and the two known sites in the same way in which they had on previous foraging excursions. Otherwise, it would be hard to see how they could treat both (or either) of their learned site-to-hive directions as relevant to the task of returning to the hive from *R*.

Bees can also resolve conflicting information about what to *do* at particular places. For example, Zhang *et al.* (2006) demonstrated that honeybees can be trained to reverse their choice preference, both at the hive and at the feeder, depending on time of day. In one experiment, the same bees learned both (i) to choose, in the morning, a black–white "sector" (or "pinwheel") pattern, over a black–white concentric rings pattern, at the feeder, and then to choose a black–white vertical grating over a black–white horizontal grating upon arrival back at the hive, and (ii) to choose, in the afternoon, the rings pattern over the sector pattern, at the feeder, and then to choose the horizontal grating over the vertical grating at the hive.

In another experiment, bees learned both (i) to choose, in the morning, a horizontal grating over a vertical grating at the feeder, and then to choose a vertical grating over a horizontal grating at the hive, and (ii) to choose, in the afternoon, the vertical over the horizontal grating at the feeder, and then to choose the horizontal over the vertical grating at the hive.

Bees appear to have a general ability to vary parameters in a pattern independently of any specific task.

3.7. Second systematicity hypothesis

The capacity of bees to reverse their choice preferences, presumably over a wide range of stimulus cues, provides us with a family of systematicity hypotheses, such as:

Ceteris Paribus: A honeybee is sensitive to the content
  [Choose *A* at the feeder and *B* at the hive]
 iff it is sensitive to the content
  [Choose *B* at the feeder and *A* at the hive].

Thus, provided that a bee can learn to choose *A* over *B* at one time while performing a certain task at a certain place (e.g., returning home in the morning), it can learn to choose *B* over *A* at another time while performing that same task at that same place. Furthermore, it seems that the bees would represent the relevant place (e.g., hive) as the same place, regardless of time of day and the choice to be made.

3.8. Sequence learning

The generality and richness of the honeybee's navigational abilities is further manifested in its ability to remember various kinds of sequences per se, as opposed to the capacity merely to remember different items recalled sequentially via trigger-response mechanisms. Honeybees have the capacity to remember a sequence of flight vectors like the following: first, fly *n* distance units in direction *d*; second, fly *m* distance units in direction *d** (T. S. Collett *et al.* [1993]).

   The same study also showed that bees have the capacity to learn a sequence of positive visual stimuli, in the process of learning to negotiate a simple maze. Thus, in order to negotiate the maze, bees learned to choose, for example, the hole marked with white rather than the one marked with black in the first chamber, the hole marked with blue rather than the one marked with yellow in the second chamber, and the hole marked with vertical stripes rather than the one marked with horizontal stripes in the third chamber. M. Collett *et al.*'s (2002) study on the effects of panoramic context on the performance of route flight segments showed that honeybees have the capacity to learn route sequences of the form: first, fly distance *n* to landmark *L*, then fly distance *m* to landmark *L**. For each of these cases of sequence learning, alternative hypotheses to the effect that the bees merely recalled separate memories in the correct order can be ruled out (see Tetzlaff [2006] for discussion).

3.9. Final systematicity hypotheses

Honeybees presumably have the general capacity to represent a wide variety of each of the above three types of sequences. These general capacities yield the following systematicity hypotheses:

Ceteris Paribus: A honeybee is sensitive to the content
    [Fly distance n in direction d, then fly distance m in direction d^*]
 iff it is sensitive to the contents
    [Fly distance n in direction d^*, then fly distance m in direction d] and
    [Fly distance m in direction d^*, then fly distance n in direction d].
Ceteris Paribus: A honeybee is sensitive to the content
    [Fly distance n to landmark L, then fly distance m to landmark L^*]
 iff it is sensitive to the contents
    [Fly distance m to L, then fly distance n to L^*],
    [Fly distance n to L^*, then fly distance m to L], and
    [Fly distance m to L^*, then fly distance n to L].
Ceteris Paribus: A honeybee is sensitive to the content
    [Choose white in the first chamber, blue in the second, vertical in the third]
 iff it is sensitive to the contents
    [Choose white in the first chamber, vertical in the second, blue in the third],
    [Choose blue in the first chamber, white in the second, vertical in the third],
    and so on.

All of the various instances of systematicity we have proposed support the generalization:

(BEE-SYS) *Ceteris Paribus*: For a range of navigational capacities,
 a honeybee is sensitive to the content [p] iff it is sensitive to F[p].

To reiterate a point we made at the start (section 2.1), the truth of our various systematicity hypotheses does not depend upon settling just which proposals about the precise content of bee states is actually correct. The candidates we have provided are simply the plausible *de re* ascriptions spontaneously provided by the researchers.

Note that systematicity does not imply productivity, or the ability to recursively generate a potential infinitude of expressions from a given base. Indeed, for all their ability to permute representations into novel ones, it appears that no non-human animal has any such recursive ability (see Hauser *et al.* [2002]). At any rate, there is so far no evidence that a bee that can represent a sequence can also represent indefinitely long repetitions of such a sequence, in the way that even small children spontaneously can do.

4. CLASSICAL VS. CONNECTIONIST PROPOSALS

There is a straightforward explanation of systematicity in terms of classical cognitive architecture. A classical system is sensitive to the content [p] iff it is sensitive to F[p] for two reasons. First, the vehicles expressing the contents [p] and F[p] have the same syntactic structure and the very same constituents: the syntax-sensitive mechanisms that would be responsible for tokening [p] are the very same as those that would be responsible for tokening F[p]. Second, the contents [p] and F[p] are determined by their vehicles' syntax and by the contents of their vehicles' constituents.[13]

Of course, it is possible to rig a classical system so that its capacities are not systematic (cf. Aizawa [1997]). But it is important to see that rigging would be required. For a proportion of the possible values of "p" (consider whatever proportion you think would warrant the label "asystematic"), to devise a classical system that is sensitive to [p] but not sensitive to F[p] would require permitting entokenings of representations of [p] while blocking entokenings of representations of F[p]. That, however, would prevent the formation of such a large proportion of syntactically well-defined representations that the system would hardly seem to be appropriately classified as a syntax-driven mechanism, contrary to what classicism requires. Thus, it is *asystematicity*, not systematicity, that has to be specifically designed into classical systems.

On the other hand, we do not have a good idea of how an explanation of systematicity could proceed in terms of non-classical architectures. Such an architecture could, of course, produce F[p] iff it produced [p], but only as a by-product of producing all other patterns, well- or ill-formed, as well: the systematicity would not be a *law* (see section 2.2 (ii) above). Such architectures, by design, do not support concatenative syntax. So an explanation of systematicity in terms of such an architecture will have to appeal to something other than such syntax.

Smolensky (1995) has shown in principle how a connectionist architecture could exhibit systematicity. His account requires positing (among

---

[13] Particularly in considering navigation, it is almost irresistible to talk about creatures using some kind of "cognitive map." We think it is unlikely in the extreme that *this* talk can be taken at face value, since it seems to us unlikely that there is literally a map *in the brain* over which computations are defined. There might, of course, be in the bee's brain isomorphisms between, say, stimulated portions of a visual ganglion and figures in ambient space. But what needs to be shown is that these isomorphisms are exploited computationally (e.g., the actual spatial properties of the representation are used to represent properties of what is represented, and are essential to the success of the computation – see Rey [1981] and Pylyshyn [2004, ch. 7] for discussion). [Editor's note: see Rescorla (chapter 3) for a dissenting opinion on the reality of cognitive maps in animals.]

other things) linearly independent syntactic-role vectors (ordered n-tuples of activation values) that bind (superimpose) with other representational vectors, a binding that provides for a sort of functional, non-concatenative syntax (Horgan and Tienson [1996]). However, this sort of architecture is capable of exhibiting systematicity only if it is provided with the capacity to entoken such syntactic-role vectors. For ultimately, syntactic-role vectors must be entokened along with vectors that represent individuals or properties in order for them to be superimposed. But then not only must the capacity to exhibit systematicity be specifically built into such an architecture, but also it must be capable of implementing a classical language of thought after all. Likewise, all such vectors must be entokened in order for the system to perform operations on its representations, particularly if, as we have seen, bees are able to access and update information about specific parameters across a wide variety of tasks. Of course, Smolensky argues that none of this is so, since, he claims, weight matrices would be available that can process vector representations without their constituents having to be entokened. But we think that this is precisely what he has not established.[14]

The general lesson is this. Representationalists of any stripe who reject classicism need to find a way to make their proposed cognitive architectures behave as if their representations have concatenative structure, even though they do not.[15] Such theorists either will not succeed, or they will only appear to succeed either by inadvertently implementing classical representations or by special rigging (cf. Hadley [2004]). Such "success" may come, but only at the cost of explanatory power.

5. INSTRUMENTALISM

Why suppose that honeybees acquire informational content at all? Why not suppose that attributing content to bees may be nothing more than our adopting an "intentional stance" (Dennett [1987]) or other "interpretive"

---

[14] Indeed, to take an analogy that Smolensky (1991, p. 225, n.7) himself has drawn, it seems as improbable that one could implement bee systematicities and information integration without entokening constituent structure as it would be that one might prove theorems in logic by Gödel numbers without factoring the numbers into their primes. Note, though, that the presence of such implementation might not be obvious: the system might *seem* to be radical connectionist on the surface, but it could (indeed, arguably must) nonetheless implement a classical structure. To insist that there is no such classical implementation requires showing a negative existential, which, notoriously, it is by no means easy to do.

[15] Editor's note: see Rescorla (chapter 3) for a representational account of the concatenative structure of cognitive maps.

kind of understanding (Davidson [1980]) toward their behavior, whereby they are regarded as "rational," but about whose actual truth there is no fact of the matter? Perhaps what we see as the systematic nature of bee cognition lies merely in our interpretation of the data rather than in any real mental capacities of bees.

Consider, however, waggle dances (section 3.1), path integration, vector flights (section 3.2), and the solar compass mechanism (section 3.3). What is striking here is that there is no question of the bees' overall rationality – certainly nothing remotely approaching their appreciating the deductive closure of their "beliefs" (Dennett [1978], p. 11). As we've noted, their representations, like those evidently of most non-human minds, don't seem productive or recursive. Indeed, our ascription of intentional content to their states, albeit provisional (section 2.1), is not based on any "norms" of rationality,[16] but rather upon observation of a number of law-like relations that obtain among, for example, the distances and compass directions of foragers' flights to particular sites, the durations and orientations in relation to gravity of their post-flight waggle runs, and the distances and compass directions of the flights of bees recruited by those foragers' dances. Moreover, as the phenomenon of default reliance on recalled flight vector information shows, these relations can obtain independently of the current landscape cues encountered during flight – they irrationally ignore what's right in front of their noses. For all that, however, honeybees seem to be able to perform vector-algebraic computations on the relevant information (sections 3.2, 3.6), integrate this information with information about features of the landscape (section 3.5), and resolve conflicts in information about the same place (section 3.6). These are precisely the kinds of phenomena that are explained in terms of computations over stored and retrieved representations. It is unclear, to say the least, how one might proceed without them. Unless the interpretivist is prepared to be an instrumentalist about all explanation, it behooves him to say why the instrument works in the specific way it does, and in this case it is hard to see how it could do so without the states it postulates being real.

---

[16] It might be claimed that they obey some sort of practical, decision-theoretic rationality. However, other than assuming in many of these cases that they navigate towards things they more or less "want," we have absolutely no evidence that they, for example, always navigate so as, e.g., to maximize expected utility. Perhaps some of the navigation is triggered by some stimulus cue and the poor things find themselves trudging off on a foraging expedition despite a strong preference to languish in the hive. The point here is that, *pace* Dennett and Davidson, the intentional ascription can be made without commitment to any overall rationality of the bees. See Rey (2002, 2007) for further discussion.

6. CONCLUSION

Honeybees have abilities to navigate as a result of a remarkable integration of information about distance, time, direction, and the location of a range of items and landmarks, much of which they can convey to each other in their famous waggle dance. These abilities display a variety of systematicities regarding distance, solar bearing, and stimulus cues, which we specified in section 3. We submit that the best explanation of these abilities and systematicities is that the bees compute over causally efficacious, syntactically structured representations, i.e., representations in a "language of thought" of the sort proposed in classical theories of mental architecture. If this is so, then it is a reason to think that bees really do have the intentional states that researchers routinely ascribe to them.

CHAPTER 5

Invertebrate concepts confront the generality constraint (and win)

Peter Carruthers

This chapter defends the claim that invertebrates possess concepts against the so-called "generality constraint," first proposed by Evans (1982). A number of different versions of that constraint are distinguished. Some are ill-motivated. Those that aren't are not only consistent with but support the claim that invertebrates possess genuine concepts, as opposed to mere "proto-concepts," and that invertebrates engage in genuine forms of thinking, as opposed to mere "proto-thinking." Indeed, it turns out that distinctively human kinds of thinking contain mere *faux*-thoughts by comparison with those that we share with non-human animals.

I. INTRODUCTION

What does it take to possess a concept? Do any non-human animals have concepts? One crucial constraint on the concept *concept* is that concepts are the building blocks of thought. Hence no creature could count as a concept-user that wasn't capable of thinking. This mightn't seem like a significant additional restriction, but actually it has some teeth, ruling out some otherwise concept-*like* phenomena. Consider the Australian digger wasp (Gould and Gould [1994]). The female builds a tower-and-bell structure above the hole in which she lays her eggs, to protect them from another species of parasitic wasp. At various points during construction she uses her own body as a yardstick. For example, she stops building the tower and begins on the bell once the former is three of her own body lengths high. Does she, then, have the concept, *three body lengths* (or some sufficiently close analog)? She does at least possess a sort of recognitional capacity which she deploys to end one phase of her activity and initiate another. (And likewise she must be capable of recognizing the materials that she

I am grateful to Elisabeth Camp, Bradley Rives, Michael Tetzlaff, and (especially) Robert Lurz for their comments on previous drafts of this chapter.

collects for the construction of the tower, as well as recognizing that one side of the tower that she is constructing is higher than the other, and so forth.) But does the wasp *believe* that the tower is now three body lengths high, and is that why she moves on to the next activity (the construction of the bell)?

There are multiple reasons for denying that she does. The most fundamental derives from the fact that the overall pattern of her behavior is *rigid* (albeit displaying flexibility of detail – collecting mud from here rather than there, placing the mud on this side rather than that side, and so on). For example, if an experimenter progressively buries the tower in sand while she is constructing it, she will just keep on building, indefinitely, because she never reaches the three-body-lengths trigger for initiating the next phase. But once she has completed the tower and begun on the bell, she takes no notice if an experimenter buries most of the tower in sand, even though the bell then ends up resting on the ground and will consequently be quite useless. Likewise if an experimenter makes a small hole in a completed portion of the tower before it is finished, she will build *another* tower-and-bell structure on top of it, rather than effecting a simple repair.

Another consideration is that the state that ends the tower-construction phase never interacts with any other "goal" states. This gives us reason to think that the state isn't genuinely a *belief*. For it is of the essence of beliefs that they should be apt to interact with desires in such a way as to issue in motor plans and behavior.[1] Moreover, we have no reason to think that the state in question factors into two (or more) conceptual components, *tower* and *three body lengths*. But again, it is of the essence of beliefs that they should be structured out of distinct conceptual components, each of which can figure in other attitudes and be suitably combined with other concepts to formulate distinct thoughts. What the wasp actually has is an abstract, innately specified, but flexibly implementable, motor plan, which is guided in its detailed execution by perceptual information, and whose various stages are triggered and/or completed by the matching of concept-like recognitional templates against the perceptual data.

From these considerations we can extract the following constraints. In order to count as having concepts, a creature needs to be capable of thinking. And that means, at least, that it must possess distinct belief states and desire states, which interact with one another (and with perception) in the selection and guidance of behavior. In addition, the belief states need to

---

[1] Editor's note: See Saidel (chapter 2) for a similar account of the distinctness condition for beliefs and desires, and Roberts (chapter 12) for an account of concepts (employed in emotions) that are not detachable or recombinable in thought.

be structured out of component parts (concepts) which can be recombined with others to figure in other such states with distinct contents. Moreover, belief and desire states need to play causal roles that are sensitive to their underlying structures, figuring in simple inferences that bring to bear belief states to select actions that will enable the realization of the creature's goals.

These constraints on concept possession are by no means trivial. Nevertheless, many invertebrates actually satisfy them (or so I shall argue in section 2). This is especially clear in the case of honeybees, whose powers of thought have been intensively studied – notably their flexible use of spatial information in the service of a multitude of goals. But the constraints are probably satisfied by Australian digger wasps, too, in respect of the states that guide their navigational (but not their nest-construction) behavior. (And there is surely no requirement that *all* of an organism's behavior should be guided by genuine concept-involving thoughts if *any* is to count as such. For much of our own routine, habitual, or "inconsequential" behavior wouldn't pass muster, either.) I have argued for these claims in some detail elsewhere (Carruthers [2004, 2006]), and will only sketch those arguments here. (But see Tetzlaff and Rey [chapter 4] for some closely related considerations.) My main focus will be on an argument purporting to establish yet further constraints on genuine concept possession (the so-called "generality constraint"), which invertebrates (together with most other animals) would turn out to fail.

Let me say a word about terminology, however, before we proceed. The use of the term "concept" in philosophy is systematically ambiguous (Laurence and Margolis [2007]). It is sometimes used to designate the *content* of a word or a component of thought. In this usage a concept is an abstract object, often identified with a "mode of presentation" of the things that the word picks out. But sometimes concepts are intended to be mental representations, concrete components of the physical tokenings of the thoughts of which they form part.[2] In the present chapter I am concerned almost exclusively with concepts in the latter sense. Our question is whether invertebrates possess the sorts of mental representations that are the components of genuine thoughts. Whenever I want to refer to one of these mental representations I shall use italics (as well as using italics for

---

[2] There is also a third usage, which equates concepts with mental *capacities*. This is what Evans himself has in mind when formulating the generality constraint (1982, p. 101). But I take this usage to be closely related to the idea of concepts as mental representations. For any capacity must have a categorical basis, and distinct capacities that bear systematic relationships to one another are likely to have distinct categorical bases (Fodor and McLaughlin [1990]). The latter can then be equated with the mental representations postulated by language-of-thought theorists.

emphasis – the difference should always be clear). And on those occasions when I do want to refer to the content of a mental representation I shall insert the relevant words or phrases within square brackets.

2. THE CASE FOR INVERTEBRATE CONCEPTS

Like many other insects, bees use a variety of navigation systems. One is dead reckoning (integrating a sequence of directions of motion with the distance traveled in each direction, to produce a representation of one's current location in relation to the point of origin; see Gallistel [1990]). This in turn requires that bees can learn the expected position of the sun in the sky at any given time of day, as measured by an internal clock of some sort. Another mechanism permits bees to recognize and navigate from landmarks, either distant or local (Collett and Collett [2002]). And some researchers have shown that bees will, in addition, construct mental maps of their environment from which they can navigate.

Gould (1986) reports, for example, that when trained to a particular food source and then carried from the hive in a dark box to a new release point, the bees will fly *directly* to the food, but only if there is a significant landmark in their vicinity when they are released. (Otherwise they fly off on the compass bearing that would previously have led from the hive to the food.) Other scientists have found it difficult to replicate these experiments directly, perhaps because bees have such a strong disposition to fly out on compass bearings to which they have been trained. But in a related experiment, Menzel *et al.* (2000) found that bees that had never foraged more than a few meters from the nest, but who were released at random points much further from it, were able to return home swiftly. They argue that this either indicates the existence of a map-like structure, built during the bees' initial orientation flights before they had begun foraging, or else the learned association of vectors-to-home with local landmarks. But either way, they claim, the spatial representations in question are allocentric rather than egocentric in character.

More recently, Menzel *et al.* (2005) have provided strong evidence of the map-like organization of spatial memory in honey bees through the use of harmonic radar. The latter technology enabled the investigators to track the flight-paths of individual bees. Bees who were just about to set out for a feeder were captured and taken to random release points some distance from the hive. Initially, the bees then traveled along the vector that they were about to fly out on when captured. This was followed by a looping orientation phase, once the bees realized that they were lost, followed by a straight flight, either to the hive, or to the feeder and then to the hive. The latter sequence (a flight straight to the feeder), in particular, would only be possible if the bees could calculate a new vector to a target from any arbitrary landmark that they know, which requires both a map-like organization to their memory and the inferential resources to utilize it.

Moreover, bees can make flexible use of the information encoded in their mental maps, in the service of multiple goals. Thus the very same information that there is nectar 200 meters north of the hive, for example, is utilized both when returning to the hive laden with nectar and when setting out to visit the nectar source from the hive once again. It is also used to guide the orientation of the bee's dance to inform other bees of the location, and it can be acquired from observing the dance of another bee as well as from personal experience. In addition, bees learn the locations of many other substances that they take as goals when appropriate, including pollen, water, and tree sap. And the data obtained by Menzel *et al.* (2005) suggests that all of these locations will be encoded on the bee's mental map, in such a way that the bee could, if appropriately motivated, fly directly from a source of water to a source of tree sap, for example.

There is much more that could be said about these and related data. To mention just one issue: does the fact that bees have memory systems with a map-like organization disqualify them from having genuine beliefs? This would be on the grounds that maps lack constituent structure, as Bermúdez (chapter 8; 2003a) claims. However, the latter claim might be true of some topographic maps, but certainly isn't true of symbolic maps. These are composed of elements representing types of entity and substance (water, trees, grassland, buildings) as well as individuals (e.g., a particular river or town) which could be recombined with one another in indefinitely many distinct configurations to represent any number of different geographical layouts.[3] The mental maps of bees are plainly of this latter sort.

Taken all together, the data warrant the claim that bees possess both belief-like states and desire-like states that interact with one another in simple practical inferences to select and guide behavior; and that the belief-like states possess a component structure, containing symbols that refer to various landmarks and substances as well as encoding the distances and directions between them. Whether this is sufficient to qualify bees (and other invertebrates) as genuine thinkers, and genuine concept-users, is the topic of the remainder of our discussion.

---

[3] Editor's note: See Rescorla (chapter 3) for a similar account of cognitive maps as structured representations.

3. THE GENERALITY CONSTRAINT

The generality constraint is introduced by G. Evans (1982) as a constraint on genuine concept possession, and thus as a constraint on a creature's capacity for authentic thought. (Others insist, in similar vein, on the "spontaneity" of thought; see McDowell [1996].) The constraint, as Evans formulates it, is this: genuine thinkers must be capable of entertaining all syntactically permissible combinations of any concepts that they possess (or almost all of them, at any rate – this qualification will be discussed in section 4). So if thinkers possesses the concepts F, G, a, and b, then they must be capable of thinking each of the thoughts Fa, Fb, Ga, and Gb (but not the "thoughts" FG or ab, which are ill-formed and uninterpretable).

A word about terminology before we proceed further. For the most part I shall discuss the generality constraint in terms of the *thinking* of thoughts. But Evans himself uses the language of *entertaining* a thought (see his [1982], p. 104). Is this a significant difference? One possibility is that Evans uses "entertain" to mean something like "suppose," in which case the generality constraint would be tantamount to the claim that any creature that has concepts must be capable of supposition. This idea will be discussed, and heavily criticized, in section 4. Alternatively, "entertain" (like "think") can be used generically, to cover all forms of propositional attitude (believing, desiring, supposing, wondering whether, etc.). Thus understood, the difference between the two ways of formulating the generality constraint is merely verbal. And note that, so understood, the generality constraint permits "cross-overs" between the different attitude types. For what one might be incapable of believing one might nevertheless be capable of supposing or wishing. Thus someone who possesses the concepts *a*, *identity*, and *negation* might be capable of *supposing* that *a isn't a*, even if she isn't capable of *believing* it. And someone who is incapable of *believing* that he has never been born might nevertheless be capable of *wishing* it.

Taken at its face, the generality constraint will very likely require us to deny thoughts and concepts to most if not all non-human animals. Hence, if it is endorsed, then animals will be capable, at best, of *proto-thoughts* composed of *proto-concepts* (Bermúdez [2003a]; Dummett [1973, 1996]). And the generality constraint will then mark a radical divide between the minds of human beings and the proto-mindedness of non-human animals. This is because, as a number of philosophers have pointed out, there are probably numerous restrictions on the ways in which the concepts (or rather, the proto-concepts) of animals can be combined and recombined. Carruthers (2006) gives the following example. A bee that is capable of thinking that there is nectar 200 meters north of the hive (or something that approximates to this), and that is capable of thinking that the brood chamber is now above it, might nevertheless be *incapable* of thinking that there is nectar 200 meters north of the brood chamber. This is because the bee's spatial navigation and mental map-building outside the hive are based on solar bearings, whereas bees navigate inside the hive in the dark, where they employ quite other (gravity-based and olfactory) ways of representing spatial relationships. And bees might very well lack any means of integrating the two sets of spatial representations into a single thought.

Likewise, many who have written on this topic have used the example of a monkey who thinks that the lion is eating the antelope: it may nevertheless be *incapable* of thinking that the antelope is eating the lion. This example is probably not a good one, however. We might well be able to get the monkey to think that the antelope is eating the lion if we rigged things up right – for example, if we could arrange so that the antelope really was eating the lion, or at least appeared to be doing so. But there will be plenty of other examples that can serve to make the point. Thus a monkey that is familiar with an aged matriarch – call her "Elsa" – might be incapable of thinking that Elsa is an infant. For what could we possibly do that might induce the monkey to entertain such a thought (whether believing it, desiring it, or whatever)?

The generality constraint is believed to be warranted by the demand that real thoughts must be compositionally structured. I endorse this demand. I agree that in order to count as a genuine thinker, a creature's thoughts must be composed out of recombinable conceptual components. But there are a number of distinctions that have been overlooked in most treatments of the topic. One is between the different notions of possibility involved, which can be *logical, causal,* or *metaphysical.* And the other is between a strong requirement that genuine concepts must be recombinable with *all* (or almost all) syntactically permissible others, and the weaker requirement that genuine concepts must be recombinable with at least *some* others. Let me briefly consider the former set of distinctions first, although it is the difference between strong and weak versions of the generality constraint that is more important for my purposes.

The requirement that it must be *logically* or *conceptually* possible for genuine concepts to recombine with others is too feeble to be of any interest. (Evans himself, however, sometimes seems to have had this reading in mind. For he writes that there should be no *conceptual* barrier in the way of thinkers entertaining the combinatorial variants of their thoughts: see his [1982], p. 102.) For even if a creature's "thoughts" possess no component structure whatever – either realized in simple (componentless) sentence-like representations or in a distributed connectionist network with limited powers of learning – it will still be *conceptually* possible for that creature to entertain novel variants of the "thoughts" that it entertains. We just have to conceive that the creature should somehow acquire new powers of representation.

In contrast, the requirement that it must be *causally* possible for genuine concepts to recombine with others is probably too strong for our purposes. For the generality constraint is meant to track the cognitive *capacities* that a thinking creature possesses, not its cognitive *performance*. For familiar reasons – having to do with contingent limitations of memory, attention, inferential skills, and so forth – it might be the case that a thinker is causally prevented from entertaining certain recombinations of its concepts, even though the creature possesses the underlying conceptual competence to do so.

What we should claim, therefore, is that it must be *metaphysically* possible for genuine concepts to be recombined with others. This allows us to idealize beyond contingent limitations on a creature's cognitive performance. But such idealization should be relative to the underlying cognitive architecture that the animal possesses. For what prevents a bee from combining solar-based spatial representations with gravity-based ones might be the modular organization of these two distinct kinds of spatial cognition, rather than mere limitations of memory or attention. In which case, to get those different forms of representation combined with one another would require a change to a novel (non-bee-like) cognitive architecture. And the resulting creature would, arguably, no longer be a bee.

The distinction between causal and metaphysical varieties of the generality constraint may be by no means easy to negotiate in practice, involving, as it does, the question of what features of a creature's cognition are *essential* to it, and what accidental. There are delicate issues here that may often be difficult to resolve. This won't matter much for present purposes, however. Although I shall continue to formulate the generality constraint in terms of metaphysical possibility, I shall place little weight on its distinctness from a causal version of the same idea. Much more important is the question of the appropriate quantifier (*all* versus *some*) that should be employed. In fact we have the following two possibilities to consider.

> *Strong generality constraint:* If a creature possesses the concepts F and a (and is capable of thinking Fa), then for *all* (or almost all) other concepts G and b that the creature could possess, it is metaphysically possible for the creature to think Ga, and in the same sense possible for it to think Fb.

Weak generality constraint: If a creature possesses the concepts F and a (and is capable of thinking Fa), then for *some* other concepts G and b that the creature could possess, it is metaphysically possible for the creature to think Ga, and in the same sense possible for it to think Fb.

I maintain that the requirement that thoughts must be compositionally structured, built up out of distinct and recombinable concepts as parts, only warrants the weak generality constraint. But this raises no difficulty for the idea of invertebrate concepts. Crucially, compositionality does *not* warrant the strong generality constraint, which is the one that creates problems for the idea that any non-human animals are genuine concept users.

Recall the claim that concepts are the building blocks of thought. Concepts are *components* of the complex representations that are thoughts. And if they really are the components of thought, then each such component must be capable of combining with at least *some* other concepts that the organism possesses in the context of a distinct thought. Conversely, if it were impossible for the concept F in Fa to combine with any other concept that the creature could possess, then that would suggest that either F or a (or both) aren't really distinct isolable parts of the larger representational state. Genuine concepts should be *detachable* from the states of which they are parts. And if they are thus detachable, then there should be no principled obstacle to them figuring along with other such parts in at least some other complex states.

The relationship between the weak generality constraint and compositionality is, arguably, an epistemic one. For consider what evidence could convince us that the concept F is a detachable component of a state with the content [Fa]. The best evidence would consist of cases in which that very concept figures in other thoughts, for example in a state with the content [Fb]. Hence if the weak generality constraint is satisfied, and we are satisfied that a creature's behavior warrants ascribing an appropriate *range* of thoughts to it, then we have reason to think that it has thoughts that are built up out of component concepts. Otherwise we may lack any warrant for thinking that the creature's state really does break up into the two separate components F and a. That is, for every concept F and every concept a that we want to attribute to the creature, we may need to find *some* other concepts G and b such that we have evidence that the creature is capable of thinking Fb and capable of thinking Ga. And the best such evidence is to actually find circumstances in which the creature thinks Fb and circumstances in which it thinks Ga.

Hence it is, arguably, the weak generality constraint that warrants us in thinking that a creature's thoughts are genuinely *composed* of concepts as parts. But this claim poses no threat to the conceptual capacities of invertebrates. Consider, for example, a honeybee's thought with the content [nectar is 200 meters north of the hive] (or some near equivalent). Is this genuinely composed of the concepts *nectar*, *200 meters* (or some roughly equivalent measure of distance), *north* (or some similar solar-based measure of direction), and *hive*? Well, yes, because we know that bees satisfy the weak generality constraint in respect of such concepts (Carruthers [2004, 2006]; Tetzlaff and Rey [chapter 4]). We know that a bee can also think thoughts with the contents [the hive is 200 meters north of the nectar], [nectar is 200 meters west of the hive], [pollen is 400 meters north of the hive], and so on for all interpretable combinations of the four candidate concepts, both with each other and with other similar concepts. And we know that the inferences in which bees engage are sensitive to such component structures.

What reason could there be for insisting that genuine concept-users must also satisfy the strong generality constraint, and be capable of combining any concept that they possess with any other concept that they possess? For this certainly isn't required by the core idea that concepts are the building blocks of thought. Of course, from our human perspective, our thought processes are the very paradigm of thinking. And the strong generality constraint, or something close to it, really is true of us. But we need to pay attention to the reason *why* it is true of us. I shall argue that this is best explained by our capacity for creative supposition, combined with our abilities to draw inferences from the things that we suppose. But thinking creatively is one thing, thinking *simpliciter* is another. The fact that most animals can't do the former provides no reason for denying that they can do the latter. There is therefore no good reason, I shall argue, to believe that a creature must be capable of entertaining all permissible combinations of its concepts in order to count as a genuine concept-user, or a genuine thinker. In which case non-human animals can count as full-fledged thinkers, after all (invertebrates included).

4. STRONG GENERALITY AS AN IDEAL

As many have pointed out, not even humans really satisfy the strong generality constraint, if the latter is taken with full generality. For although they are syntactically well-formed, we can't actually interpret or do anything with such thoughts as *Julius Caesar is a prime number* or *Green ideas sleep furiously*. One response to this point has been to claim that the generality constraint shouldn't require all syntactically possible combinations of concepts, but only those that conform to the right *categories*. Thus for these purposes the concept *prime number*, to be real, only needs to be combinable with other number concepts, not with any singular terms whatever. This is the line that is generally taken in the philosophical literature, following Evans (1982).

Camp (2004) argues that placing categorical restrictions of this sort on the generality constraint is a mistake, however. For combinations of concepts that seem like nonsense in one era, and which would therefore have motivated a categorical restriction, can not only be interpreted in another, but can even be recognized to be true. The thought *Matter is energy* would provide one clear example, and metaphors like *Juliette is the sun* would provide another. Rather, Camp thinks, the strong generality constraint should be thought of as an *ideal* to which actual organisms approximate (and to which humans come pretty close). On this account, then, the question whether non-human animals have concepts might not always admit of a yes-or-no answer. Rather, most animals might meet the generality constraint to *some* degree, and can therefore be described as *approximating* to genuine thought and concept deployment to a greater or lesser extent.

Although concept possession is here regarded as a matter of degree, there are surely positions at either end of the spectrum where stronger, yes-or-no language would be warranted. Thus humans approximate so closely to the ideal set out in the strong generality constraint that it would be misleading to say anything other than that we *are* genuine thinkers and genuine concept-users (just as it would be misleading to describe someone with a slightly receding hairline as anything other than hirsute, or not bald). And conversely, many animals fall so far short of meeting the strong generality constraint that it would be quite inappropriate to describe them as having concepts at all (just as it would be inappropriate to describe someone with only a few tufts of hair over his ears as hirsute, and equally misleading to deny that he is bald). Rather, the language of "proto-concepts" and "proto-thoughts" is better warranted when describing most species of non-human animal (Camp [2009]).

Camp thinks, then, that the strong generality constraint is an *ideal* to which organisms can approximate. The use of evaluative language, here, prompts one to ask: Ideal with respect to what? In the service of what value? Camp replies: with respect to the purposes for which thought is required. Her idea is that a creature whose capacities for representation fall a long way short of what the generality constraint would require isn't getting the full benefit from those capacities. But of course, whether a capacity to generate novel combinations of concepts counts as a benefit must be relative to the cognitive powers (and also the ecological niche) of the creature in question. There is no benefit in being able to entertain a new range of thoughts if you can't do anything useful with those thoughts. But this is, I claim, a function of the range of attitudes available to the creature, as well as its inferential abilities, not its capacity to think per se. I shall elaborate these points in turn.

4.1. Creative supposition

What is it that enables humans to approximate to the strong generality constraint? There is no single answer: it is actually a cluster of abilities. One is our capacity to *suppose* – to entertain a thought without commitment to its truth, evaluating it or drawing inferences from it. This capacity is first manifested in infancy in the form of childhood pretend play, as when the child (perhaps struck by the similarity in shape between a banana and a telephone handset) supposes that the banana is a telephone, and pretends accordingly (Nichols and Stich [2003]). No other species of animal on earth engages in pretence in normal circumstances. (Some hand-reared chimpanzees have, as adults, been observed to engage in behavior that at least looks very much *like* pretence, however. See Jolly [1999].) And it is extremely doubtful whether any animals outside of the great ape clade are capable of supposing. (There is some reason to think that chimpanzees might occasionally entertain states that are the functional equivalent of supposition, at least, mentally rehearsing potential actions in advance of decision-making. See Carruthers [2006].)

Moreover, the capacity to generate suppositions *creatively* is a crucial ingredient in human problem-solving abilities. Consider, for example, its role in science, specifically in our practices of inference to the best explanation. When confronted by puzzling data, scientists often need to generate a range of potential explanations before devising experiments to test between the resulting candidate theories. This will often require considerable creativity, since explanatory hypotheses can't in any sense be derived from, or "read off from," the data. Indeed, there is no way to routinize hypothesis generation. For example, consider what took place when scientists first hypothesized that light is a wave, or that light is a stream of particles. Such ideas were, at the time, genuinely novel.

It isn't just in science that creative supposition is important to us. The same is true in much of ordinary life. And the same is equally true of hunter-gatherers. For as Liebenberg (1990) demonstrates, hunters when tracking prey will often need to develop speculative hypotheses concerning the likely causes of the few signs available to them. (And these can be extremely subtle, such as the precise manner in which a pebble has been disturbed, say, or the way in which a blade of grass has been bent or broken.) These hypotheses are then subjected to extensive debate and further empirical testing by the hunters concerned. Constructing these hypotheses will often require creative uses of imagination, since they concern the unobserved (and now unobservable) causes of the observed signs, and the circumstances in which they may have been made.

It should be plain, in fact, that a capacity for creative supposition forms an essential component of human life-history, entering into almost everything that is distinctive of us and our unique forms of flexibility and adaptability. It is also plain that it provides a significant part of the explanation for the fact that human thought approximates to the strong generality constraint, since it is what enables us to put together old ideas in novel ways. (And it may be, in turn, our unique capacity for recursively structured language that underlies this capacity, to a significant degree. For we can, at will, select novel combinations of lexical items to be formulated into a sentence, which we can then rehearse and consider. See Carruthers [2006, 2007a] for extensive discussion.)

In light of this account of why human forms of thinking approximate to the strong generality constraint, it should be plain that the latter is simply irrelevant to the question whether a creature is capable of genuine thought (i.e., possesses beliefs and desires), and likewise irrelevant to the question whether a creature is a genuine concept-user. What it *is* relevant to is the question whether a creature is capable of certain *kinds* of thought, specifically suppositional and creative thought. But supposition is a distinctive type of attitude. The question whether a creature is capable of *supposing that P* has no bearing on the question whether it is capable of belief, and capable of desire. And likewise the question whether a creature is capable of freely and creatively generating novel thoughts/suppositions is irrelevant to the question whether it is capable of thought per se, and to the question whether it possesses concepts. To put the same point somewhat differently: the reason why humans approximate to the strong generality constraint isn't because they have concepts, and because there is something about the nature of concepts, or the nature of propositional attitudes, that requires it. It is rather because we are – perhaps uniquely in the animal kingdom – capable of supposition, and of creatively generating thoughts to be taken as objects of supposition. (And even if our unique capacity for language isn't itself responsible for the latter, it certainly greatly enhances it.)

Someone might respond to these points by proposing a doctrine of *the unity of the attitudes* (modeled after Aristotle's doctrine of the unity of the virtues). The claim would be that a creature can't possess *any* attitude type unless it possesses *all*. Hence a creature doesn't really count as having beliefs or desires unless it is also capable of supposing. But what could possibly motivate such a claim? One suggestion would be that we take humans as our paradigm cognizers, and then subject the different types of human attitude to functional definition. In which case, since beliefs can interact with creative suppositions in humans, it will be of the essence of beliefs that they should be capable of doing so.

I have two things to say by way of reply. One is that it is very doubtful whether we should select the human mind as our paradigm of what a mind is like. (I shall return to develop this point in section 5.) The other is that, even if we do do this, we plainly shouldn't define the different attitude types holistically, in terms of their interactions with *all* others. For consider the consequences: if it is true that psychopaths are incapable of guilt (as it seems to be; see Blair [1995]), then it would turn out that they are incapable of believing anything or desiring anything, either (and nor would they count as having concepts). And even if it were felt that one could reply to this objection by noting that psychopaths are defective members of the species (which is actually far from clear: they might rather be in balanced dimorphism with normal folk; see Murphy and Stich [2000]), then consider Mr. Spock from the television series *Star Trek*. He is said to be incapable of emotion. Is he thereby incapable of thinking at all? Does he have no beliefs, and no concepts? This would plainly be an absurd thing to say.

These points leave an opening, of course, for someone to claim that possession of beliefs and desires doesn't require a creature to be capable of *all* other attitude types, but just creative supposition. That would still leave most non-human animals beyond the pale of genuine thought. But this claim looks equally ill-motivated (and for the same reason). And it is likewise subject to counterexample. We just have to imagine a human who is especially "literal minded," being capable of all other attitude types *except* creative supposition. (It may be that some autistic people are actually like this. Certainly one of the diagnostic features of autism is that autistic children fail to engage in pretend play.) Yet it would surely be absurd to deny that such a person was capable of thinking at all.

4.2. Two systems of reasoning

I have argued that one reason why human thinking approximates to the strong generality constraint doesn't have anything much to do with our possession of concepts, as such, but rather with our capacity for creative supposing. Yet this is by no means the whole story. For there would be little point in entertaining creative suppositions if we couldn't also develop new and flexible reasoning strategies for drawing inferences from those suppositions. If we were limited to the same set of fixed inferential capacities employed by non-human animals, then arguably creative supposing would bring us little advantage. (What would a chimpanzee be able to *do* with the hypothesis that light consists of particles, for example, even if it could be induced, somehow, to entertain such a thought?) But we aren't so limited. Indeed, there is a growing consensus in cognitive science that humans possess a unique system for reasoning and drawing inferences. Let me elaborate.

It is now widely accepted by those who work on the psychology of reasoning that humans possess two different *types* of cognitive system for thinking and reasoning (Evans and Over [1996]; Kahneman [2002]; S. Sloman [1996, 2002]; Stanovich [1999]). Most believe that what is now generally called "system 1" is really a collection of different systems that are fast and unconscious, operating in parallel with one another. The principles according to which these systems function are, to a significant extent, universal to humans, and they aren't easily altered (e.g., by verbal instruction). Moreover, the principles via which system-1 systems operate are, for the most part, heuristic in nature ("quick and dirty"), rather than deductively or inductively valid. It is also generally thought that most, if not all, of the mechanisms constituting system 1 are evolutionarily ancient and shared with other species of animal.

System 2, on the other hand, is generally believed to be a single system that is slow, serial, and conscious. The principles according to which it operates are variable (both across cultures and between individuals within a culture), and can involve the application of valid norms of reasoning. These system-2 principles are malleable and can be influenced by verbal instruction, and they often involve normative beliefs (that is, beliefs about how one *should* reason). Moreover, system 2 is generally thought to be uniquely human.

There is an important sense, then, in which distinctively human reasoning abilities (realized in system 2) are socially constructed. This is, no doubt, a large part of the explanation of the fact noted earlier, that thoughts that seem "nonsensical" in one era can be made sense of, and found to be true, in another. But again, this has nothing to do with the capacities to entertain thoughts, or to possess concepts, per se. Whether a creature is capable of having beliefs built up out of component concepts is one thing, and whether it possesses an indefinitely flexible socially constructed reasoning capacity is surely quite another.

5. PROTO-THOUGHT VERSUS FAUX-THOUGHT

Someone might seize upon the distinction drawn above between system-1 and system-2 thinking to propose that *genuine* thinking and *genuine* concepts should be reserved to system 2, with the sorts of system-1 thoughts and concepts that we share with the rest of the animal kingdom being described as mere *proto*-thoughts and *proto*-concepts. For after all, doesn't our own human case constitute the very paradigm for both the concept *thought* and the concept *concept*?

One thing wrong with this proposal is that there is actually nothing special about most of the concepts that get deployed in creative supposing, or in system-2 thinking more generally. On the contrary, most system-2 thoughts are built up out of some of the same system-1 concepts that might be available to a non-human animal. Thus many animals might possess the concepts *light* and *particle*, for example, which figure in the thought *Light consists of particles*. And while it is true that there are also many distinctively human concepts, perhaps arrived at – either directly or indirectly – via the operations of system 2, the generality constraint was never supposed to be about the *number* of concepts that a creature possesses. Rather, the question at issue in the strong generality constraint is whether a creature's concepts can be combined with all other concepts that *it* can have. So the fact that humans possess many more concepts than do invertebrates is, in itself, no objection to the claim that the latter possess genuine (as opposed to proto-) concepts.

(Indeed, in light of this point, it seems likely that invertebrates might approximate to the strong generality constraint much more closely than do other non-human animals, who possess a wider range of concepts. If invertebrate concepts are largely drawn from the domain of navigation, it may well be that most such concepts are capable of being combined in thought with most others. If the minds of monkeys, in contrast, are highly modular [Carruthers (2006)], containing multiple specialist systems for forming beliefs of particular types, then there might actually be many *more* restrictions on their capacities to combine together concepts drawn from these different domains. Hence, although monkeys possess many more concepts than do honeybees, it may be that the latter come closer to complying with the strong generality constraint.)

Another thing wrong with the proposal that system-2 thinking should be taken as the paradigm of thought is that system 2 doesn't really constitute a natural kind (nor a set of natural kinds). Rather it is, as we pointed out above, to a significant extent socially constructed. Its operations are highly variable between cultures, and between individuals within a culture. (In some people, for example, system 2 is largely verbal, running on rehearsed natural-language sentences in the form of "inner speech," while in others it is largely visual, consisting of sequences and manipulations of visual images.) And the operations of system 2 depend, to a significant extent, upon the individual subject's normative beliefs about how she *should* reason.

The system-1 processes that we share with non-human animals, in contrast, do constitute a cluster of natural kinds. There are systems for doing dead reckoning, for extracting geometrical information about the environment, for judging the approximate numerosity of a set, for calculating rates of resource-availability, and so on and so forth (Gallistel [1990]); as well as systems for generating novel desires, of various types, and for selecting appropriate actions in the light of one's desires (Carruthers [2006]). These systems, when present, will be universal to all members of the species, and many will be highly conserved across species. Each represents a legitimate object of scientific study: our goal should be to figure out how each such system works, how it is structured, and how it interacts with other systems in the mind–brain of the organism in question.

Moreover, the most plausible accounts of system 2 on the market maintain that its processes are actually *realized in* the operations of system 1, to a significant degree, rather than existing alongside of the latter (Frankish [2004]; Carruthers [2006, 2009a]). For example, it is by interpreting a given utterance in inner speech as a *commitment*, or a "making up of mind," that the functional equivalent of a new belief, desire, or intention results (depending on the sort of commitment that gets self-attributed) – provided, that is, that one has a standing system-1 desire to execute one's commitments. Thus, suppose that an utterance is interpreted as a commitment to the truth of the proposition that it expresses, and the subject therefore forms a system-1 belief that a commitment of that kind has been made. This will then interact in future with the system-1 desire to honor commitments, issuing in further overt or covert verbalizations. If asked whether he believes the proposition in question, for example, the subject will reply that he does. For one of the things that one ought to be prepared to do, if one has committed oneself to the truth of a proposition, is assert it. And likewise, during one's system-2 practical or theoretical reasoning, one will be prepared to rely upon the sentence in question as a premise. For if one has committed oneself to the truth of a proposition, then one ought also to commit oneself to any other proposition that one believes follows from it. And so on.

Thus although system-2 thinking is the variety that is most familiar to us (since its operations are to a significant degree conscious), it is system 1 that is the more basic, both ontologically and for explanatory purposes. For system-2 processes are largely realized in those of system 1. (One difference, in my view, is that system 2 always involves the activity of the motor system, whereas system 1 needn't do so. See Carruthers [2009a].) In which case, although ordinary folk might be inclined to take system-2 thinking as their paradigm of thought, it is plain that they *shouldn't* do so – or not for explanatory purposes or in the context of cognitive science, at any rate.

Even more importantly, it turns out that there aren't really any attitudes at the system-2 level (Carruthers [2007b, 2009b]). For the events that occur within system 2 don't occupy the right sorts of causal roles to be a judgment, for example, or to be a decision. Thus it is surely a requirement on any event that is to qualify as a judgment that it should be immediately available to inform the agent's practical reasoning, without the mediation of any further cognitive process. For a judgment is supposed to be the event that brings a new belief into existence. For example, judging $P \supset Q$ issues in a belief with that content, and should be available to interact with a desire for Q immediately, issuing in a desire to bring about P, without the intervention of any other belief or desire. But a system-2 event like the inner verbalization of the sentence "If P then Q" plays no such role. On the contrary, it first has to issue in a belief that one has committed oneself to the truth of the proposition *if P then Q*, and then this together with one's desire to execute one's commitments leads one to feel committed to wanting to bring about P in the presence of a desire for Q. And since what happens in system 2 doesn't really contain or involve any propositional attitudes, as such, there is good reason for us to insist that system-2 thinking consists of mere faux-thoughts, rather than in the real thing.

Instead of it being the case that animals possess mere *proto-thoughts* in comparison to human forms of thinking, then, distinctively human thoughts are mere *faux-thoughts* compared to those that we share with non-human animals. Each individual token of system-2 thinking is a real enough event, of course, involving the activation of real (system-1) concepts. And such events – individually and collectively – can have immensely important consequences. (Witness the march of scientific discovery and technological invention.) But the processes that issue in such events aren't natural kinds, and nor are there any beliefs and desires at the system-2 level. From the standpoint of cognitive science, then, distinctively human thinking consists of mere faux-thoughts. The real thing is done by animals (and by humans insofar as they share the same cognitive systems as other animals).

CHAPTER 6

A language of baboon thought?

Elisabeth Camp

I. INTRODUCTION

Does thought precede language, or the other way around? How does having a language affect our thoughts? Who has a language, and who can think? These questions have traditionally been addressed by philosophers, especially by rationalists concerned to identify the essential difference between humans and other animals. More recently, theorists in cognitive science, evolutionary biology, and developmental psychology have been asking these questions in more empirically grounded ways. At its best, this confluence of philosophy and science promises to blend the respective strengths of each discipline, bringing abstract theory to bear on reality in a principled and focused way. At its worst, it risks degenerating into a war of words, with each side employing key expressions in its own idiosyncratic way – or worse, contaminating empirical research with a priori dogmas inherited from outmoded philosophical worldviews.

In *Baboon Metaphysics* (2007), Dorothy Cheney and Robert Seyfarth offer an analysis of baboon cognition that promises to exemplify the very best interaction of philosophical theory and empirical research. They argue that baboons have a language of thought: a language-like representational medium, which supports the sophisticated cognitive abilities required to negotiate their complex social environment. This claim is intended to be surprising in its own right, and also to shed light on the evolution of spoken language. Because our own ancestors likely lived in a similarly complex social environment, Cheney and Seyfarth propose that the earliest humans also developed language first as a cognitive medium, and that spoken language evolved as a means to express those thoughts.

There are two potential difficulties here. First, "Language of Thought" (LOT) is a term of art, with much associated theoretical baggage and often comparatively little careful exposition. Thus, evaluating the claim requires getting clearer about just what LOT implies in this context. Second, if

Cheney and Seyfarth are right, then we seem to be left with a rather surprising model, on which baboons think in a way very like we do but fail to talk. According to Cheney and Seyfarth, this is because they lack a theory of mind. But this still leaves a dramatic mismatch between the expressive potential of baboons' postulated representational system and the complexity of the behavior they manifest in other areas. Thus, it's worth examining whether an alternative form of thought might better explain the distinctive contours of their conceptual abilities and limitations.

2. FROM CONTENT TO FORM

The claim that thought is in language or is language-like is a claim about the form of thought. Information itself – how things are in the world – doesn't have any form: the same information, such as the shortest route between two locations, can be represented in multiple ways; that's why the question of form can even arise. However, while we have an intuitive understanding of the differences in form among ordinary external representations, it's harder to know what it means for thought to have one or another form: surely we don't mean that minds are ethereal sheets on which a homunculus writes or draws pictures, as we inscribe marks on paper. Rather, claims about thoughts' forms are usually intended functionally: as concerning a level of description at which distinct token thoughts share certain structural features despite lower-level differences. The features that constitute a given thought-type X are determined by the functional role X plays within the overall system: by what other thoughts, perceptual inputs, and behavioral outputs X is produced by and produces when the system is operating correctly. The formal features of X are then determined by abstracting away from, first, X's attitude – e.g., belief or desire – and second, its informational content: by isolating the transitions and co-instantiation relations that obtain regardless of what particular state in the world X represents.[1]

Predicate logic provides the most familiar case in which we distinguish formal or syntactic features from contentful or semantic ones; and it serves as the model for thought on the "Language of Thought Hypothesis" (LOTH). However, we need to distinguish at least two operative interpretations of LOTH (for discussion, see Camp [2007]). On the first

---

[1] "Content" is a loaded term, and many theorists will object that contents do already have formal properties, given either by the structure of the objects and properties in the world (*à la* Russell) or by the structure of the mode of presentation (*à la* Frege). Because we need a term for what is being thought about that doesn't already fix form, I use the term in a more coarse-grained way (*à la* Stalnaker).

interpretation, LOTH starts with the observation that representational abilities appear to be complex, in the sense of employing multiple simpler, interacting abilities; it then argues that those complex abilities must be underwritten by analogously complex vehicles (ultimately, neural configurations), such that the constituents and structure of those vehicles mirror the constituents and structure of what is represented by the corresponding abilities. Thus on this interpretation, LOTH is primarily a way of spelling out computationalism, and it remains neutral about the specific formal features of the vehicles' parts and structure. On the second interpretation of LOTH, which is the version that is relevant for Cheney and Seyfarth's discussion, the claim is that mental representations, however these are implemented, have a specifically language-like structure.

These interpretations are not always clearly distinguished, for at least two reasons. First, most philosophers have been exclusively concerned with human thought, and it is plausible that the structure of human thought often shares a common structure with the sentences we use to express them. Second, the claim that thought is language-like is typically opposed to the claim that thought is imagistic (e.g., Pylyshyn [1973]), and most philosophers assume that images lack formal structure in the relevant sense. The governing assumption is that there are just two kinds of representation: imagistic or *iconic*, which is analog and employs direct resemblance between signifier and signified; and sentential or *propositional*, which is digital and employs a merely conventional or causal referential connection between signifier and signified. However, as we will see in sections 4 and 5, there are other representational formats – most notably, maps and diagrams – which mix iconic and non-iconic, analog and digital elements in different ways, and which are governed by their own distinctive formal principles (Camp [2007]). In many ways, these mixed systems, rather than imagistic ones, represent the most theoretically interesting alternatives to language.

Because form is an abstract property of thought, it cannot be accessed directly. However, we can make provisional inferences about a thought's form by examining the overall pattern of contents that can be represented within the cognitive system and how the system manipulates those contents (where these features are themselves inferred indirectly from behavior). Most representational formats exhibit distinctive limitations in what information they can represent. For instance, because imagistic systems represent by replicating the physical appearances of particular objects, they cannot directly represent disjunctive information.[2] Further, different sorts

---

[2] Although a larger cognitive system might be able to deduce from a picture that either P or Q must obtain.

of information are easier to access, compile, and update in different formats. For instance, in cartographic, but not linguistic, systems, altering the location of any one represented individual automatically alters the represented relations between it and every other represented individual. Thus, we can glimpse the distinctive contours of different forms of thought by attending to limitations in the contents that a system is capable of representing, and to how it clusters and distinguishes distinct contents in processing.

Finally, it's worth noting that insofar as we construe form functionally, a representational system need not be implemented in a way that looks like the formats we ordinarily employ. Instead, a physical substrate implements a system in virtue of there being some consistent, causally operative mapping from formal to physical properties. For instance, there must be some properties of the implementation of a functional map that correspond to "being east of" or "being to the left of," although they need not themselves be being to the east or left. Moreover, those properties must be appropriately related to each other, and to further properties like "being north of" and "being in front of," in such a way that one could construct a normal physical map just by substituting the functionally appropriate counterparts.

3. BABOON CONTENTS

Although Cheney and Seyfarth don't distinguish form and content as explicitly as I have, the argument of their book implicitly moves from a claim about the contents that baboons represent to a conclusion about how they represent them. By far the most notable feature of baboon cognition is their ability to track complex social dynamics. Each baboon troop consists of around eighty members, in which females form a fairly stable dominance structure while males migrate and change rank frequently. Females' social ranks are determined by two factors: first, by which (matrilineal) family they belong to, and second, by their birth order within that family.

Social rank has a pervasive effect on everyday interactions, determining who is allowed to eat what, sit where, groom or mate with whom, or handle whose baby. And baboons clearly behave in ways that indicate their awareness of others' and their own relative ranks: for instance, if a dominant baboon approaches two lower-ranking ones, the most subordinate typically retreats, as if she recognizes that she is subordinate to both of the others (p. 92).[3] Female baboons also regularly act to preserve and improve their rank, including in indirect ways. For instance, they join alliances with their

---

[3] All page numbers without author or date are from Cheney and Seyfarth (2007).

close relatives or higher-ranking females against opponents with whom they have no independent conflict, and they employ the close kin of baboons with whom they've recently fought as proxies for direct interaction – indeed, "kin-mediated reconciliation" is twice as common as direct reconciliation (p. 83).

Much of baboons' social interaction takes the form of vocalizations, especially threat grunts, fear barks, and reconciliation grunts. Although these vocalizations themselves lack any real internal syntactic structure, baboons who overhear unseen callers are able to recognize the caller and type of call being made. This information can in turn affect their own behavior: for instance, if two unrelated baboons are sitting near one another and overhear a call that represents a conflict between their relatives, the baboon from the higher-ranking family is then more likely to go assert her own dominance over the other than if they heard a call involving baboons they weren't related to (p. 97). They also demonstrate surprise when they hear (artificially constructed) sequences of calls that violate their expectations about social order. In particular, baboons respond with more surprise to sequences that represent a subordinate threatening a dominant from a different family than they do to calls that represent an analogous intra-familial conflict, even when the difference in overall rank order is the same (p. 108). This difference in evinced surprise provides compelling evidence for the hypothesis that baboons represent social rank in a two-tiered, hierarchical manner – a hypothesis we'll examine more closely in the next section. More direct evidence for this hypothesis comes from the fact that when a conflict between two baboons does lead to a change in dominance, the effects of that change depend on whether the baboons are related: intra-familial changes in rank affect only those two baboons, while a change in rank involving baboons from different families may cause many members of the losing baboon's family to lose rank, and even fall to the bottom of the overall order (p. 70).

4. LANGUAGE-LIKE FEATURES OF BABOON THOUGHT

Given this background, our question now becomes: what do the contents of baboons' thoughts reveal about their form? Why should we believe that they think in a language-like way? In keeping with many discussions of LOT, Cheney and Seyfarth merely claim that baboon cognition is importantly *like* natural language (p. 250). However, in contrast to many such discussions, which remain extremely vague, Cheney and Seyfarth identify six specific respects of similarity, which they summarize in the following passage:

The vocalizations of monkeys clearly lack any properties that we would be tempted to call syntactic. Nevertheless, their social knowledge, their assessment of call meaning, and their parsing of call sequences display a number of syntactic properties. First, knowledge is *representational,* and highly specific. Second, social knowledge is based on properties that have *discrete values*... Third, animals combine these discrete-valued traits to create a representation of social relations that is *hierarchically structured.* Baboons, for example, create a nested hierarchy in which others are placed in a linear rank order and simultaneously grouped according to matrilineal kinship in a manner that preserves ranks both within and across families. Fourth, social knowledge is *rule-governed and open-ended*... Fifth, knowledge is *propositional*... That is, they represent in their minds (albeit in a limited way) the individuated concepts of "Sylvia," "Hannah," "threat-grunt," and "scream," and they combine these concepts to create a mental representation of one individual's intentions toward another... Sixth, knowledge is *independent of sensory modality*... These properties of non-human primates' social knowledge, while by no means fully human, bear important resemblances to the meanings we express in language, which are built up by combining discrete-valued entities in a structured, hierarchical, rule-governed, and open-ended manner. (pp. 268–269, italics in original)

I'll condense their six properties into three broad categories:

- Representational/propositional/independent of sensory modality
- Discrete-valued/rule-governed/open-ended
- Hierarchically structured

Taken together, these features appear to make a strong case for the claim that baboons think in something very like language. They are the features most commonly cited in discussions of LOT and of what constitutes a language; and I agree with Cheney and Seyfarth that baboon cognition is like language in all these respects. However, in this section I argue that none of these features are sufficient to make baboon cognition *distinctively* language-like, because they can also be exhibited by other representational systems, such as maps and diagrams. If this were just a disagreement about what constitutes a language or being language-like, it wouldn't be very substantive. In section 5, though, I argue that language differs from these other systems in a crucial further respect – its combinatorial principle lacks a substantive, dedicated semantic significance – and that this difference explains its comparatively greater expressive capacity. In section 6, I argue that this feature is likely absent from baboon cognition, even though at several points Cheney and Seyfarth talk as if it were present. Thus, the particular contours of baboon cognition are better explained on the hypothesis that baboons employ a representational format that differs importantly from language.

4.1. Representational thought: representational, propositional, and independent of sensory modality

The first property that Cheney and Seyfarth mention, of being *representational*, is fairly obviously a necessary condition on being a linguistic system; but just as obviously, it's also not sufficient: maps, pictures, and diagrams are all also representational. Likewise, die-hard behaviorists aside, nearly all parties will agree that baboon cognition is representational, simply in virtue of being a kind of thought.[4] However, this leaves open the very question we're asking: what form do those representations take?

The second property, *propositionality*, can be construed in two ways. Sometimes "propositional" is used in a way that's basically equivalent to "representational": it just means being truth-assessable, or representing a state of affairs, in which case it is again necessary but not sufficient for language.[5] In its other use, "propositional" is tied specifically to sentential structure: to say that thought is propositional in this sense implies that it has subject–predicate structure.[6] On this interpretation, though, the claim that baboon cognition is propositional is question-begging: it simply attributes linguistic structure to baboon cognition without further evidence.

The third property is *independence from sensory modality*; for example, baboons incorporate information derived from overheard vocalizations and from directly observed interactions into a single representation of social rank.[7] Again, though, this feature can be implemented in a variety of formats. For instance, the thought of *A* threatening *B* might be represented by an image of the two fighting, even if it is caused by overhearing a sequence of calls. And while images can only explicitly encode visual

---

[4] Some theorists (e.g., Gibson [1966]) do deny that thought is representational.

[5] This usage seems to be employed in the following passage from Cheney and Seyfarth:

> Applied to humans, the language of thought hypothesis assumes that people – even preverbal infants – have propositional attitudes: mental states with representational content. To have a certain propositional attitude is to be in a specified relation to an internal representation: to know, believe, or fear that something is the case. (p. 250)

[6] Cheney and Seyfarth appear to be employing this sense when they write that "the baboon's alarm wahoo seems best described as a proposition: a single utterance or thought that simultaneously incorporates a subject and a predicate" (p. 256). Likewise, immediately prior to the passage cited in footnote 5, Cheney and Seyfarth write: "Like natural languages, [the Language of Thought] includes some mental representations that correspond to objects in the world and others that specify the relation between these objects" (p. 250).

[7] I have argued (2009) that a related feature, of *stimulus-independence* – the ability to compile information from multiple sources and occasions, and to apply it in flexible ways in variable contexts – is a necessary condition on genuine conceptual thought.

properties, maps frequently represent objects and properties that lack any sensory appearance, such as an earthquake's epicenter.

4.2. Compositional thought: discrete-valued, rule-governed, and open-ended

The next class of properties that Cheney and Seyfarth discuss are more closely associated with LOTH. First, baboon cognition is *discrete-valued*: for example, baboons represent each baboon in their troop as a distinct entity. They also classify vocalizations into discrete categories with sharply different meanings, such as *Hannah's threat grunt*, *Shashe's threat grunt*, or *Shashe's fear bark*, even though in terms of their purely physical acoustic properties, those vocalizations form a continuum (p. 231). Second, baboon cognition is *rule-governed*: for instance, if a baboon observes a dominant lose a fight to a subordinate, this has systematic effects on the represented ranks of those two baboons and possibly of other troop members as well. Similarly, if a baboon hears an audio sequence that is ambiguous between two interpretations – say, it displays two baboons making threat-grunts and a third making a fear-bark, which could be a response to either threat – she will respond as if she "parses" the sequence according to a "rule" given by the established dominance order (p. 266). Third, baboon cognition appears to be *open-ended*: baboons are not just capable of representing specific dominance relations among specific baboons, but can represent nearly any configuration of relations among all the baboons they know.[8] Indeed, Cheney and Seyfarth's experimental methodology exploits just this feature: they present baboons with artificially constructed audio sequences that are unlikely to occur naturally. The baboons don't merely find such sequences anomalous, as they might if they heard an entirely new sound. Rather, they appear to find the sequences surprising precisely because of the information conveyed: for instance, they look at relatives of the individuals whose calls are being played, as if to check their reactions.[9]

Taken together, these three properties imply that baboon cognition is *compositional*: it combines discrete representational parts into larger wholes, such that (nearly) any combination of parts licensed by the system's

[8] Not absolutely all combinations need be possible: in particular, baboons are likely unable to represent alternative kinship relations, such as Sashe belonging to Hannah's family. For a discussion of what would underwrite such cognitive flexibility, see Camp (2009).

[9] This contrasts with a structurally analogous experiment involving honeybees who were confronted by bee dances representing the surprising information that nectar was located in the middle of a lake (Gould and Gould [1988]; Tautz *et al.* [2004]). The bees' "response" – inaction – doesn't give us reason to distinguish surprise or disbelief from incomprehension (Camp [2009]).

combinatorial rules is well-formed and significant.[10] The combinatorial rules of such a system are (relatively) *general* or *systematic*, in the sense that they apply to (nearly) all parts of the relevant formal types, regardless of their particular content. As a result, such systems also display (relative) *productivity*: the system can represent any of a large range of contents by combining a fairly small pool of basic elements in different ways.

Compositionality is traditionally taken to be an essential, even definitive, feature of language. There is significant debate about just how fully compositional natural languages really are, both because the intuitive meaning of a whole sentence often seems to depend on factors that are not explicitly coded by its constituent terms or mode of composition (e.g., Travis [1994]), and because the syntactic categories that govern the well-formedness of whole sentences are often quite narrow and overlapping (e.g., Johnson [2004]). But it is nearly undeniable that language is compositional to some large degree. Further, classic arguments for LOT rely exclusively on these features: because our own and other animals' cognitive abilities appear to be systematic and productive, the argument goes, the vehicle that underwrites those abilities must be language-like in its form.[11] The implicit assumption is that only language is compositional, and hence capable of producing systematic, productive representational outputs.

However, language isn't the only type of compositional system (Camp [2007]). Most obviously, diagrammatic systems, such as Venn diagrams, are compositional. But further, many maps are also constructed from discrete elements – a city map might employ black lines for streets, green squares for parks, and red dots for ATM locations, for instance – which may or may not bear any resemblance to what they represent, and which can be recombined in different ways according to a uniform principle to represent a wide range of different states of affairs.[12] Indeed, maps can be even more systematic than language, insofar as they don't impose any syntactic restrictions on which types of elements can be combined, as language does.

---

[10] Cheney and Seyfarth explicitly claim that baboons' vocalizations – or more properly, their interpretation of other baboons' vocalizations – are compositional (p. 266).

[11] Editor's note: See Tetzlaff and Rey (chapter 4) and Carruthers (chapter 5) for such an argument applied to honeybee and (other) invertebrate cognition.

[12] I use the term "map" narrowly, to refer to spatial depictions of isomorphic spatial situations. I call spatial depictions of, for example, abstract information "diagrams." One might object that maps are not discrete, because the elements are typically put together in, and represent locations in, a continuous space, and because they often employ icons that vary continuously, such as the shape of a blue line depicting the shape of a river. However, maps' signs need not be iconic and often carry discrete semantic import, and maps can employ discrete representational spaces, such as a seating chart.

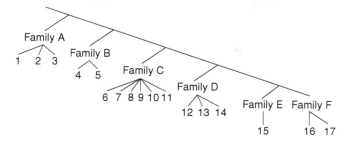

Figure 6.1 Hierarchical dominance relations in baboons (after Cheney and Seyfarth [2007], p. 107).

I discuss the implications of the combinatorial principles employed by these various systems in section 5.

4.3. Hierarchically structured thought

The final property that Cheney and Seyfarth identify in baboon cognition, of being *hierarchically structured,* is the most surprising. In section 3, I sketched the evidence that female baboons' social ranking is hierarchically structured: whole families are ranked relative to each other, and individuals are in turn ranked within each family, producing an overall absolute order. Further, baboons themselves seem to be aware of this hierarchical structure, insofar as they react differently to inter-familial and intra-familial conflicts involving baboons with the same absolute rank difference. From this evidence about the contents of baboons' representations of social order, Cheney and Seyfarth conclude that the form of their thought is also hierarchically structured: as they say, "the picture that emerges in a baboon's mind can be diagrammed as a branching, hierarchical tree" (p. 277), of the sort depicted in Figure 6.1.

It should be relatively uncontroversial that we *can* represent baboons' awareness of social rank as in Figure 6.1. The controversy comes, first, in moving to the claim that we need to represent their awareness in this way, and second, in drawing a conclusion from this about the form of baboon cognition across the board. In particular, if all we had to go on was static evidence about the social relations that baboons represent at a given moment, we wouldn't have much reason to prefer a two-layered structure over a linear ordering: it might just be coincidence that individuals from the same family all happen to cluster together, or it might be a by-product of some further factor, like size or aggressiveness. However, the postulation of a two-layered structure gains significant support from the dynamics of baboon cognition, and specifically from the fact that baboons treat intra- and inter-familial rank reversals so differently. Thus, at least for current purposes, I want to grant that baboons do have some sort of two-tiered representation of social rank.

Next, we need to get clearer on the sense in which such a two-layered representation is hierarchical. Cheney and Seyfarth don't specify exactly what they mean. Baboons' thought about social structure shouldn't count as hierarchical simply in virtue of representing one individual or family as ranked higher than another – after all, Cheney and Seyfarth don't claim that the purely linear dominance structure among males requires a hierarchical representation. Rather, we are seeking to identify a formal, structural property of baboons' thought. More specifically, to support the hypothesis that baboons think in a language-like format, the hierarchical structure in question should be as closely analogous as possible to the hierarchy in language. I believe what Cheney and Seyfarth have in mind is this: baboons' representation of social relations is hierarchical in the sense that the same relation – *dominant to* – which is represented as holding between individuals is also represented as holding between units that are comprised of those individuals. This is a lot like the sort of hierarchical relationship we find among phrases in language. For example, in a sentence like "The girl who kissed the boy with the red shirt is wearing a blue dress," the noun phrase "the red shirt" is embedded within the larger noun phrase "the boy with the red shirt," which is itself embedded within the noun phrase "the girl who kissed the boy with the red shirt," so that the same operation which creates the second noun phrase from the first is applied again to form the entire noun phrase.[13]

Suppose we grant, then, that both baboon cognition and language exhibit the following sort of hierarchical structure: a relation which applies to individual elements can also be applied to relate units that are constructed from those individual elements. How language-like does this show baboon cognition to be?

One important difference between baboon cognition and language is that actual languages can generate structures of potentially infinite depth; but it seems quite unlikely that baboons' representations are capable of more than two layers of structure. For instance, although baboons rank all the families within their troop, it seems unlikely they are capable of

---

[13] More generally, modern grammars aim to employ a single construction rule – e.g., functional application, conjunction, or Merge – which operates on expressions of various types to produce larger phrases from smaller ones by a uniform operation.

ranking whole troops in relation to one another: there simply aren't the kinds of interactions among whole troops that would make this sort of ranking feasible. However, I don't think this difference matters much for current purposes.[14] A language-like system capable of just one layer of embedding, supplied with concepts for the contents that Cheney and Seyfarth argue baboons can think about – such as social relations, causal processes, patterns of food availability, and threats from predators – would still be a quite powerful representational medium.

Even putting these differences to the side, though, the mere presence of hierarchical structure is not enough to make baboon cognition distinctively language-like, because once again, other representational formats can also exhibit this feature. To take an example of particularly direct relevance, Linnean taxonomic trees employ branching lines to depict phenotypic differentiation. Here we have the same type of functional structure as in baboons' representations of social relations, simply with phenotypical similarity replacing dominance. Individual animals are classed together as a functional unit (a species) in virtue of sharing certain micro-features, and those functional units are in turn classed together with other such units to form a larger group (a genus), on the basis of sharing certain macro-features.[15]

Other non-linguistic forms of representation can also exhibit hierarchical structure. Thus, a Venn diagram might partition a collection of Venn diagrams, each of which represents some relation among the extensions of specific properties, according to whether those diagrams themselves possess certain features. It is even arguable that maps can exhibit hierarchical structure. For instance, a map collector might draw a map of the locations of the maps in his library. One likely difference between both of these cases and baboons' representations of dominance is that in the latter, the hierarchical relation is transitive: individuals from different families are represented as ranked in dominance in virtue of the represented ranking between their families. However, an especially eccentric map collector might arrange a library of maps of the United States according to the

---

[14] Cheney and Seyfarth (p. 252) explicitly include the closely related property of recursion among the features specific to modern natural languages that they're not claiming baboon cognition to possess. Another potentially significant difference is that in language, the application of the relevant operation (say, functional application) is what binds individual constituents together into a functional unit, whereas in baboon social cognition, a distinct operation – kinship – constitutes those units. Even so, I think the analogy between the two cases is tight enough, in the respect specified in the text, to warrant the claim that baboon cognition is like language in being hierarchical.

[15] Taxonomic trees are now often taken to represent phylogenetic history as well, though the phenotypic and phylogenetic interpretations do not always produce the same overall structure.

location in the country that the maps depict, so that maps of New Jersey are located on the east wall, maps of Texas on the south, and so on. In that case, the first-order functional unit would be an individual map, in which the spatial configuration of individual signs purports to replicate the spatial configuration of cities and other depicted entities. But in turn, those maps would themselves serve as signs representing the regions they depict, so that the overall arrangement of maps within the library replicates the spatial configuration of those regions.

Even putting these more recherché cases aside, the case of taxonomic trees shows clearly that hierarchical structure is necessary but not sufficient for language. Hence, it is invalid to infer from the presence of hierarchical structure to the conclusion that baboon cognition must be distinctively language-like. Further, because all of the representational formats we've been discussing can also possess all of the other features that Cheney and Seyfarth identify, the inference from the presence of all of these features to the conclusion that baboons have a language of thought is likewise invalid.

5. GENERALITY, FLEXIBILITY, AND THE CONTENTS OF THOUGHT

So far, we've established that appealing to structural features like compositionality or hierarchical structure doesn't suffice to establish the form of baboon cognition. To make further progress, we need to get clearer on how these various representational formats differ from language, and specifically on what implications this has for the contents that cognitive systems employing them are capable of representing.

I think the most important difference is this. In all of these formats, including language, we have a combinatorial principle – a rule for combining the system's basic parts into larger wholes – which is applied repeatedly, and potentially at distinct levels. In language, this principle is highly abstract, and has a very thin semantic significance. Predication, for instance, signifies instantiation or property-possession, so that the significance of combining "Socrates" with "is wise" is that the referent of the former instantiates the property expressed by the latter; and this relation is sufficiently abstract and general that it can relate nearly any property and object.[16] Further, in language the referential relation mapping basic expressions to objects and properties in the world is conventional or causal. Taken together, both the referential relation and the combinatorial principle are

---

[16] Other combinatorial principles for language, such as functional application, conjunction, and Merge, are even more general and abstract.

abstract enough that they don't impose substantive in-principle limitations on what can be assigned as referents to those basic expressions.[17]

Like languages, maps and diagrams can also employ arbitrary signs as their basic representational elements, and so they have a much wider expressive range than imagistic systems do. However, in maps and diagrams the basic combinatorial principle often has a quite robust semantic significance. And of course, a representational system can only represent the referents of its signs as being related by the relation that is represented by its combinatorial principle. When that combinatorial principle does have a robust significance, however, then this in turn constrains what objects and properties can be assigned as referents for the system's basic signs. So, for example, in maps (as opposed to diagrams) the combinatorial principle is one of (approximate) isomorphism, up to a scaling factor, between the signs' spatial configuration and the configuration of the objects and properties that they refer to. Because they are constructed this way, maps are only capable of depicting spatial relations among particular objects and properties. A map cannot, for instance, represent just that George is happy, or that someone somewhere is wearing a red shirt and carrying a gun, without placing George or some particular individual in some particular location; nor can a map assign a non-spatial relation, like dominance, as the referent of a basic expression (Camp [2007]). Likewise, the combinatorial principle that governs Linnean taxonomic trees is that entities on lower branches share a set of common features, which is represented by the node from which the branches radiate. As a result, Linnean trees cannot represent spatial relations among objects – nor can they even explicitly represent the shared and differentiating properties that determine each level of the tree.

The fact that a representational system's governing combinatorial principle can so heavily constrain the range of contents it is capable of representing provides, I think, a rather surprising justification for a very traditional intuition behind the Language of Thought Hypothesis. Theorists typically justify LOTH by appealing to the generality or systematicity of thought, by which they mean the general recombinability of one's basic concepts. As I said in section 4.2, an argument that moves straight from this sort of generality to the distinctively language-like form of thought is invalid, because maps and diagrams can be at least as recombinable as language. As we might put it, all of these formats are equally capable of representing a complete range of contents within a certain domain.

---

[17] However, because language is digital or discrete it cannot directly represent continuous values (Camp [2007]).

However, theorists have also ascribed another, arguably more profound sense of generality to thought, which is more distinctively connected to language. This is generality in the sense of the size of the domain the system can represent. Many theorists have held that it is an essential feature of thought or reason, as opposed to mere automatic response, that it be flexibly adaptable to a wide range of situations. Thus, Descartes (1637/1988, p. 140) concludes that men's souls must have an entirely different nature from those of animals, because even the stupidest man can invent and combine signs to make himself understood, whereas no animal or robot can do the same. Turing (1950) took a closely related criterion – the ability to converse in a way indistinguishable from a man, on any topic that might be presented – as an operational definition of intelligence. For both thinkers, it is not the ability to use language per se that is criterial of intelligence; rather, it is the ability to flexibly adapt to any situation. However, both also assume that only language provides an expressive medium that is flexible enough to manifest this cognitive adaptability.

We can now see why language should be so tightly connected to flexible, adaptable thought: it exploits referential and combinatorial principles that are abstract enough not to substantially constrain the range of contents the system can represent. By contrast, insofar as other systems employ combinatorial principles with more substantive semantic significance, the domain of contents that they can represent is more restricted. Neither Descartes nor Turing was interested in claims about thought's form; rather, they wanted to identify "sure signs" for discerning intelligence from a third-person perspective. But the same considerations apply if we turn to the medium of thought: maximal expressive generality is most easily achieved in a language-like format.

Unlike Descartes, I don't think we should restrict thought or reason to humans. Many other animals clearly do represent states of affairs in the world, and manipulate those representations in systematic ways to produce action. Further, some other animals clearly achieve a significant degree of both compositional and expressive generality (Camp [2009]). Rather than seeing thought or reason as an all-or-nothing affair, we should treat it as a matter of degree.[18] But if we do, then we should also acknowledge that thought can be implemented in many formats, with different degrees of expressive generality. In particular, while maps and taxonomic trees are expressively quite limited, Venn and Pierce diagrams are much more

---

[18]   Editor's note: See Carruthers (chapter 5) for a comment on this point.

flexible – indeed, they can achieve expressive equivalence to first-order monadic predicate logic (Shin [1994]).[19]

6. BABOON THOUGHT

What are the implications of this theoretical discussion for baboon cognition? For one thing, we can clearly rule out the possibility that baboons represent dominance relations using maps, since dominance is a non-spatial relation, and maps can only explicitly represent spatial relations. More relevantly, it seems plausible that baboons might well represent female dominance relations in a form that can be drawn as the sort of branching tree depicted in Figure 6.1, as Cheney and Seyfarth suggest. However, this is fully compatible with the tree's branches and nodes having a dedicated semantic significance, as in a taxonomic tree. If that were the case, then baboons would have a form of thought with much less expressive generality than language, despite being discrete, rule-governed, open-ended, and hierarchical. And this would in turn explain the fact that they don't seem to exploit the full expressive generality that even a language capable of a single layer of embedding would provide.

At some points, it appears that Cheney and Seyfarth are only committed to the weaker claim that baboons' social knowledge alone forms a hierarchical, compositional, representational system: for instance, they write that "[Baboons'] social knowledge constitutes a discrete, combinatorial system of representations – a language of thought – that shares several features with human language" (p. 251). If baboons' hierarchical compositional system were indeed restricted to representations of dominance, then the claim that they think in a language-like format with a non-restrictive combinatorial principle that operates on a highly restricted conceptual domain would be empirically indistinguishable from the claim that they employ a system with a semantically restricted combinatorial principle. But in that case, the additional expressive generality of the language-like system would be doing

---

[19] Such systems are still limited by the fact that they exploit the spatial structure of the representational vehicle: for some contents, the appropriately intersecting figures cannot be drawn in a single plane (Lemon and Pratt [1998]). On the other hand, many theorists have held that language also falls short of full expressive generality. (We saw in section 4.2 that it falls short of full compositional generality.) That is, various philosophers and linguists have wanted to impose limitations on the range of terms that can be significantly combined, even when those combinations are syntactically well formed. This reflects, I think, an intuition about the semantic significance of predication: that, for example, you can't meaningfully predicate "is a prime number" of Julius Caesar because he's not the kind of object that could possibly possess that property. In Camp (2004), I argue against such restrictions on recombinability.

no explanatory work, and so it would be more parsimonious to explain baboons' cognitive abilities by hypothesizing that they employ a tree-like structure whose combinatorial principle has a dedicated significance, of dominance.

At other points, though, Cheney and Seyfarth commit themselves to the stronger claim that all of baboon cognition is robustly language-like, as in the following passage:

The lack of syntax in non-human primate vocalizations cannot be traced to an inability to recognize argument structure – to understand that an event can be described as a sequence in which an agent performs some action on an object. Baboons clearly understand the difference between *Sylvia threatens Hannah* and *Hannah threatens Sylvia*. Nor does the lack of syntax arise because of an inability to mentally represent descriptive modifiers (a *big* leopard as opposed to a *small* one) and prepositions that specify locations (a leopard *in* a tree as opposed to one *under* a tree) . . . In their natural behavior, therefore, non-human primates and other animals certainly act as if they are capable of *thinking*, as it were, in sentences. But the ability to think in sentences does not lead them to *speak* in sentences – in our view, because their lack of a theory of mind causes them not to understand what others might need to know. (p. 264)

Here, Cheney and Seyfarth go beyond simply attributing some sort of hierarchical, compositional format for social knowledge: they speak as if all of baboon cognition occurs in a format whose structure fairly closely resembles that of natural language. And indeed, the considerations in section 5 might seem to provide an important motivation for this stronger view. Baboons don't just think about dominance: they also represent food, mates, predators, and other things, and their actions are often informed by information about multiple topics; as Cheney and Seyfarth say,

A baboon's ability to acquire the most nutritious food depends, simultaneously, on both her ecological knowledge of plants and her skill in competition with others. Her ability to detect and evade predators depends, simultaneously, on both her knowledge of predator behavior and her ability to live cooperatively in a large group, where she benefits from predator detection and defense. (p. 122)

The fact that baboons can bring thoughts about various topics together to produce unified action seems to suggest that they have a general medium of thought. But since only language provides enough expressive generality to cover all of these domains, it appears that baboons must think in language after all.

Against this stands the fact that baboons don't manifest an ability to think hierarchically structured thoughts in any domain *except* dominance. For instance, they don't engage in any sort of tool use, as chimpanzees do, and as we might have expected if they could entertain thoughts with complex clausal structure, such as "Hitting the nut *with* a rock *causes* tasty nutmeats to come out." Cheney and Seyfarth explain a different lack of ability – the fact that baboons don't make syntactically complex, language-like vocalizations – by appealing to the hypothesis that they lack a theory of mind. The relationship between theory of mind and communication is complex enough to merit its own discussion.[20] But given how sophisticated baboons' social awareness already is, their very lack of theory of mind constitutes another domain where they don't manifest an ability to think hierarchically structured thoughts which would be quite useful for them.

Of course, there are many explanations for the absence of these abilities which are fully compatible with baboons' thinking in a language-like way: language is – at most – only a necessary condition on abilities like tool use and theory of mind. However, there is also no positive evidence in favor of their having a general hierarchically structured cognitive system. There is just evidence for hierarchically structured thoughts about dominance, on the one hand, and a general ability to represent various topics, on the other. But the latter ability is demonstrated by many, perhaps most, other animals; and Cheney and Seyfarth don't intend to claim, as for example Fodor and Pylyshyn (1988) do, that all thought is language-like. Rather, they intend to be advancing a bold claim specifically about baboon thought, with specific relevance for the evolution of spoken language in humans – where the most distinctive aspect of baboon thought is just the hierarchical structure of their representation of dominance.

The evidence presented by Cheney and Seyfarth is thus compatible with the hypothesis that baboons have multiple cognitive modules, perhaps encoded in different formats, with only the dominance module being hierarchically structured, as in a taxonomic tree. Proponents of modularity have offered various responses to the challenge to explain how thoughts from different modules might interact to produce action. It's worth noting, though, that if there were a dominance module, all the information about intra- and inter-matrilineal structure could be isolated within it. The only information that would need to be fed in and out would concern relations

---

[20] In humans, theory-of-mind deficits produce systematic impairments in linguistic production and comprehension, although the deficits are more pragmatic than semantic. Cheney and Seyfarth point out (p. 244) that a Gricean account of meaning presupposes a robust theory of mind; but Grice intended his account as a rational reconstruction of speaker meaning, rather than a psychological analysis (see Camp [2006]). In practice, something less than fully explicit mental-state attribution and closer to mere coordination might suffice for the evolution of a syntactically complex communicative system (Skyrms [2004]), so long as the number of messages that needed to be communicated was sufficiently high (Nowak *et al.* [2000]).

between particular individuals: who is related to whom, and who has, or is likely to, defer to or supplant whom.[21] Thus, there would be no need for other modules, or a general faculty of cognition, to process hierarchically structured representations.

7. CONCLUSION

Thus, we have seen that all six of the features that Cheney and Seyfarth identify are indeed respects in which baboon cognition is plausibly like language. Nonetheless, we shouldn't conclude that baboons think in language, because we get a simpler and more efficient explanation of the distinctive contours of their cognitive abilities and limitations if we hypothesize that their representational system also differs from language in at least one crucial respect: that the component of their thoughts which is hierarchically structured employs a combinatorial principle with a robust function, that of representing dominance. If we adopt this weaker view, then Cheney and Seyfarth's "social origins hypothesis" could be reformulated as the still-substantive claim that the hierarchical structure in the analogous module employed by our ancestors was eventually appropriated to represent other relations, and ultimately to represent something as abstract as predication.[22]

Beyond baboon cognition and the origins of language, we can also draw two more secure, if also more purely methodological, morals. The first is that speculating about the form of thought is a dangerous business. It can seem almost irresistible to assume that thought has a form; but because this claim is usually understood functionally, it cannot be tested directly. Nor is it generally possible to determine the form of thought just by examining structural features, like being discrete, rule-governed, or even hierarchical. Instead, we need to appeal to the particular contents that an agent is and is not capable of representing, and to how they manipulate those contents. Even then, though, inferences from content and processing to form will always be inferences to the best explanation; and such inferences are always vulnerable to the charge of imaginative failure. In this sense, Cheney and Seyfarth's discussion provides a valuable case study.

Second, in general, theorists have neglected alternative representational possibilities because they have too unreflectively subscribed to a dichotomy between imagistic and linguistic formats. One way in which philosophers

---

[21] Other modules or general cognition might have representations of dominance and kinship; the claim is just that they wouldn't need to represent hierarchical structure.

[22] Though, as several authors (e.g., Pinker and Bloom [1990]) have pointed out, hierarchical organization may be a feature of many complex cognitive systems.

might usefully contribute to debates about the form of thought is by developing a more general understanding of the combinatorial and referential principles that govern various representational systems and of the relations among those systems. This would enable us to systematically delineate the space of representational possibilities, with special attention to the functional strengths and weaknesses of each system.

CHAPTER 7

Animal communication and neo-expressivism

Andrew McAninch, Grant Goodrich, and Colin Allen

I. INTRODUCTION

One of the earliest issues in cognitive ethology concerned the meaning of animal signals. In the 1970s and 1980s this debate was most active with respect to the question of whether animal alarm calls convey information about the emotional states of animals or whether they "refer" directly to predators in the environment (Seyfarth *et al.* [1980]; see Radick [2007] for a historical account), but other areas, such as vocalizations about food and social contact, were also widely discussed. In the 1990s, ethologists largely came to a consensus that such calls were "functionally referential" (Evans and Marler [1995]) even if they did not satisfy all the semantic requirements imposed by philosophers of language. More recently, though, it has been argued that ethologists should eschew the concept of reference and return to a focus on the affective aspects of animal communication (Rendall and Owren [2002]). We propose to take a new look at this debate in the light of recent developments in the philosophy of language under the heading of "neo-expressivism" (Bar-On [2004]). This view provides two different senses in which an utterance satisfies an *expressive* function. We intend to use neo-expressivism to provide a philosophical framework for understanding the relationship between the affective and referential aspects of animal signals by seeing them as *both* acts that express some motivational state of the animal *and* products that express propositions with truth-evaluable content. Defending the second part of this claim requires us to reject the recent proposal that non-conceptual content is entirely adequate for understanding the cognition and communication of animals.

We wish to thank the participants of the 2006 University of North Carolina, Chapel Hill, Expression Workshop – with special thanks to Dorit Bar-On.

2. WHAT IS NEO-EXPRESSIVISM?

Neo-expressivism was first proposed as a way to account for some of the distinctive features of avowals, where an avowal is understood as a self-ascription of a present mental state (Bar-On [2004]). Neo-expressivism employs two corresponding distinctions, one between utterances as *acts* and as *products* and one between the notion of "expression" in the *action* sense and in the *semantic* sense. Consider the act/product distinction first. With respect to "avowal," Bar-On writes:

> It can be read as referring to someone's act of avow*ing*, which is an event in the world with a certain causal history and certain action properties. But it can also be read as referring to the result or product of such act – a linguistic (or language-like) token, an item with certain semantic properties. (Bar-On [2004], p. 251)

An utterance, such as an avowal, then, can be expressive either as an act or as a semantic product. Expression in the *action* sense – what we will call "a-expression" – occurs when "a *person* expresses a state of hers by intentionally doing something" (Bar-On [2004], p. 216).[1] However, expression in the *semantic* sense – what we will call "s-expression" – occurs when "a *sentence* expresses an abstract proposition, thought, or judgment by being a (conventional) representation of it" (Bar-On [2004], p. 216).[2] Thus, on a neo-expressivist account of avowals, an utterance of the sentence "I am tired and hungry" a-expresses the speaker's fatigue and hunger, while the product of this act s-expresses a truth-evaluable proposition, which is semantically continuous with other ascriptions, such as "She is tired and hungry" and "I was tired and hungry yesterday" (Bar-On [2004], p. 23), and can be embedded in truth-preserving inferential contexts involving statements such as "If I am tired and hungry, then I should stop working."

Bar-On and Chrisman (in press) apply the neo-expressivist machinery to ethical claims, which is of particular interest to us because the affective approaches to animal communication seem closely aligned with the view to which Bar-On and Chrisman are responding, namely traditional expressivism – the view that an ethical claim is nothing over and above the expression of a non-cognitive mental state, whose content is not truth-evaluable. Although traditional expressivism nicely accounts for the

---

[1] The requirement that the expressive act be intentional here is only that it is goal-directed, but not that it necessarily involves the goal *of* expressing something (Bar-On and Chrisman [in press]).

[2] One might question whether animal alarm calls represent content *conventionally* in the appropriate sense. We hold that, to the extent that such calls are *arbitrarily* related to their contents, they are at least minimally conventional representations.

apparent, *internal* link between the making of an ethical claim and some motivation to act in accordance with it, it has trouble reconciling its main thesis with the apparent truth-evaluability of ethical claims, as indicated by their surface similarity with straightforward declarative sentences. Bar-On and Chrisman argue that neo-expressivism can accommodate both features of ethical claims. The idea is that, while the act of making a genuine ethical claim does require that the agent a-express the appropriate (possibly non-cognitive) motivational state, the product of that act s-expresses some proposition with truth-evaluable content (Bar-On and Chrisman [in press], p. 141). Thus, while the *act* of making an ethical claim, such as "Torture is wrong," might express some conative mental state in the same way that the act of saying "Boo!" or "Hooray!" does, the *product* of making an ethical claim is semantically on par with a sentence such as "Torture is legal." Bar-On and Chrisman employ the notion of *felicity conditions* on acts to explain the internal link between the two types of expression at work in ethical utterances. The main idea is that an ethical claim is *genuine* only when the act of making such a claim expresses, in the action sense, an appropriate motivational state. The felicity conditions on offering an apology provide a familiar analog to this idea. The norms governing such conditions are informed, in part, by pragmatic considerations, by what practical purpose acts of apology are supposed to serve. In the case of apologies, at least, part of that purpose simply is the expression of regret on the part of the apologizer. Thus, although saying "I'm sorry" has as its product a certain truth-evaluable content regardless of whatever attitude is a-expressed, if the speaker a-expressed no sentiment of regret, then he is guilty of an expressive failure or impropriety – he fails to make a proper or genuine apology (Bar-On and Chrisman [in press], p. 149). We'll have more to say about this role of felicity conditions, as it applies to animal signals, later in the chapter.

Our aim in this chapter is to exploit the neo-expressivist apparatus to provide a new philosophical perspective on the meaning of animal alarm calls and on animal communication more generally, applying the idea that what Bar-On has identified is a subset of utterances that are *both* expressions of certain emotional or motivational states *and* expressions of some content that is truth-evaluable. Our suggestion is that some animal signals are members of this subset. Thus, for example, a vervet monkey's leopard alarm call could be an act that a-expresses the monkey's fear, as well as an act whose product s-expresses the proposition that the predator is present. Now Bar-On herself is careful to emphasize that not all verbal or gestural expressive acts have products that are s-expressive. For example, suppose a person smiles upon seeing a child helping an elderly woman with her groceries. This person a-expresses a feeling of *happiness*. But the product of this expression of happiness – the smile itself – does not, according to Bar-On, meet the conditions of truth-evaluability that, for example, the sentence "I am happy" does. A smile does not seem to s-express a truth-evaluable proposition. Bar-On writes, "The product of an act of avowing, unlike a smile or a wince, or even a verbal cry such as 'Ouch!,' is a *semantically articulate* self-ascription, an item with *semantic structure* and truth-conditions. It is a product whose properties allow it to serve, and be caught up, in other kinds of distinctively linguistic (and mental) acts" (Bar-On [2004], p. 251, our italics). The operative question for our purposes, then, is whether animal signals, or at least some of them, should be grouped with avowals and ethical claims or rather with smiles and winces. We, of course, argue for the former, but this argument requires a defense of the claim that the animal signals in question meet the requisite criteria of articulate semantic structure. We will turn to this question in section 4. But first we will look more closely at some of the extant views on the meaning of animal communication and how they map onto the position of neo-expressivism.

3. FROM AVOWALS AND ETHICS TO ETHOLOGY

In this section, we lay out three approaches to the study of animal communication: an approach that emphasizes its affective function, an approach that emphasizes its referential function, and an approach that combines both. Just as some traditional expressivists regard ethical statements as mere expressions of emotion, many ethologists interested in the vocalizations of animals have also focused on the affective aspects of these vocalizations. Darwin himself had noted that certain features of animal vocalizations appear to be correlated with emotional arousal – high-pitched calls correspond to high arousal, for instance (see Hauser [1996], esp. ch. 7, for a review). In light of such observations, one way to understand animal signals is to treat them simply as natural expressions of affective states, which have their effect by inducing an affective state in their receiver (see, e.g., Bastian [1965]; Rowell and Hinde [1962]). Rendall and Owren (2002) go so far as to claim that it is *only* the receiver's affective response that is important to understanding the evolutionary function of animal signals. Thus they dismiss questions of the semantic content of animal alarm calls, claiming instead that such calls are best explained in terms of their function of influencing "the behavior of others in ways that are, on average, beneficial to signalers (and potentially, though not necessarily, also to listeners)" (Rendall and Owren [2002], p. 307; see also Dawkins and Krebs [1978]; Krebs and Dawkins [1984]). This leads them to say that their approach "emphasizes subcortical systems like the brainstem and limbic structures that control attention, arousal and affect" (Rendall and Owren [2002], p. 311).

Rendall and Owren are in fact reacting against the preceding thirty years of research into the semantic or referential properties of animal signals, an approach which, they write, "is a bit peculiar in that it uses a single, recent, and potentially highly derived system of communication (language) to model scores of phylogenetically older and evidently simpler systems" (Rendall and Owren [2002], p. 307). Nevertheless, recent scientific consensus among ethologists has been that a semantic, referential framework is appropriate for investigating animal communication. One very influential set of field studies was conducted over multiple years by Robert Seyfarth and Dorothy Cheney (Seyfarth *et al.* [1980]; Cheney and Seyfarth [1990]). This research was conducted in the Amboseli National Park, Kenya, and was begun when Cheney and Seyfarth were postdoctoral advisees of Peter Marler. Struhsaker (1967) had reported that vervet monkeys at Amboseli produced a variety of acoustically distinct "alarm calls" when confronted with different predators. Cheney and Seyfarth recorded these alarm calls and played them back to the monkeys from loudspeakers hidden in the bushes. Using the results from these experiments and their other direct observations, they argued that alarm calls elicit responses that are keyed to a predator type and not to the caller's motivational state. As Seyfarth and Cheney (2003) summarize their argument, "[v]iewed from the signaler's perspective, animal vocalizations are unlikely to be caused exclusively by emotions because they can be given or withheld depending on many different social factors and because – in encounters with different predators, for example – animals give acoustically different calls in situations with similar emotional valence" (p. 51). These studies and others conducted by scientists associated with Marler's research group have led many ethologists to the view that alarm calls in many species are at least "functionally referential" in conveying information about predators and are not just expressive of a caller's own state of alarm (Evans and Marler [1995]; see also Hauser [1996]).[3]

---

[3] The conditions that Evans and Marler list for functional referentiality include production specificity, discrete structure, and context independence (Evans and Marler [1995], p. 347). They avoid using "referential" *simpliciter* because they are concerned about the possibility of empirically investigating

Marler (1992) recognized the utility of treating alarm calls as simultaneously conveying information about a predator and the caller's emotional
state, and many ethologists would agree. This position is easily assimilated
to neo-expressivism. Indeed, these observations from ethology and the
position of neo-expressivism are mutually supportive. On the one hand,
ethologists, who have clearly been reading some of the philosophical literature on reference, have been worried that such philosophical accounts of
reference involve issues that they cannot resolve empirically (e.g., Quine's
[1960] "Gavagai" problem), or seem to require cognitive capacities beyond
those that are plausibly attributed to animals (e.g., the higher-order intentional states in the Gricean framework advocated by Dennett [1983]).[4] We
think neo-expressivism provides a better option for ethologists seeking a
philosophically rich account of communicative expression, although its
application to animal communication may present its own empirical challenges. On the other hand, philosophers can benefit from this assimilation
to the extent that neo-expressivism can be applied or could be developed
to apply to a wider range of communication than initially thought. Our
suggestion is that the best explanation of the meaning of animal alarm
calls is that they are acts that a-express some motivational state of the animal and whose products s-express some proposition with truth-evaluable
content. Indeed, this not only widens the scope of neo-expressivism but
also suggests how the study of animal communication may be relevant to
understanding the evolution of human language.

4. CONCEPTUALITY AND TRUTH-EVALUABILITY

We recognize, however, that some philosophers and scientists will be skeptical of the idea that alarm calls and other communicative acts of animals
are usefully assimilated to linguistic utterances that have truth-evaluable
content. Davidson (1982), for example, argues that non-human animals
lack the interpretive abilities necessary for genuinely conceptual thought
or semantically interpretable communication. More recently, some philosophers have suggested that animal cognition lacks the kind of conceptual
structure that is paradigmatic of human cognition. (The recent literature

---

additional conditions imposed by various philosophical theories of reference by, e.g., Grice (1957),
Quine (1960), and Dretske (1981).

[4] Dissatisfaction with the Gricean framework has also motivated some cognitive ethologists (e.g.,
Bekoff and Allen [1992]) to look toward Millikan's (1984) teleosemantic approach, but it too creates
empirical difficulties because it depends on knowledge of natural selection in the distant past that is
hard to obtain.

on non-conceptual content is full of examples of this position; see Gunther [2003]). Perhaps there is trouble looming when Bar-On claims that avowals, unlike natural expressions such as smiles or winces, are "semantically artic-ulate" and have "semantic structure," if this articulate semantic structure requires a degree of conceptuality that animals, and the products of their expressive acts, do not possess (Bar-On [2004], p. 251).

Two strategies for responding to this worry about the applicability of neo-expressivism to animal signals are available. One is to accept that animals lack conceptual capacities but also to show how a notion of non-conceptual content (NCC) could be sufficient for truth-evaluability.[5] The other strategy is to accept that conceptual content is required for truth-evaluability but to argue that at least some animals have sufficient concep-tual capacities to support truth-evaluability.[6] In this essay we'll pursue the latter strategy, which is in keeping with the main thrust of Bar-On's neo-expressivist approach. In section 6 we will criticize recent attempts to treat NCC as adequate for explaining the entire cognitive and communicative repertoire of animals, but first we must say more about the relationship of conceptuality to articulate semantic structure and truth-evaluability.

Although Bar-On, in her discussion of avowals, has given some indi-cation of what a semantically articulate product is, we need to say more about what we mean by "enough semantic structure to support truth-evaluability." Here we'll adopt two generally Fregean ideas. One is of pred-ication as the basic structure of any propositional content. The other is of propositions as the bearers of truth. In predication, an object is "brought under" a concept, and content that is thus structured is "conceptual." Gunther (2003, p. 8) characterizes four "conceptualist" principles which he claims are derived from a Fregean characterization of conceptual content. These four principles are as follows.

(1) *Compositionality* is the idea that complex contents are determined by their constituents. It is typically taken as a corollary that these con-stituents can recombine to form other complex contents. For example, the content of the sentence "John is a philosopher" is determined by the simpler constituents "John," "philosopher," etc.

(2) *Cognitive significance* connects perceptual and other mental contents to beliefs. According to this principle, the conceptual content of any men-tal state or communicative signal is a possible belief content. Cognitive

---

[5] Editor's note: See Tetzlaff and Rey (chapter 4) for an account of non-conceptual content in the mental representations of honeybees.

[6] Editor's note: See Carruthers (chapter 5) for a defense of conceptual content in invertebrate mental representations.

agents typically form beliefs on the basis of such contents, but are capable of learning when to withhold judgment. For example, perceiving that one object is larger than another typically leads to a belief with this content, but some cognitive agents can flexibly learn that a distorting mirror undermines this perception–judgment link. An organism that lacks any flexibility of this kind would have states without cognitive significance.

(3) *Reference determinacy,* as the name suggests, is about how conceptual content is related to its reference. There are several different ways of construing this principle, but the one that fits best with the present subject is what Gunther (2003) calls the "recognitional construal." An agent is able to recognize the referent of its conceptual content.

(4) *Force independence* concerns the idea that agents may have different attitudes to one and the same content. One may believe that it is sunny today, or one may desire that it be so. This principle enables intercommunicability of conceptual content. If one thought that the conceptual content of the belief that it is sunny was different from the conceptual content of the doubt that it is sunny, then the two attitudes would be about different things. Furthermore, if these two different attitudes (i.e., belief and doubt) were not separable from their conceptual contents, then a single individual would not be able to entertain different attitudes toward the same contents.

Gunther suggests that for a putative semantic content to fail to conform to any one of these principles is for that content to be non-conceptual. We are inclined to draw a less sharp line, but we do not wish to argue a merely terminological point. Nonetheless, we believe that a more fruitful approach is to consider how animal signals may approximate the conditions described by the four principles. We contend that conformity with all four principles is not required for fruitful application of notions such as truth-evaluability and semantic continuity to animal communication. Consequently, our strategy is not to try to prove that the utterances of any non-human animals satisfy all four criteria simultaneously. Instead, we will be satisfied if we can make it plausible that, by approximating one or more of these features, specific instances of animal communication are appropriately understood in conceptualist and neo-expressivist terms.

5. GRUNTS, SQUEALS, AND OTHER ARBITRARY SIGNALS

In this section we discuss the application of the four principles of conceptuality identified by Gunther to animal communication. It is important to realize that we can only scratch the surface of the diversity of animal signals. Monkeys grunt to convey the presence of predators, or chutter to indicate their social intentions. Rats "laugh" ultrasonically when tickled (Panksepp and Burgdorf [2003]). Recently, we have even been told that the release of air from the rear ends of herrings may actually say something that need not be regarded as a fish faux pas (B. Wilson *et al.* [2004]). No one should think that the study of animal communication is glamorous work. Nor should they think that any firm generalizations about animal communication can be derived from inspecting just one or two examples. Ethologists have made it their goal to unpack the meanings of all manner of signals, auditory, visual, and perhaps even tactile and olfactory. Nevertheless, because space would not allow us a full review of all forms of animal communication, we shall focus in this section mostly on auditory vocalizations of mammals, although we shall also briefly discuss the canid play bow, which is a visual display. We shall argue that the four principles of compositionality, cognitive significance, reference determinacy, and force independence can be associated to different degrees in various examples of non-human mammalian vocal communication. And to the extent that these four principles do apply to some animal signals, these signals satisfy the criterion of articulate semantic structure and, thus, meet the requirement for truth-evaluability.

We will not take the four principles in the order that Gunther lists them. Instead, we begin with *reference determinacy*, since this topic has been explicitly discussed by ethologists themselves. For example, when discussing the meaning of vervet monkey alarm calls, the issue of specificity of content comes up very quickly. Vervet monkeys produce at least three acoustically distinct calls in connection with predatory eagles, leopards, and snakes. Seyfarth, Cheney, and their former student Hauser have considered determinacy of reference against the background of what they discovered about the ontogenesis of alarm calls. Young vervets, for instance, begin by producing "eagle" alarm calls in response to many things moving overhead, including such things as falling leaves. But over time they narrow their responses to just those species that actually prey on vervets. At the Amboseli research site, adult vervets typically produced alarm calls in response to two species (martial eagles and crowned eagles), but not to a third species of eagle that is morphologically more similar to one of the predatory species than either of the two predatory species are to each other.

This production specificity seems to be shaped by the response of adult monkeys to the calls of juveniles. When juveniles give an alarm call, the adults scan the appropriate direction and may or may not repeat the call.

The responses of juveniles are rapidly shaped by adult repetition of their calls. Caro and Hauser (1992) describe an instance observed by Hauser of a young monkey producing the "leopard" call in response to an elephant. Coincidentally, there was a leopard nearby that elicited a call from an adult. It took months for the juvenile to stop giving alarm calls to elephants despite the absence of any further reinforcement from adults.

These facts and others were taken to help solve the question of what content the signals convey. Clearly "eagle" is too generic for the "eagle alarm call" (although most people continue to refer to it as such). But to gloss the signal's content with the phrase "martial eagle or crowned eagle" might seem too specific insofar as it hooks the content to a human taxonomic scheme. "Threatening bird overhead" might be more like it, but even here there is a skeptical tug – do monkeys really understand the distinction between birds and other animals? This worry, pulling one to doubt whether any phrase of English is adequate to the job of conveying the content of animal signals, was paramount among philosophers such as Davidson, Dennett, and Stich around twenty-five years ago. We're not going to address their arguments here (instead, see Allen [1992]; Allen and Bekoff [1997], ch. 4).[7] Our point here is simply to establish that there was and remains interest among ethologists in assigning specific meanings to the vocalizations and other signals of non-human animals (see also the studies cited below).

We turn now to another of Gunther's principles: *force independence*. In the background to the discussions about the content specificity of vervet alarm calls was also the question of "illocutionary" force of animal calls: do alarm calls have declarative (assertoric) force, such as "eagle," or imperative force, such as "take cover!"? Some reasons for thinking that for vervets, at least, the force might be considered declarative include (i) that the calls continue even when all are appropriately situated and (ii) that appropriate responses vary from individual to individual, so there is no univocal command being given. If one were to gloss the calls as having imperative force, one might need to gloss the content as something like "do whatever is appropriate for a predatory bird overhead!" thereby involving reference to the predator in the content.

Of course, to concede that utterances might have different force is not yet to say that the content of those utterances is force-independent – i.e., that animals might express different attitudes to the same content.

---

[7] Editor's note: See Jamieson (chapter 1) for an interpretivist/instrumentalist solution to the issue of specifying the content of animal thoughts.

Nevertheless, it remains an empirical possibility. Consider, for example, the play bows of dogs and other canid species, a stereotyped lowering of the animal's front end while the rear is kept at its normal height. Play bows preceding play bouts appear to serve as invitations to play, or as expressions of a desire to play. Bekoff's (1995) analysis of the placement of play bows during play indicates that these are best understood as declarations that what just preceded the bow or is about to follow it (e.g., a bite) is still play. Hence, the same content ("play is ongoing") appears in one context (prior to play) to have the force of a desire or request and in the other context (during play) to have the force of an assertion.

So far, then, we have identified some possible analogs to reference determinacy and force independence in animal communication. What of *compositionality*? It has generally been assumed that the calls of vervet monkeys lack compositional structure. Since Cheney and Seyfarth conducted their studies, however, the technology for playback experiments in the wild has improved, making it much more possible to test the reaction of animals to combinations of signals. Such studies (pioneered by Zuberbühler, who is a former student of Cheney and Seyfarth) suggest a semantic role for different components of the acoustic signals in other primates such as Diana monkeys (Zuberbühler [2000]), putty-nosed monkeys (Arnold and Zuberbühler [2006, 2008]), gibbons (Clarke *et al.* [2006]), and chimpanzees (Crockford and Boesch [2005]).

Although the expressive power of combinations of discrete elements have been the focus of these recent investigations into primate vocalizations, researchers interested in other systems of mammalian vocalization have been interested in other ways in which such vocalizations may be modified to produce semantically compositional messages. Slobodchikoff and colleagues (1986, 1991) have used recordings and playbacks to investigate the alarm calls of Gunnison's prairie dogs. They have provided evidence not just of predator-specificity for the alarm calls of prairie dogs, but also for specific modulations of pitch and frequency of the calls to describe features of predators. For instance, Ackers and Slobodchikoff (1999) analyzed the vocalizations of prairie dogs elicited by artificial silhouettes of predators and concluded that fundamental harmonic frequency and a combination of the dominant harmonic frequency and the interharmonic interval are the components describing the size and shape of the eliciting stimuli. Based on such results Slobodchikoff claims to have identified noun-like, adjective-like, and verb-like elements in the calls of Gunnison's prairie dogs, enabling them to convey information not just about predator type, but about physical features such as size and color, and about the speed with which a potential predator is moving (see Slobodchikoff [2002] for a review). Slobodchikoff's description of prairie dog communication in terms of noun-like, adjective-like, and verb-like elements is, we concede, controversial. Nonetheless, the work makes clear that compositionality in animal communication systems is a matter for careful empirical investigation.

We have saved *cognitive significance* until last because it is perhaps the most obscure of Gunther's four criteria. However, the issues of learning and flexibility have been discussed in the context of animal behavior. For instance, in their discussion of animal concepts Allen and Hauser (1991) stress the difference between the relatively inflexible behavior of ants with respect to dead nestmates, and the kind of learning that humans would display under conditions where evidence of death was undermined by contrary evidence. To many authors, cognitive significance and the role of evidence is further related to the social, norm-guided practice of giving reasons for beliefs. While non-human animals don't engage in the full range of normative practices that are characteristic of human social groups, Bekoff's research on "playing fair" (Allen and Bekoff [2005]) provides one context in which normative notions may be appropriately deployed. Using comparative data between various canid species, including dogs, wolves, and coyotes, Bekoff has shown that play bows are sometimes used dishonestly, in that, after soliciting play, an animal may use this opportunity to establish dominance. This is most frequent in coyotes, the most aggressive of the three species. But Bekoff argues that dishonest signaling can eventually lead to ostracization from the group. This discussion of play bows is congruent with Bar-On's discussion of the felicity conditions governing avowals and ethical claims. An avowal or ethical claim, according to such conditions, is *genuine* or *proper* only when the agent a-expresses an appropriate motivational state in uttering it. Similarly, we might claim, an animal's play bow is *genuine* only when the animal a-expresses a desire to play, as opposed to (for example) a desire to establish dominance. It is the fact that the animals themselves seem to be assessing the genuineness of each other's signals (e.g., as the coyotes do by ostracizing conspecifics who use the signals infelicitously) that leads us to the view that some notion of cognitive significance applies here. Animals aren't just passive responders to signals with pre-determined meanings, but active epistemic agents capable of adjusting their responses to signals in light of evidence about the reliability of the signalers.

One might worry that the cognitive significance of play bows, alarm calls, etc. is of significance only to the scientist, and not to the animal subjects themselves. An experiment by Cheney and Seyfarth (1990) suggests, however, that vervet monkeys do assess the reliability of other individuals and adjust their behavior to unreliable signaling. In their experiment, one call of a target monkey was repeatedly played back to other members of the target's group, when the target herself was out of sight. Once the others had habituated, no longer showing an overt response to this individual's vocalization, Seyfarth and Cheney played back a different call from the same individual, or a call of the same type recorded from a different individual, and observed the reactions of the members of the group. They found no habituation to the calls of other individuals, but they found an interesting pattern with respect to calls from the target individual. If the others had been habituated to an alarm call, the monkeys showed no transfer of habituation to a different alarm call from the same individual – in other words they responded normally to leopard alarm calls even though they had learned to ignore the target's eagle alarm calls. But if they had been habituated to a call with a social function (such as the "moving-into-the-open grunt"), then the habituation transferred to other calls with social functions (such as a "contact" call) – in other words, they ignored all of the target's calls within the social category, despite the fact that these calls have very different acoustic properties. From this, Seyfarth and Cheney argued that the vervets categorized the social calls semantically – in terms of the kinds of activities and situations they refer to – rather than syntactically in terms of the audible features.

Our conclusion from this too brief discussion is that the non-conceptuality of animal communication is not a foregone conclusion. The extent to which animal signals satisfy the principles of conceptuality identified by Gunther requires additional empirical investigation. Nevertheless, the recent trend in the empirical literature has been towards recognizing more semantic structure rather than less. Thus we submit that the *s-expressive* dimension of the neo-expressivist stance is fruitfully applied to non-human animals.

6. TRUTH-EVALUABILITY WITHOUT CONCEPTS?

In this section, we bolster the case for the conceptualist stance by taking a critical look at how the notion of non-conceptual content has been applied by philosophers to animal cognition and communication. It has been quite commonplace among philosophers writing about non-conceptual content (NCC) to make claims about animals. Thus, Andy Clark writes, "[T]he idea of nonconceptual content seems well suited to describing the cognitive states of many animals" (2003, p. 172). As well as suggestions that NCC might be useful for ethologists, there is a class of arguments that appeals explicitly to non-human animals to bolster the case for the very existence of NCC. For instance, Gareth Evans, the archetypal proponent of NCC, takes it for granted that various non-human animals perceive and remember things, and that these states have intentional content even though the animals possessing them lack concepts of the things about which they carry information. In its most general form, the argument can be schematically presented like this.

1. Animals possess representational states with content.
2. Animals lack concepts.
C. The content of animals' representational states is non-conceptual.

As it stands, this argument does not wear its validity on its sleeve, but we will presume for the sake of discussion that some reasonable way can be found to state the connection between concepts and contents that would justify the inference.

Evans and others extend the basic argument further, arguing for the significance of NCC by asserting that it accounts for what is shared between human and non-human animal cognition. This view is sympathetically echoed by Peacocke (2001), who claims that, while it is plausible to deny concepts to lower animals, it is also plausible to affirm some properties – e.g., certain spatial representations – as common to the perceptions of both humans and lower animals. "If the lower animals do not have states with conceptual content," Peacocke concludes, "but some of their states have contents in common with human perceptions, it follows that some perceptual representational content is nonconceptual" (p. 614).

Another major source of motivation for defenders of NCC comes from reflections on the character of perception. It is observed that the exact content of any perceptual state seems ineffable: no matter how much one says about one's present visual experience, for example, one is bound to run out of words to express the sheer variety of hues and textures contained in that experience. This inexpressible residue, it is argued, does not fall under any concepts we possess. Such arguments rely on an introspective appeal to the richness or "fine-grained" nature of perception, and, as outlined here, they commonly rely on implicating words and concepts (calling them "lexical concepts" is simply to label the connection without justifying it). Such a tight connection between conceptual content and language further reinforces the idea that the mental states of languageless animals must be non-conceptual in content.

The discussion of the applicability of NCC to animals in the literature has largely been carried out at an intuitive (armchair) level. Gunther (2003) remarks that "[l]ike Evans and McDowell, many assume that animals don't have concepts (although the relevant principle and rendering are generally not identified)" (p. 23). This is a bit harsh, as authors from Evans to Clark have made some stab at justifying their acceptance of premise (2), that animals lack concepts. Clark (2003), for example, writes:

To have (properly) the concept *fly* involves more than being able to find your way around (like the frog) in a fly-infested domain. It involves having a whole web of concepts in which your concept of fly is embedded. This consciously echoes Evans' Generality Constraint (Evans 1982, pp. 100–105), which insists that to truly possess a concept "*a*" you must be able to think *a* in all the (semantically sensible) combinations which it could enter into with other concepts you possess. (p. 173)

To be sure, "having a whole web of concepts" is not a particularly clear rendering of a principle. (And see Fodor [1998] for a contrary defense of conceptual atomism.) We could (and perhaps should) also put pressure on Clark's notion of being "semantically sensible," for what seems a semantically sensible thought about a fly from one point of view need not seem semantically sensible given another. (Was the original idea that light waves propagate in a vacuum semantically sensible?) Clark actually suggests using hyphenated phrases to express "unstructured" animal contents. (So the content is not "eagle threatening" but "eagle-threatening.") From the point of view of the practicing ethologist, this suggestion has little utility, for it provides no help in answering the question of what words are appropriately inserted around the hyphens (for example "eagle-threatening" vs. "overhead-predator-threatening"). Concepts or non-concepts, the ethologist is still going to be thrown back on notions articulated by Marler and the scientists he has influenced (see also Allen and Saidel [1998]).

José Bermúdez (2003a, 2003b) is among the more empirically informed defenders of NCC for animals, although his appeals to actual cognitive ethology are made with a view to supporting premise (1). He cites cognitive ethologists for their commitment to using intentional/representational notions to explain animal behavior (2003b, p. 4), and he takes the success or failure of this research program to be an empirical matter (2003a).

Bermúdez's view of the defense of premise (2) is that it "depends upon a substantive philosophical account of what it is to possess a concept" (2003a). Like Clark, Bermúdez mentions Evans' generality constraint in this context as essential to concept possession.[8] Bermúdez also argues that

---

[8] Editor's note: See Carruthers (chapter 5) for a different version of the generality constraint, as well as an argument that, on its most plausible construal, many animals (including invertebrates) satisfy it.

the allegedly domain-specific nature of animal cognition is incompatible with the generality constraint. But Bermúdez raises the bar further by talking about "concept mastery" as a criterion for having thoughts with conceptual content. According to Bermúdez, "genuine concept mastery involves an ability not simply to make judgments involving those concepts but also to justify those judgments and to reflect on the grounds for them." These he takes to be "paradigmatically language-dependent activities" (2003b, p. ix) and *ipso facto* beyond the range of non-human animals. It is unclear why one should equate concept mastery with concept possession, but we'll leave this point aside for now. It's sufficient for our current purposes that the introduction of NCC does not clarify ethological practice or suggest further empirical work. In contrast, a conceptualist take on animal communication suggests various fruitful lines of research that, as we described in the previous section, already have counterparts in the ethological literature.

If the issue for understanding non-human animal communication were that of truth-evaluability alone, perhaps either a conceptualist or non-conceptualist account would be appropriate – even NCC can be true or false. However, the notion of s-expression in the neo-expressivist account also invokes semantic continuity across the variety of utterances produced by an actor. We submit that such continuity requires a way to connect the content of different utterances to each other. NCC provides no account of these connections. Even if the content of animal signals falls short of the full inferential promiscuity of human language, there is nonetheless sufficient evidence that animal signals are not interpreted as isolated semantic units. A conceptualist take on the s-expressive power of animal communication is warranted.

7. FUTURE DIRECTIONS

We conclude by proposing some future directions that a continuation of the present discussion might take. We have argued that at least some animal signals are best understood as acts that express some motivational state of the animal, as well as acts whose products express some proposition with truth-evaluable content. With respect to some animal signals, we have speculated about what particular motivational state is a-expressed and what propositional content is s-expressed, but we happily concede that support for such speculations requires further investigation, both scientific and philosophical. Another question, though, is why the a-expression of some particular motivational state would correspond to the s-expression of some propositional content in the first place. Bar-On's suggestion is that the "internal" link between the motivational state and the propositional content is fixed by the conditions on what constitutes a *proper* performance of the expressive act in question. And the norms governing the proper performance of such acts are fixed, in part, by what function these acts have in the practices in question. Consider, for example, how Bar-On and Chrisman (in press) describe this internalist thesis with regard to ethical claims:

[W]hat is distinctive about ethical claims – what renders them *ethical* claims – is the fact that a person who issues an ethical claim is supposed to give voice to a (type of) motivational state using a linguistic (or language-like) vehicle that involves ethical terms or concepts. This . . . is not offered simply as a generalization about what regularly happens when people issue ethical claims; rather it is a characterization of a certain category of acts – acts of making ethical claims – in terms of their point, which distinguishes them from other kinds of claim-making acts, and has implications for their proper performance. (pp. 144–145)

We think this reading of the internalist thesis holds promise for the study of certain categories of animal communication as well. Consider the case of the insincere use of canid play bows: the bowing individual, in this case, fails to a-express the appropriate motivational state required to make this act a *genuine* play bow. The conditions governing what counts as a genuine play bow, on this view, include at least the requirement that the bowing individual a-express a motivation to play, as opposed to a motivation to fight, for instance. The expression of a motivation to play is part of the very *point* of play bows. Likewise, genuine alarm calls require a-expression of a state of concern or fear about a predator. And given the observations of ethologists going all the way back to Darwin about the acoustic properties of such calls, it seems likely that their evolution has in part been driven by their capacity to carry emotional information. The neo-expressivist interpretation of the internalist link between the a-expression of some motivational state and the s-expression of some propositional content opens up a new facet of inquiry with respect to animal communication: investigations into what particular motivational state is a-expressed, what propositional content is s-expressed, and what social function is performed in the utterance of some animal signal are most fruitfully pursued in concert.

CHAPTER 8

Mindreading in the animal kingdom

José Luis Bermúdez

I. INTRODUCTION

Can non-human animals think and reason about what other creatures are thinking, reasoning, or experiencing? Experimentalists, ethologists, and theorists have answered this deceptively simple question in many different ways. Some researchers have made very strong claims about so-called *mindreading abilities* in animals (Byrne and Whiten [1988, 1990, 1991]; Dally *et al.* [2006]; Hare *et al.* [2001]; Hare *et al.* [2002]; Premack and Woodruff [1978]; Tomasello and Call [2006]; Tschudin [2001]). Others have been critical of such claims (Heyes [1998]; Penn and Povinelli [2007b]; Povinelli and Vonk [2006]). Even a cursory look at the extensive literature on mindreading in animals reveals considerable variation both in what mindreading abilities are taken to be, and in what is taken as evidence for them. The first aim of this essay is to tackle some important framework questions about how exactly the mindreading hypothesis is to be stated. In sections 2 and 3, three importantly different versions of the mindreading hypothesis are distinguished. The first (which I call *minimal mindreading*) occurs when a creature's behavior covaries with the psychological states of other participants in social exchanges. The second (which I call *substantive mindreading*) involves attributions of mental states. In section 3, substantive mindreading is further divided into *propositional attitude mindreading* and *perceptual mindreading*. In section 4, I present reasons for thinking that the role of propositional attitude psychology in human social life is very much overstated and show that this very much weakens the analogical case for identifying propositional attitude mindreading in non-linguistic creatures. And in section 5, I present a revised version of an argument I have given elsewhere (Bermúdez [2003a]) to show that the most sophisticated form of substantive mindreading (the type of mindreading that exploits the concepts of propositional attitude psychology) is only available to language-using creatures.

2. MINIMAL AND SUBSTANTIVE MINDREADING

My starting point is that many types of animal are genuine thinkers. I have discussed this at length elsewhere (Bermúdez 2003a) and will not rehearse the arguments again here. The evidence from comparative psychology and cognitive ethology overwhelmingly supports taking some forms of animal behavior to be genuinely psychological, generated by primitive forms of belief and desire via processes that have significant commonalities with the forms of reasoning engaged in by language-using creatures.

Animals are capable of sophisticated social behaviors. Many of these social behaviors do not have any sort of psychological dimension. Schooling and flocking behaviors are obvious examples. And there are behaviors with a psychological dimension that do not involve any social coordination, as in cases of emotional contagion. But there do appear, at least at first sight, to be forms of social coordination in the animal kingdom that have a psychological dimension and that involve a sensitivity to the psychological states of other participants in the interaction.

Here is an example of how non-linguistic creatures can exploit social cues. A well-known set of experiments by Brian Hare and collaborators have revealed that domestic dogs are strikingly successful on object choice tasks with social cues (Hare *et al.* [2002]). One reason these results are striking is that most primates, which are generally thought to have quite sophisticated social-cognitive skills, seem unable to perform above chance on object choice tasks. In a standard object choice task, an experimenter hides a food reward in one of two opaque containers. The subject, who did not see the food being hidden, has to choose between the two containers. Before the animal is presented with the choice, the experimenter "signals" which container the food is in by using one of a range of communicative cues (such as pointing to, marking, or looking at the correct container). Hare *et al.* found that domestic dogs master object choice tasks very quickly, often without any learning.

The success of domestic dogs in picking up and exploiting social cues to solve object choice tasks is a paradigm example of social coordination with a psychological dimension – as opposed to coordinated group behaviors, such as schooling or flocking, where (to simplify somewhat) an individual's behavior depends simply upon changes in the behavior of other participants in the coordinated group behavior. That there is social coordination is obvious. What makes it social coordination involving sensitivity to psychology is that the dogs behave in ways that depend upon changes in the psychological states of the other participant in the interaction. The dogs in the object choice tasks are able to respond to different visual cues. These cues all have something in common. They all have a common cause in the psychological profile of the experimenter – namely, the experimenter's intention to signal to the animal the location of the reward. This allows us to extrapolate to predictions about how the dogs will behave in future tests – namely, that they will respond to visual cues that have the same cause and origin. In essence, we assume that the dogs are responding to cues in the abstract, rather than to the physical gestures by which those cues are made – a "multi-track" sensitivity, as opposed to a set of contingencies between particular responses and particular stimuli.

This account of social coordination involving sensitivity to psychology is *quasi-operational*. While it goes beyond observed behavior in making reference to the psychological states of the experimenter, it does not go beyond the observed behavior of the experimental subject. The experimental subject is characterized in purely behavioral ways. Saying that a non-linguistic creature displays psychological sensitivity in this quasi-operational sense does not attribute to it any psychological states. Displaying sensitivity to psychology only requires behaving in ways that depend upon the psychological states of another participant in the interaction. It is neither implied nor required that an animal displaying sensitivity to psychology should represent (or even be capable of representing) the psychological states of the other participant(s) in the exchange.

I will use the expression "minimal mindreading" to describe what is going on in instances of social coordination involving sensitivity to psychology of this type. Here is the official definition:

A creature engages in *minimal mindreading* when its behavior is systematically dependent upon changes in the psychological states of other participants in the interaction.

Characterizations of minimal mindreading are *descriptive* rather than *explanatory*. To say that an animal is engaged in minimal mindreading is simply to assert that certain contingencies hold between its behavior and the psychological states of the creatures with which it is interacting. It is not in any sense to say *why* those contingencies hold.

The expression "substantive mindreading," in contrast, is intended to be explanatory. Attributions of substantive mindreading are made in order to explain how and why an animal's behavior depends systematically upon the psychological states of other participants in the interaction. What explains the dependence, it is typically claimed by those who identify substantive mindreading in the animal kingdom, is the fact that the animal engaged in a social interaction is mentally representing the psychological states of other participants in the interaction.

Here is the matching official definition:

A creature engages in *substantive mindreading* when its behavior is systematically dependent on its representations of the psychological states of other participants in the interaction.[1]

Although the notion of systematic dependence features in the definition both of minimal and of substantive mindreading, it is doing different work in each. In the definition of minimal mindreading, the systematic dependence is not intended to be causal. Minimal mindreading is covariation pure and simple. In contrast, claims of substantive mindreading are intended to be causal. The animal's behavior is caused by (and hence can be explained by appeal to) how it represents the mental states of others.

3. TWO TYPES OF SUBSTANTIVE MINDREADING

Substantive mindreading occurs when a creature behaves in ways that depend systematically upon how it represents the psychological states of other participants in the interaction. But there are different types of psychological states and, correspondingly, different types of substantive mindreading. In this section I articulate what I take to be the most important distinction in this area, both from a theoretical and from an experimental perspective.

We can start from the obvious fact that psychological states do not typically generate behavior on their own. Behavior is the product of complexes of psychological states – of what might be thought of as psychological profiles. We can only think about the behavioral implications of individual psychological states through the prism of the subject's psychological profile. This is part of what makes studying the psychology of non-linguistic creatures so challenging. A well-designed experiment tries to find behavioral criteria for the presence or absence of a particular form of psychological state. No interesting psychological states have unambiguous and unequivocal implications for behavior, however. So assumptions have to be made about the subject's more general psychological profile and, of necessity, these assumptions are not themselves under investigation and scrutiny. This means that there is always an element of boot-strapping going on when we explore the psychological lives of non-linguistic creatures.

[1] Behavior can be understood in a thin sense here. Preferential looking counts as a behavior, for example.

Fortunately, psychological states lie on a continuum in terms of the directness of their implications for behavior. At one end of the continuum are psychological states with more or less immediate implications for behavior. At the other end lie the psychological states that feed into action only very indirectly. We can think about where an individual psychological state lies on the continuum in terms of the complexity and particularity of the background psychological profile required for it to issue in action. In some cases the background psychological profile is very simple, given by a relatively fixed set of drives and goals that may well be constant across individuals within a given community, or even across a given species. In other cases the background psychological profile is highly complex and highly individual.

This basic fact about the relation between psychology and action has important implications for thinking about substantive mindreading. A creature engages in substantive mindreading to the extent that its behavior depends systematically upon how it represents the psychological states of others. A mindreading creature behaves in ways that reflect its predictions about how other creatures are going to behave – predictions derived from representations of their psychological states. It is clear that certain conditions have to be met for these predictions to be successful. It is not enough simply that the mindreading creature represent the psychological states of other participants. Or even that it represent those psychological states accurately. The success of behavioral predictions stands or falls with their being in conformity with the background psychological profile of the creature whose behavior is being predicted. I say that a prediction is in conformity with a background psychological profile when the predicted behavior is the behavior that would result from the combination of the (accurately represented) psychological state and the background psychological profile.

What does it take to secure conformity with the background psychological profile? One way to secure conformity would be through explicitly (and accurately) representing the background psychological profile in order to apply some set of principles that connect psychology with behavior. These principles may be proto-theoretical, as proposed by adherents of the "theory of mind" approach to mindreading. In this case the principles themselves are explicitly represented. Or they may be principles governing the subject's own decision-making processes, as suggested by supporters of the simulationist approach.[2] On the simulationist view the principles are not

---

[2] For the debates between simulationist and theory-theory approaches to mindreading see the papers in Davies and Stone (1995) and Carruthers and Smith (1996).

explicitly represented. The particular principles, and how they are applied, are less important than the "raw materials" on which they operate. In this case the raw materials are representations of psychological profiles.

But conformity can also be achieved without explicit representation. In cases where the relevant elements of the background psychological profile are generic and widely held it is possible simply to trade on them. So, for example, if I put a $100 bill in plain view on the sidewalk and I correctly identify someone as catching sight of it, I am fairly safe in predicting that they will bend over to pick it up. The background psychology required to generate this behavior is nothing more than a desire for free money, which we can safely assume to be constant across the human population – so constant in fact that there is no need explicitly to represent it, and certainly no need to delve any deeper into the particularities of the individual's psychology. In this case a reasoner will move directly (and with justification) from the observation that a person has seen the $100 bill to a prediction that the person will bend over to pick it up. In almost every case this prediction will be accurate.

Again, we have two end-points on a continuum. The more complex and variable the relevant elements of the background psychological profile, the more necessary explicit representation becomes, and the more extensive it has to be. I am taking complexity and variability here to be distinct phenomena. Complexity itself does not mandate explicit representation. Predictors can trade on constant elements of the background psychological profiles when those elements are generic and widely held, no matter how complex they are. The real problem is created by variability. If there are many different ways in which an agent's psychology might be configured relative to the behavior being predicted, then there are all sorts of ways in which a prediction might go wrong, even if the prediction is based on a completely accurate psychological attribution.

Making predictions that involve explicitly representing a background psychological profile can be a substantial intellectual achievement. It typically involves, for example, representing the range of different motivational states that an agent has, together with the information they currently possess about the environment and a range of more general beliefs. But it is not enough, of course, simply to represent the states. The representer must also represent how they fit together and how they might jointly determine a particular action. To put it another way, the representer must reason about how the agent might reason their way to a particular action. This reasoning is typically conscious – and even when it proceeds below the threshold of consciousness it is consciously accessible. The activity of explanation and prediction is a personal-level activity (in the sense of Dennett [1969] – see Bermúdez [2005, chap. 1] for further discussion).

These general observations about the different ways in which identifying another's psychological state can generate predictions of behavior have important implications for how we think about substantive mindreading in non-linguistic creatures. Both experimentalists (Tomasello and Call [1997, Pt. 2; 2006]) and philosophers (Bermúdez [2003a]) have noted that substantive mindreading is not a unitary phenomenon. There are different types of mindreading, varying according to the type of psychological state that they involve. Predictions based on representations of perceptual states, for example, reflect a different type of mindreading from predictions based on representations of beliefs and desires. Standardly these types of mindreading are distinguished simply as a function of differences between the relevant represented psychological states, on the tacit assumption that if psychological states are different in type then representing them requires distinct abilities. The current observations give us a principled way of categorizing mindreading abilities that lines up in important respects with the standard distinctions.

Consider, for example, the psychological states that philosophers standardly term propositional attitudes. These includes beliefs, desires, hopes, fears, and so on. What they have in common, from a philosophical point of view, is that they can all be analyzed as attitudes that thinkers and reasoners have towards propositions. We will look in more detail later on at what propositions might be and why this is important for thinking about the mindreading abilities of non-linguistic creatures. For the moment the important point is that the propositional attitudes are collectively located at one end of our continuum. They typically do not have direct implications for action. There is no single way that a particular belief or desire will feed into action. Individual beliefs and desires feed into action only indirectly, as a result of an agent's specific psychological profile.

This holistic character of the propositional attitudes places a very specific burden on mindreading that involves attribution of propositional attitudes, because it brings into play the distinctiveness of the agent's background psychological profile. Any creature that exploits propositional attitude attributions in order to predict the behavior of another agent will need also to represent explicitly that agent's background psychological profile. The success of the prediction will ultimately depend upon the accuracy both of the propositional attitude attribution and of the representation of the background psychological profile. Let us call this complex form of mindreading *propositional attitude mindreading*.

Perceptual mindreading is typically far less complex. In many contexts what a creature perceives has obvious and immediate implications for action – seeing a predator, or a food source, for example. The only elements of the background psychological profile that need to be brought into play are generic and universal. In these cases, therefore, there is correspondingly little or no need for the creature explicitly to represent the agent's background psychological profile. Of course, not all cases of perceptual mindreading are straightforward. Sometimes predicting how an agent will respond to something in plain view requires delving deep into the agent's psychology. But experiments exploring the mindreading abilities of non-linguistic creatures tend to lie at the straightforward end of the spectrum. They typically exploit the fact that seeing a food item has immediate implications for action, as in the much-discussed food competition paradigm developed in Hare *et al.* (2001).

For these reasons propositional attitude mindreading is a more complex and sophisticated intellectual activity than perceptual mindreading. It involves explicitly representing elements of an agent's background psychological profile, and then reasoning about how the agent will act in the light of what is known of their psychology. The complexity of the explicit representation and the scope of the reasoning will vary depending on the particular propositional attitude. But there will always have to be some explicit representation and some reasoning on the part of the propositional attitude mindreader. Perceptual mindreading is not like this. It is perfectly possible for a creature to be a perceptual mindreader without any capacity for explicitly representing an agent's background psychological profile, and without any capacity to reason about how psychology issues in action. This is because perceptual mindreaders can often exploit and trade on direct connections between perception and action. The holistic character of the propositional attitudes means that there are no comparable direct connections between propositional attitudes and action.

4. THE DOUBLE ANALOGY

Something like the following pattern of reasoning is implicit in many discussions of animal minds.

(1) Certain species of non-human animals solve many problems of social interaction and coordination that are analogous to problems solved by humans.
(2) Humans solve these problems through mindreading strategies.
(3) Hence non-human animals also have to be mindreaders.

There is a double analogy here. The first analogy is between the types of social situations confronted by human and non-human animals. The second analogy is between the strategies that humans and nonhumans employ to navigate those situations. There are many important questions that might be raised about whether and how arguments from analogy should be used in these contexts. I will prescind from these questions here. What I want to focus on is the basis on which the second analogy is made. Even if one thinks that it is acceptable to reason analogically from the mindreading strategies of human animals to those of non-human animals, it is important to start from an accurate picture of how humans solve problems of social interaction and social coordination.

Many philosophers assume without argument that some version of what is standardly called *folk psychology* or *common-sense psychology* is the principal tool that we employ to navigate the social world. This is standardly understood to involve attributing propositional attitudes. In previous work I have expressed skepticism about this assumption. There are many forms of social understanding and social coordination that proceed without attributions of propositional attitudes. One example that I have discussed (Bermúdez [2003a, 2005]) are highly stereotypical interactions that can be modeled using frames and routines. This is particularly relevant for thinking about mindreading in non-linguistic creatures.

Many of the social interactions that we engage in are highly stereotypical. We negotiate them successfully because we are able to predict what other participants will do. But those predictions need not, and in fact rarely do, involve forms of propositional attitude mindreading. When one goes into a shop or a restaurant, for example, it is obvious that the situation can only be effectively negotiated because one has certain beliefs about why people are doing what they are doing and about how they will continue to behave. I cannot effectively order dinner without interpreting the behavior of the person who approaches me with a pad in his hand, or buy some meat for dinner without interpreting the person standing behind the counter. But these beliefs about what people are doing do not involve second-order beliefs about their psychological states. Ordering meals in restaurants and buying meat in butcher's shops are such routine situations that one need only identify the person approaching the table as a waiter, or the person standing behind the counter as a butcher. Simply identifying social roles provides enough leverage on the situation to allow one to predict the behavior of other participants and to understand why they are behaving as they are.

Social understanding and social coordination exploiting shared knowledge of social routines and stereotypes is a form of reasoning. However, this reasoning is similarity-based and analogy-based. Social understanding becomes a matter of matching perceived social situations to prototypical social situations and working by analogy from partial similarities. We do not store general principles about how social situations work, but rather have a general template for particular types of situation with parameters that can be adjusted to allow for differences in detail across the members of a particular social category.

Research in computer science and artificial intelligence provides one way of modeling this type of social reasoning. Motivated in part by the intractability of rule- and logic-based solutions to these everyday social interactions, computer scientists have proposed what are known as *frame-based* systems (Nebel [1999]). Here is Minsky's (1975) original articulation of the notion of a frame:

> Here is the essence of the theory: when one encounters a new situation (or makes a substantial change in one's view of the present problem) one selects from memory a structure called a *frame*. This is a remembered framework to be adapted to fit reality by changing details as necessary.
>
> A *frame* is a data structure for representing a stereotyped situation, like being in a certain kind of living room, or going to a child's birthday party. Attached to each frame are several kinds of information. Some of this information is about how to use the frame. Some is about what one can expect to happen next. Some is about what to do if those expectations are not confirmed.
>
> We can think of a frame as a network of nodes and relations. The top levels of a frame are fixed, and represent things that are always true about the supposed situation. The lower levels have many *terminals* – slots that must be filled by specific instances or data. Each terminal can specify conditions its assignments must meet. (The assignments themselves are usually smaller sub-frames.) Simple conditions are specified by *markers* that might require a terminal assignment to be a person, an object of sufficient value, or a pointer to a sub-frame of a certain type. More complex conditions can specify relations among the things assigned to several terminals. (pp. 111–112)

The frame-based approach gives a concrete example of the form that a routine-based approach to social understanding and social coordination might take. The key point is that, as stressed earlier, the parameters for the frame (what Minsky calls the terminals) need not be propositional attitude attributions. Social interactions that are sufficiently stereotypical to be modeled in terms of frames can proceed without propositional attitude mindreading. Where they do involve mindreading this can simply be perceptual mindreading.

Frames and routines provide a framework for interpreting some of the observational and ethological evidence often cited for propositional attitude mindreading in primates. An important part of the case (as reviewed, for example, in Tomasello and Call [1997], Pt. 2) comes from observation of behaviors in the wild that seem to involve tactical deception (Byrne and Whiten [1990]) and/or communication. Leaving aside the methodological issues raised by the analysis of what has seemed to some observers to be rather anecdotal observations, one issue to explore is whether the observed behaviors could not be viewed as stereotypical and patterned interactions where the parameter-setting does not involve one creature forming beliefs about the desires and beliefs of another creature.

Consider communicative behaviors, such as the much-discussed alarm calls of vervet monkeys (Cheney and Seyfarth [1990]). One of the key features of vervet monkey alarm calls is that they use different types of alarm call in response to the presence of different types of predator – and that monkeys hearing the alarm call respond in different ways to each type of call. This seems to fit very closely the frame model just outlined, with relatively fixed responses (the calls and the behaviors to which they give rise) triggered by different perceptual experiences (playing the role of the terminals in Minsky's frames). This interpretation of the vervet alarm calls is consistent with many of the claims that have been made about the degree of cognitive sophistication that they reflect. So, for example, it is consistent with the vervet alarm calls carrying information about events in the environment (as opposed to being expressions of the monkey's state of arousal).[3] And yet it does not involve bringing into play the machinery of propositional attitude mindreading. The routine does not involve one monkey intending to bring it about that the other monkeys believe that a predator is nearby – or that the other monkeys recognize the first monkey's intention to bring it about that they form this belief.

Tactical deception has been less systematically and longitudinally studied than vervet monkey alarm calls. It is certainly possible that what have been interpreted as episodes of primates intentionally manipulating (or attempting to manipulate) the propositional attitudes of conspecifics will turn out to be complex and sophisticated routines of the type analyzed by Minsky. It is plausible that the parameter-setting will involve a degree of mindreading, but the default assumption (particularly in the light of the considerations that will emerge in the next section) should be that this

---

[3] Editor's note: See McAninch, Goodrich, and Allen (chapter 7) for the latest discussion on the supposed contrast between referential and emotive accounts of vervet alarm calls.

will be perceptual mindreading. Certainly, many of the reported instances of tactical deception do seem to be interpretable in terms of intentions to manipulate a conspecific's visual perspective (rather than their propositional attitudes). Consider the following well-known description of an instance of tactical deception in a troop of baboons in Ethiopia.

An adult female spent 20 min in gradually shifting in a seated position over a distance of about 2m to a place behind a rock about 50 cm high where she began to groom the subadult male follower of the group – an interaction not tolerated by the adult male. As I was observing from a cliff slightly above [the animals] I could judge that the adult male leader could, from his resting position, see the tail, back and crown of the female's head, but not her front, arms and face: the subadult male sat in a bent position while being groomed, and was also invisible to the leader. The leader could thus see that she was present, but probably not that she groomed. (Report by Hans Kummer quoted in Byrne [1995], p. 106)

We can understand what is going on here in terms of a Minsky-style routine. The female baboon is engaging in a complicated pattern of quasi-stereotypical behavior in which the terminals are filled by instances of perceptual mindreading. One terminal is filled by her calculation of the alpha male's line of sight. Another by her perception of the rock between the alpha male and the subadult male. There is no need to appeal to the female baboon's intention to manipulate the beliefs of the alpha male.

5. THE LIMITS OF NON-LINGUISTIC MINDREADING

In the previous section I tried to weaken the temptation to think that the complex forms of social interaction and social coordination that we see in the animal kingdom demand explanations in terms of propositional attitude mindreading. In this section I take a more direct tack. I present a version of an argument I first proposed in Bermúdez (2003a). The argument aims to show that propositional attitude mindreading is not available to creatures that lack a public language. In order to make the structure of the argument more perspicuous I make each step explicit, adding comments where applicable.

(A) *Unlike perceptual mindreading, propositional attitude mindreading involves representing another creature's attitude to a proposition.*

A representation of another creature as, say, believing that the food is hidden behind the tree is tripartite in nature. It involves representing

 (i) a particular individual as
 (ii) bearing a particular propositional attitude to
(iii) a particular proposition.

Perceptual mindreading is also tripartite in nature. It involves representing
  (i) a particular individual as
  (ii) perceiving
  (iii) a particular object or state of affairs.
Despite this similarity in structure, however, the representations required
for propositional attitude mindreading are far more complex than those
required for perceptual mindreading.

Consider a perceptual mindreader M representing another agent α as
perceiving a state of affairs S. The perceptual mindreader is already perceiving S. In order to represent α as perceiving S, M needs simply to add
to its representation of S a representation of a relation between α and S. As
we saw in the previous section, in many cases of perceptual mindreading
this additional representation can be very straightforward. It can be simply
a matter of representing S as lying in α's line of sight. The representational skills required are basic geometric skills, on a par with those involved
in working out possible trajectories of objects (including the agent's own
body) through the environment. As we saw in section 3, moreover, the
fact that S is in α's line of sight can often have very immediate implications for action. This means that moving from a representation of α
as perceiving S to a prediction of how α will behave is often completely
straightforward.

Now consider a propositional attitude mindreader M* representing
another agent β as believing a proposition P. Here it is not typically the case
that P corresponds to a state of affairs in the distal environment that M*
is already perceiving. In fact (as we saw in the last section), in many of the
cases where propositional attitude mindreading is identified in the animal
kingdom P is actually false. The aim in tactical deception as standardly
interpreted, for example, is to generate false beliefs in another agent – that
is, the deceiver must intend to bring it about that an agent believe that p
where p is false. So, the question arises: what is it to represent a proposition
(particularly one that one does not oneself believe)?

One answer here is that propositions just are states of affairs, and so
representing a proposition is no more and no less complicated than representing states of affairs. On this interpretation propositional attitude
mindreading does not come out as fundamentally different in kind from
perceptual mindreading. It is true that propositional attitude mindreading
can involve representing states of affairs that do not exist (as in tactical
deception cases), but it is widely accepted that many types of non-human
animals can represent non-existent states of affairs. After all, we can only
explain the behavior of non-linguistic creatures in psychological terms if we

attribute to them desires, and having a desire often involves representing a non-existent state of affairs.

The obvious problem with this view is that states of affairs lack some of the fundamental characteristics of propositions. In particular, propositions are true or false, while states of affairs are not the sort of things that can be either true or false. On many standard ways of thinking about propositions and states of affairs, states of affairs are the things that make propositions true or false – precisely because propositions are representations of states of affairs that can be true or false.[4]

The "truth-aptness" of propositions is absolutely fundamental to the whole enterprise of propositional attitude mindreading. Propositional attitude mindreading allows us to explain and predict the behavior of other subjects in terms of the representational states that generated it. It is such a powerful tool because it works both when other subjects represent the world correctly, and when they misrepresent it. Moreover (as will become very important in the following) the truth-aptness of propositions is what explains the inferential connections between propositional attitudes that are not belief-like. Desires, for example, are not true or false in the way that beliefs are. But desires have contents (propositions) that stand in logical relations to the contents of desires and other beliefs. These logical relations are constantly exploited in practical reasoning.

In sum, my claim is that propositional attitude mindreading involves representing another agent's representation of a state of affairs. I will use the term "proposition" to abbreviate "representation of a state of affairs." Anyone who thinks about propositions in a different way is invited to use the unabbreviated expression.

(B) *Propositional attitude mindreaders must represent propositions in a way that allows them to work out how the relevant propositional attitudes will feed into action.*

This should not be controversial in the light of discussion earlier in this chapter. Propositional attitude mindreading is a way of explaining and predicting behavior. Obviously it is not enough simply to represent the propositional attitudes of another agent. Those propositional attitudes

---

[4] Things are not quite as simple as this, since propositions can be logically complex and it is not clear that there are logically complex states of affairs. Even if one thinks that the proposition that *the table is red* is made true by the state of affairs of the table being red, it is far from obvious that the proposition *the table is not red* is made true by the state of affairs of the table not being red. Many philosophers would deny that negative states of affairs exist. Nonetheless, the fact remains that when *the table is not red* is true, its truth consists in the holding of some state of affairs (the table being black, for example).

must be represented in a format (what is sometimes called a vehicle) that can be exploited in reasoning that leads to explanation and prediction.

(C) *Working out how a particular set of propositional attitudes will feed into action depends upon the inferential relations between those propositional attitudes and the agent's background psychological profile.*

This is an immediate consequence of the earlier discussion in section 3. Propositional attitudes do not feed directly into action in the way that many perceptual states do. Exploiting propositional attitude attributions to explain and predict behavior requires working out the different possible inferential connections between those propositional attitudes and the agent's background psychological profile, as well as the information that they have through perception about the distal environment. A propositional attitude mindreader must be able to represent propositions in a way that makes clear the logical and inferential relations between the attributed propositional attitudes, the assumed background psychological profile, and the anticipated action.

(D) *The representations exploited in propositional attitude mindreading are consciously accessible constituents of a creature's psychological life.*

When a propositional attitude mindreader forms beliefs about the mental states of another agent, those beliefs are integrated with the rest of the mindreader's propositional attitudes – with their beliefs about the distal environment, with their short-term and long-term goals, for example. This integration is required for the results of propositional attitude mindreading to feature in a creature's practical decision-making. And, since practical decision-making takes place at the conscious level, beliefs about the mental states of other agents must also be consciously accessible.

(E) *The representational format for propositional attitude mindreading must be either language-like or image-like.*

The basic distinction here can be put in a number of different ways – as the distinction between digital representations and analog representations, for example. It is a very basic distinction for cognitive science, as reflected for example in what has come to be known as the imagery debate.[5] The central idea is straightforward, although there are many different ways of working out the details. A language-like representational format allows complex representations to be built up in a rule-governed way from basic representational units. The representational units and complex representations built up from them function as symbols, with no intrinsic connection

---

[5] For classic discussions see Anderson (1978) and Pylyshyn (1981). Kosslyn *et al.* (2006) is a more recent contribution.

to what they represent. An image-like representational format, in contrast, functions as a picture. It is not built up from basic representational units and it represents through similarity relations between the structure of the representation and the structure of what is being represented.

As far as propositional attitude mindreading is concerned, the most obvious candidates for an image-like representational format comprise mental models theory in the psychology of reasoning (originally proposed in Craik [1943] but most comprehensively developed in Johnson-Laird [1983]) and the conception of mental maps put forward by Braddon-Mitchell and Jackson (1996). The idea of structural isomorphism is key to both approaches. Mental maps and models are isomorphic to what they represent, in the sense that the relations holding between elements in the map/model can be mapped onto relations holding between elements in what is represented.

(F) *The representational format for propositional attitude mindreading must exemplify the structure of the represented propositions.*

This follows from (B) and (C) above. Propositional attitude mindreading allows mindreaders to navigate the social world by making sense of and predicting the behavior of other agents. Attributions of propositional attitudes do not lead immediately to predictions and explanations – precisely because propositional attitudes themselves do not feed directly into action. So, a propositional attitude mindreader needs to be able to work out the implications of the attributed propositional attitudes for the agent's behavior, in the light of what is known (or conjectured) about the agent's background psychological profile. This is a matter of reasoning about the logical and inferential relations between propositional attitudes. Accurate predictions depend upon the predictor being able in some sense to track the reasoning that the agent might themselves engage in.

This means that propositions (and hence, of course, propositional attitudes) must be represented in a way that allows the mindreader to reason about the logical and inferential connections between propositions. In particular, they must be represented in a way that makes clear the structure of the relevant propositions. This is because many of the most basic logical and inferential relations between propositions hold in virtue of their structure.

Consider, for example, the most fundamental form of logical thinking – that codified in the propositional calculus and involving the basic logical connectives, such as disjunction, conjunction, and the material conditional (if... then...). It is hard to see how a mindreader could reason about the propositional attitudes and background psychological profile of another agent without attributing to them conditional beliefs. These conditional beliefs might, for example, dictate possible behaviors contingent upon particular environmental factors (e.g., if the prey goes into the woods then I will follow it). Or they might record regularities and contingencies in the environment (e.g., if it rains then there will be more insects on the leaves). In order to reason about how an individual with these conditional beliefs might behave they must be represented in a way that reflects their structure – in a way that reflects the fact that they are attitudes to a complex proposition that relates two other propositions. Unless the conditional belief is represented in this way it will be impossible to reason, for example, that since the agent has seen the prey going into the woods it will follow it.

(G) *Representing propositions in a pictorial or image-like format does not reveal their canonical structure.*

It is certainly true that images have a type of structure. So do mental models and maps. We can identify distinct parts in analog representations and indeed identify them across different representations. Without this it would be impossible for analog representations to represent in virtue of their isomorphic structural resemblance to the state of affairs that they represent. But this is not the right sort of structure for them to represent propositions in the way that (F) requires.

Braddon-Mitchell and Jackson (1996) themselves bring out both how imagistic representations can be structured, and why that is not enough to represent propositions in a manner that will allow them to feature in inferences.

> There is no natural way of dividing a map at its truth-assessable representational joints. Each part of a map contributes to the representational content of the whole map, in the sense that had that part of the map been different, the representational content of the whole would have been different. Change the bit of the map of the United States between New York and Boston, and you change systematically what the map says. This is part of what makes it true that the map is structured. However, there is no preferred way of dividing the map into basic representational units. There are many jigsaw puzzles you might make out of the map, but no single one would have a claim to have pieces that were all and only the most basic units. (p. 171)

As this very helpful formulation brings out, analog representations do not have a *canonical structure*. Their structure can be analyzed in many different ways (corresponding to many different jigsaw puzzles that one can construct from it), but none of these can properly be described as giving *the* structure of the map.

This is why maps (and other analog representations) are not well-suited to represent propositions. Propositions have what might be termed a canonical structure and in order to understand the inferential connections in which a proposition might stand a thinker needs to understand that canonical structure. The canonical structure of a proposition corresponds to what Braddon-Mitchell and Jackson describe as the "preferred way of dividing" the proposition into basic representational units. The canonical structure of a conditional proposition, for example, is "If A then B," where "A" and "B" are the basic representational units (in this case the basic representational units are themselves propositions). But it is clear that this canonical structure cannot be captured in any sort of analog representation. We have no idea what a conditional map might look like, for example.

(H) *The canonical structure of a proposition is only revealed when propositions are represented in a linguistic format.*

According to (E), propositions must be represented in either an image-like or a language-like representational format. From (F) we have that an image-like representation of a proposition cannot reveal its canonical structure. So, (H) will follow provided that language-like representations of propositions can reveal their canonical structure. But it is obvious that the canonical structure of a proposition is revealed when it is represented linguistically. Viewed in the abstract, language is a mechanism for creating complex representations through the combination of basic representational units according to independently identifiable combinatorial rules. Language contains markers (such as the logical connectives) corresponding to the basic inferential connections between propositions. Indeed, for many philosophers it is almost a tautology that sentences express propositions.

(I) *The linguistic representations required for propositional mindreading must involve natural-language sentences.*

(H) tells us that propositions must be represented in a linguistic format for propositional mindreading. But it does not say anything about that linguistic format, beyond that it must be capable of revealing the structure of a proposition. There are two different candidate formats. On the one hand, the vehicles for propositional attitude mindreading might be the sentences of a public language. Or, on the other, they might be the sentences of what is sometimes termed the language of thought. The language of thought is proposed as a representational format for certain types of cognitive information-processing (Fodor [1975]). It is a key element in what is sometimes called the computational or representational model of the mind. There is no need, however, to explore the details of the arguments for and against the language-of-thought hypothesis and the computational model of the mind (for further discussion see Bermúdez [2005] and Bermúdez [in press]). The important point is that the language-of-thought hypothesis is an explanatory hypothesis in cognitive science. It is a hypothesis about the machinery of subpersonal information-processing. Information-processing that exploits sentences in the language of thought takes place below the threshold of consciousness. This means that sentences in the language of thought cannot be consciously accessible constituents of a creature's psychological life. But we saw in (D) that the representations exploited in propositional attitude mindreading must be consciously accessible constituents of the mindreader's psychological life. They must be capable of featuring in a creature's conscious practical decision-making.

6. CONCLUSION

This essay has introduced two fundamental distinctions to be kept clearly in view when thinking about mindreading in the animal kingdom. The first is between minimal mindreading and substantive mindreading. Minimal mindreading occurs in a social interaction when a creature's behavior depends systematically upon changes in the psychological states of other participants in the interaction. In contrast, a creature engages in substantive mindreading when its behavior is systematically dependent upon how it represents the psychological states of other participants. Substantive mindreading is not a unitary phenomenon. There is a principled distinction between perceptual mindreading and propositional attitude mindreading, stemming from the holistic character of the propositional attitudes. Using attributions of propositional attitudes to predict and explain behavior involves complex forms of reasoning that exploit information about the agent's background psychological profile.

The principal aim of this essay was to argue that propositional attitude mindreading does not and cannot exist in the absence of language. The temptation to identify propositional attitude mindreading in the animal kingdom often rests on the tacit assumption that most if not all of the complexities of human social understanding and social coordination depend upon propositional attitude mindreading. We looked at an important type of interaction that can be modeled without making this assumption, and considered how that model might be applied to behaviors in the animal kingdom that are sometimes taken as evidence for propositional attitude mindreading. Finally, I developed an argument to the effect that propositional attitude mindreading cannot exist in the absence of language. If this argument is sound, it shows that perceptual mindreading is the only form of substantive mindreading that can exist in the (non-human) animal kingdom.

CHAPTER 9

The representational basis of brute metacognition: a proposal

Joëlle Proust

I. INTRODUCTION

Self-confidence is based on two sources. One is the current evidence on which our judgments are built – i.e., on the way the world is. A second source of confidence comes from evaluating one's past ability to reach true judgments.[1] Is such a reflexive ability uniquely human? Surprisingly, the answer is no: there is growing evidence that some non-human animals who have not evolved any mindreading capacity, such as macaques and dolphins, are able to evaluate appropriately their self-confidence level in perceptual and memory tasks. This result is quite surprising, and suggests interesting new hypotheses about the evolution of the mind, the role of non-conceptual content in self-knowledge, the foundations of rational decision-making, and epistemology.

The set of dispositions that allow self-confidence to develop over time as a consequence of prior mental exercise has been studied in detail by experimental psychology, under the heading "Metacognition." This term, however, has also been used independently by philosophers and cognitive scientists interested in the philosophy of mind to designate the ability to form mental concepts referring to one's own intentional states or to oneself as a cognitive agent. Thus the two communities are presently using the word "metacognition" to refer, respectively, to the ability to control and monitor one's own cognition, and to the ability to attribute mental states to oneself and others. This equivocacy can only encourage some researchers to make

This work, as part of the European Science Foundation EUROCORES Programme CNCC, was supported by funds from CNRS and the EC Sixth Framework Programme under Contract no. ERAS-CT-2003–980409. I thank Hannes Leitgeb for attracting my attention to the fact that the same formal limitations apply to certain forms of belief revision and to metacognition. I thank Robert Lurz for his editorial suggestions. I am grateful to Dick Carter for his remarks about a prior draft and for his linguistic help. I also thank Jérôme Dokic, Frank Esken, Anna Loussouarn, and Claudine Tiercelin for helpful comments.

[1] As already noticed by David Hume (1739/1978, I, 4, 1).

inappropriate generalizations, either using mindreading as a criterion for the control of subjective uncertainty (thus excluding a priori the possibility of non-human self-confidence), or taking mindreading capacities to be necessarily mastered by self-confident animals and humans (thus over-attributing mindreading capacities to them). To prevent ambiguity, I will use "mindreading" to refer to mentalizing abilities and "metacognition" to refer to the control and monitoring of one's cognitive capacities.

My present aim is not just to dispel the various misunderstandings associated with the use of the same term for different purposes. It is, in addition, to clarify the nature and semantic properties of metacognition in non-humans. As is the case for every philosophical inquiry concerning animal minds, studying animal metacognition should provide new perspectives on the structure of mental content *and* on mental activity in general.

This exploration will proceed in four steps. First, the experimental evidence for animal metacognition will be briefly presented (section 2) and the difficulties of a metarepresentational view on metacognition summarized. Second, the possibility of alternative, non-propositional semantic structures will be discussed (section 3). A specific representational format that might be sufficient for animal metacognition to develop will be examined (section 4). Finally, some objections will be addressed, and further developments of the proposal will be considered (section 5).

2. EXPERIMENTAL EVIDENCE ON ANIMAL METACOGNITION: A PUZZLE

In the psychology of human metacognition, one typically collects evidence about what subjects think they are able or will be able to perceive,[2] or remember,[3] or how well they think they did (or will do) on a task, by using a simple method: one asks them. Experiments on animal metacognition, *mutatis mutandis*, follow the same pattern. Perceptual or memory tasks are offered to animals, with or without an "opt-out" structure. In certain trials, once presented with the stimuli for that trial, animals can choose to perform the task or not. In others, they are forced to respond. A metacognitive animal should tend to use the uncertainty key on a stimulus in those cases in which, in a forced choice condition for that stimulus range, its responses are produced at random. It is rational for the animal to opt out,

---

[2] On metaperception, see Levin (2004).
[3] On metamemory, see Koriat (2000) and Nelson and Narens (1992).

i.e., express its uncertainty, in those cases where it predicts that it cannot meet the informational demands of the task.[4] We can illustrate the opt-out paradigm with Hampton's (2001) experiment. Animal subjects have to evaluate their ability to remember which stimulus was previously presented to them: after a variable delay, they must either report that a probe just presented was or was not included in what they saw in a former episode (the temporal interval varies between 15 and 100 sec), or decide to opt out.

The first striking result of the metacognitive experiments conducted in comparative psychology is that animals such as rhesus monkeys and dolphins can reliably express their self-confidence, with no access to rein-forcement scheduling.[5] Animals that solve a metacognitive task for a set of stimuli prove able to transfer their ability to new stimuli and new tasks. Capuchin monkeys[6] and pigeons, however, tend to use the "uncertainty key" randomly.[7] A second striking result is that subjects, whether humans or non-humans, seem to have personal preferences for using particular metacognitive strategies. Some seem to be quite ready to admit that they are uncertain, while others seem to prefer to incur a risk and pay the associated cost, by offering direct tentative answers. This variation, in the eyes of comparative psychologists, shows that metacognition is indeed a decisional process, which reflects a subject's general epistemic attitudes and motivations.[8]

These results clash with a well-established view, according to which metacognition necessarily involves a metarepresentational capacity, a capac-ity that develops in human children between 4 and 5 years of age and allows them to attribute mental states to themselves or to others – to "read minds."[9] Granting that vertebrates have a form of propositional represen-tation of states of affairs, the classic view entails that subjective uncertainty is expressed in thought by recursive representations in which first-order representations are embedded in second-order representations (e.g., "my perceiving/judging/believing that this is a dense presentation"), the latter having in turn the property of being uncertain to degree p. How then could metacognition be available to monkeys and dolphins, which do not master mental concepts?

---

[4] Obviously, this kind of experiment must meet various methodological constraints in order to make sure that the animal has not been reinforced to press the uncertainty key when specific stimuli are presented to him. On these constraints, see Smith *et al.* (2006).

[5] Smith *et al.* (1998). For a review, see Smith *et al.* (2003) and Son and Kornell (2005).

[6] Michael Beran, personal communication.

[7] Inman and Shettleworth (1999), Kornell *et al.* (2007), and Smith *et al.* (2006).

[8] Smith *et al.* (2003) and Smith *et al.* (2006).

[9] Flavell (2004). For a detailed discussion of this view, see Proust (2007).

A philosopher confronted with this puzzle, however, will want to take a closer look at the empirical evidence. Peter Carruthers (2008) claims that a combination of first-order attitudes is sufficient to explain animals' use of the uncertainty key in Smith *et al.*'s metaperceptual paradigm. He presents two distinct "rules" that, on his view, suffice to account for the data. The first states that when a task-stimulus is processed at a sensory threshold, the beliefs expressing the two possible perceptual categorizations between which the animal is oscillating, e.g., [that the pattern is sparse] and [that the pattern is dense], are both weak conclusions. In such a case, the belief that wins is the stronger one. And given that the opt-out key has a reward associated with it, the animal will choose this stronger conclusion. A second rule is meant to explain the cases where, although the attitudes have different strengths, the animal "is reluctant to act, and seeks either further information, or some other alternative for action."[10] The key idea here is that conflict in input or in plans with equal or closely similar strengths (that is, first-order perceptions or categorizations) motivates the animal to switch modes of response. A "gate-keeping mechanism" allows animals to opt out when uncertainty reaches a critical level.

Can Carruthers' two rules account for the opt-out response pattern in non-humans? I will only briefly summarize my response to this question, as a full discussion can be read elsewhere.[11] Carruthers' first rule indeed can explain part of the opt-out responses *if* trial-by-trial reinforcement is provided: for the animals can in such cases associate a given predictive value with each individual stimulus, without having to evaluate their subjective uncertainty. If, furthermore, the uncertainty key is selectively reinforced by a small amount of food, then it is represented in the task as a state of the world (as a predictor for a small amount of food). At the present stage of research, however, these two potential problems are dealt with. Reinforcement of the uncertainty key is not offered, novel test stimuli are used, and transfer of the ability to novel tasks is tested. One cannot invoke the strength of a stimulus as guiding the animal's behavior, when this stimulus is not reinforced: the first rule cannot apply any longer. The second rule, however, does apply, but is perfectly coherent with a metacognitive reading. Having conflicting impulsions, over time, to act or not to act on a given stimulus, the subject is not certain of his ability to categorize, even though it believes that the world is one way or another. So the switching does depend on subjective – not objective – features, such

---

[10] Carruthers (2008, section 3.2).   [11] See Proust and Smith (in preparation).

as a sense of ability, combined with the practical knowledge of a given cost/benefit ratio.

If this line of reasoning is correct, we are now confronted with the puzzle in clearer terms. If metacognition exists in non-humans, and supposing that non-humans have propositional thinking, what is the representational format allowing flexible metacognitive calls in non-humans?

3. WHICH REPRESENTATIONAL FORMAT FOR METACOGNITION?

3.1. Particular-based and feature-based systems

If it is granted that animal metacognition is made possible by *comparators* (i.e., control equivalents of gate-keeping mechanisms) whose function is to monitor and control subjective uncertainty, it need not be taken to consist of a single ability reflected in many different contexts; it might rather result from multiple forms of regulation that have separately evolved to monitor specific cognitive mechanisms: each with its informational source, its learning dynamics, its anatomical substrate, and its selective pathology. It can be argued, however, that these various metacognitive mechanisms might nevertheless have a common representational format, and share basic anatomical resources (implementing, *inter alia*, working memory and inhibitory devices). The term "representational format" refers to the general way in which information is captured and used by a system to guide behavior. Philosophers often take for granted that a propositional format is the only possible way of forming thoughts. It is quite plausible that full-fledged rational, communicable thoughts that humans are able to form require a propositional structure; but it may well be that animal thinking, as well as human thinking on certain occasions, relies on other representational formats to collect, combine, retrieve, and evaluate emotional, perceptual, and motor information.

As Frege (1892/1951) recognized, and as Strawson (1959) emphasized, a propositional analysis of thought contents comes with a metaphysics: the world appears to be composed of independent particulars as bearers of properties and relations, which themselves are dependent universals. Basic particulars are reidentifiable, independent entities: material objects or persons. Universals are either sortals (often expressed by common nouns allowing us to count particulars, like "three apples") or characterizing universals (expressed by verbs and adjectives). A propositional format offers a general framework for referring to objects, and to truth values, in a unified spatiotemporal system. Let us call forms of language or thought with this structure *particular-based representational systems* (from now on: PBS).

On a view widely shared among philosophers, human rationality depends on propositional format because it maps the structure of the world onto the mental, allowing thinkers to recombine the constituents at will, and to form conceptual deductions and inferences based on probabilistic regularities. It is uncontroversial that not all animals have access to such a form of thinking (most invertebrates may lack it, and most vertebrates would have access only to primitive forms of propositional thinking).[12] There are, in particular, two properties of human learning which most invertebrates seem to lack. They may not have any way of reidentifying objects, or themselves, as the same over time: their representational system does not respond to the principle of objectivity. Let us use "protoconcepts" for the protosymbolic classifiers that non-verbal animals use to categorize properties and events, and possibly infer other properties from them without fulfilling the objectivity constraint. When animals cannot reidentify independent objects, their protoconcepts fail to subsume individual entities. If, however, protoconcepts do not apply to individual, numerically distinct property-bearers, they fail to be "strictly determined," as concepts normally are. As Frege made clear (after Kant), it must be the case, for any individual, that it either falls, or does not fall, under a given first-order concept (vague concepts do not have this property; this is why they pose a serious problem for propositional thinking). Protoconcepts, having no individuals in their scopes, should present a property similar to vagueness: they should fail to be well-determined. Protoconcepts, like vague predicates, have no exact boundaries. They have, rather, similarity-based conditions of application. The protoconcept of [prey], for example, will apply to visual patterns similar to a prototypical prey pattern. This in turn makes it questionable to say that a protoconcept *truly* applies to some particular (currently perceived) pattern. It would be more adequate to say that protoconcepts are more or less efficient classifiers: they have conditions of well-formedness and of efficiency, without being truth-evaluable.

A second closely related difference concerning the application of protoconcepts has to do with breadth of scope: protoconcepts with no objectivity should also fail to fulfill the generality constraint. In virtue of the generality

---

[12] See Proust (1997, 1999) and Bermúdez (2003a). [Editor's note: see Bermúdez (chapter 8) for a similar view, and Carruthers (chapter 5) for a defense of conceptual and propositional forms of thinking in invertebrates.]

constraint,[13] grasping the truth-conditions for "Peter will come" and for "Anna is late" would allow one to grasp the truth-conditions for "Anna will come" and for "Peter is late": predicates are not tied in thought to particulars, and neither are particulars tied to predicates. The *generality constraint* emphasizes the role, in rational thinking, of the ability to combine atomic sentences in arbitrary ways using rule-governed operations. If an animal cannot represent complex thoughts, involving negation, quantification, hypothetical reasoning, it cannot be said to think in the way humans think.

A plausible hypothesis is that the articulation, in human thought, of conceptual and non-conceptual contents reflects the evolutionary succession of two different, generatively entrenched,[14] representational formats. The more recent particular-based representational system (PBS) would be generatively dependent on a former representational system, which will be identified below as the *feature-based representational system* (FBS). PBS would thus be able to enrich FBS.[15] Several characteristics of FBS might survive in the enriched format, such as analog representation, embodiment, and vagueness.

My hypothesis is that metacognition, perception, and action are represented – at least in part – in an FBS format. In order to examine the possible structure of FBS representations, we will contrast the proposed view with the closely related notion of feature-placing representational systems (FPS).

3.2. Feature-placing representational systems

Several authors have tried to capture the ability of animals to navigate through space, and register states of affairs in a way that does not involve reference to objects or attribution of properties.[16] On this view, the act of placing a feature is a basic competence that can be exercised without concept possession, generality, or objectivity. A feature, as opposed to a property, can be represented as exemplified or "incidental"[17] with no sense of a contrast between a representing subject and a represented object. A standard example of a feature-placing sentence is:

(1) Water! (here, now)

---

[13] See Dummett (1973), Evans (1982), and Strawson, (1959). [Editor's note: see Carruthers' (chapter 5) discussion on the generality constraint.]
[14] On this concept, see Wimsatt (1986) and Proust (2009).
[15] On the formal properties of the process of enrichment, see Carnap (1937).
[16] See Bermúdez (2003a), Campbell (1993), Cussins (1992), Dummett (1993), and Smith (1996).
[17] Glouberman (1976).

In this type of sentence, a mass-term (e.g., "water") is presented as holding at a given time and at a given place – no individual referent can be specified, no "completeness" (understood as "saturatedness"), no place-identification is presupposed. Sortals, also called "count nouns," cannot be expressed in this format. You cannot, for example, count water. What you can do, however, is evaluate the degree to which an affordance is present (there may be little or much water). A minimalist view of features takes them to be close to Gibson's "affordances" (i.e., informational patterns with survival significance).[18] Features, as affordances, belong to an ontology where no subject–world division is operating.[19] These patterns inform the animal that something valuable or dangerous needs to be acted upon in a certain way (captured, ingested, fled from).

As anticipated in section 3.1, the representation expressed by (1) is not a belief, for it is not structured propositionally: it cannot be true or false. But, as a representation, it obeys formal constraints (e.g., graduality), and it can be misapplied: it has success conditions. What is expressed in a feature-placing episode like (1) is a conative/expressive relation characterizing an "environmental experience."[20] It can fail either because the efficient conative dimension does not offer the best control given the environment, or because the environment does not include the affording factor (the feature is misplaced). Both errors may occur in one single FPS episode.[21] What deserves to be emphasized is that FPS representations need to produce an evaluation combining the urgency of the need and the quantity or intensity of the associated outcome. One can suggest, then, the following basic structure for an FPS representation:

(2) Some (much, little) drinking affordance!

What kind of thinking, then, does an animal perform with FPS representations? It identifies an affordance, categorizes it for its intensity on a gradient

---

[18] See Bermúdez (1998).

[19] Affordances are relational, rather than being objective or subjective properties. As Gibson observes:

> An important fact about the affordances of the environment is that they are in a sense objective, real, and physical, unlike values and meanings, which are often supposed to be subjective, phenomenal and mental. But, actually, an affordance is neither an objective property nor a subjective property; or it is both if you like. An affordance cuts across the dichotomy of subjective–objective and helps us to understand its inadequacy. (Gibson [1979], p. 129)

[20] The expression is borrowed from Cussins (1992), p. 669. Ruth Millikan describes such thoughts as "Pushmi-Pullyu" (Millikan [1995]). There is no indication in her article, however, that she is trying to characterize a distinctive non-propositional representational format.

[21] There are cases where failing to relate conative states with their proper targets may be lethal for animals. Consider, for example, how traps and lures work.

scale, and triggers the associated motor programs. Thinking in FPS is predictive: the conative and epistemic expectations largely determine which features are attended to. Emotions can be further amplified when a given feature has been perceived, in order to select appropriate actions.

3.3. Feature-based representational systems

Our present problem is not to determine how objectivity and spatial thinking interact, for metacognition has very little to do with spatial information. We can transform FPS, however, so that it can express what needs to be expressed in a system able to exercise metacognition. Given this goal, we need to distinguish a "feature-placing" representational system (FPS) from a "feature-based" system (FBS). The basic difference between an FPS and an FBS is that the first evaluates an *environmental* affordance as being incident (at a time and at a location) while the second evaluates a *mental* affordance as being incident (at a time). Just as an environmental affordance is represented in order to predict the outcome of the associated motor program, a mental affordance is represented in order to predict the outcome of the associated mental action. For example, if a high-benefit, high-risk task requires detailed perception (or memory) of a visual display, the animal needs to decide whether or not it is appropriate to act on the information it has. Expressed in words, an example of an FBS representation would be something like

(3) Poor (excellent, etc.) *A*-ing affordance!

Here "*A*-ing" points to the current mental disposition exercised as part of the task (categorizing, remembering, comparing, etc.). For example, the animal appreciates whether it is able to perform a task requiring what the theorist calls "remembering a test stimulus." The metacognitive part of the task does not consist in remembering a test stimulus, but in predicting whether one's ability to remember is sufficient given the task demands. Just as human beings sometimes need to evaluate whether they have reliable information in store before performing a given task, the animals studied by Hampton, Smith, and their colleagues have to determine not only whether what they perceive or remember is an X, but *whether they can perceive or remember at all*. Affordances, in this analysis, are relations between the status of a mental disposition and a given outcome: a "good" disposition predicts success, a "poor" one predicts failure. Mental affordances are thus similar to physical affordances, for which bodily dispositions are relevant as well as mental ones. One can only hypothesize, at this point, that physical and mental affordances are presented to subjects through specialized indicators. Before we come to this point, we first need to consider an objection to the analysis of FBS using (3).

A reader might, indeed, object that the term "*A*-ing" only makes sense when we attribute to the animal the possession of the associated mental concept of *A*-ing; non-human animals, however, cannot employ mental concepts. Let us insist, in response, that the animal may represent *A*-ing without having to represent it *as a mental disposition*. It does not need to have the concept of remembering to remember, and it does not need to identify a memory condition as a memory condition to evaluate its memory when deciding what to do. As we saw above, an FBS only represents *global affordances*, in a way that does not need to distinguish the subjective from the objective contributions. If it is granted that affordances can be represented through features, then one should admit that mental affordances are also possible targets for feature-based representations. (This argument is developed in section 4 below.)

In summary, let us compare an FPS representation like (2) with an FBS representation like (3). The former only requires that the animal be properly coordinated with an environmental affordance to be able to represent the associated feature (in space, but not *as spatial*). Similarly, representing (3) only requires that the animal be properly coordinated with a mental affordance to represent it in a mental, normative "space," but neither *as* mental, nor *as* normative. To clarify how a representation can be adequately coordinated in the absence of environmental cues, we need to pursue the comparison with how coordination occurs in FPS.

3.4. Features as non-conceptual contents

In order to flesh out the parallel between FPS and FBS, we need first to understand how an animal can use information that features in FPS. For example, how might an animal use the following FBS representation

(4) [in front, big prey affordance]

to guide its behavior? In answering this, we want to know:
  (i) What are the cues that spatially lead to the affordance?
 (ii) How much "prey stuff" is there in front as compared to other areas?
(iii) Is the acting option still available or not?
(iv) What is the optimal route to the goal?
These various dimensions of information indeed constrain any action developing in space: "where," "what," "when," and "how" questions need to be answered for an action to be triggered. Is the semantic structure of

FPS thoughts, as articulated in (1)–(4), sufficient to make this information available to a decision system?

Answering this question requires two steps. The first is to recognize the role of embodiment in generating non-conceptual contents. As first shown by Evans (1982), a theorist interested in capturing the semantics of non-conceptual content needs to refer to an animal's skills and abilities;[22] these abilities constrain how non-conceptual content is generated and used. They are not, however, *constituents* of the representation that the animal forms in its interaction with the environment (just as space is not a constituent of an FPS representation). Or, in Cussins' words, the "realm of embodiment" is needed to specify the "realm of reference," without being part of the latter.[23] These skills and abilities therefore qualify as basic elements in a non-objective, dynamical ontology.[24] Cussins calls them "cognitive trails."

Here is an example of how embodiment constrains cognitive trails. A salticid "jumping" spider, *Portia labiata*, preys mostly on other spiders rather than on insects. It is thus equipped to prey either inside or outside its own web.[25] Having, in contrast to other spiders, high-resolution vision, *Portia* has an innate disposition to form visual search-images for preferred prey (other spiders). If the spider categorizes specific prey patterns rather than independent objects, it offers a model of a feature-placing representational system.[26] The ability to exercise visual search in diverse neighbourhoods clearly depends on how *Portia*'s cognitive capacities are embodied (other spiders stay in their webs, and track their prey through felt vibrations). Evolution and learning explain *Portia*'s behavior and motivation as based on non-conceptual representations: its search-images. Now what about *Portia*'s *experience*? An agent, according to Cussins, does not have conscious access to the cognitive trails it uses, since these are mere dispositions. What *can* be experienced, however, is *trail tracking*: features are presented non-conceptually as constituting a situated intensive affordance – in a way that allows fine-grained perceptual recognition and action.[27]

---

[22] See Evans (1982) and Cussins (1992).   [23] See Cussins (1992), pp. 655–656.

[24] The term "embodiment," when used from the animal's perspective, is used by Cussins to refer not to an animal body/mind, which would presuppose an unwanted contrast between body/mind and world, but rather to holistic "way-finding abilities through an environmental feature-domain" (Cussins [1992], p. 673). Affordances thus relate to way-finding abilities as types of these abilities.

[25] See Jackson and Li (2004).

[26] Section 3.1 offers reasons to deny spiders access to a PBS, due to lack of objectivity.

[27] I will not discuss here the issue of the applicability of the notion of non-conceptual content to subpersonal states. I will simply accept the view defended in Peacocke (1994) and Bermúdez (1994) that it is so applicable. It seems admissible that *Portia*, although it may not have a first-person-level type of experience, still has non-conceptual contents that motivate it to act as it does.

A second step consists in pointing out that the relation of a cognitive trail to trail-tracking can be redescribed as the relation between a regulation space available to an animal as a consequence of its phylogenetic and ontogenetic history, and a given control episode within the space of possible regulations. A regulation space indeed offers (i) a description of all possible trajectories to a given goal (where "trajectory," in contrast with "trail," may not be spatial, but refers to a succession of commands), and (ii) a selection of trajectories (in that framework) currently available to the agent (a selection constrained by his positioned scenario). A regulation space thus includes all the possible trajectories already present in the animal's repertoire, and their possible *combinations*; it corresponds closely to Cussins' set of available cognitive trails.

On this background conception, non-conceptual contents are thus determined by a regulation space (rather than merely by a type of embodiment). It is, on this view, not primarily embodiment that makes non-conceptual contents non-conceptual, it is their being dynamically generated by control episodes, which happen to involve, in most cases, one or several bodies moving through space as a main source of internal and external feedback.[28] Thus the second step only involves a theoretical interpretation of step one. *Portia's* total set of cognitive trails composes her regulation space. *Portia's* jumping on another spider is made possible by the non-conceptual content of her vision, which also motivates her to act (i.e., track a given trail or select and operate a given command).[29]

Our framework, as completed, offers straightforward answers to our four questions above. Question (i) can be answered, following the Evans–Cussins line, in control terms. When there exists a cognitive trail to the goal (i.e., when a control model is available in the regulation space), embodied non-conceptual content (in this case: visual feedback) allows a spider to know where, in its peripersonal space, the prey is located, even though it cannot identify places as individual locations.

Question (ii) is much easier to solve given our control apparatus. The question of how much prey stuff there is in front as compared to other areas or times would seem to be beyond reach for an animal who cannot form representations of objective space, or represent alternative contexts. There is, however, a simple way of constructing comparative intensity for a control system. It is enough, in this system, to have established a mean value over

---

[28] A body, actually, can itself be analyzed as an integrated set of regulations, decomposing into a control part and an image part.

[29] The question of whether an animal which has only FPS or FBS – and therefore has no concepts – can entertain non-conceptual contents will be dealt with in section 5.

prior encounters with the same affordance type to be able to compare it with the present encounter. This mean value can also be established innately, as is the case for primary emotions. Therefore, the norm does not need to be explicitly represented to be active in triggering an intensity judgment. The animal only needs to have a calibrating mechanism that reflects or resonates to the intensity of the affordance type. The representation of intensity is successful *insofar as it predicts affordance sufficiency* for adequate behavior given a motivation level. Intensity might be coded non-conceptually by a set of subpersonal features. In *Portia*, for example, affordance intensity might be calibrated by the mean value of the search-image, as well as by the emotions and dispositions to act that are associated with visually capturing its prey. In this way, an animal incapable of propositional thinking is able to represent the contrast between intensities.

To know whether an affordance is still available, or whether it is too late to act, as question (iii) asks, the animal can rely on the time and frequency aspects of its non-conceptual representation, a form of content that plays a major role in timing its actions or effecting dynamic couplings with the actions of others. Again there are specific forms of non-conceptual content that can be used to select the correct command and monitor its successful application. *Portia* may rely on motor representations to know when and how to act on a given affordance appropriately, given the specific size and agility of its prey.

Finally, the answer to question (iv) – how to determine an optimal, or at least satisfactory, route to the goal – depends on inverse modeling. In so-called "modular" theories for inverse modeling, a system stores pairs of inverse and direct models, associating a given realized goal with a given command.[30] Embodied non-conceptual contents have been shown to play a role in representing these pairs.[31] For example, the seen orientation of a cup helps select the hand used to grasp it and the orientation of the wrist.

If these considerations are on the right track, FPSs express affordances through their specific non-conceptual contents; the same contents that underlie featural recognition of affordances also structure an animal's control of these affordances. It is thus clearer that non-conceptual contents are the ingredients of the dynamic models that are made available to an animal (innately and through learning) to control perception and action. One might thus propose (5) as offering the fine-grained non-conceptual structure that is included in a given FPS representation:

---

[30] See Wolpert and Kawato (1998).   [31] See Jacob and Jeannerod (2003).

(5) Affordance A (intensity I, direction D, in temporal interval dt, with control C)

Let us now turn to the feature-based representational system (FBS). Can a similar account be offered of how an animal can exercise metacognition?

4. NON-CONCEPTUAL CONTENTS IN A FEATURE-BASED FORMAT

Our way of representing affordances in metacognition was exemplified by

(3) There is (poor, excellent) A-ing affordance,

where "A-ing" refers globally rather than subjectively to a mental disposition (e.g., remembering, perceiving, etc.). Is our two-step strategy able to account for the information that (3) expresses? In particular, how are we to respond to the following questions, parallel to those that were raised about FPS:

(i) What is the cognitive trail that leads to a mental affordance?
(ii) How much "affordance" is there now as compared to other times?
(iii) Is the affordance still available or is it too late to act?
(iv) What is the optimal route to the mental affordance?

Responding to these questions again requires finding out whether there is a systematic way in which such information can be structured by embodied skills and abilities in the animal: can non-conceptual contents also be used by a control system to select mental goals (such as obtaining qualitatively and quantitatively adequate information)? The difficulty for FBS, compared with FPS, is that animals using an FBS cannot rely on spatial non-conceptual features, such as shapes, colors, or search-images. But this difficulty can be overcome, if one observes that there are other types of information that may be extracted, which are already used in an FPS: in particular, intensity in proprioceptive signals and time information.

To characterize these two types, I will start with a human example for the sake of clarity. The common tip of the tongue experience, or TOT,[32] is the experience of having muscular activity in the tongue, felt not as an odd bodily manifestation, but as a predictor for the ability to come up with a missing word. Research on phenomenology in TOTs shows that there may be three qualitative dimensions fused in this feeling. One is *intensity of a felt bodily signal.* A second aspect of non-conceptual content is *intensity of a felt emotion* involved in the TOT experience. A third aspect

---

[32] For a review of TOT research, see Brown (1991).

resides in the *feeling of imminence* (i.e., the sentiment of being able to soon recover the word). A high value on each dimension seems to predict high subjective confidence and likelihood of prompt retrieval.[33] The affordance that a TOT allows one to grasp is the availability of a particular word in one's memory.

This example will help us answer the four questions above. Question (i) requires qualifying the cognitive trail to a mental affordance. Just as space is processed by *Portia* in an embodied way, a non-human animal can have access to a mental affordance by using a reinforced cognitive path. There is indeed a *temporal contiguity* between the experience of making a choice (categorizing a pattern as dense or sparse by pressing key A or B) and the experience of a delay generated by uncertainty. A temporal lag presents the animal with an error-signal: as compared with normal behavior, the present activity is impaired. Here is the essential point: although the delay is a natural consequence of task difficulty, it becomes in addition a natural signal carrying information *about a need to know what the affordance is.* A plausible hypothesis therefore is that a temporal comparison between expected time for completion of the task and observed time, occurring as part of a given controlled activity (i.e., including a comparator), offers a key to making a mental affordance salient to the animal.

Question (ii) has to do with how an animal can non-conceptually grasp the amount of a mental affordance. The way an affordance is evaluated as high or low is reflected by what is called, in the literature on human metacognition, an "epistemic feeling." As our TOT example suggests, comparators can monitor *several* non-conceptual aspects of these features represented in thoughts like (3) above. Epistemic feelings can be felt as weak or strong, according to the activity in their dedicated somatic markers.[34] They can carry the sense of a more or less imminent resolution. Lastly, they can be endowed, to a greater or lesser extent, with motivational force. Such motivation to continue performing a mental task – such as trying harder to remember – might be a non-conceptual indicator for the associated affordance.[35] An additional source of non-conceptual emotional content consists in the specific dynamical intensity pattern characterizing a mental affordance. Some epistemic feelings have a distinctive "acceleration"

---

[33] See Schwartz *et al.* (2000).

[34] A somatic marker, as defined by Damasio, is a bodily signal whose function is to influence the processes of response to stimuli. We here take somatic markers to influence the processes of rational decision in general – including metacognition. See Damasio *et al.* (1996).

[35] For an analysis disentangling the control and the monitoring aspects of a feeling of knowing, see Koriat (2000) and Koriat *et al.* (2006).

aspect that naturally represents a high-valued dynamic affordance (compare insight and exhilaration).[36] The feelings that can be used by Smith's macaques are plausibly generated by perceptual fluency, an oculo-motor ability developing over time; here too, intensity in fluency, duration of hesitation, opposite motivations for acting and reaching the reward, might help the animal evaluate its internal level of uncertainty.

Question (iii) asks how an animal can know whether an affordance is still available or not. In mental as well as in bodily action, the estimated time of a course of action can only be appreciated by extracting the information through partial simulation of the execution of the associated task.[37] The animal can compare the mean values of the respective timings for (a) the required action (based on prior experiences for a type of task), and (b) his prior efforts to reach similar mental affordances. It is therefore arguable that the estimated time for a mental action to attain its goal is given by a forward model simulating that action, just as in the bodily case. Non-conceptual contents constitute significant landmarks in such covert simulatory activity.

Interestingly, answering question (iv) is much simpler in the case of metacognition than in the case of bodily action. When acting to grasp an affordance in space, on the basis of an FPS, one needs to select one of the cognitive trails that are in the repertoire, which creates competition between solutions. In contrast, mental affordances (such as the disposition to remember something) seem to be quite constrained as to how they can be exploited. A subject who needs to retrieve a cue from her memory in FBS seems to have a single trail available. This may be related to the fact that the types of information used to trigger the action are restricted to time and intensity: the paths cannot be easily varied for lack of alternative feedback. It is a different story, however, when a human subject has access to a propositional store of information. In this case, she has potential access to folk theories about the mind, and may use alternative strategies to predict her mental affordances (for example, using heuristics from popular wisdom). These considerations suggest the following fine-grained non-conceptual structure of feature-based predictive metacognitive representations:

(6) Affordance A (intensity I, in temporal interval dt, with control C).

---

[36] On this difference, see Carver and Scheier (1998).   [37] For a full defense, see Proust (2006).

5. OBJECTIONS, RESPONSES, AND NEW QUESTIONS

The interpretation of animal cognition presented above aims to offer a realist reconstruction of the information that is causal in generating behaviors and practical decisions in non-humans. The basic idea is that cognition operates in two generatively entrenched formats. The most ancestral format has two subtypes: *feature-placing*, which helps the animal to navigate, categorize, and exploit environmental affordances, and *feature-based*, which allows the animal to exploit mental affordances.[38] Metacognition is hypothesized to be represented as a feature-based system, which would explain how some non-human species might have evolved it. The more recent format is *propositional* – that is, particular-based. Only the latter format can be used recursively to form metarepresentations.

A reader might object that our solution is purely ad hoc, inventing a representational format when there is no independent reason to do so. It is true that the distinction between the propositional and the two feature-involving formats was initially introduced to explain how metacognition might work, given the various puzzles generated when describing its operation in metarepresentational terms, and the unsatisfactory explanation that reduces it to objective uncertainty.[39] There are, however, additional arguments in favor of the present hypothesis. First, it explains the *emergence* of flexible informational use in phylogeny. Many non-human animals, having no sense of objectivity, hence no ability to represent an independent world, are clearly able to adjust to world changes. Such flexibility presupposes an ability to control one's behavior in an endogenous way (by extracting and exploiting regularities in the outer world and in monitoring one's own cognitive condition), which in turn requires representational use.[40] The present proposal is that featural representations are the basis of such flexibility.

A second reason is that it helps explain how propositional content *evolved* from prior representational formats. It makes little evolutionary sense to say that propositional thought appeared with the emergence of linguistic abilities, for linguistic abilities themselves require flexible controls to be exercised. The idea that a propositional system redescribes or enriches contents delivered by a more ancient memory store is supported by

---

[38] The present proposal has concentrated on predictive metacognition. Future empirical research should also investigate whether non-human animals can also retrospectively evaluate their own mental actions in a metacognitive way (for example: regret a decision).

[39] See Proust (2007).   [40] See Proust (2006).

recent neuroscientific evidence about the two-storage structure of working memory.[41] It furthermore explains the presence of non-conceptual contents within propositional thought.

A third reason is that this assumption promises to clarify some puzzles concerning non-conceptual content. If it is true that FPS and FBS exist independently of, and prior to, propositional representation, the question whether they coexist with propositional thought in humans, or whether they have been replaced by propositional thought, might become a subject for interdisciplinary research. The present proposal suggests that, whichever position is adopted on this issue, non-conceptual contents should be treated as autonomous relative to concept possession, as they are present in a format that does not include predication. Such autonomy is independently supported by the fact that non-conceptual contents provide non-circular access to the possession conditions of perception and action concepts.[42]

A second objection is that a system with no objectivity cannot involve the normative constraints associated with mental content. This second objection takes up a famous argument for rejecting the autonomy of non-conceptual content: objective place reidentification is a fundamental pre-condition for having an integrated representation of a situation.[43] With no correctness conditions for spatial representations, however, such integration is impossible, and the concept of content itself is lost. Thus feature-placing and feature-based systems would *not* generate thought contents.

There are various ways to counter this objection. One is to show that rejecting autonomy leads to severe problems for concept acquisition.[44] Another is to define non-conceptual content independently of the semantics for propositional systems, as is done in this chapter, in the wake of Cussins' (1992) contribution. Non-conceptual contents, on this alternative view, are viewed as *stabilizing features* in affordance control.[45] Stabilization has two facets crucially conjoined in non-conceptual content. It plays a functional role in recognizing features over time (remember that features have no strict boundaries) and mediates successful interactions with the environment. Denying an animal the ability to form non-conceptual representations would accordingly entail denying that it can recognize affordances, act upon them, and revise its featural models. Finally, one might develop a notion of epistemic normativity that does not exclusively apply to propositions.[46] In cases where it represents a situation featurally,

---

[41] See Gruber and von Cramon (2003).   [42] See Cussins (1992) and Bermúdez (1994).
[43] Peacocke (1992), p. 90.   [44] See Bermúdez (1994).   [45] As suggested by Cussins (1992), p. 677.
[46] Success conditions can be used in a semantic theory. See Stalnaker (1984) and Bermúdez (2003a). But success semantics for a non-propositional format has not yet been proposed.

an animal does not aim at grasping the truth-value of its thoughts, for indeed it does not form an explicit representation of itself, nor can it represent propositional thoughts that can be true or false. This does not entail that feature-placing does not engage well-formedness conditions and semantic norms. Some controls are clearly recognized as more cognitively efficient than others and tend to be selected and exploited because they are represented as more cognitively efficient. Therefore, sensitivity to norms of cognitive adequacy might emerge in FPS and FBS. This is a topic for ongoing research.

Third, some readers might be tempted to object that a number of animals, such as *Portia* the salticid spider, do not use any representations worthy of the name, since their decisions to act are strictly based on conditioning mechanisms. Thus reconstruction of their mental states would be a vain effort: they do not have any. This argument, however, has been rejected since the late sixties: as Rescorla and Wagner (1972), Gallistel (2003), and others have shown, associative learning indeed depends on the information that is represented by an animal, it does not bypass it. The conditioned stimulus must provide information about the unconditioned stimulus to generate a response; temporal pairing is not the crucial causal factor, as was first believed, but contingency.[47] Feature-placing is a representational format that is compatible with an associative learning theory, in which cues are selected for their predictive value in relation to a certain affordance.

6. CONCLUSION

This chapter has attempted to sketch a view in which metacognition can be present in non-humans. Much still remains to be done to compare human with non-human metacognitive ability. More interdisciplinary work, in particular, needs to be conducted on the four dimensions of non-conceptual content that might be instrumental for metacognitive episodes (i.e., mental actions) to be performed. The concept of enrichment suggests that a thinker may use her folk-theoretical generalizations to describe and influence her alternative, feature-based epistemic feeling. The question of whether human metacognition uses a separate feature-placing format, or is absorbed within the propositional mode of thinking, is still open. But current research may soon come up with interesting new constraints.

---

[47] See Gallistel (2003) for a review.

CHAPTER 10

Animals, consciousness, and I-thoughts

Rocco J. Gennaro

I. INTRODUCTION

I-thoughts are thoughts about one's own mental states or about "oneself" in some sense (Bennett [1988]). They are closely linked to what psychologists call "metacognition": that is, cognitions about other cognitions or mental representations (Metcalfe and Shimamura [1994]; Koriat [2007]).[1] There seems to be growing evidence that many animals are indeed capable of having I-thoughts as well as having the ability to understand the mental states of others (Hurley and Nudds [2006]; Terrace and Metcalfe [2005]).

There is also a relevant philosophical theory of consciousness: namely, the *higher-order thought* (HOT) theory of consciousness which says that what makes a mental state conscious is the presence of a suitable higher-order thought about that state (Gennaro [2004a]; Rosenthal [2005]). For various reasons, such thoughts are typically understood to take the form "I am in mental state M now." A higher-order thought, then, is a kind of metacognition. It is a mental state directed at another mental state. So, for example, my desire to write a good book chapter becomes conscious when I am (non-inferentially) "aware" of the desire. Intuitively, it seems that conscious states, as opposed to unconscious ones, are mental states that I am "aware of" in some representational sense (Lycan [2001]). In a case of subliminal perception, I am not aware that I am in that perceptual state. Thus, it is unconscious. However, when I become aware that I am having that perception, it becomes conscious.

An often cited problem, however, is that the HOT theory rules out animal consciousness because animals (or at least most animals) are incapable of having such thoughts; they do not possess such sophisticated "I-concepts" and "mental concepts." This is a common objection

Thanks to Robert Lurz for numerous helpful comments on an earlier draft of this essay.
[1] Editor's note: See Proust (chapter 9) for a non-metarepresentational definition of "metacognition."

normally offered by non-HOT theorists, such as Fred Dretske (1995), Robert Lurz (2002), and Bill Seager (2004). Moreover, one prominent HOT theorist, Peter Carruthers, actually embraces this alleged consequence of the HOT theory (Carruthers [2000, 2005]). I have had my say elsewhere on Carruthers' contention that animal consciousness is very unlikely given the truth of some form of HOT theory (Gennaro [1996, 2004b, 2006]). I won't repeat those arguments here except to say that a higher-order thought need not be as sophisticated as it might seem. Since most of us believe that many animals have conscious mental states, a HOT theorist must explain how animals can have the higher-order thoughts necessary for such states. One reason most of us believe that animals have conscious states is simply because our folk psychology is a theory of conscious mental states and it works well in explaining and predicting much of animal behavior.

Thus, there is a three-way tension among the following claims that needs to be relieved: (a) most animals have conscious mental states (i.e., there are generally positive common-sense grounds for believing that animals have conscious states); (b) the HOT theory is true, which, in turn, entails having I-thoughts; and (c) few (if any) animals are capable of having I-thoughts based on various empirical and theoretical considerations.

Carruthers rejects (a) and embraces (b) and (c), while Dretske, Lurz, and Seager endorse (a) and (c) but reject (b). I reject (c) and accept (a) and (b). Thus, this chapter has a double purpose: to discuss and elaborate upon the evidence for higher-order thoughts (or I-thoughts) in animals but also to show that the HOT theory is indeed consistent with animal consciousness. In section 2, I will argue that recent experimental evidence on animal memory and metacognition strongly suggests that many animals have the self-concepts and mental-state concepts necessary to form I-thoughts. In section 3, I reply to the claim that having I-thoughts requires having thoughts (and thus concepts) directed at others' mental states. The stakes are high because if the HOT theory is true, any evidence indicating the absence of I-thoughts would also cast doubt on animal consciousness itself.

It is also crucial at the outset to note one important subtlety of the HOT theory. When a conscious mental state is a first-order world-directed state, the higher-order thought is *not* itself conscious. When the higher-order thought is itself conscious, there is a yet higher-order (or third-order) thought directed at the second-order state. In this case, we have *introspection* which involves a conscious higher-order thought directed at an inner mental state. When one introspects, one's attention is directed back into one's mind. For example, what makes my desire to write a good book chapter a conscious *first-order* desire is that there is an (unconscious) higher-order thought directed at the desire. In this case, my conscious focus is directed at the entry and my computer screen, so I am not consciously aware of having the higher-order thought from the first-person point of view. When I introspect that desire, however, I then have a *conscious* higher-order thought (accompanied by a yet higher, third-order, thought) directed at the desire itself. An additional rationale for this aspect of the HOT theory is to serve as a reply to the objection that it is circular or leads to an infinite regress. It might seem that the HOT theory results in circularity by defining consciousness in terms of higher-order thoughts. It also might seem that an infinite regress results because a conscious mental state must be accompanied by a higher-order thought, which, in turn, must be accompanied by another higher-order thought ad infinitum. The standard reply is to remind the objector that the initial higher-order thought need not itself be conscious.

Of course, the very concept of "consciousness" is notoriously ambiguous, but perhaps the most commonly used contemporary notion of a "conscious" mental state is captured by Thomas Nagel's famous "what it is like" sense (Nagel [1974]). When I am in a conscious mental state, there is "something it is like" for me to be in that state from the subjective or first-person point of view. This is how I will use the term.

2. I-THOUGHTS AND HIGHER-ORDER THOUGHTS IN ANIMALS

It is sometimes said that all or most (non-human) animals cannot "mind-read"; that is, they do not understand that others (or even they) have mental states. And adherence to the so-called "theory-theory" view of mind-reading, whereby understanding mentalistic notions presupposes having a "folk-psychological" theory of mind, seems to rule out that animals have I-thoughts (or higher-order thoughts).[2] In addition, Carruthers (2005), for example, cites experimental work by Povinelli (2000) suggesting that chimps (and very young children, for that matter) lack the mental concepts "appear" or "see," which is then treated as necessary to have I-thoughts about *one's own* experiences. Such experiments are designed to determine if chimps take notice of whether or not the experimenter is looking at something (e.g., food) or unable to see something (e.g., due to blindfolding).

---

[2] Theory-theory is usually contrasted with "simulation theory," though many theorists hold some hybrid theory. There is much discussion about such "theories of mind" in the contemporary literature (Carruthers and Smith [1996]; Goldman [2006]; Nichols and Stich [2003]). One issue centers on those who think that one's concepts of mental states are acquired through a process of simulating another's mental activity with one's own, and those who argue that some kind of background theory of mind is presupposed in the ability to mindread.

However, there seems to be growing evidence that many animals can indeed have some I-thoughts and read (other) minds in some sense. Moreover, as we will see in section 3, it is not at all clear that having I-thoughts requires reading *other* minds.

In any case, there are two main concepts in an I-thought (or higher-order thought): namely, a self-concept ("I") and mental state concept ("M"). Let us consider them in turn.

2.1. Self-concepts and episodic memory in animals

Episodic memory is an explicitly conscious kind of remembering involving "mental time travel" (Tulving [1983, 2005]). It is, for example, often contrasted with *semantic* memory, which need only involve knowing that a given fact is true or what a particular object is, and *procedural* memory whereby memory of various learned skills is retained. Tulving also uses the term "autonoetic consciousness" for that kind of episodic remembering. The link to I-thoughts is fairly clear: some notion of self or "I" seems necessary to have a genuine episodic memory. I recognize the memory as *mine* and representing an event in *my* past. Tulving speaks of episodic memory's "dependence on a remembering 'self' [and] . . . relation to subjectively apprehended time" (Tulving [2005], p. 14).

Tulving himself strongly resists the idea that non-human animals have episodic memory. But his case is less than convincing and he even seems to retreat from this position in the very same essay. For example, he concedes "that some of [his] assertions may be too strong" (2005, p. 27). In speaking, by analogy, of amnesic patient KC, he explains that "it is possible that he [KC] has a little left of one or more of the properties of episodic memory and that we are dealing with a case of severe impairment in episodic memory rather than its total absence" (pp. 27–28). Now this naturally makes one wonder why the same should not be said for most non-human animals if indeed KC has at least a limited ability for episodic memories as well as an ability to think about the short-term future. It is hard to see how, for example, KC can play various card games and even chess without having *some* ability for mental time travel (both into the past and future). Tulving also tells us that KC's short-term or working memory is "normal" and that "he remembers what happened a short-term while (1 to 2 minutes) ago" (p. 23).[3]

---

[3] Interestingly, Tulving (2005, p. 26) acknowledges that KC clearly has metacognitive abilities and believes that he would pass various tests which measure the ability to understand other minds (or "theory of mind").

Turning more directly to non-human animals, Tulving often qualifies his strong negative claim by speaking approvingly of the more cautious con-clusion (reached in W. Roberts [2002]) that chimps' ability to imagine their *extended* future is in doubt and that their ability to mentally travel into the future and past is *limited* (p. 39). Perhaps most telling is Tulving's concession that Clayton and Dickinson and their colleagues (in, e.g., Clayton *et al.* [2003]) have "reported ingenious and convincing demonstra-tions of memory for time in scrub jays" (p. 37). Scrub jays are food-caching birds and when they have food they cannot eat, they hide it and recover it later. Because some of the food is preferred but perishable (e.g., crickets), it must be eaten within a few days, while other food (e.g., nuts) is less preferred but does not perish as quickly. In cleverly designed experiments using these facts, scrub jays are shown, even days after caching, to know not only *what* kind of food was *where* but also *when* they had cached it (see also Clayton *et al.* [2006]).

There is even more positive recent evidence for episodic memory in animals not mentioned by Tulving. Evidence in primates is discussed in the same volume in which Tulving's (2005) chapter appears. Menzel (2005), for example, describes experiments in which a female chimp (Panzee) recovers food hidden by a trainer by coaxing a different trainer (who was unaware of its location) to let her get it. This was done even after quite a bit of time delay between the observation and the time at which the second trainer appeared. A similar result can be found in Schwartz (2005) with respect to a gorilla named King. And Hampton (2005) found that a monkey was able to successfully match-to-sample even after delays. The subject had to decide whether to submit to a test of the sample *after* the stimulus display had been removed but *before* the test has been presented. The results indicate that monkeys both know when they remember and when they have forgotten, indicating both a capacity for episodic memory as well as a form of metacognition.

Additional evidence is presented in Eichenbaum *et al.* (2005) whereby rats can remember the temporal order of the odors of various objects. And Dere *et al.* (2006) extensively review the expanding literature strongly suggesting episodic memory in a variety of animals, including dolphins, birds, and rodents (such as mice and rats). Finally, it is interesting to note that there are also reports of animals able to plan for the future, such as is found in western scrub jays (Raby *et al.* [2007]). They show that the jays plan for future need by preferentially caching food in a place where they have learned that they will be hungry the following morning. It is often observed how an ability to think about the future (i.e., "prospective memory") is closely related to the capacity for episodic memory (a point Tulving [2005] repeatedly stresses; cf. Zentall [2005]).

Some interpretations of the above data are, to be sure, not uncontroversial in some circles and we should of course not jump to unwarranted conclusions. However, there is little reason to hold the very strong view that animals have *no* episodic memory or have no ability at all to mentally time travel. If this is correct, then there is also no reason to deny an animal's ability to form at least some minimal self-concept which, in turn, can figure into a higher-order thought.

Three other points are worth making here. First, it is important not to equate having episodic memories with having *accurate* episodic memories. That is, if an experiment really shows a lack of the accuracy of an episodic memory, we should not conclude that the animal in question has no episodic memory at all. If we compare this to human adults, we quickly see the problematic inference. Human eyewitness reports, for example, are often mistaken but we would not and should not infer any general lack of episodic memory on the part of the subject. We must be careful not to hold animals to a higher standard than we hold ourselves.

Second, I have previously argued at length that there is a compelling a priori Kantian-style argument showing that having at least some form of episodic memory is necessary for even being a conscious creature (Gennaro [1996], chapter 9). The basic idea is that having concepts of outer objects involves some understanding of those objects as enduring through time (since we do not take them to be mere fleeting subjective states of mind), which, in turn, requires us to think of ourselves as temporally enduring subjects with a past (mainly because we recognize that those objects are the same objects at different times). That is, if a conscious organism can reidentify the same object at different times, then it implicitly understands itself as something which endures through time.

Third, we should recognize that there are degrees of self-concepts. We might distinguish the following four I-concepts, moving from the least to most sophisticated (initially presented in Gennaro [1993]):

Level 1:   I *qua* this thing (or "body"), as opposed to other physical things.
Level 2:   I *qua* experiencer of mental states.
Level 3:   I *qua* enduring thinking thing.
Level 4:   I *qua* thinker among other thinkers.

Interestingly, one also finds a willingness to talk of a continuum of self-consciousness in the experimental literature (e.g., Kinsbourne [2005]) as well as corresponding levels of consciousness in human development, including the purely physical "self-other contrast" (Nelson [2005]).[4] In any case, all that is needed for having most higher-order thoughts is the kind of minimal "bodily self-consciousness" self-concept found in level 1: that is, being able to distinguish one's own body from other things. And it is surely fairly uncontroversial that most animals at least have this most unsophisticated I-concept. My own view in the end is that most animals are at least capable of a level 3 self-concept and perhaps even a level 4 concept, as is evidenced by the results and arguments offered in this and the next section.

2.2. Attributing mental states to oneself and others

It is also important to point out some of the evidence for *mental state* attributions in animals (i.e., the "M" side in a higher-order thought). Some of it suggests that animals have metacognitive states but only directed at themselves: thus, I-thoughts. We have already seen some significant evidence for this in section 2.1 in what is sometimes termed "metamemory." If an animal has a metamemory state, then it not only has a self-concept but it is also able to form a thought directed at a memory, which is itself a mental state.

In addition, there is the much discussed work on uncertainty monitoring with animals such as monkeys and dolphins (J. D. Smith *et al.* [2003]; J. D. Smith [2005]). For example, a dolphin is trained in a perceptual discrimination task, first learning to identify a particular sound at a fixed frequency (the "sample" sound). Later, he learns to match other sounds to the sample sound. When presented with a sound that is either the same or different in pitch as the sample sound, he has to respond in one way if it is the same pitch (e.g., press one paddle) and another way if it is a different pitch (press another paddle). Eventually, the dolphin is introduced into a test environment by being forced to make very difficult discriminations. To test for the capacity to take advantage of his own uncertainty, the dolphin is presented with a third "uncertain" response that is rewarded if he is uncertain. He is presented with a third paddle, the Escape paddle, which is virtually equivalent to declining the trial. The dolphin does indeed choose the Escape paddle with expected frequency and a similar response pattern to humans and rhesus monkeys, which in turn is taken by many to suggest that he is aware of his state of uncertainty; that is, he has some knowledge

---

[4] Editor's note: See DeGrazia (chapter 11) for a similar ranking of degrees of self-concepts and self-awareness.

of his own mental state. This is a metacognitive state: the dolphin is aware that he doesn't know something (e.g., whether or not a sound matches or is very close to matching the sample sound). It seems reasonable to seek a common underlying explanation for all of the subjects involved (Browne [2004]).

A related paradigm has to do with testing a subject's (e.g., a monkey's) ability to accurately respond, not to an external stimulus, but to the level of its own confidence in the accuracy of a response (Hampton [2005]; Son and Kornell [2005]). Such "meta-confidence judgments" are treated as evidence of metacognition because the experiments are designed to elicit a "betting" judgment of the form "I am confident that I know." I won't describe this experiment in any detail, but, for example, two rhesus macaques were tested in this way using a system of low- and high-risk bets. In brief, the monkeys did indeed tend to bet "high risk" much more often when they were able to make accurate confidence judgments, and bet low risk more often when responding incorrectly. Thus, they seem able to express feelings of confidence or lack of confidence about their cognitions, and so display metacognitive ability.

It is also crucial to note here that some authors do speak of degrees of metacognition or self-awareness in ways arguably similar to the distinction between conscious and unconscious higher-order thoughts (as described in section 1). For example, Son and Kornell (2005, pp. 300–301) interestingly speak of "*implicit* meta-cognition," which sounds very much like "unconscious higher-order thoughts." They refer to the "*tacit* meta-judgment of uncertainty" as opposed to *explicit* metacognitions or *self-reflective* consciousness, which clearly has an affinity to the more sophisticated conscious higher-order thoughts. We may not often have evidence of self-reflective consciousness in monkeys, Son and Kornell state, because monkeys cannot verbally express their judgments. However, if there were such evidence, they claim, "we would then have evidence of *meta*-metacognition" in monkeys (p. 318). Again, a clear example of meta-metacognition would be a *conscious* higher-order thought, but this is more than is required for one to have a conscious state. Thus, animals can still have unconscious higher-order thoughts continuously accompanying all of their conscious states. As Son and Kornell (2005) put it: "according to this view, we make meta-cognitive judgments *constantly* and without explicit knowledge of them" (p. 317, emphasis added).

Let us turn now to the ability of animals to attribute mental states *to others*, which is another kind of higher-order thought, albeit a thought about *another's* mental state. Despite the Povinelli (2000)-style experiments briefly noted at the beginning of section 2, the evidence seems to be growing that at least some animals can "mindread" under other conditions. For example, recent work by Laurie Santos and colleagues shows that rhesus monkeys attribute visual and auditory perceptions to others in more competitive paradigms (Flombaum and Santos [2005]; Santos *et al.* [2006]). Rhesus monkeys preferentially attempted to obtain food silently only in conditions in which silence was relevant to obtaining food undetected. Monkeys would take grapes from a silent (i.e., not noisy) container while a human competitor was looking away: thus, apparently understanding that hearing leads to knowing on the part of human competitors. Subjects reliably picked the container that did not alert the experimenter to the fact that a grape was being removed. This suggests that monkeys take into account how auditory information can change the knowledge state of the experimenter. In addition, rhesus monkeys also chose to take food from human competitors who could not see them, either because the humans' eyes were facing away or because their faces were blocked by an opaque barrier.[5]

It is important to point out that controls were used to eliminate various non-mindreading (or "behavior-reading") interpretations of the data. For example, it is shown that monkeys do not prefer to steal grapes from the non-belled containers simply because the sound of bells frightens them. There was also no historical link between the competitor's observable features and his future actions; that is, subjects had no past experience with the competitor responding in a certain way to the sound of a bell.

Now, it may be the case that a non-mindreading interpretation *could* still be given for virtually all such experiments. It may indeed *always* be *possible* to construct creative and very elaborate alternative first-order mental or even purely behavioral explanations for any given set of animal behaviors (Carruthers [2008]; Povinelli and Vonk [2006]). A very thorough reply would be a topic for another paper. I'll only say here, first, that just because an alternative explanation is *possible*, it doesn't follow that it is the best or most reasonable explanation. Second, there comes a point where such deflationary interpretations might even work for much of *human* behavior or for, say, the behavior of a deaf mute human who is incapable of verbal communication. Third, as Browne (2004) puts it: "it is parsimonious to explain similar, complex, stimulus-response patterns by similar psychological mechanisms" (p. 648). Thus, I side with those

---

[5] Earlier related results using a competitive paradigm are reported for chimps in Hare *et al.* (2001); Hare and Tomasello (2004); and Tomasello and Call (2006).

who hold that attributing higher-order mental states (and consciousness for that matter) is often the more parsimonious move to make. This is all the more clear when one considers other similarities between humans and other animals, such as evolutionary history and brain structure.[6]

Finally, it is worth mentioning that results similar to those described in section 2.1 regarding caching and episodic memory are applicable here as well. For example, many crows and scrub jays return alone to caches they had hidden in the presence of others and re-cache them in new places (Emery and Clayton [2001]). This suggests that they know that *others* know where the food is cached and thus, to avoid having their food stolen, they re-cache the food.

Taken together with the earlier evidence presented, it seems reasonable to think that many animals have I-thoughts of some kind or other. Although many subjects of the above experiments are primates, many other animals are also tested, such as dogs, pigs, and even mice and rats.

In the next section, I'll consider two problematic claims which underlie some of the opposition to the above conclusions.

3. TWO PROBLEMATIC CLAIMS

Some insist that if an animal cannot pass a given mindreading task (directed at another), it is therefore incapable of having any thoughts about its own mental states. This is a very problematic claim. The thesis to be challenged, then, is:

(1) Having I-thoughts requires having thoughts directed at others' mental states.

The obvious corollary of (1) is:

(2) If an organism O cannot form *concepts* of another's mental states, then O also cannot have I-thoughts of any kind.

3.1. A reply to thesis (1)

To be sure, despite the recent evidence presented in section 2, many animals do not pass various tests designed to show the ability to mindread (such

---

[6] See also J. D. Smith (2005, pp. 257–260) for a very forceful similar line of argument. To give just one example on this point, Carruthers (2008) needs to posit the existence of a "gate-keeping mechanism" (among other capacities) to try to explain how it is possible to interpret much of the evidence cited above as involving only first-order (unconscious) mental states. And as Robert Lurz has impressed upon me (email correspondence), it even remains unclear why the gate-keeping mechanism is not itself metacognitive, despite Carruthers' claim to the contrary.

as the Povinelli [2000]-style experiments mentioned early in section 2). Nonetheless, I disagree with the notion that one should conclude from these negative results that most animals therefore do not have *any* higher-order thoughts. That is, I think that (1) is false. First, it is not clear that so much should be read into the failure of animals in such experiments. For one thing, their failure in such situations might be explained because the situations don't typically arise in the animal's native environment. As we have seen, many primates, at the least, do much better in similar tests when performed in more natural or competitive settings. Moreover, it is odd to treat such experimental results as if the paradigms used indicate an undeniably clear *necessary* condition for having other attributing mental capacities. This is somewhat reminiscent of treating failing the Turing Test as indicating the utter absence of any intelligence or even consciousness.

More to the point here, even if some or most animals cannot, say, engage in intentionally deceptive behavior (to use just one example) and so arguably do not have thoughts about the mental states *of others*, it still does not follow that they cannot have *unconscious* higher-order thoughts about *their own* mental states. Recall that only self-directed unconscious higher-order thoughts are required for conscious states, according to the HOT theory. Thus, I agree with Ridge (2001) that the opposing view rests on the false assumption "that there could not be an agent capable of having HOTs about its own mental states but incapable of having HOTs about the mental states of others" (p. 333). The latter at least seems far more sophisticated and does not seem necessary for there simply to be conscious mental states, especially simple conscious pains or perceptions. Moreover, as Ridge also points out, the move from "no deceit" to "no HOTs whatsoever" is much too quick and unjustified (p. 322). Just because evidence of intentional deception would be the *best* evidence of mindreading, it clearly does not follow that the lack of such evidence indicates a lack of higher-order thoughts.[7]

Finally, it seems to me that some tests for other-attributing thoughts in the theory-of-mind literature are aimed at determining whether or not animals (or infants) can have *conscious* thoughts directed at another's mental state. Speaking of "intentional deception," for example, seems to suggest that the animal is *consciously* intending to cause a false belief in another animal. To the extent that this is what experimenters have in

---

[7] For a further defense of the view that self-attribution of mental states is prior to our capacity to attribute mental states to others, see Goldman (2006). A more modest view, offered by Nichols and Stich (2003), is that the two capacities are independent and dissociable.

mind, then there is again no reason to think the HOT theory is in trouble even if animals lack this ability. As we have seen, the HOT theory allows for the presence of conscious states even in the absence of *any* (either self-attributing or other-attributing) *conscious* higher-order thoughts. If a higher-order thought is itself conscious, then one is in a more sophisticated *introspective* state which is not necessary for having a more primitive first-order conscious state. Thus, thesis (1) is, at best, on very shaky ground.

3.2. Concept possession and the generality constraint

One might reply to the above that adherence to the so-called "generality constraint" dictates that if one can self-attribute a mental concept, then one should be able to other-attribute that mental concept. In an effort to show this to be a serious problem for the HOT theory, Seager (2004) also cites evidence suggesting that animals do not other-attribute mental states, and then says the following:

[A]ll animals also lack the ability to attribute mental states to themselves because those who can self-attribute will be a subset of those who can other-attribute . . . It is . . . [a] doubtful logical possibility that a being which lacked the ability to attribute mental states to others could attribute them to itself . . . such an asymmetry would seem to run counter to Evans's (1982) "generality condition" on concept possession (the claim that one cannot have a concept C unless for any object O, one can have the thought that "O is C") . . . What is incoherent is the notion that one could conceptualize one's own possession of mentalistic attributes while being completely unable to form a thought of another being having mental states. (pp. 264–265)

For the sake of clarification, the generality constraint is sometimes put as follows: the attribution of thoughts to any organism of the form "a is F" and "b is G" commits us to the idea that the organism should also be able to think that "a is G" or "b is F." Moreover, we might even agree that "the content of all propositional attitudes is said to be subject to this constraint" (Toribio [2007], p. 446). Thus, we might also think of the generality constraint as involving a commitment to the idea that belief and desire states (which are also composed of concepts) can be recombined with other such states, and perhaps even that the organism can make appropriate simple inferences among them.[8]

---

[8] For more on this line of argument and varieties of the generality constraint, see Carruthers (chapter 5).

In any case, Seager's quotation, at a minimum, indicates an endorsement of thesis (2) above: if an organism O cannot form *concepts* of another's mental states, then O also cannot have I-thoughts of any kind. However, the generality constraint is a very strong condition on concept possession. For example, Tye (2006) calls it a "stronger requirement" than others he considers because it requires that I am capable of thinking *any* thoughts that can be formed from combining a concept with other concepts I possess. This makes all concept-users into idealized rational agents with a complete grasp of all its concepts and capable of combining into thoughts all concepts that one possesses. One might instead opt for the view that possessing a concept C is one of degree which allows for a partial understanding of C. "On this intuitively attractive view," Tye (2006) explains, "one cannot possess the concept FORTNIGHT, for example, unless one grasps that a fortnight is a period of time" (p. 9).[9]

Even among human beings we sometimes distinguish between those who have a "partial" concept of, say, DOG and those who have, on the one extreme, "no concept at all" and, on the other, an expert biologist's dog concept. The same might be said for the understanding that a young child has of TREE compared to an adult's increased understanding and then finally to a botanist's tree concept. Treating concept possession in this way would also not require all concept-users to be able to draw all possible connections among one's stock of concepts. We sometimes might not "see" the connection between two concepts or thoughts containing those concepts because we only have a partial grasp of the concepts involved. This should also be said for various animals; that is, it may be that animals have a (partial) understanding of VISION, SEE, PERCEPTION, and the like without always being able to apply those concepts to others in certain experimental situations. We should not conclude that animals have *no* concept of X if they are unable to pass a test for a more advanced understanding of X. This, I suggest, is what skeptics often do when, say, a chimp doesn't infer a concept of VISION or SEEING from certain particular movements (or lack of movements) of another's eyes. Instead, we have seen how various experiments (e.g., Santos *et al.* [2006]) indicate at least some partial grasp of the concepts SEEING and HEARING. This notion of concept possession can thus help to explain *why* certain connections between thoughts and other propositional attitudes are not

---

[9] Editor's note: A standard practice in philosophy, and in this chapter, is to refer to concepts by writing the words that express them in the upper case. So, for example, "DOG" refers to the concept of dog and not to dogs (i.e., the actual animals).

made by some animals. It can also explain how an animal can fail to attribute a mental concept to another, but still apply that (or a very similar) concept to itself.

Of course, one central issue then becomes: what is it to have a mental concept "M" anyway? Again, the answer will in part depend on which notion of concept possession one holds. If we accept the idea that one can have a concept C based on a partial understanding of C, then it is very unclear what reason we have for withholding such concepts as PERCEP-TION, PAIN, and DESIRE from most animals. To be sure, most animals may not have a very sophisticated concept of these mental states, but yet it seems that they are aware that they are in such states (e.g., a dog seems to be aware that it is seeing as opposed to, say, blind or hearing). Similarly, an animal knows when it is in pain even if it has a difficult time determining or understanding when another creature is in pain. Thus, having at least a partial understanding of the concept PAIN would involve the notion that "this hurts," as opposed, say, to comprehending philosophical writings on pain. An animal with a DESIRE for food understands that it "wants something." And a partial understanding that one is having a VISUAL PERCEPTION involves at least grasping that one is "seeing" as opposed to, say, "hearing." As Allen (1999) puts a similar point: "philosophers have been tempted by the argument that . . . for example, a dog does not believe there is a squirrel in the tree because it lacks 'the' . . . concept of squirrel. But there is no reason to think that having [that] belief requires that animals have that specific concept, nor that lacking the canonical concept of squirrel means that they lack any concept whatsoever" (pp. 35–36).

Thus, another question arises when considering the plausibility of the generality constraint: namely, do we even apply the *same* exact mental concept to ourselves as we would to another? It is assumed by many that the concept PAIN or VISUAL EXPERIENCE that one might attribute to oneself is the same as that which one attributes to another. Then, as we have seen, the reasoning goes that since many animals can't attribute the latter, they can't attribute the former. This is a highly questionable claim. For one thing, if the above account of concept possession is viable, then it may just be that an organism O has a *better* understanding of a mental concept C when self-attributing C than when attributing it to another. And so, *contra* Seager and the generality constraint, it would be perfectly reasonable for an animal to be able to conceptualize its own mental states *to some extent* without being able to conceptualize another's mental state to the same extent or in the same way.

Moreover, perhaps we should even suppose that there is a difference between the concepts *MY* PAIN and *YOUR* PAIN, or *MY* VISUAL EXPERIENCE as opposed to *YOUR* VISUAL EXPERIENCE. That is, since we only *directly* experience our own mental states, it might just be that the concept MY always implicitly accompanies my mental-state concepts. The lion or chimp has more immediate first-person access to its own mental states and thus can acquire concepts of its own mental states in a more direct way. However, acquiring and then attributing mental states to others (such as YOUR PAIN or YOUR BELIEF) involves an additional, or at least different, inferential process. To put it bluntly: it is normally *much harder* to know about another's mental states than it is to know about one's own mental states. There is a reason why the problem of *other* minds is an age-old problem in the history of philosophy. One need not hold some radical Cartesian infallibility view to appreciate this point, since even the most anti-Cartesian skeptic will typically acknowledge that the admittedly fallible access to our own minds (as opposed to other minds) is at least more immediate in some important sense.[10] For example, I need not interpret my *behavior* in any obvious way when I think that I have a simple desire for food or a pain in my back. Thus, if there are two distinct concepts involved in the self-attribution and other-attribution of mental concepts (because of the "my" and "your" qualifiers), then it is not even clear that the generality constraint is violated when an animal cannot other-attribute a mental state that it can self-attribute. And this would be yet another reason not to accept the logic that failure of some animals to other-attribute mental concepts means that they cannot attribute them to themselves. Attributing mental states to others seems to involve additional cognitive abilities, such as making certain inferences based on behavioral evidence, which some animals may not have. But this does not mean that they are incapable of having mental concepts at all or self-attributing them.

In any case, if I am right thus far, this bodes well for the HOT theory which only requires an (unconscious) I-thought with a self-attributing mental concept in order for an animal to have conscious mental states.

Now, much of the above raises the very difficult issue of under what conditions is it reasonable to attribute any concept to a non-linguistic animal. I cannot fully address this issue here. Nonetheless, one core idea in the animal cognition literature is that the attribution of concepts is

---

[10] *Contra* Carruthers (2008), who cites well-known problems with infallibility (e.g., from Nisbett and Wilson [1977]) as one reason to favor the opposing view. This is really not the issue; rather, it is whether or not it is typically *harder* to know about another's mental state. In other words, aren't we *more often* wrong when attributing mental states to others?

justified if there is evidence supporting the presence of a mental representation that is independent of solely perceptual information (Allen and Hauser [1991]). This view fits well with the attribution of concepts in the experiments described in the previous section. Following up on this, Allen (1999) proposed the following account:

An organism O may reasonably be attributed a concept of X (e.g., TREE) whenever:

(i) O systematically discriminates some Xs from some non-Xs; and

(ii) O is capable of detecting some of its own discrimination errors between Xs and non-Xs; and

(iii) O is capable of learning to better discriminate Xs from non-Xs as a consequence of its capacity (ii) (pp. 36–37).

As Allen notes, the above is not meant as a definition of "concept," but rather a criterion for when it is reasonable to attribute a concept X to an animal. Of course, if we are going to use it as a guide for attributing *mental* concepts to animals, then the X in question cannot be TREE or some external object but rather a mental concept (of which an animal arguably has at least a partial conception). We have seen that many animals seem to be able to meet condition (i) where "X" ranges over mental states; that is, they are able to distinguish one mental state from another, such as seeing from not-seeing, or hearing from not-hearing, or remembering from not-remembering. For some, this may even be enough for an animal to have a mental concept, since it shows at least some understanding of those concepts by way of comparison.

A case could also be made that some of the above experimental results indicate an ability to meet clauses (ii) and (iii) for mental states. For example, when a chimp or dolphin or rat detects its own error in, say, a metaconfidence or metamemory task, and then goes on to learn to perform the task better on that basis, it seems to have met (ii) and (iii). So when an animal learns to improve its performance on memory or confidence tasks, it seems to have understood how to *better* discriminate its own mental states from one another. In addition, Allen's own example (1999, p. 38) of pigs' "backout behavior" seems suited for this purpose. He describes cases where pigs display a self-monitoring of performance. Some pigs would attempt to back away from the choice they had made after committing to a response they had given (on, say, a same/different perceptual task), but before any feedback was provided.

In any case, I also find little reason to accept thesis (2), that if an organism cannot form concepts of another's mental states, then it cannot have I-thoughts of any kind.

In closing, then, it is at the least very premature to claim that animals cannot have I-thoughts at all. At best, there seems to be growing positive evidence that animals can mindread and have I-thoughts, which include various degrees of conceptual sophistication. And even if mindreading others is not found in very many animals, it doesn't follow that no I-thoughts are present. Finally, this also means that if the HOT theory is true, we need not deny that most animals are conscious.

CHAPTER II

Self-awareness in animals

David DeGrazia

I. INTRODUCTION

Many animals are self-aware. At any rate, I claim, the cumulative force of various empirical data and conceptual considerations makes it more reasonable to accept than to deny this thesis. Moreover, there are importantly different sorts of self-awareness. If my arguments are on the right track, then scientists and philosophers have significantly underestimated the case for animal self-awareness.

2. TYPES OF SELF-AWARENESS

The most primitive type of self-awareness is *bodily self-awareness*, an awareness of one's own body as importantly different from the rest of the environment – as directly connected with certain feelings and subject to one's direct control. Because of bodily self-awareness, one does not eat oneself. And one pursues certain goals. Bodily self-awareness includes *proprioception*: an awareness of body parts, their position, their movement, and overall body position.[1] It also involves various *sensations* that are informative about what is happening to the body: pain, itches, tickles, hunger, as well as sensations of warmth, cold, and tactile pressure. These forms of awareness are essential to any creature that can feel features of its body and environment and act

Thanks to Robert Lurz, Marc Hauser, and my colleagues in the Department of Philosophy – especially Tad Zawidzki and Eric Saidel – for feedback on a draft.

[1] For an outstanding discussion of proprioception and its relationship to self-awareness, see Bermúdez (1998, chapter 6). Addressing how self-awareness is possible without language, the book gradually develops a case – drawing primarily from developmental psychology – that the most sophisticated forms of self-awareness can be built up from primitive beginnings. Thus, Bermúdez represents a notable departure from common assumptions about self-awareness challenged in this essay. Notably, Robert Mitchell has also emphasized different types of self-awareness among animals, but he apparently assumes that there are literally different *selves* associated with a given individual (e.g., Mitchell [1994]). By contrast, I maintain that (at least in non-pathological cases) there is just one self, the individual, who may be self-aware in various ways.

appropriately in response. In sum, bodily self-awareness includes both an awareness of one's own bodily condition and an awareness of one's *agency*, of moving around and acting in the world. Somewhat radically, I suggest that most or all sentient animals have this type of self-awareness.

Social self-awareness – awareness of oneself as part of a social unit with differing expectations attaching to different positions – is present in highly social creatures. It enables such animals to interact with each other effectively. By understanding the expectations that come with one's position, and the ways in which particular interactions among group members affect how one can best deal with them, an animal improves her chances of surviving and passing along her genes. Wolf X, for example, understands that he is subordinate to wolf A, the alpha, and that wolf B has recently formed an alliance with A, so X had better not attack B for fear of A's retribution. Social self-awareness in animals presupposes bodily self-awareness insofar as deliberate social navigation is possible only in creatures aware of their own agency.

Introspective awareness is awareness of (some of) one's own mental states such as feelings, desires, and beliefs. Is this phenomenon exclusive to language-users? After all, it requires not just having mental states, but awareness of having them; one might suppose that such mental reflexivity requires the conceptual rocket of language. On the other hand, assuming a rabbit can be hungry – can *have* the sensation of hunger – it may be plausible to hold that the rabbit is also *aware that she has the sensation*. Indeed, insofar as bodily self-awareness rests partly on having various sensations, and noting their connection with one's body, bodily self-awareness may implicate a basic sort of introspective awareness. I leave that possibility open. As we will see, there is independent evidence from metacognition studies involving monkeys that certain non-linguistic creatures are introspectively aware.

Let us turn to the arguments.

3. DESIRES AND INTENTIONAL ACTION

Many animals have *desires*. That is, they *want* certain things such as food, refuge, or access to a mate. Given a choice between two substances to eat, or two places to sleep, they often *prefer* one to the other. The thesis that desire abounds in the animal kingdom seems strongly supported by common sense. But further support is available.

There is a strong case that all animals capable of having pleasant and unpleasant experiences – let's reserve the term *sentient animals* for them – have desires. To find X pleasant entails, *ceteris paribus*, wanting that the experience of X continue. To find Y unpleasant entails, *ceteris paribus*, wanting the experience of Y to discontinue. Hence a conceptual connection between desires and hedonically valenced experiences, assuming many animals have the latter, provides a good reason to believe they have desires.

Their behavior also suggests that many animals have desires. Why does your dog zoom into the kitchen when she hears you pouring food into her dish? Presumably, because she wants to eat. Why does she jump excitedly and head to the back door, where the leash is, when you look at her and say it is time for a walk? Presumably, because she wants to go for a walk. Appeals to animal behavior as evidence for desires, however, must be advanced carefully. Behavior *alone* might suggest that all animals have desires, but that inference would be unwarranted. We would be on questionable ground saying that the spider builds a web because it wants to or, worse, that the jellyfish follows its desire in swimming around. At least as I am using the term "desire," one must be capable of conscious states, and in particular pleasant and unpleasant feelings, in order to have desires; unconscious desires are possible, but only in beings capable of having conscious desires.[2] So desire-like behavior requires independent evidence that the creature in question is sentient, for responsible attribution of desires. Here I simply assume that such independent evidence is available in the case of mammals, birds, and probably at least reptiles and amphibians.[3]

Let us now consider studies focusing on animals' preferences. Marian Stamp Dawkins has studied *what* animals want in choice situations and *how much* they want it: "For instance, when a pigeon has learnt to peck a key for food, will it still keep pecking when instead of having to give just one or two pecks per item of food, it has to peck four, eight or even 50 times?" (Dawkins [1993], pp. 147–148). Of course, a pigeon can prefer pecking for food over resting with no food only if he *has* preferences or desires. Similarly for any animal who prefers to go into one enclosure over another. For example, when hens were offered a choice between standing on wire floors and standing on a floor of wood shavings, even those hens who had never before encountered the second sort of floor chose it, consistently, as soon as they had the option (ibid, p. 153). Their preference or desire was evident.

---

[2] More formally, A desires X only if (1) A is disposed to bring X about, (2) this disposition is potentially conscious, and (3) A is disposed, *ceteris paribus*, to have pleasant feelings upon attaining X and unpleasant feelings at prolonged failure to attain X (DeGrazia [1996], p. 130).

[3] See ibid., chapter 5 for arguments and citations to empirical evidence.

Much behavior among sentient animals suggests desires. Much of this same behavior, I submit, is best understood as reflecting *beliefs* that, together with the relevant desires, produce *intentional action*. Your dog heads for the kitchen upon hearing you pour food into her dish not only because she wants to eat, but because she believes that by going to the right place she will be able to eat. Thus she intentionally heads for the kitchen. She goes to the back door when anticipating a walk not only because she wants one, but also because she believes going there in this situation will enable her to take a walk. So she intentionally heads there. To be sure, there are other ways of interpreting such familiar behaviors without attributing either desires or beliefs, much less intentional action. But these alternative interpretations seem strained in view of the evidence.[4] Better to maintain that cognitive ethology – the study of animal behavior, in the context of evolutionary theory, that attributes intentional states such as beliefs and desires to animals (Jamieson and Bekoff [1993]) – is on the right track. If so, then a belief-desire model of intentional action (Davidson [1980]) supports the attribution of the latter to animals.[5]

But now we face an important objection. In the philosophy of mind, desires and beliefs are classified as *propositional attitudes*, mental states that take propositions or sentences as their objects. For example, in desiring food, I desire *that I eat food*. Similarly, I believe *that there is food in the kitchen*. But can my dog, or any non-linguistic creature, mentally entertain such propositions? To do so, he would seem to need *concepts*. Does he really have the concepts of food, eating, kitchen, and so on? Presumably he doesn't have *our* concepts of food as nourishing, eating as applicable to all creatures with mouths, and kitchens as rooms used for cooking. But perhaps he has *his own* concepts that pick out these items even if the conceptual scaffolding differs from that of our concepts – and, from the building blocks of his concepts, we could in principle construct the relevant propositional attitudes. That's one possibility I would take seriously. But one might doubt it. One might reasonably suppose that possession of concepts requires capacities for abstraction that surpass non-linguistic beings. In that case, my dog, lacking concepts, would also lack desires and beliefs as propositional attitudes.

---

[4] See DeGrazia (1996, chapter 6) for my full case.
[5] I attribute the model, not its extension to animals, to Davidson. Eric Saidel persuasively argues that this model incontrovertibly applies wherever animals' behavior reveals an ability to consider novel means to an end or familiar means to a novel end (Saidel, this vol., chapter 2). Some of the examples I present meet even this conservative standard.

Suppose that's correct. We should still agree that behaviorist and stimulus-response interpretations of relevant animal behavior are less credible than interpretations informed by cognitive ethology. Thus, even if we don't attribute to animals full-blown desires and beliefs, which are concept-laden, we may in good epistemological conscience attribute to them *proto-desires* and *proto-beliefs*. These states, we may say, interact in producing *proto-intentional action*. The idea is that these mental states, though not conceptual, nevertheless have *content.*[6] Their content is supplied by something like *generalized features of perceptions*. My dog's proto-desire for food will pick out relevant instantiations of food as things suitable for him to eat even if it does not employ a universal concept of food as stuff that nourishes.

Again, I attribute real desires and beliefs to many animals. But even if I am wrong on this point, I'm on solid ground in attributing at least proto-intentional states to them. And that will suffice for my arguments. (Although I will hereafter drop cumbersome references to *at least proto-* intentional states, let us bear the qualifications in mind.)

Desires to do certain things and intentional actions that involve doing them suggest at least some rudimentary awareness of oneself as persisting through time. Your dog's intentionally running to the back door with a desire to go for a walk requires that she represent herself as being around long enough to go outside. The very desire to do something, even if the action is obstructed, is similarly future-oriented and self-implicating. For the desire and intention amount to a rudimentary plan, which necessarily includes a representation of completing the intended action. If this is correct, then a common-sense appreciation of the ordinary behaviors of many animals suggests a kind of self-awareness – namely, bodily self-awareness, here with an emphasis on the agency aspect.

Strengthening the case for intentional action, and therefore for bodily self-awareness, is evidence of more sophisticated behaviors in animals involving planning, complex problem-solving, and/or tool use. In such cases, denying that animals perform intentional actions seems absurd, because the actions are so obviously deliberate. Consider some examples.

Chimpanzees use natural objects in pursuing certain goals – for example, moss as a sponge, rocks as nut-crackers, and stems to probe for insects (McGrew [1992], pp. 44–46). They have also been observed using sticks to cushion the soles of their feet when climbing or walking over thorns (Stanford [2001], p. 126). Such behaviors are clearly intentional, not to

---

[6] See Bermúdez (1998, chapter 4) for a way of developing this idea.

mention intelligent. For those who reserve the term "tool use" for instances in which one *fashions* an inanimate object before employing it, several feats will make the grade. Chimpanzees have been observed doing all of the following (Hauser [2000], pp. 35–36): stripping leaves off sticks and inserting them into the homes of ants and termites, waiting for them to climb aboard only to become primate dinner; chewing leaves to create an absorbent sponge, which is used to soak up excess water or sap from tree holes; fashioning sticks to produce a sort of dental probe for an unusual method of grooming group members.

Dolphins also furnish examples of highly deliberate problem-solving. Some dolphins wear cone-shaped sponges over their beaks, apparently a protective measure as they nose along the bottom in search of food (Connor and Peterson [1994], pp. 195–196). They engage in cooperative hunting that is responsive to immediate circumstances (Mann *et al.* [2000]). There are even reports of dolphins apparently "asking" humans in the water for assistance in removing a fishing hook from a group member's mouth or tail (White [2007], pp. 93–94).

Some examples come from birds, specifically New Caledonia crows, who fashion two different types of twigs to extract insects from different sorts of holes (Hauser [2000], p. 36). One crow was videotaped making a complexly shaped tool out of a wire:

> Betty tried to obtain the food with the straight wire but when that proved impossible she took it away, wedged it in a crevice in her tray and bent it to the appropriate hook shape. Then she went over and used it as a tool. She even corrected the shape of the hook. (Anderson and Kacelnik [2004], p. 46)

Your own experience with pets may furnish an impressive feat of problem-solving (even if not tool use). My best example features my family's Labrador retriever, who, apparently frustrated at being confined to the study, reared on her back legs and attempted to turn the doorknob.

Such planning and problem-solving are instances of intentional action. Again, intentional action is possible only if the animal agent has some sense of herself as persisting long enough to complete the action or plan. This sense of self involves, most basically, a sense of one's own body as importantly distinct from the rest of the world and as subject to one's direct control.

4. FEAR

Few will doubt that many animals experience the primitive emotion of fear. Like anger and sexual arousal, fear is associated with the sympathetic autonomic nervous system. This system facilitates action in what we may broadly call *emergency* situations. Fibers in the system increase heart rate, sweating, and general arousal while decreasing digestion and other processes associated with rest. Also implicated is the limbic system, a group of neurological structures (e.g., the amygdala, hippocampus, thalamus) that are essential to motivation and emotion. Importantly, the sympathetic autonomic nervous system and limbic systems are evolutionarily primitive, common to all vertebrates. It seems responsible to assume that any creature that is endowed with these two systems, and sentient, can experience fear.

What is fear? It is an emotional response to the perception of danger, a response that facilitates attention to promote protective action. What is the object of fear? It is something one perceives to pose a threat of harm to oneself. When? Some time in the future. These mundane implications of the concept of fear suggest that those who can be afraid have some sense of themselves as persisting into the (possibly very near) future. That is, anyone who can fear has at least a rudimentary bodily self-awareness. Moreover, if the subject who fears perceives the harm threatened as *being hurt*, this would entail an awareness of the possibility of having pain in the future, a type of introspective awareness. These basic points suggest that an enormous range of animals are self-aware in some way and to some degree.

5. ANTICIPATION OF ONE'S OWN FUTURE

Like intentional action involving a plan, fear requires some awareness that one will continue into the future. Is there independent evidence that animals can anticipate their own futures?

Note that, from an evolutionary standpoint, a sense of time would be highly adaptive for creatures capable of complex behaviors in a changing environment. Anticipation is useful for getting a jump on predictable events and selecting behaviors accordingly. Moreover, anticipation would presumably work in conjunction with memory. Animals who can anticipate the movement of prey and predators, based partly on memory of their past behavior in similar circumstances, would enjoy a major advantage in determining what to do.

A skeptic might reply, however, that what is adaptive is the capacity to *encode* information gained from experience and *use* that information in modifying future behavior. There is no additional adaptive value, the challenge continues, to representing that information *consciously*, as would be required for any forms of memory or anticipation relevant to self-awareness.

This objection misfires, for two reasons. First, there is good reason to think some self-representing memories and anticipations in animals are conscious. There is probably additional adaptive value to being able to represent one's own past and future consciously. In humans, the ability to manage complexity and novelty, to improvise in unfamiliar circumstances, is associated with conscious mental states, whereas unconscious information-processing often suffices in familiar terrain. But, again, animals must deal with variable environments: moving predators and prey, changing weather and food supplies, and – in social species – evolving social dynamics. So conscious anticipation and remembering would be advantageous in novel or highly variable situations. Second, even if the relevant self-representations were all unconscious, they would still manifest self-awareness. There is no reason to require that self-representations be conscious to count as manifesting a rudimentary self-awareness (at least in creatures conscious of some features of their world through pleasure, pain, proprioception, and external senses such as vision and hearing).

In addition to evolutionary considerations, there is specific empirical evidence suggesting certain animals' ability to anticipate their own futures. Consider two examples. In one, squirrel monkeys were initially given a choice between one piece of date (a fruit they like) and four. Naturally, they took four. Then the scientists began to withhold water – for three hours if the monkeys chose four pieces of date, for thirty minutes if they chose one piece. The monkeys learned to anticipate the consequences of their choice. Although not thirsty when choosing, they anticipated becoming thirsty and chose a smaller bounty of food in order to drink more readily when thirsty (Zimmer [2007]). In another study, scrub jays were permitted to feed freely during the day for six days, except in the morning, when they were confined either in a compartment where they got breakfast or in another where they did not. On the evening of the seventh day, the jays received extra food. Although not then hungry, they stashed the surplus in the compartment where they had learned they would not receive breakfast, anticipating the possibilities for the next morning (Raby *et al.* [2007]). Importantly, in these instances, the animals not only anticipated future events, but anticipated their own situation in the future – being thirsty or hungry or not – providing further evidence of bodily (and perhaps introspective) self-awareness.

6. MEMORY OF ONE'S OWN PAST

Consider now some data suggesting animals' awareness of their own recent behavior. Researchers trained a dolphin to understand a particular gesture as meaning "repeat": do again what you just did before. The dolphin was able to execute this command, repeating his immediately preceding action when this command was given but not when other commands were given (Mercado *et al.* [1998]). In an earlier study, rats were trained to press one of four levers right after hearing a buzzer, the correct response depending on their behavior – immobility, face-washing, walking, or rearing – at the time of the buzzer. The rats demonstrated their ability to discriminate among their immediately preceding behavior types (Beninger *et al.* [1974]). Awareness of what one just did would seem to implicate memory and bodily self-awareness.

Also of interest are studies in which researchers focused on the possibility of *episodic* memories. The latter involve conscious recollection of *experiences from one's past*. Implicit memories, by contrast, are stores of information based on past experiences, where those experiences are not consciously recollected, though the information can influence present behavior. You may remember (having seen) the face of a character in a movie without remembering when you saw it, what the movie was, or whose face it is – implicit memory. If you recall the experience of watching the movie, you have an episodic memory.

Now consider another experiment involving scrub jays, who prefer to eat moth larvae rather than peanuts if the larvae are fresh but prefer peanuts if larvae have been dead a few hours (de Kort *et al.* [2005]). The jays were given a chance to hide both kinds of food, and then were removed to a cage. The birds kept away from their caches for four hours tended to dig up larvae whereas those who had to wait five days ignored the larvae and dug up peanuts. (The experiment was controlled to rule out the hypothesis that the birds were following their sense of smell.) If jays appear to have episodic memory, it should be unsurprising that other studies suggest that mammals, including rats (Babb and Crystal [2005]) and gorillas (Schwartz *et al.* [2005]), do as well. Since any such episodic memories would be memories of having done something, or having had a particular experience, they would suggest at least bodily self-awareness.

Does room remain for skepticism? What if the jays, for example, simply remembered *that* they hid food a short time ago or a long time ago without remembering *doing so*? This would be implicit rather than episodic memory. Nevertheless, it would involve an awareness of something one did in the past, manifesting bodily self-awareness.

7. IMITATION

In *imitation*, one intentionally does what someone else has done. More precisely, one individual learns from another *the form of a particular behavior* and copies it. Imitation differs from *goal emulation*, in which one learns from another a particular goal to pursue; from *observational conditioning*, in which one learns from another in what circumstances to apply a behavior already in one's repertoire; and from *stimulus enhancement*, in which one learns from another what in the environment to attend to, leading to one's discovery of an action that resembles that performed by the other (Whiten and Ham [1992]). In genuine imitation, one's intention implies some representation of oneself. For the imperative "Do what that individual did" has an implicit subject: oneself. There is no claim here that the intention and associated representations are linguistic, nor even that they're conscious, just that whatever form they may take, their contents imply an awareness of oneself as an agent capable of acting in the same way.

Convincing instances of imitation include the following. An orangutan was observed using kerosene to start a fire and a trash can lid to tend it after observing the same actions by a human (Russon and Galdikas [1993]). The chimpanzee Washoe "adopted" a young chimp who eventually mastered thirty-nine signs of sign language, without human instruction, by imitating Washoe (Fouts *et al.* [1984]). Chimpanzees raised in homes have apparently imitated a plethora of actions performed by caretakers (for a list see Whiten and Ham [1992], pp. 263–264). The same is true of Chantek, a language-trained orangutan, who imitated many signs and actions by the time he was two – including in response to the sign "DO SAME" (Miles [1993], p. 49). Dolphins, meanwhile, have an extraordinary capacity to imitate the actions and postures of conspecifics, humans, and seals, as well as human speech (Connor and Petersen [1994], pp. 188–91; Herman [2002], pp. 277–278). Perhaps the most remarkable instance occurred when two captive dolphins who had been trained to perform for audiences were accidentally put in each other's shows – which had different cues and required different actions. One performed the other's show correctly, without training, based entirely on having observed the other dolphin's training (discussed in White [2007], pp. 88–90). Whether animals other than apes and dolphins can imitate is uncertain.

8. SELF-RECOGNITION WITH MIRRORS

Since Gordon Gallup's pioneering experiments in the 1970s, self-recognition with mirrors has often been cited as evidence of self-awareness in animals. Before considering those experiments, let us note that mirror self-recognition involves more than perceiving oneself in a mirror. Any dog, for example, can perceive an image in the mirror; and when the image is of herself, she can perceive (what happens to be) herself in the mirror.

But the sort of recognition that is relevant to bodily self-awareness involves perceiving one's own image as *an image of one's own body*.

In Gallup's studies, primates who had become familiar with mirrors were anesthetized and painted with odorless markers on parts of their heads that were visually inaccessible without the use of mirrors. After awaking, the primates used mirrors to pick at the marks (something they did not do without mirrors). Initially, only chimpanzees and orangutans exhibited the ability to use mirrors for self-examination. Only they – and humans – it seemed, could perceive their reflections as reflections of their own bodies (Gallup [1977]).

More recently, representatives of other species have passed the mirror test, though some controversy remains. Bonobos, or "pigmy chimpanzees," have succeeded (Hyatt and Hopkins [1994]). Among gorillas, Koko, the most proficient language pupil of her species, has apparently made the grade (Patterson and Gordon [1993], p. 71), but it is unclear whether any other gorillas have (Parker [1994]; Gallup *et al.* [2002], pp. 326–327). Meanwhile, after some early inconclusive studies, a carefully controlled experiment indicated that dolphins can examine themselves in mirrors and other reflective surfaces (Reiss and Marino [2001]). More recently, a well-regarded study confirmed mirror self-recognition in elephants (Plotnik *et al.* [2006]). Studies on tamarin monkeys suggested they *might* have recognized themselves, but a later attempt to replicate these results failed, leaving uncertain how to interpret the initial data (Hauser [2000], pp. 107–109; Gallup *et al.* [2002], p. 327).

Thus, certain non-human species are clearly capable of recognizing themselves – as themselves – in mirrors, but we don't know how far into the animal kingdom the capacity extends. Although it is silly to maintain, as some commentators have, that mirror self-recognition is the only valid indication of self-awareness in animals, it is surely one relevant consideration in the case for bodily self-awareness.

9. TAKING INTO ACCOUNT ANOTHER'S SPATIAL PERSPECTIVE

The behavior of some animals indicates that in pursuing particular objectives they can take into account another individual's spatial (and perceptual?) perspective. In one case (Kummer [1982]), a troop of baboons were resting when, over some twenty minutes, a female gradually moved about two meters, ending up behind a rock where she groomed a male. Had the dominant male observed the grooming, there would have been hell to pay. But from where he sat, he could see only the female's back, tail, and the top of her head. He could not see the male being groomed, who had bent down behind the rock, presumably so the dominant male could not observe the transaction. Jane Goodall (1986, pp. 570, 577–580), meanwhile, provides these instances of suggestive behavior in chimpanzees: A young chimpanzee leads a female out of view of higher-ranking males in order to copulate. A subordinate courting a female covers his erection when a superior male suddenly appears. While fighting a rival, a male hides signs of fear – which might embolden the rival – by suppressing instinctive facial expressions and vocalizations or by manually covering his mouth. A chimpanzee avoids looking at food that only she knows about until other chimpanzees have departed, securing exclusive access to the prize.

In these and similar examples, observers have understood an animal's behavior as evincing an awareness of another individual's spatial perspective, taking it into account in an effort to conceal something about the first animal's situation or behavior – thereby advancing some objective such as a rewarding transaction with a conspecific or exclusive access to food. Wherever such an attribution is correct, it would seem to imply bodily self-awareness. For in each case, the other's perspective is salient *in relation to the agent's own physical position or situation*, of which the agent must be aware for the behavior to be effective.

The most rigorous available evidence of animals' taking into account another's spatial perspective suggests a more radical thesis: that the animals have a "theory of mind," that is, some grasp of other individuals' mental states. In a series of carefully controlled studies (Hare *et al.* [2001]), a subordinate and a dominant chimpanzee competed for food, which was arranged in various ways on the subordinate's side of two opaque barriers. In each setup, the subordinate saw the baiting procedure and could monitor the dominant's visual access to the food. If subordinates could determine what dominants could see, they should preferentially get the food that dominants had not seen hidden or moved. This is exactly what happened. Moreover, when a dominant who witnessed the baiting was replaced with another dominant who had not, subordinates adjusted their behavior accordingly, demonstrating some ability to keep track of who had seen what. A similar set of experiments involving capuchin monkeys (Hare *et al.* [2003]), interestingly, did not furnish evidence that they are sensitive to what conspecifics can see. Yet later, differently designed experiments suggested that not only chimpanzees, but also tamarins and rhesus monkeys, distinguish human investigators' goal-directed and accidental behavior – based on how their actions relate to environmental constraints – in making inferences about the investigators' goals (Wood *et al.* [2007]). If this interpretation of the data is correct, then monkeys too have a theory of mind.

Besides being interesting in its own right, the question of whether particular animals have a theory of mind is relevant to whether they are capable of true deception (see next section). Moreover, evidence that animals can think about others' mental states makes it more believable that they can think about their own mental states (see discussion of metacognition below, section 12).

10. DECEPTION

Do some of the cases described above involve deception? We might initially define deception as an intentional action – or omission – that is misinterpreted by another to the agent's advantage.

The cases of surreptitious grooming and of resisting the urge to look at food seem to meet this standard. And something like this conception is assumed in Byrne and Whiten's attribution of deception to primates' "Machiavellian" manipulations of each other (Byrne and Whiten [1988], chapters 15, 16). Baboons make distinct gestures of "looking" when they see predators or another baboon troop. Other baboons spontaneously follow the gaze. In one instance discussed by the authors, a male attacked a younger baboon, who screamed, provoking several adults to run toward them. The running adults were making aggressive calls, apparently preparing to attack the offending male, who – seeing their approach – suddenly "looked" into the distance, despite the absence of predators or baboons in that direction. The adults stopped and followed his gaze, at which time he escaped. Very effective manipulation, but was it deception?

Deception, as ordinarily understood, involves not merely intentional action that in fact misleads, but *intentional misleading*. The deceiver intends to misrepresent a situation so that another individual will fail to grasp how things really are. Thus, one who deceives has a theory of mind – specifically, a belief or sense that the targets of deception have mental lives (which can be confounded). But it remains debatable whether animals such as those just described have a theory of mind. Whether or not they really see other animals as *conscious subjects* or *thinkers*, surely they see other animals as unlike inanimate objects: they grasp that certain animals will *respond* in predictable ways to particular provocations, not just *move around* the way a ball or balloon might. One might therefore find congenial a suggestion that these animals have a *proto-understanding of agency*:

[an ability] to recognize that certain things in one's environment, such as con-specifics, prey, or predators, can be manipulated in very specific ways – ways that do not apply to various other things, including many other animals, trees, rocks, and the like. What is emphasized is the recognition of another, not so much as a *thinker*, but as a *doer*. (Güzeldere *et al.* [2002], p. 356)

Even such proto-understanding of agency would suggest a sort of self-awareness: an awareness that one's own behavior can induce certain actions in others. This involves more than the agency aspect of bodily self-awareness, for it implicates an awareness of others as doers or actors, an important component of social self-awareness.[7]

II. COMPLEX SOCIAL UNDERSTANDING

That your own actions can influence those of others, especially if they are members of your social group, is an insight of social understanding. Many mammals have complex social lives featuring group living, domi-nance hierarchies or more equitable relations, a sense of kin to particular others, shifting alliances, and the like. Individuals may keep track of salient interactions with others, such as whom they have fought with, whom they have groomed or been groomed by, etc. Each group member has to understand her position in the group and her relation to particular others as well as what behavioral expectations follow from these factors. This understanding manifests social self-awareness. To the extent that memory is involved – for example, that so-and-so recently groomed me, or attacked me – such understanding also implicates a non-trivial awareness of one-self as persisting over time. Examples of complex social understanding in particular species will add flesh to these skeletal remarks.

It is common knowledge that wolf packs feature nuanced social dynam-ics. Moreover, as many human caretakers notice, domestic dogs (a species that evolved from wolves) engage in pack behavior within a human house-hold; even if there is only one dog, he may assess which human is the "alpha" and work to forge an alliance with him or her. Though less actively social than dogs, domestic cats work out dominance hierarchies among themselves.

---

[7] We have considered whether non-human primates have a theory of mind. What about dolphins? According to one extraordinary account, a sailor had fallen overboard in rough waters and out of sight of his crew. Later, a group of dolphins surrounded the struggling sailor. Two dolphins from the group swam to the boat and "told" the human crewmates where the lost sailor was by approaching the boat, swimming away in the direction of the swimmer, and repeating this sequence until the boat followed them and found the sailor (White [2007], p. 163).

Primate social life has been the subject of extensive ethological study. Cheney and Seyfarth's leading work on vervet monkeys, for example, demonstrates that vervets know who is a relative, who is a dominant, who's a relative of a dominant, and how other group members rank against each other (Cheney and Seyfarth [1990]). The authors argue that monkeys' innate disposition to group others in hierarchies and family structures evolved to facilitate the ability to predict the behavior of conspecifics (Seyfarth and Cheney [2002]). This plausible conjecture may apply as well to other highly social mammal species.

Apes recognize group members, remember favors and grudges, have long-term relationships, and build and shift alliances (Goodall [1986]; Stanford [2001]). The structures of social life characterizing different ape species reveal differences, however. For example, while chimps are very hierarchical and not infrequently violent, bonobos cooperate more, communicate with recreational sex, and excel at building alliances (Stanford [2001], chapter 1).

Though harder to study in the wild than land animals, cetaceans (whales) have been found to have exceptionally complex social lives. Inasmuch as the ocean habitat provides such large animals no refuge from predators, it is unsurprising that these most intelligent of aquatic mammals have evolved elaborate social abilities and group structures: they are utterly dependent on cooperation and mutual defense (Simmonds [2006], p. 109; Connor and Peterson [1994]).

Perhaps the most extensively studied cetacean is the bottlenosed dolphin. As Louis Herman (2002) explains, what young members of the species have to learn about social life is extensive and time-consuming:

To function effectively within these units, the young dolphin must undergo extensive learning about the conventions and rules of the society, about cooperative and collaborative activities, and about the identities and even personalities of group members . . . The protracted period of development and dependence of young dolphins on their mothers and other group members allows the time and opportunity for extensive social learning to take place. (p. 275)

One joint activity is cooperative hunting, which features role specialization: "driver dolphins" herd fish towards the "barrier dolphins." Another example of role specialization is the "broker dolphin" who acts as a link of communication among various subgroups within the larger social unit (Simmonds [2006], p. 110).

These and many other data support the thesis that a wide range of mammalian animals have rich social lives featuring relatively sophisticated social understanding. Such understanding, I have argued, evinces social self-awareness.

12. METACOGNITION

Our discussion so far has focused on evidence that strongly suggests bodily self-awareness, social self-awareness, and, cutting across these two types, temporal self-awareness (i.e., an awareness of oneself as persisting over time). What about introspective awareness, an awareness of one's own mental states? Does this require such extensive abstraction that only linguistic beings possess it? There is reason to suppose not.

Of special interest are recent studies on metacognition in animals. Metacognition involves having cognitive states about other cognitive states. Strictly speaking, a theory of mind involves metacognition insofar as, say, X has beliefs about what Y believes, sees, or intends. But what is generally meant by "metacognition" in recent ethology literature is having cognitive states about *one's own* cognitive states. Any creature capable of metacognition (in this sense) is capable of introspective awareness because such meta-states involve awareness of the contents of one's own mind.

Some of the best evidence of metacognition in animals comes from studies of monkeys by David Smith and colleagues (for summaries, see Smith and Washburn [2005]; Phillips [2006]). Monkeys learned to control a joystick to choose answers in discrimination tests about visual patterns on a computer screen. They received food pellets for correct responses and timeouts (delays before further trials) – which they hated – for incorrect responses. Then they learned to choose an on-screen icon for "pass" when a test was too difficult. If they chose pass, they received no food and there was no delay; they simply moved to the next trial, a consequence more desirable than a timeout but less desirable than immediate food. Their ability to use the pass option provided initial evidence that they assessed their own level of confidence and understood that they were unsure – an instance of metacognition.

But what if the monkeys were not assessing their own confidence or understanding, but merely doing something to move faster to another trial? Or, conflicted about which answer was correct, simply selecting the pass option by default? Further data renders such skepticism more difficult to maintain. First, less cognitively sophisticated animals, rats, never learned the pass option (Smith and Schull [1989]), suggesting that the monkeys might be doing something special. Second, the researchers changed the monkey trials so that they received food or timeouts only after a series of trials, rather than after each trial. Third, the investigators found that some monkeys can use the pass option in a brand new cognitive test rather than having to wait to learn its consequences anew (as would seem necessary for a conditioned response). Moreover, recent trials have had the monkeys demonstrate the ability to *remember* previously shown images rather than discriminate among present images (Hampton [2001, 2005]). In these trials the monkeys who master the task apparently attempt to recall an image, compare it with current images, and decide whether they can make a match. In addition to providing evidence for introspective awareness, this cognitive achievement strongly suggests episodic memory. Finally, new research suggests that monkeys who learn a pass response in a perception task can immediately apply it not only to different perception tasks but to memory tasks as well (Kornell *et al.* [2007]). At the same time, it is worth noting that one leading scholar has proffered alternative, "deflationary" explanations for the data (Carruthers [2008]), keeping the issue open.[8]

13. CONCLUSION

Our discussion has supported several claims about self-awareness that are not widely accepted. First, self-awareness is not a single phenomenon; rather, it admits of types that are worth distinguishing. Second, and relatedly, self-awareness can exist in quite humble forms. Any creature with an awareness of its own body as importantly different from the rest of the world – as directly connected with certain feelings and as subject to one's direct control – has bodily self-awareness. A vast range of animals, it seems, has this sort of self-awareness. A smaller set of animals, members of highly social species including primates, cetaceans, and many other mammals, possess social self-awareness (which presupposes bodily self-awareness). It is therefore abundantly clear that self-awareness is neither exclusively human nor dependent on linguistic competence. There is also good, if not conclusive, reason to believe that certain non-human animals have a degree of introspective awareness.

---

[8] Space constraints prevent me from discussing another type of evidence for self-awareness in animals: reports of linguistic self-references by apes trained in sign language. For example, when asked "WHO THAT?" as she gazed in the mirror at herself, the chimpanzee Washoe allegedly signed "ME WASHOE" (Gardener and Gardener [1969]). For several examples involving the gorilla Koko, see Patterson and Gordon (1993).

CHAPTER 12

The sophistication of non-human emotion

Robert C. Roberts

A little dose . . . of judgment or reason often comes into play, even in animals very low in the scale of nature.

(Charles Darwin, *The Origin of Species*)

I. INTRODUCTION

I am going to explore the nature of emotions or their counterparts as exemplified in the lives of non-human animals. *Emotion* is a somewhat indeterminate concept, as is that of *sophistication*. So I will start with a concept of emotion that I have proposed in the past as useful in human moral psychology, and with several dimensions of sophistication that we find in human emotions as so understood. Then, by considering some observations about some animals' capacities, I will estimate the degrees to which such animals approximate such sophistication.

I have proposed (R. Roberts [1988, 2003]) that the central cases of human emotions are "concern-based construals." This conception makes emotions out to be a special kind of perception. Perception is not merely sensory reception, but reception that is so structured as to make some kind of *sense* of the object. The paradigm human emotions are events of receptivity structured by a synthetic unity of "factual" and "evaluative" attribution. Thus emotions ascribe some character or other to the situations they are about, and this character is both "descriptive" and "evaluative" (concern-based – a matter of care or interest to the emotion's subject).

In human beings, the sensory content of perception is subject to extreme reduction or attenuation relative to the perception's content or intentional object – what is perceived. Consider, for example, a sketch consisting of two or three deftly drawn lines in which one can see a man running. Or, for an even more extreme case, the characters printed on a page of *War and Peace* that mediate the intelligent reader's being struck with an impression of the dramatic personal significance of prince Andrei's encounter with

Anatole Kuragin in the field hospital (Tolstoy [2007], book three, part two, chapter 37). In the first case sensory content provided by the drawing at most *suggests* what the subject sees in it, and in the second case, the sensory content taken in by the reader's eyes bears *no* resemblance to the reader's impression of the scene. In fact, in a good reader's practice, the printing on the page may be virtually invisible, phenomenally; the narrative, and not the printing, has become the vehicle of the construal. In the broad sense of perception that I intend by "construal," the reader's impression of what is going on in the field hospital scene is a perception. It is characterized by an immediacy of presentation that is analogous to sensory impressions, despite the extreme divergence of current sensory content from the mental impression.

The other crucial part of my proposal has been that emotions are "concern-based." This view involves resistance to the supposition that "cognition" and "conation" are such that no mental event has the properties of a desire or concern (such as world-to-mind direction of fit) inextricably bound to the properties of a belief or perception (such as mind-to-world direction of fit). The idea of a concern-based construal is that of just such a mental event. Thus, my fear that I have cancer is not just the "cognition" that cancer can cause death and that I probably have cancer, *plus* the dispositional desire to avoid things that can cause death, and thus the episodic desire to be safe from what seems to be growing in my abdomen.

This principled separation of belief-like states from desire-like states seems to be a product of the belief-desire orthodoxy, plus an effort to account for the mental status of states like fear, rather than a sensitive description of the mental state. On the view I am proposing, this fear-episode is a way of "seeing" my situation in which it "looks" ("feels," "impresses me as") dire, threatening, bad, menacing, ominous, or something of the sort, and so something to be avoided. The threatening look of the situation belongs not just to some desire added onto the perception, but to the perception itself – perception being the structured, sensorily underdetermined presentation noted above. The badness of the object is an aspect of the subject's impression. This evaluative look is based in a concern – in the present case, a concern for survival. So if, as a result of a professional consultation, I come to see the lump in my abdomen as intestinal impaction, my fear may change immediately to the rather opposite evaluative perception of hope. The hope and the fear are based in a common concern.

I specifically tailored the model of emotions as concern-based construals to human emotions, and more specifically to throw light on their moral dimensions and to allow for the subtlety and complexity of their content that must be accounted for in an analysis of the nature of human moral virtues. Nevertheless, I have argued (R. Roberts [1996; 2003, pp. 115–119]) that the construal view throws light on the emotions of very young children and some non-human animals. Even philosophers who deny that any non-human animals possess rationality tend to admit that they have perception and desire. In the present essay, I want to extend and qualify this claim. I will argue that the conception of emotion as concern-based construals allows us to see degrees of sophistication in animals' emotions that would seem improbable if we thought of emotions as requiring the ability to have thoughts (Neu [2000]; Nussbaum [2001]; Solomon [2003]).

I will argue that a crucial key to appreciating both the continuity and discontinuity between human emotions and the emotions of many non-human animals is the distinction between concepts and thoughts. If we think of possessing a concept as the systematic ability to recognize things in terms of their functions relative to oneself and thus both distinguish them from one another and relate them to one another and to oneself, we will see that the possession of concepts, either unlearned or learned, is widespread among non-human animals. Indeed, *some* of such capacity is necessary for perception. It is natural to think of the possession of thoughts as a much more sophisticated mental power, involving the ability to detach a concept from its role in perception and consider it reflectively, apply it intentionally, and compare it with and relate it to other thoughts. If any non-human organisms have this capacity, they have it to a much smaller extent than we, and a number of the differences between human and non-human emotional capacities derive from the difference between the capacity to have a concept and the capacity to have a thought.[1]

2. ANIMAL EMOTIONS

Adult human beings are capable of emotions with the following properties, which I here lump together as kinds of sophistication. I have tried to approximate an exhaustive list of dimensions of sophistication, but within the limits of this essay I will discuss some of them more thoroughly than others.

- Emotions are situational
- Emotions can occur in the absence of the object
- Emotions can occur in response to a complex narrative

---

[1] Editor's note: See Carruthers (chapter 5) for such an account of the nature of concepts and their existence in animals (in particular, invertebrates).

- Emotions can be felt
- Emotions can be dissented from
- Emotional dispositions are plastic
- Emotions can be reflexive in being
  (a) about their subject
  (b) about an emotion of their subject
- Emotions can be about other people's mental states

2.1. Emotions are typically situational

The "object" of an emotion is a situation rather than a simple or singular item (a "stimulus"?). It has features or aspects related to one another in such a way that the nature of those aspects and the relations they bear to one another determine the type of emotion in question. Jealousy, for example, attributes to a situation such features as a rival, a beloved, oneself, and the beloved's attention or affection. A subject in a state of jealousy "reads" his situation as having such features.

Thus the emotion is *conceptual* and *propositional*. To say that the emotion is conceptual is to say that it exhibits the subject's ongoing ability to distinguish and relate the items in the situational object. In the case of jealousy one of the distinct things in the array is the *rival*, another the *beloved*, another *oneself*, another the attention or *affection* of the beloved that is being transferred or risks being transferred from oneself to the rival. To say that the emotion is propositional is to say that these various distinct things are ordered to one another in distinct ways (the rival is *my* rival, the beloved *my* beloved, the affection is the *beloved's* and it is being diverted *from* me *to* the rival). Thus the mental content of jealousy has a propositional form something like *the rival is diverting my beloved's affection (which I want to have all to myself) from me to himself.*

One might initially think that the emotions of non-linguistic creatures are tropism-like reactions to "stimuli," and thus non-conceptual and non-propositional, for example that prey animals simply react to their natural predators with flight- and freeze-behaviors. On this view, emotions no doubt register the presence of the predator by sense perception in one or more of its modalities, but such perception only mediates the triggering of an automatic response-mechanism of a particular kind.

The thinking behind this picture of animal emotion might be that the ability to distinguish the things that need to be distinguished in the situation and relate them to one another in the way that is expressed in the italicized sentence by which I characterized human jealousy depends on language, and the animals in question lack language. Thus, John Deigh

(2004) says, "propositional thought presupposes linguistic capacities, which are unique to human beings and, in fact, human beings who have grown past infancy. Consequently, if one represents the thought content of every intentional state as a proposition, one cannot account for primitive [for example, animal] emotions" (p. 10). Thus, the account I sketched above of a perception that is both conceptual and propositional could not apply to any non-human animal, according to Deigh.

But there is conceptual space between the notion of an emotion that depends on thought and an "emotion" that is nothing but a tropism. Deigh's criticism of the neo-Stoic theory of emotions by strictly associating "thought" with language seems plausible enough; but my claim is about concepts and perceptions with a propositional form (see R. Roberts [2009a]), not about thoughts. It seems pretty clear that many mammals have the power of situation perception with respect to things they care about. They do not respond mechanically to the presence of a predator. They are afraid of their predators only in certain situations, and are highly sensitive to differences of situation. Temple Grandin cites a typical but striking example. A squirrel in a tree taunts a cat for about half an hour. The squirrel creeps down the trunk, looking the cat straight in the eye, until the cat springs. The squirrel scampers up to safety and the cat has to drop to the ground since the distance to where the branches begin exceeds the cat's ability to climb. The scenario is repeated several times. Grandin comments that this squirrel "definitely [isn't] frightened, because a frightened squirrel, just like a frightened rat, displays very specific behaviors like freezing in place. This [is] not a frightened squirrel" (Grandin and Johnson [2005], p. 205). The squirrel responds to the predator not in the manner of a tropism and its stimulus, but quite intelligently, judging just how close it can allow the cat to get in the peculiar circumstance of placement on the side of the tree. It would be a different matter altogether were the squirrel the same distance from the cat as in the above scenario, but on the ground, with the cat between itself and the tree. The implication is that when the squirrel *is* frightened of the cat, it is because it perceives the situation as one in which the cat is a real threat to its well-being. And it can accomplish this feat without having the capacity to detach the concept of a threat, or of a predator, or of an unsafe distance, or any of the other concepts involved in its emotional discrimination of the situation, *from* the situation for separate processing.

Human fear involves some estimation of the probability of the aversive event occurring. The squirrel seems to be making just such an estimation (judgment) in taking into consideration such dimensions of the situation as the cat's facility at climbing the tree and the speed with which the squirrel can scurry up the tree when the cat lunges for it relative to the speed of the cat's lunge. Grown human beings too make such estimations without the intervention of language. Think of how intuitively one makes estimations of speed and distance when driving in traffic. Driving would be impossible if we had to have linguistically expressible *thoughts* about all these relativities. Here we function mostly on the basis of perception and inarticulate skill. When we perceive ourselves as in real danger, we get scared (and this is typically before we *think* the situation through), just like the squirrel that's caught between the cat and the tree. But most of the time we negotiate the "dangers" of driving quite calmly, just like the squirrel that (purely perceptually) judges itself to be well out of reach of the cat.

I mentioned at the beginning that the concepts of an emotion and of cognitive sophistication are somewhat indeterminate, and offered suggestions for making them somewhat more determinate, for the purpose of clear discussion. The concept of a concept has a similar indeterminacy (see Glock [1999]). One might, for example, require that the subject be able to consider the category in question (e.g., *predator*) independently of any current perceptual instantiation (e.g., to be able to think critically: "What is the difference between hawks and ducks, such that the former are my predators and the latter not?"). This power of perception-independent concept manipulation is mightily enhanced by language, if not strictly dependent on it, and so might well be thought to be peculiar to animals with syntactical language. Here, I propose, we have the idea of a *thought*, as contrasted with that of a mere concept. If so, the ability to make concern-based construals does not depend on the power of thought.

The concept of possessing a concept that I just sketched allows ample room for the possession of concepts by animals that lack words for categorizing, picking things out, and relating the things thus picked out. By the same token it allows for the possibility of animals having propositionally structured mental states. Such structure does not require that the animal have sentences in which to express the propositions whose structure is reflected in its situational construals, or that it be able to deploy these concepts in perception-free thoughts; but the construals have a structure that *would* be expressed in the corresponding sentences or their rough equivalents.

The animal grasps its situation, via perception, as having one or another kind of bearing on itself (for good or for ill). Thus the dog delights in *the prospect of getting my supper*, and the squirrel is alarmed by the fact that *the cat is located between me and the only tree in the vicinity.* In these cases, animals seem to grasp the situation they are in (just about to get dinner, vulnerable to being caught by the cat), and achieve this without the mediation of language. In these very ordinary cases, the animal grasps or understands its situation *in the perception*, the same situation (more or less) that humans can depict in syntactical language.

2.2. Emotions can occur in the absence of the object

A human being can feel jealousy without being in the presence of either the rival or the beloved, or at a time when the beloved's affection or attention is not fixed on the rival. To what extent can animals have emotions in the absence of what the emotion is about?

The absence of language limits the extent of the ability. Hope, anxiety, and grief are emotion types that involve essentially, or at least paradigmatically, absent objects, and it seems clear that animals can display episodes of such emotions. Cows can experience grief or anxiety about an absent calf, and dogs can hope for the return of their master (waiting expectantly at the door at about the time of the master's usual return home). Thus the cow seems to be using the concept of the calf in the absence of the calf, the dog the concept of the master in the absence of the master. This ability requires a fairly high degree of cognitive sophistication, and makes a great gulf, most likely, between these animals, on the one hand, and insects, worms, and reptiles on the other.

Jealousy, by contrast, does not *essentially* involve the absence of the object. Dogs sometimes display jealousy when a new (human) baby is born into the family, or even when its master and mistress cuddle in its presence. But it seems unlikely that a dog would experience jealousy just by "thinking" about the supposed rival, much less by being told a story of the beloved's unfaithfulness. It seems similarly improbable that any dog would feel anger at an offender that was not immediately present. If any animal can do this, it is likely to be among the ones at the top of the social IQ chart.

2.3. Emotions can occur in response to a complex narrative

In human beings, the "situation" grasped in an emotion often has aspects that reside in the past and are accessible only through a historical or quasi-historical narrative or the memory that such a narrative would represent. The emotions that come to pass between two long-time lovers are an obvious example; their feelings about one another are laden with the history of their relationship. The scene in the field hospital from *War and Peace* is understandable emotionally and "moves" the reader appropriately only if the reader knows about Kuragin's seduction of Prince Andrei's fiancée Natasha Rostov, and the fierce vengefulness with which Prince Andrei has pursued Kuragin for months across Russia and into Turkey. All this narrative information and more feeds into the reader's construal of the situation depicted in book three, part two, chapter 37, partially determining the special and particular character of the reader's emotion. Linguistic ability is of course necessary to such reading-emotions, as it is to the emotions of old lovers when these are fed by reminiscing together and reading love letters from their past.

Animals that are unable to tell stories to one another have less access to such historical aspects as sometimes make human emotions so rich and deep, yet many animals do have memories that enter into the structure of their emotions. Dorothy Cheney and Robert Seyfarth (2007) provide an especially striking and well-documented example in their recent book on baboon minds.

The baboons that Cheney and Seyfarth study live in matriarchally structured troops of sixty or so individuals with a fairly stable dominance hierarchy among the females. Generally, the daughters of high-ranking mothers have high rank, and those of low-ranking mothers low, but it is possible for daughters of low-ranking mothers to outrank daughters of higher-ranking mothers. The baboons make a variety of distinct sounds – threat grunts, screams, conciliation grunts, alarm barks, copulation calls, contact calls, lipsmacking – each of which has a social meaning and is governed by social rules. For example, a fear bark is a typical response to a threat grunt, and indicates submission. Fear barks are given only to individuals ranked higher than oneself, while conciliation grunts may be directed at individuals ranked either higher or lower than oneself. Individuals recognize the individual voices of each other member of the troop, and thus can tell which individual originates any sound even when the individual in question is hidden from sight.

One kind of experiment exploited the emotion-like state of *surprise*. Cheney and Seyfarth recorded individual calls of various kinds, and then in the bush set up loud speakers through which these sounds could be broadcast. When a selected individual came into the area, the experimenter would sound pairs of calls that were paradoxical relative to the existing dominance hierarchy in the individual's troop. For example, the experimenter might sound a threat grunt of lower-ranking Shashe and then a fear-bark of higher-ranking Beth. From the fact that the observed animal does a sort of double-take in response to the simulated exchange and shows unusual interest in this sequence, Cheney and Seyfarth infer that she has performed the following mental feat: she has distinguished the types of calls given, presupposed the rules that govern each kind of call, identified the calling individuals, and accessed their respective dominance ranks; the animal synthesizes all this information in the mental event of surprise.[2] Knowledge of the particular matrilineal membership of the individuals also affects the experimental subject's perception of the situation:

And to recognize that the sequence "Champagne threat-grunts and Luxe screams" is more portentous than "Champagne threat-grunts and Hanna screams" – even though both sequences violate the dominance hierarchy – the listener must add matrilineal membership to her calculations. Baboons make these complicated calculations very quickly, and probably unconsciously. (Cheney and Seyfarth [2007], p. 109)

Here and throughout the book Cheney and Seyfarth use discursive-thought language to characterize the baboons' mental processes. They write of "calculation," "assumptions," "inference," "considering," "recalling," "deciding," "taking into account," and such-like mental-procedural language (see pp. 179–80), but they also comment, as in the above quotation, that the animals probably do these things "unconsciously." Cheney and Seyfarth's inferences from the baboons' behavior to their mental states are a bit speculative in any case; they recognize that just about any appearance of mentality in non-human animals can in principle be explained by reference to learned behavioral contingencies (though the complexity of the baboons' supposed behavioral learning strains behaviorist credulity).

Once one recognizes the possible richness of perception, it is generally safer to infer perception than to infer mental procedures. In the quotation above, I think "unconsciously" does not mean "without consciousness," but rather, "without discursive, sequential thought." The baboons' surprise in response to the experimenter's concocted paradoxical social information seems to be a simultaneous "take" on the situation in which the baboon grasps the whole situation, in all the impressive distinguishing and connecting that goes into it, in a single impression. This is what I call a construal. My guess is that baboons do very little inferring or calculating, but they do some very impressive perceiving.

---

[2] Editor's note: See Camp (chapter 6) for a further account and assessment of Cheney and Seyfarth's theory of the cognition underlying baboon vocal communication and comprehension.

When the human being, after reading the first 950 or so pages of *War and Peace*, comes to the scene in the field hospital, he too automatically invests it with social information that he has picked up in the course of his reading. He may, but does not necessarily, draw some inferences. Most likely, as soon as it becomes clear that the very unhappy amputee on the cot across from Prince Andrei is Kuragin, the reader construes that sufferer in terms of his elopement with Natasha and his offense against her and Prince Andrei. This present sufferer is the scoundrel of the narrative past.

Seyfarth and Cheney report that female dominance hierarchies are pretty stable among baboons, but that male ranking changes frequently. In either case, however, the ability to collect this much detailed social information from witnessed interactions across time certainly reflects something like a capacity to construct a narrative, and it appears that baboons base emotional and practical responses on that narrative-like knowledge. But in the absence of the power to construct and present thoughts in the long sequential strings that constitute the universal human phenomenon of story-telling, what the baboons manage is not really narrative, but only something like the capacity that human beings have to construct one.

2.4. The subject can feel his own emotion

Emotions are essentially states of *consciousness*, but only sometimes are they *felt*. Thus we must distinguish *functional-access consciousness* (consciousness of what the emotion is about) from *phenomenal consciousness* (the subject's direct awareness of being in the emotional state – feeling the emotion). As situational perceptions, emotions necessarily access what they are about (their very "aboutness" guarantees this). If the Epicurean therapist is right in explaining my inordinate acquisitiveness by reference to my unconscious fear of death, then I must be aware of my approaching death as a disagreeable prospect, even if I am not aware of being aware of it in this way. When we speak of "functional" access we mean that the access to the emotion's object has a behavioral function (in the above case, causing my acquisitive behavior); only thus can it figure in a true explanation of the behavior.

But to *feel* an emotion is to have more than functional-access consciousness of the emotion's object: it is to be non-inferentially aware of being in the emotional state. It is thus to be in a position to acknowledge, note, evaluate, remember, or report the presence of the emotion as a direct result of the subjective experience of it. The Epicurean client is not aware in this way of fearing death; he has to learn this, as a matter of testimony at first, from his therapist. Such phenomenal consciousness comes in varying degrees of vivacity and accuracy. The Epicurean client may gradually become more and more aware of his fear of death, over a course of many weeks of therapy.

Can any non-humans feel their emotions? Peter Carruthers (1989) has argued that consciousness of one's mental states depends on the ability to think *about* or turn one's attention *to* the candidate mental state.[3] This account of phenomenal consciousness bears some resemblance to the account of feeling emotions that I gave in chapter 4 of R. Roberts (2003): to *have* an emotion E (say, anger) is to construe a situation in the concern-based way as being ε (e.g., as involving a culpable offender against something important); but to *feel* E is to construe oneself as construing the situation as ε. The purpose of that discussion was to explain how people can feel emotions they *don't* have – say, to feel anxious when in fact one is just coming down with the flu, or to feel contempt for a person one really only envies. I argued that this possibility requires a power of second-order construal that depends on having an emotion vocabulary. One needs an emotion vocabulary because feelings of emotions that are not there have to be *concocted*, and such concoction requires that the subject construe himself as in an emotion-state of a type. This requires that he have the power to think about emotions, which in turn seems to require that he have an emotion vocabulary. The implication would be that no animal incapable of thinking about his own emotional responses to situations, using a language of emotion, will feel an emotion he is not having.

Were that account true of all emotional feeling, including veridical feelings of emotion, animals would be excluded from feeling any emotions at all. But the account places too much weight on the power of second-order perception to function as a general account of emotional feeling. In the case of a human being feeling an emotion where his self-perception is *not* deceptive, what he perceives in the second-order perception is a first-order *perception* or immediate *impression* of the situation as ε. This first-order impression differs from a mere belief or knowledge that the situation is ε. Perceptual impressions are a special kind of content to which the subject of the impression has special access. My psychoanalyst may know my emotions better than I do, but only I am in a position ever to feel them. And what puts me in a position to have phenomenal awareness must itself

---

[3] Editor's note: See introduction to volume for a description of Carruthers' higher-order thought (HOT) theory of consciousness and its implication for animal consciousness, as well as Gennaro (chapter 10) for a defense of animal consciousness in terms of the HOT theory.

be a kind of quasi-phenomenal or potential-phenomenal awareness. Most phenomenal consciousness and unconsciousness in human beings is partial. It has the nature of "subception," "peripheral awareness," or "implicit consciousness," in varying degrees. The blindsight that is produced by the selective destruction of certain cortical areas is both at the extreme of the dissociation of phenomenal consciousness from functional-access consciousness, and is a degradation of functional-access consciousness, both in human beings and in monkeys (Stoerig [1996]). By contrast, a skillful basketball player's unconsciousness of just how he makes his deft moves on the court accompanies undegraded functional-access consciousness, but is, by the same token, only partial phenomenal unconsciousness.

Thus, I think the weakness of animals' powers of second-order consciousness should not be taken as implying that they lack phenomenal consciousness of their emotions altogether. Like vision and hearing, emotions will usually be, so to speak, partially self-lit. Animal minds are less complicated motivationally than human minds, so that fewer, if any, mechanisms like repression and self-deception degrade consciousness of their emotions. On the other hand, this advantage of the animals is strongly offset by their weaker or absent powers of thought. We humans do gain awareness of our emotions through talking about them, both by virtue of focusing more specifically on them (categorizing them by way of our emotion vocabulary) and by explaining them in terms of our character traits, our life story, and one or another theory about them. These implements and strategies both enhance our powers of self-awareness and make us prey to much deception; the simpler minds of animals limit their access to the truth and shield them from much deception.

2.5. Emotions can be dissented from

Grown people can dissent from their own emotions. For example, a person may judge, at the time of her fear, that what she is fearing is not in fact fearsome, or at the time of feeling guilty that she is not in fact guilty of what she is feeling guilty about. That is, people can sometimes disagree with what their emotions are "telling" them, just as they can, on occasion, disagree with what their eyes are "telling" them. Compare the visual experience of someone looking at the Mueller-Lyer Illusion, having just measured the two lines carefully. His visual experience "tells" him one of the lines is longer, but he doesn't believe his visual experience.

One of my chief reasons for resisting the neo-Stoic view that emotions *are* judgments (Nussbaum [2001]; Solomon [2003]) is the human capacity to deny the propositional content of one's own emotional states while in the emotional state. Judgments necessarily involve assent to the content, and in human emotions such assent isn't fully automatic; so emotions can't just *be* judgments, any more than ordinary sensory perceptions are. Of course, like other kinds of perceptions, emotions *tend to produce* the corresponding judgments, and the default position for emotions (when not critically examined) is that they do so. In an animal that is not able to adopt a critical stance on her own emotions, this possible wedge between emotion and judgment is lacking, and so emotions in such animals are, for practical purposes, judgments. However, knowing the human case, we might still want to hold, theoretically, that, say, squirrel emotions are not judgments, but only perceptions that always and automatically generate judgments.

But does it make sense to ascribe judgment to animals that cannot dissent from any content that is presented to them? I think it does, because there are other criteria besides assent by which we ascribe judgment to a subject. Earlier, when I said that Temple Grandin's squirrel made judgments about how dangerous the cat was, the stress was not on the squirrel's assent to the proposition, but on its flexibility, skill, and intelligence at estimating danger. A third aspect of judgment, closer to assent, is the readiness to act on a perception. So we might say that if the squirrel is willing to creep down the tree looking the cat in the eye, it doesn't judge itself to be in much danger. Even if the squirrel is not capable of a separate act of assent to (dissent from) the propositional content of its perception, it is certainly capable of the two other aspects of what we call judgment, and perhaps this is enough to warrant the ascription of judgment to the squirrel. In the human case, too, a separate act of assent (say, after consideration of evidence for and against the propositional content of the emotion) may be relatively rare.

Still, I doubt that any non-human animal dissents from its emotions. There seem to be at least three conditions for an animal's being able to present to himself the situation "I feel guilty, but I'm not" or "I'm afraid, but there's nothing to be afraid of." He needs (1) to feel his emotion (see section 2.4 above); (2) to feel it as involving the claims that emotions of that type make; and (3) to be able to think about the situation targeted by the emotion, as distinct from his emotional construal of it. Abilities (2) and (3) require a power of *thought*, as I distinguished it, above, from a conceptual power and its correlative, the ability to perceive states of affairs that have a propositional structure. To think "I'm afraid, but there's nothing to be afraid of," I have to have the thought of my being afraid while also having a thought about the situation as having a character independent of my emotional construal of it. So an animal that lacks the power of thought cannot dissent from his emotions.

2.6. Emotional dispositions are subject to shaping

In most animals, some emotional dispositions are not fixed beyond revision. Just as human beings can learn to negotiate steep precipices without panic, though initially programmed to panic, squirrels and pigeons and many other wild animals can, through lots of benign contact with human beings, learn to be relatively fearless of fairly close approach. Such flexibility is no doubt a kind of sophistication that is very widely distributed in the animal kingdom.

Human emotional dispositions can be brought to line up better with reality by way of reflection and training. For example, the natural panic response to looking down a precipice can be overcome by a combination of desensitization (which I assume to be the mechanism by which the reduction of the fear disposition in most animals is brought about) and rational judgment about one's actual safety (say, considering the fact that the glass elevator was reliably designed for safety). And moral maturity involves acquiring a proper selectivity with respect to one's anger and other emotions. Robert Solomon offers the following illustration of the more distinctively human power:

I'm at a new neighborhood shop, in a great rush. The salesman is amiably chatting with the customer before me, and I get extremely irritated. I would be furious, but I think, "This is a new shop; this is exactly what this person ought to be doing. I'm the one whose haste is out of place." And so I do not get furious, I just remain impatient, which I try to hide. After a moment or two, I start enjoying the conversation, as I think, "Isn't it nice to live in a city where people still treat each other so nicely." I'm not suppressing my emotion; I have *transformed* it through reflection. (Solomon [1995], p. 222)

Anger's propositional structure involves the perception of offense in the situation – a crossing of proper boundaries or the doing of improper harm. Solomon's rational approach to his own anger-disposition exploits this fact about anger by a reconstrual of the situation in terms that counter the impression of offense, and he presumably does this out of some consideration to the effect that it is the right thing to do, or that his life will go better if he can avoid anger in this situation. Thus he quite purposefully looks for and finds a plausible alternative way to see the situation.

Solomon is what Aristotle would call a rational animal. Many animals are rational in some ways, some very impressively so. But the *way* Solomon displays rationality in the above example depends on the ability to have thoughts. He manages his anger by calling on thoughts that are quite radically underdetermined by anything in his perceptual field (thoughts about the age of the shop and the virtues of an excellent neighborhood, for example). And such management of anger, thought Aristotle (1980, pp. 17–19 [I.9], pp. 96–98 [IV.5]), can, with repetition over time, become a stable disposition. Dispositions of this kind make people excellent specimens of their kind. Since the kind of thoughts that Solomon deploys here in the interest of emotional self-management are within his voluntary control, Aristotle (1980, pp. 48–53 [III.1]) thought that animals like Solomon could be praised, in an ethical way (as agents, that is, and not merely as artifacts), for their emotional dispositions. This kind of emotional plasticity, a plasticity that puts the animal's emotional dispositions within the voluntary control of the animal himself, is a distinctive feature of human beings. And it is the ability to have thoughts (which seems at least strongly linked to the ability to speak a syntactically complex language) that grounds this kind of rationality.

Bonobos are among the smartest non-human animals, but I would be surprised to find out that they manage their emotional dispositions in the way Solomon does in this example. They manage their anger, all right, notably by having (hetero- or homo-) sexual intercourse with the offender. Frans de Waal (2005) reports:

I witnessed a minor squabble over a cardboard box, in which a male and female ran around and pummeled each other until all of a sudden the fight was over and they were making love! (p. 10)

We cannot deny for certain that the couple thought, "It's silly to be squabbling this way, not worthy of an adult bonobo [or something to that effect]. How can we feel better about each other? – Oh yes, sex!" It seems more likely that there is some bonobo mechanism (say, by way of all the touching and chasing) that triggers, without reflection, the sexual urge, which leads to behavior that resolves the anger.

2.7. Adult human emotions can be reflexive in at least two degrees

An emotion is reflexive when its subject is an important aspect of its situational object. An emotion's having a subject does not entail that the subject of the emotion is an aspect of the emotion's situational object. All emotions have subjects; they are by nature states of a subject. But only some of them are (partly) *about* the subject.

Some emotions are reflexive *by type*. For example, in pride and shame the subject is necessarily an important element in the situational object. If I am proud that a team won, or ashamed of its performance, I must construe it as in some sense *my* team. Other emotions, such as fear and anger, are not reflexive by type, but many instances of them are reflexive. A mother can fear for the well-being of her children, but she may also fear for her own safety. Apparent instances of animal emotions that are reflexive by type may be explainable as fear (guilt in dogs; see Ross and McKinney [1995], pp. 71–72) or as tropism-like (strutting in male turkeys). But emotions that are *incidentally* reflexive are very common. The squirrel that's afraid of the cat is afraid for itself; thus, in its perception of the situation, it must distinguish itself from the other things in that situation. It could not have the situational construal that it does have unless it had some rudimentary concept of itself.[4]

In human beings, emotions can be not only about the subject, but about an emotion of the subject. For example, a person might be proud of his anger, afraid of his anxiety, or ashamed of hoping for the death of his parent. This kind of reflexivity requires not only that the animal have a concept of himself, but that he have a concept of the emotion-type which his secondary emotion is about (thus in the examples, a concept of anger, of anxiety, and of hope), along with some evaluative concept that can be applied to it. I suspect that this kind of reflexivity is unique to human beings. To apply the evaluative concept (say, *contemptible* or *praiseworthy*) to the instance of emotion in question may require the capacity to *think about* emotion-types, and this capacity may be tied rather strictly to the possession of a vocabulary of emotion types.

2.8. *Emotions can be about other people's mental states*

Human emotions can be about other people's mental states. For example, someone might be glad that another person envies her, or feel contempt for another's fear. This ability underlies much of the profundity of human interpersonal relationships, both good and bad, and thus of morality, broadly speaking. We are friends not so much with people who behave in a kindly manner to us, but with ones who wish us well, who rejoice and grieve "with" us; and we are enemies, not only of people who

---

[4] Editor's note: See Gennaro (chapter 10) and DeGrazia (chapter 11) for accounts of self-awareness and self-concepts applied to animals.

do us actual harm, but also of people who feel contempt for us or wish us ill. Our personal relationships thus have a kind of emotional "depth" that depends on our emotional sensitivity to the mental states of other people (R. Roberts [2009b]).

Ethologists debate the extent to which animals of various species have a "theory of mind." The term has a comical ring, given what we usually call theories. An animal has a "theory of mind" if it has a concept of the mental states of other animals, and thus is able to know or estimate what another knows or does not know, is feeling or not feeling, is intending or not intending to do.[5]

De Waal (2005, p. 193f.) is confident that the great apes (chimpanzees, bonobos, gorillas, orangutans) genuinely recognize others' mental states and adjust their behavior in accordance with what they know and how they care about them. He tells a story about two chimpanzees:

Puist, a heavy, older female, pursues and almost catches a younger opponent. After her narrow escape, the victim screams for a while, then sits down, panting heavily. The incident seems forgotten, and ten minutes later Puist makes a friendly gesture from a distance, stretching out an open hand. The young female hesitates at first, then approaches Puist with classic signs of mistrust, such as frequent stopping, looking around at others, and a nervous grin on her face. Puist persists, adding soft pants when the younger female comes closer. Soft pants have a particularly friendly meaning; they are often followed by a kiss, the chimpanzee's chief conciliatory gesture. Then, suddenly Puist lunges and grabs the younger female, biting her fiercely before she manages to free herself. (De Waal [2005], p. 158)

The younger animal seems to be asking herself, "What's going on in Puist's mind?" and it looks as though, to strategize as Puist seems to do, Puist needs to have a concept of the younger chimp's belief (trust, mistrust) concerning her (Puist's) state of mind (intention, friendly or hostile). Thus Puist has a belief about the effect her own behavior will have on the younger chimp's belief about Puist's intention.

Cheney and Seyfarth (2007) are less generous than de Waal in attributing mental-state concepts to apes and monkeys. They distinguish the ability to recognize beliefs and knowledge in others from the ability to recognize "simpler" mental states such as emotions and intentions (pp. 158–159). Cases like the one from de Waal invite three explanatory options: (1) the animals have a concept of mental states similar to ours; (2) the animals' behavior can be explained without recourse to mental-state attribution, as purely a

---

[5] Editor's note: See Bermúdez (chapter 8) and Fitzpatrick (chapter 14) for a fuller discussion of the empirical and theoretical issues surrounding the possibility and the extent of theory-of-mind (mindreading) abilities in animals.

matter of behavioral contingencies; (3) the animals have a dawning or quasi-concept of mental states, being able, in perceptual-cue-rich contexts, to recognize "simple" mental states like emotions and intentions, but not more sophisticated ones, such as belief and knowledge. I think what they mean by "simpler" is that whereas emotions and intentions are often expressed in some perceptible posture or movement of the body or face of the assessed animal, beliefs (insofar as these are not embodied in behavioral-cue-rich intention or emotion) have to be "inferred" from information and thus have a more "abstract" character for the animal doing the assessing.[6] In the terms of my present discussion, they require thinking and not just conceptually sophisticated perceiving. Cheney and Seyfarth no doubt have in mind the kind of intention that John Searle (1983) calls "intention-in-action" (e.g., intentionally swerving to avoid hitting a deer that runs across the road) rather than "prior intention" (e.g., the intention to make it to Toronto before nightfall). Prior intentions would have to be classified with belief and knowledge, if I am right about the gist of Cheney and Seyfarth's distinction. I think their distinction is helpful and that it fits nicely this essay's proposal to credit animals with conceptual powers far more than with powers of thought.

Trading on our earlier distinction between thought and concept, the more generous interpretation (de Waal's) of this chimp interaction involves explicit deliberative thinking. After the failed first chase, Puist asks herself, "How can I give that youngster what she deserves?" and hits on the idea of the deception: "If I make friendly gestures, she'll think it's safe to let me get close; and when I get close enough, I'll bite her." Similarly, the younger chimp thinks, "Despite Puist's friendly gestures, she may be planning hostilities. But then again, maybe not. What shall I do? I wish I knew what she's thinking. Can I trust her?" Such attributions of thought are explanatorily unnecessary. We can explain the interaction (in the style of Cheney and Seyfarth) with recourse to nothing more than concepts embodied in perception. On this view, the chimps have powers of discrimination. They distinguish each other from other members of the troop; they remember the first chase. Both animals distinguish hostile behavior from friendly. They know behavioral contingencies, such as that friendly behavior will allow close approach and that close approach makes harm possible. But these concepts are deployed only, or almost only, in perception and behavior, not in reflection and rumination, as in the first

[6] Cheney and Seyfarth admit that there is some, but not decisive, evidence that under competitive conditions chimpanzees take into consideration other individuals' knowledge (belief) in the absence of direct behavioral cues (2007, pp. 168–171).

interpretation. It seems plausible that such reflection and rumination more or less detached from the perceivable immediacy of the situation is greatly enhanced by the power of syntactically complex language. Human beings frequently engage in such explicit thinking, and this thinking is done *sotto voce* or quasi-*sotto voce* in some natural language. This explicit thinking is also used in retrospect to explain mental processes that did not involve discursive thinking. And we know that such processes need not involve discursive thinking, by the fact that we too sometimes act intelligently yet "without thinking."

3. CONCLUSION

Conceiving emotions as concern-based perceptions (construals), I have examined eight dimensions of sophistication of emotions as mental states. My explorations suggest that non-human animals exhibit a perhaps surprising degree of sophistication in several of these dimensions. I have suggested that a key to seeing the sophistication, without losing sight of undeniable differences between humans and other animals, is the distinction between conceptual powers and powers of thought.

CHAPTER 13

Parsimony and models of animal minds

Elliott Sober

I. INTRODUCTION

Dennett's (1971, 1987) ideas about the intentional stance have elicited different reactions from philosophers and scientists. Philosophers have focused on Dennett's alleged anti-realism about the mental while scientists have focused on his three-way distinction among zero-order, first-order, and second-order intentionality. For most philosophers, anti-realism (at least concerning the mental states of human beings) is a *no-no*; for most cognitive scientists, the three-way distinction is useful. This contrasting reaction is typical of a larger pattern: philosophers are more inclined to cite work with which they disagree while scientists are more inclined to cite work on which they wish to build.

Dennett (1987, 1991b) has denied that he is an anti-realist, but that has not stopped philosophers from continuing to affix a scarlet letter "A" to his work. Nor has the specter of anti-realism stopped cognitive ethologists from using the three-way distinction to articulate a central methodological principle, which they call "the principle of conservatism." According to this principle, hypotheses that explain an organism's behavior by attributing lower-order intentionality are preferable to hypotheses that explain the behavior by attributing higher-order intentionality (see, for example, Cheney and Seyfarth [1990, 2007]).

My subject here is the principle of conservatism. What, exactly, does it say and what is its justification? Cognitive scientists often regard the principle as an instance of a more general methodological maxim, namely the principle of parsimony, *a.k.a.* Ockham's razor. They reason as follows: since Ockham's razor is a sound principle of scientific inference, there is no special question about why the principle of conservatism should be used in cognitive science. My main goal in this essay is to trace how the

My thanks to Martin Barrett, Tom Bontly, Simon Fitzpatrick, Chuck Kalish, Robert Lurz, Carolina Sartorio, Armin Schulz, Larry Shapiro, and Shannon Spalding for useful discussion.

general principle is related to the specific one. This tracing suggests that the principle of conservatism needs to be refined. Connecting the principle in cognitive science to more general questions about scientific inference also will allow us to revisit the question of realism versus instrumentalism. Realist philosophers of science often have no problem with the principle of parsimony. Maybe they should not be so sanguine. Finally, connecting the principle of conservatism to more general inferential issues suggests that the principle can be more than a qualitative tie-breaker. If two explanations fit the observations *equally* well, one is told to prefer the explanation that is more parsimonious. The view of parsimony that I'll describe also allows theories to be compared that fit the data *unequally* well. If a complex theory fits the data better than a simpler theory does, which theory is better overall? Many philosophers think there can be no principled answer to this question; they think it is a matter of taste how much weight you put on simplicity compared with goodness-of-fit. The view of parsimony provided by the part of statistics called "model selection theory" suggests that there is room for skepticism about this conventionalist view.

I have argued in earlier publications that invocations of parsimony in science often should be viewed as expressions of subject-matter-specific background theories (Sober [1988, 2005]); it follows that different invocations in different scientific problems may rest on very different foundations (Sober [1990, 2001]). Thus conceived, the way to understand the use of parsimony in a given scientific domain is to uncover the background theory in play. Fitzpatrick (chapter 14) adopts this strategy to assess the principle of conservatism. This is not the strategy I will pursue here. The framework deployed in model selection theory is very general; it is not specific to the subject matter of any one science (which is not to say that there are no assumptions that must be satisfied for the apparatus to apply). How does that general framework help clarify the principle of conservatism?

2. PRELIMINARIES

The usual definition of orders of intentionality is this: a first-order mental state is a mental state that is not about (the presence or absence of) any mental state, a second-order mental state is a mental state that is about (the presence or absence of) a first-order mental state, a third-order mental state is a mental state about (the presence or absence of) a second-order mental state, and so on. Aboutness is judged by the state's propositional content (if it has one). Consider a dog, Fido, and his master, Louise. If Fido believes that a bone is buried in the backyard, this is a first-order mental state, since the content of Fido's belief (*that there is a bone buried in the backyard*) does not describe anyone's mental state. If Fido believes that Louise *sees* that he is digging in the backyard, this is a second-order state, since the content of Fido's belief adverts to Louise's mental state. And if Louise believes that Fido *realizes* that she is *watching* him, Louise's state is third-order. By convention, a zeroth-order mental state is a limiting case; it denotes a state in which there is no mentation at all.

It is customary in the literature to say that adult human beings have second-order (and higher) intentionality, that apes and monkeys have at least first-order intentionality though it is controversial whether they have second-order intentionality, and that thermostats have only zeroth-order intentionality. This suggests that we should define how orders of intentionality are assigned to organisms (or to "systems") as follows:

Organism O has nth-order intentionality

$=_{def}$ O has at least one nth-order mental state.

Notice that this definition is consistent with a single individual's having multiple orders of intentionality. It usually is assumed that if an organism has second-order mental states, then it also has first- and zeroth-order states. I will adopt this assumption here.

The definitions and the assumption just mentioned suggest the following simple probability argument. The statement that a system has second-order intentionality is logically stronger than the statement that it has first-order intentionality, since the former entails the latter, but not conversely. It is a consequence of the axioms of probability that logically stronger statements can't be more probable than logically weaker statements. This means that:

$\Pr(O$ has 2nd-order intentionality$)$

$\leq \Pr(O$ has 1st-order intentionality$)$

$\leq \Pr(O$ has 0th-order intentionality.[1]

The axioms of probability also entail that this ordering of probabilities must remain in place regardless of what new observational evidence is obtained:

(1a) $\Pr(O$ has 2nd-order intentionality$|E)$

$\leq \Pr(O$ has 1st-order intentionality$|E)$

$\leq \Pr(O$ has 0th-order intentionality$|E)$, for any evidence E.

---

[1] These inequalities will be strict if $\Pr[O$ has $(n+1)$th-order intentionality$|O$ has nth-order intentionality$] < 1$.

Is this enough to justify C. Lloyd Morgan's famous "canon"? Morgan (1894) describes his principle as follows:

In no case may we interpret an action as the outcome of the exercise of a higher psychical faculty, if it can be interpreted as the outcome of the exercise of one which stands lower in the psychological scale. (p. 53)

Even if Morgan's "higher" and "lower" are taken to correspond to the orders of intentionality just defined, the answer is *no*. As (1a) makes clear, no evidence can ever make it more probable that an organism has (at least) second-order intentionality than that it has (at least) first-order intentionality. In just the same way, the axioms of probability entail that

$$Pr(\text{there are at least two apples in the basket})$$
$$\leq Pr(\text{there is at least one apple in the basket})$$

and

(1b) $Pr(\text{there are at least two apples in the basket}| E)$

$\leq Pr(\text{there is at least one apple in the basket}| E)$, for any evidence E.

Proposition (1a) doesn't capture what Morgan is after since Morgan thinks that evidence *can* sometimes justify the attribution of "higher psychical faculties."[2] The same goes for modern cognitive scientists and how they understand their principle of conservatism.

The thought behind these principles is that we should adopt hypotheses that attribute higher-level intentionality to an organism only if the data force us to do so; in the absence of such data, we should assume that the organism has only lower-level intentionality. This proposal is independent of the axioms of probability theory because the hypotheses of interest are *incompatible* with each other. A natural Bayesian representation of the principle of conservatism is to formulate it as a claim about the prior probabilities of three incompatible hypotheses:

(2a) $Pr(O$ oth-, 1st-, and 2nd-order intentionality)

$< Pr(O$ has oth- and 1st-order intentionality only)

$< Pr(O$ has oth-order intentionality only).

---

[2] In the book's second edition, Morgan (1903) restates the canon and adds: "To this, however, it should be added, lest the range of the principle be misunderstood, that the canon by no means excludes the interpretation of a particular activity in terms of the higher processes, if we already have independent evidence of the occurrence of these higher processes in the animal under observation" (p. 59).

This inequality is no more a consequence of the axioms of probability than is the following claim about apples:

(2b) Pr(there are exactly two apples in the basket)
< Pr(there is exactly one apple in the basket)
< Pr(there are no apples in the basket).

The ordering of prior probabilities described in proposition (2a) may be revised as new evidence is acquired. The priors embody a "default assumption" that subsequent evidence may displace. In just the same way, proposition (2b) might be a default assumption about a basket – an assumption we make before we have observed it; adopting this assumption does not preclude our obtaining evidence that makes it very probable that the basket contains exactly two apples.

Although (2a) is more in tune with what Morgan and modern cognitive scientists have in mind, there is a catch. What justification does (2a) have? When it comes to apples, we want empirical evidence for a claim like (2b). This evidence might come from frequency data or from a well-confirmed empirical theory. I submit that the same is true for (2a). Morgan attempted to furnish an empirical argument for his canon based on Darwin's theory of evolution, an argument that I think fails (Sober [1998b]). What about frequency data? If we knew that few organisms have second-order intentionality, that more have only first-order, and that still more have only 0th-order intentionality, that would do the trick. But the intent of Morgan's canon and of the principle of conservatism is to provide inferential advice *before* we know any such thing. Nor do we have an empirical theory that provides the needed justification. Perhaps, then, we should regard (2a) as a "primitive postulate." The problem with this approach is the one that Russell (1919, p. 71) described in another context: *it has all the advantages of theft over honest toil.*

3. MODEL SELECTION

Rather than pursue the question of whether Bayesianism is able to explain why the principle of conservatism makes sense, I want to outline some non-Bayesian ideas that have been developed in model selection theory. These, I think, provide an attractive format for characterizing, and for improving upon, what the principle of conservatism says. These ideas are non-Bayesian, in that they do not appeal to the prior or posterior probabilities of the hypotheses considered.

Table 13.1. *Number of individuals with lung cancer out of 1000 in each of four treatment cells*

		Asbestos exposure	
		+	−
Smoking	+	50	30
	−	20	3

Table 13.2. *Probabilities of lung cancer in four treatment cells*

		Asbestos exposure	
		+	−
Smoking	+	$b + a + s + i$	$b + s$
	−	$b + a$	b

I'll begin with a non-psychological example. Suppose you want to model how smoking and asbestos exposure influence lung cancer. Your information is to come, not from some antecedently well-established theory, but from data on how often people in different "treatments" contract the disease. To simplify, let's suppose that smoking and asbestos are dichotomous variables, and that the same is true of lung cancer. Suppose that there are 1,000 people in each "treatment cell" and that the number of individuals in each cell who get the disease is as shown in Table 13.1.

The task is to model how smoking and asbestos affect the probability of lung cancer. The probability in each treatment cell of contracting the disease is represented in Table 13.2: "b" represents the "baseline" probability of lung cancer when an individual does not smoke and is not exposed to asbestos; "s" is the effect of smoking alone; "a" is the effect of asbestos exposure alone; and "i" is an interaction term. Here are some causal models to consider:

(Null)	$s = a = i = 0$. The value of b is left open.
(Only smoking)	$a = i = 0$. The values of b and s are left open.
(Only asbestos)	$s = i = 0$. The values of b and a are left open.
(Two additive causes)	$i = 0$. The values of b, a, and s are left open.
(Two interacting causes)	The values of b, a, s, and i are left open.[3]

---

[3] It wouldn't matter to the framework of model selection theory if the parameters in a model that are not set equal to zero were constrained to be non-zero (rather than having their values left entirely open, as above).

The Null model is the simplest one listed; it has a single adjustable parameter (b) and says that smoking and asbestos make no difference to one's risk of lung cancer. The models of Only Smoking and Only Asbestos each have two adjustable parameters, the model of Two Additive Causes has three adjustable parameters, and the model of Two Interactive Causes has four.

How might these models be tested against each other? The fact that all contain adjustable parameters makes it difficult to see what they predict about the data. Model selection theory solves this problem by shifting attention from a model M to the instantiation of the model, $L(M)$, that assigns the free parameters in M the values that maximize the probability of the data. For example, consider the model of Two Interacting Causes and the data in Table 13.1. This model maximizes the probability it assigns to the data if its adjustable parameters are set at $b = 3/1000$, $s = 27/1000$, $a = 17/1000$, and $i = 3/1000$. These are the maximum likelihood estimates of the parameters. This model is able to fit the data perfectly; the maximum likelihood estimates exactly match the frequencies in the data. The other models cannot do this; however, they are simpler.

H. Akaike, the father of model selection theory, introduced two innovations into statistics (Forster and Sober [1994]). The first was the description of a goal that models might be asked to attain; the second was a theorem that throws light on how one might estimate a model's ability to attain that goal. The new goal was predictive accuracy. Rather than asking whether a model is true or probably true, one asks whether it will accurately predict new data when its parameters are fitted to old data. We have seen that the model of Two Interacting Causes can fit the old data perfectly. If four new groups of people are sampled from the same population from which the people in the old data set were drawn, how well will the fitted model predict their frequencies of lung cancer? Akaike's second contribution was a theorem. Akaike (1973) proved, from some surprisingly general assumptions, that

An unbiased estimate of the predictive accuracy of model M
$= \log\{\Pr[data|L(M)]\} - k.$

Here k is the number of adjustable parameters in M; it measures the model's complexity. This theorem is the basis for a proposed criterion for estimating the predictive accuracy of models. The Akaike Information Criterion (AIC) scores a model by calculating its value for the quantity $\log\{\Pr[data|L(M)]\} - k$. More complex models will have higher values for $\log\{\Pr[data|L(M)]\}$, but they will incur a larger penalty by virtue of having a larger value for k. The point of AIC is to compare models with each other. What matters is not a model's absolute AIC score, but how its score compares with those of other, competing, models. Whether a simpler model has a better score than a complex model depends on the data.

Akaike's theorem shows why the complexity of a model (as measured by the number of adjustable parameters it contains) is not an aesthetic frill; it is relevant to estimating predictive accuracy. The framework that Akaike proposed is interesting for the additional reason that it explains why it makes sense in science to test models that everyone knows are false. Null models frequently have this feature. If the goal were simply to discover which models are probably true, idealized models could be dismissed summarily. However, if the goal is predictive accuracy, it makes sense to test idealized models against each other. Surprisingly, the Akaike framework shows that a model known to be false can sometimes be expected to be more predictively accurate than a model known to be true. AIC embodies an instrumentalist epistemology.

Although philosophers often describe the principle of parsimony as a tie-breaker, AIC and the other model selection criteria discussed in statistics are more than that. They not only entail that the more parsimonious of two models is better when they fit the data equally well; they also indicate how models should be compared when they differ in both simplicity and goodness-of-fit. This resource may come in handy for cognitive scientists who want parsimony to be more than a qualitative and informal criterion.

4. ALTRUISM AND SPITE IN CHIMPANZEES

Silk *et al.* (2005) and Jensen *et al.* (2006) conducted experiments that were designed to discover whether chimps have other-directed preferences or are indifferent to the welfare of others. There are differences between the two studies, but the conclusions are on the same page: the former concludes (p. 1357) that "chimpanzees do not take advantage of opportunities to deliver benefits to familiar individuals at no material cost to themselves," the latter (p. 1013) that "chimps made their choices based solely on personal gain."

All the experiments place a chimp in a situation in which it must choose among actions. Silk *et al.* (2005) studied whether chimps choose to send food to both their own cage and to another cage more often when there is another chimp in the other cage or when the other cage is empty. They found that the frequencies of provisioning both cages in these two settings are not significantly different. Evidently, the chimps care only about

Table 13.3. *Frequencies of four types of behavior*

		Benefit to other	
		+	−
Benefit	+	49%	46%
to self	−	3%	2%

Table 13.4. *Probabilities of four types of behavior*

		Benefit to other	
		+	−
Benefit	+	$b + s + a + i$	$b + s$
to self	−	$b + a$	b

getting food for themselves; the presence or absence of another chimp – a potential recipient of their donation – does not matter. Jensen *et al.* (2006) tested how often actors choose to provide food to both self and other as opposed to providing food only for self. The amount of food that actors obtain for themselves is the same in both cases and there is no more effort involved in choosing "both" rather than "just me." Jensen *et al.* also studied what chimps do when they cannot benefit themselves. Will they provision another chimp? Here again, it appears to be a matter of indifference to the actor what happens to the would-be recipient.

In order to mimic the structure of the lung cancer modeling problem described before, I want to consider the following experiment, which is inspired by Silk *et al.* (2005) and by Jensen *et al.* (2006). The point is not that this is a good experimental design; rather, I want to start exploring how model selection ideas apply in intentional psychology. When it is time for a meal, an actor and a second chimp ("the other") are in facing cages. The actor has the option of producing the four outcomes shown in Table 13.3. Actors can cause food to be provided to both self and other, just to self, just to other, or to neither. The four outcomes are equally easy for actors to achieve and donating to the other chimp does not affect the amount of food that actors obtain for themselves. Suppose the frequencies of these four types of behavior are those given in Table 13.3.

Now let's consider some models of the chimps' behaviors that are expressed in terms of the probabilistic parameters shown in Table 13.4: "b" represents the probability of performing an action that provides food to neither self nor other; "*s*" is the probability of performing an action that provides benefit to self; "*a*" is the probability of performing an action that provides benefit to others; "*i*" is an interaction term.

(Null)	$s = a = i = 0$. The value of b is left open.
(Pure selfishness)	$a = i = 0$. The values of b and s are left open.
(Pure altruism)	$s = i = 0$. The values of b and a are left open.
(Additive motivational pluralism)	$i = 0$. The values of b, s, and a are left open.
(Interactive motivational pluralism)	The values of b, s, a, and i are left open.

The Null model says that chimps are "nihilists": they care neither about self nor other. The next two models, Pure Selfishness and Pure Altruism, are both monistic models: they say that chimps care only about self or only about others. The last two models are pluralistic: they say that chimps care about both self and other (Sober and Wilson [1998]). As before, the most complex model can achieve perfect fit-to-data. Nonetheless, depending on the frequency data and the sample size, it may turn out that Pure Selfishness is the model that receives the best AIC score.

5. MODEL EVALUATION VERSUS HYPOTHESIS TESTING

Jensen *et al.* (2006) touch on a possibility that can arise in any study, one that I think shows that the comparative and instrumentalist framework of model selection theory is superior to the accept/reject framework of conventional Neyman–Pearson hypothesis testing. Their experiments led them to conclude that chimps do not have other-directed preferences (at least when it comes to food sharing in the kind of circumstance they investigated). This conclusion was based on pooling data from all the chimps in the study. This leaves it open that when chimps are considered one by one (each participated in multiple experiments that each involved a number of trials), the evidence may indicate that some of them have other-directed preferences. Indeed, Jensen *et al.* (2006, p. 1019) say that "two of the six actors showed some possible signs of altruism."[4]

---

[4] Jensen *et al.* (2006) note that "these individuals were also the only two individuals who begged from, or harassed, the recipients" and speculate that the two chimps who provisioned others may have

This illustrates a paradoxical possibility that can arise in Neyman–Pearson hypothesis testing. You are testing Pure Selfishness against Motivational Pluralism. If you pool your data, you conclude that the chimps are egoists rather than pluralists. But if you consider the chimps one by one, constructing a different pair of models for each, you conclude that some are egoists while others are motivational pluralists. Neyman–Pearson theory sanctions both conclusions. This is odd: how can it make sense to accept egoism and reject pluralism for *all* the chimps but to do the reverse for *some* of them? Shifting to a model selection framework provides a solution to this puzzle. There are two prediction problems you might contemplate. One is predicting a new set of pooled data from the six chimps (or from six new chimps drawn from the same population); the other is predicting the separate outcomes on new experiments on each of six chimps. It is not paradoxical that different models might be better in different prediction tasks.

6. HIGHER AND LOWER

The principle of conservatism, like Morgan's canon, describes a preference concerning *kinds* of parameters, not *numbers* of parameters. It says that a model that postulates only lower-level intentionality is preferable to one that postulates higher-level intentionality if both fit the data equally well. This principle does not care if the lower-level model has a very large number of adjustable parameters while the higher-level model has only a few. It is hard to see how this principle can make sense from the point of view of model selection theory. Consider the lung cancer example. Smoking is one possible cause and asbestos exposure is another; the model that says that only smoking makes a difference is more parsimonious than a model that says that both do; and the two monistic models (Only Smoking and Only Asbestos) are equally parsimonious. Higher and lower kinds of causes don't matter.

Not only does AIC not care about the number of kinds of causes; it also doesn't care about numbers of causes (unless this count is mirrored in the number of adjustable parameters). I suppose that the additive and the interactive models of the causes of lung cancer both postulate two

---

expected the recipients of their largesse to have given them food. The point the authors are making here pertains to whether these two chimps have ultimate or merely instrumental other-directed preferences (Sober and Wilson [1998]). It does not undercut the conclusion that these chimps have other-directed preferences. The experiments addressed the latter issue and did not address the question of ultimate versus instrumental.

causes, smoking and asbestos exposure. The point is that they differ in their number of adjustable parameters, and that is what matters.

Increasing the number of causes in a model need not increase the number of adjustable parameters; everything depends on how those new causes are modeled. Consider the following example from genetics. Suppose you suspect that the three genotypes (*AA*, *Aa*, *aa*) found at a locus may influence an organism's probability of surviving to adulthood. One of the models you consider has two parameters (*b* and *d*); it says that $\Pr(\text{surviving}|aa) = b$, $\Pr(\text{surviving}|Aa) = b + d$, and $\Pr(\text{surviving}|AA) = b + 2d$. You then wish to consider the possibility that *n* loci, each with two alleles, affect survivorship. It isn't true that every *n*-locus model must have more than two parameters. Consider a model that says that at each locus, the organism has zero, one, or two "plus" alleles and that the probability of surviving is an additive function of the number of plus alleles: $\Pr(\text{surviving}/i \text{ plus alleles}) = b + id$. There may be *n* causes of survivorship (the *n* loci), but there are just two parameters.

If we drop the fixation on "higher" and "lower," a better formulation of the principle of conservatism becomes available: a model that postulates only lower-order intentionality (using *n* parameters to do so) is better than a model that postulates *both* lower-order intentionality (using *n* parameters) *and* higher-order intentionality (using *m* additional parameters) if the two models fit the data equally well. However, if introducing higher-level intentionality permits one to have *fewer* parameters overall while still fitting the data equally well, parsimony will speak in favor of introducing higher-level intentionality. This possibility will be discussed soon.

7. IDENTIFIABILITY

To apply AIC to a model *M*, there must be a unique maximum likelihood estimate for each of the parameters in *M*. When this fails to be true, the model is said to be *unidentifiable*. Here's a simple example. Suppose you heat a kettle on your stove to different temperatures and measure how much pressure there is in the kettle at each temperature. You do this *n* times and display your *n* observations as *n* data points in Cartesian coordinates, the *x*-axis representing temperature, the *y*-axis representing pressure. You now face a curve-fitting problem. What is the general relationship between temperature and pressure in your kettle? You want to draw a line in the *x-y* plane. Which line should you draw?

You should consider various models. One of them might be the linear model LIN, which says that $y = mx + b + e$. This model has three adjustable parameters, the last one being an error term that allows you to represent the possibility that your thermometer and pressure gauge may be subject to error. If you have a large number of data points, there is a single straight line that fits the data best; this is L(LIN). But suppose you have just one data point. There are infinitely many straight lines that pass exactly through this point. They make different predictions about new data. Since there is no such thing as *the* best-fitting straight line, the problem of estimating how accurately LIN will predict new data when fitted to old cannot be addressed. LIN is not identifiable. In general, for a model with n adjustable parameters to be identifiable, you need more than n data points. In practice, scientists recommend that you restrict your evaluation to models that have far fewer parameters than the number of observations you have (see, for example, Burnham and Anderson [2002]).

In the lung cancer example and also in the present example about pressure and temperature, you observe the values of candidate causal variables and also the values of the effect term. However, in cognitive science, you can't observe the beliefs and desires and other mental states that individuals have, though you can observe their behavior. How, then, is model selection theory applicable in this science?

In the experiment I invented on food sharing, you observe the frequencies of four types of meal-time behavior. You don't observe the chimp's preferences. However, this isn't necessary. Rather, for each model M, you need to find a quantitative representation of the preferences allowed by M that renders the observations maximally probable, thereby finding $L(M)$. For example, the model of Pure Selfishness makes the observations maximally probable when it sets $b = 0.02$ and $s = 0.45$. The second of these parameters represents how much chimps prefer receiving food themselves rather than going without. To find L(Pure Selfishness), what is required is not that

$$\Pr(\text{Pure Selfishness} \ \& \ s = 0.45 | \text{data}) \text{ is high}$$

or that

$$\Pr(s = 0.45 | \text{Pure Selfishness} \ \& \ \text{data}) \text{ is high,}$$

but only the more modest thesis that

$$\Pr(\text{data} | \text{Pure Selfishness} \ \& \ s = 0.45)$$
$$> \Pr(\text{data} | \text{Pure Selfishness} \ \& \ s = x), \text{ for any } x \neq 0.45.$$

Seeing that this inequality is true does not require that you find the model of Pure Selfishness plausible.

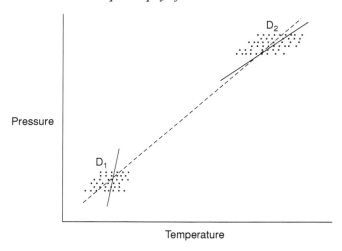

Figure 13.1 The disunified model DIS fits the two data sets D_1 and D_2 better than the unified model UNI does. L(DIS) is depicted by two solid lines, L(UNI) by a single dashed line, and data points by dots.

8. PARSIMONY, UNIFICATION, AND ORDERS OF INTENTIONALITY

The model selection approach to parsimony helps explain why unification is a theoretical virtue. Consider a unified model that applies the same n parameters to multiple data sets and a disunified model that applies a different set of n parameters to each data set. The unified model is more parsimonious, so if the two models fit the data about equally well, a model selection criterion such as AIC will estimate that the unified model can be expected to have greater predictive accuracy (Forster and Sober [1994]).

Figure 13.1 represents a simple example. Suppose the experiment you run on the kettle in your kitchen produces the two data sets D_1 and D_2. Consider the following two models:

(UNI) $y = mx + b + e$.

(DIS) $y = m_1 x + b_1 + e_1$ for the first data set.

$y = m_2 x + b_2 + e_2$ for the second data set.

The unified model has three adjustable parameters; the disunified model has six. Depending on the models' fit to data, UNI may receive the better AIC score.

This difference between unified and disunified models is the key, I believe, to understanding how the model selection framework applies to

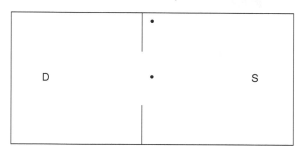

Figure 13.2 The subordinate chimp S can see both food items (represented by dots); the dominant chimp D can see just one. From Hare *et al.* (2000).

Table 13.5. *Frequencies of events in four experiments (Hare et al.*
[2000, 2001])

1	$f(S$ takes $x \mid$ an opaque barrier is between D and $x) = f_{1a}$	$f_{1a} > f_{1b}$
	$f(S$ takes $x \mid x$ is out in the open$) = f_{1b}$	
2	$f(S$ takes $x \mid$ a transparent barrier is between D and $x) = f_{2a}$	$f_{2a} \leq f_{2b}$
	$f(S$ takes $x \mid x$ is out in the open$) = f_{2b}$	
3	$f(S$ takes $x \mid$ only S was present during food placement$) = f_{3a}$	$f_{3a} > f_{3b}$
	$f(S$ takes $x \mid S$ and D both present during food placement$) = f_{3b}$	
4	$f(S$ takes $x \mid S$ was present during food placement, D was not present though another dominant individual was$) = f_{4a}$	$f_{4a} > f_{4b}$
	$f(S$ takes $x \mid S$ *and* D are both present during food placement$) = f_{4b}$	

S is a subordinate chimp, D is a dominant chimp, and x is a food item. In all the experiments, S and D both have the opportunity to try to grab food.

issues about orders of intentionality. Consider, for example, the experiments conducted by Hare *et al.* (2000, 2001) in which a subordinate chimp chooses which food items it will attempt to grab while a dominant chimp is present. In the first experiment (depicted in Figure 13.2), one food item is out in the open where both individuals can see it while the other food item is visible only to the subordinate (because there is an opaque barrier between the dominant and that food item). The result is that subordinates tend to go for the food item that the dominant individual cannot see. Hare *et al.* ran other experiments, accumulating the kind of frequency data represented in Table 13.5. For example, they used a transparent barrier instead of one that is opaque, and found that subordinates do not preferentially go for the object in front of that barrier. They also dispensed with barriers entirely and compared what subordinates do when they alone have watched where food is hidden and what subordinates do when they and a dominant both watch. Hare *et al.* defend the hypothesis that subordinates decide what to do by forming beliefs about what the dominant chimp has and has not seen. (See Fitzpatrick [chapter 14] for further discussion.)

If you look at these experiments one by one, it isn't hard to invent a first-order explanation for *each*; what is more difficult is inventing a single first-order explanation that works for *all* (Tomasello and Call [2006], p. 371).[5] In contrast, a unified explanation is easy to achieve if you resort to a second-order hypothesis. But so what? The two interpretations *seem* to fit the data equally well and they *seem* not to disagree with each other about any possible observation. And why is the fact that one explanation is unified while the other is disunified epistemologically significant (Heyes [1998])? Things look decidedly different when we view this problem through the lens of model selection theory. In fact, the two models fit the data *unequally* well, they assign *different* probabilities to what will happen in new experiments, and the difference in parsimony is relevant to estimating which will be more predictively accurate.

The simple point with which to begin is that the investigators pooled the behaviors of the different chimps that participated in each experiment, yielding a pair of frequencies for each experiment, as shown in Table 13.5. We must use these frequencies to estimate the values of the parameters used in two models. Here is a second-order model that has two adjustable parameters:

(Second) $\Pr(S \text{ takes } x \,|\, S \text{ believes that } D \text{ did not see } x) = p$

$\Pr(S \text{ takes } x \,|\, S \text{ believes that } D \text{ saw } x) = q$

The frequencies f_{1a}, f_{3a}, and f_{4a} help one estimate the first probability while f_{1b}, f_{3b}, f_{4b} as well as f_{2a} and f_{2b} bear on the second.

How should a first-order model be formulated? Here's an example to consider:

(First) $Pr(S \text{ takes } x \,|\, S \text{ believes that an opaque barrier is}$
            between D and $x) = p_1$

$Pr(S \text{ takes } x \,|\, S \text{ believes that no opaque barrier is}$
            between D and $x) = q_1$

$Pr(S \text{ takes } x \,|\, S \text{ believes that a transparent barrier is}$
            between D and $x) = p_2$

[5] Lurz (2009) proposes such a unified first-order account and describes as an alternative experimental protocol for distinguishing second-order accounts from their complementary first-order rivals.

$Pr(S$ takes $x \mid S$ believes that no transparent barrier is

between D and $x) = q_2$

$Pr(S$ takes $x \mid S$ believes that D was not present during

food placement) $= p_3$

$Pr(S$ takes $x \mid S$ believes that D was present during food

placement) $= q_3$

Data from the first experiment is relevant to estimating the first pair of parameters, data from the second experiment is relevant to estimating the second pair, and data from the third and fourth experiments is relevant to estimating the third. Since First has more adjustable parameters, it will fit the data better than Second will. However, it may turn out that the simpler model receives the better AIC score.[6]

In applying the model selection framework to First and Second, you need to find maximum likelihood estimates of parameters that represent $Pr(A \mid B)$ by attending to frequency data concerning $f(A \mid P)$, where A is an action, B is a belief state, and P is a physical property of the experiment (e.g., where food items are located). How can these data be used to estimate these probabilities? The axioms of probability entail that

$$Pr(A \mid P) = Pr(A \mid B \& P)Pr(B \mid P) + Pr(A \mid -B \& P)Pr(-B \mid P).$$

If P, B, and A form a causal chain, with B screening off P from A, which means $Pr(A \mid P \& B) = Pr(A \mid B)$ and $Pr(A \mid P \& -B) = Pr(A \mid -B)$, this equality simplifies to

$$Pr(A \mid P) = Pr(A \mid B)Pr(B \mid P) + Pr(A \mid -B)Pr(-B \mid P).$$

If we adopt the assumption that $Pr(B \mid P) = 1$, which entails that $Pr(-B \mid P) = 0$, we obtain

$$Pr(A \mid P) = Pr(A \mid B),$$

which allows $Pr(A \mid B)$ to be estimated from $f(A \mid P)$. The assumption that $Pr(B \mid P) = 1$ means that the physical circumstances of the experiment, along with the chimp's other mental states,[7] *determine* what its belief state will be. Perhaps there is a way to secure identifiability without making this assumption, but I don't see what it would be. Notice that the assumption that $Pr(B \mid P) = 1$ reduces the number of *adjustable* parameters in both

---

[6] This kind of argument also applies to the comparison of zeroth- and first-order models of intentionality.

[7] It is assumed that subordinates want food and don't want to be punished by dominants.

models. The data are no longer asked to supply estimates for parameters that describe $Pr(B|P)$ but need only do so for parameters of the form $Pr(A|B)$.

I have no stake in claiming that First is the best first-order model nor that Second is the best model of second-order. First and Second are just the examples I have used to illustrate how model selection applies to the problem at hand. These models differ by four parameters. If there were more qualitatively different data sets from additional experiments, the difference in parsimony between the first- and second-order models might increase. In model selection, the difference in parsimony defines a threshold: it indicates how much better the more complex model must fit the data for it to have the better AIC score. The larger the difference in parsimony, the higher the bar is set.

How does this comparison of First and Second connect with the assumption, mentioned earlier, that an organism that has second-order beliefs also must have first-order beliefs? This assumption does not mean that a second-order model must have *parameters* that represent the impact of first-order beliefs. By the same token, even if an organism with a psychology must extract energy from its environment, it does not follow that a psychological model must contain parameters that represent those energetic processes. The Second model does not contain parameters that represent any first-order beliefs, though the model is perfectly consistent with the thought that second-order beliefs occur only when they are caused by first-order beliefs. The two models I have considered are shown in Figure 13.3.[8]

Does it make sense to insist that we should not compare First and Second but should instead compare First with a new model that has parameters that represent both first- and second-order beliefs? This new model, which I'll call First+Second, is represented in Figure 13.4.

To consider the competition between First and First+Second in a model selection framework, we need to figure out how each can be rendered identifiable. If we pursue a strategy similar to the one I described in connection with the competition between First and Second, the result will be that there is no real difference between First+Second and Second: if we assume $Pr(B_i|P) = 1$ and that $Pr(B|B_i) = 1$, the only adjustable parameters that remain in First+Second are of the form $Pr(A|B)$. Understood in this way, First+Second is in fact more parsimonious than First. That may seem strange, but the question remains of how the two models can be identified without our being driven to that conclusion. There is another problem with

---

[8] See the discussion of thirst in Whiten (1996, p. 284); see also Sober (1998a).

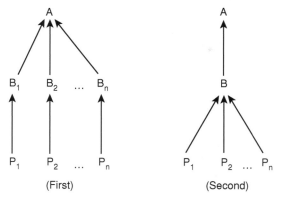

Figure 13.3 The second-order model says that the diverse physical circumstances P_1, $P_2, \ldots, P_n$ all cause the same second-order belief state B, which in turn causes action A. The first-order model says that different physical circumstances cause different first-order belief states $B_1, B_2, \ldots, B_n$, which each cause A.

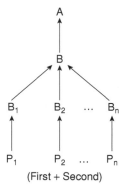

Figure 13.4 The Model First+Second says that different physical circumstances P_1, $P_2, \ldots, P_n$ cause different first-order beliefs $B_1, B_2, \ldots, B_n$, which each cause the second-order belief B, which in turn causes the action A.

rejecting the comparison of First and Second and insisting that the only relevant comparison is of First with First+Second, where First+Second is required to have adjustable parameters for all the beliefs it mentions. To do so is to refuse to consider the possibility that a model that introduces second-order intentionality might in fact be more parsimonious than one that restricts itself to first-order intentionality. Think how unmotivated it would be to take that stance in connection with the competition between a zeroth- and a first-order model. Do we really want to say that introducing intentionality cannot simplify the resulting model? If it can, some of the parameters representing zeroth-order states must be dropped.[9]

9. ANTI-REALISM

Responding to philosophers who interpret him as an instrumentalist, Dennett (1991b, p. 29) says that he advocates "a mild and intermediate form of realism" about intentional psychology and that he thinks it isn't useful to try to locate his position in the dichotomous choice between realism and instrumentalism (p. 51). Even so, there are instrumentalist themes in his essay that connect it with ideas from model selection theory. Dennett (p. 36) emphasizes the role of simplified idealizations in science and sees this as the right context in which to understand folk and scientific psychology. Even though idealized models are false, they can be useful in making predictions. Another point of contact occurs in Dennett's discussion of "real patterns." What is the difference between a finite data set that has a pattern and one that is random? Dennett (p. 32) employs an idea from computer science according to which an n-member sequence is random if it cannot be compressed – if it cannot be generated by a rule that requires fewer than n symbols to state. If the sequence is random, the most succinct way to generate it is by brute enumeration. Minimum description length has developed into a criterion for model selection; it has been given an instrumentalist interpretation and it has been related to model selection criteria like AIC (Grünwald [2007]).

In spite of these links, there are some differences between the way I've understood instrumentalism in connection with model selection and Dennett's (1991b) discussion of realism and instrumentalism in intentional psychology. Dennett frames the philosophical question as follows. It is agreed that folk psychology is predictively successful. The question is how one should explain why this is so. Is the best explanation that beliefs and desires exist, or that they are useful fictions, or is there a coherent third alternative to consider? Whatever the best answer is to this question, it is not one that model selection theory addresses. This is because the Akaike's framework allows one to be an instrumentalist about *models*; it doesn't support instrumentalism about other propositions. A "model" (in the sense of that term used in statistics) is a special kind of beast. It contains

---

[9] This bears on the criticisms that Povinelli and Vonk (2006) make of Hare *et al.*'s experiments. See Fitzpatrick (chapter 14) for discussion.

adjustable parameters that can be fitted to data. Not every statement is a model in this sense. The statement that physical objects exist is not a model, nor is the statement that beliefs and desires exist. Not every consequence of a model is a model. Consider the models of lung cancer discussed earlier. One may want to be an instrumentalist about these models while at the same time being a realist about smoking, asbestos exposure, and lung cancer. Surely there is no reason to regard smoking, asbestos, and cancer as useful fictions. By parity of reasoning, instrumentalism about models that postulate beliefs and desires does not entail instrumentalism about beliefs and desires.

The thought that instrumentalism is appropriate for some propositions but not for others finds another application in the distinction between models and fitted models. I have described AIC as a device for estimating the predictive accuracy of a model M, but it is equally true that it estimates the closeness to the truth of $L(M)$, when closeness is measured by Kulback-Leibler distance. This is why I have defended the mixed philosophy of *instrumentalism for models, realism for fitted models* (Sober [2008]).

If AIC is a device for estimating a model's predictive accuracy, where does that leave the issue of explanation? Philosophers often object to Dennett's intentional stance (instrumentalistically understood) because they think it robs intentional psychology of the power to explain behavior. But surely an idealized model can be explanatory even though it is false. This doesn't just mean that it would be explanatory if it were true. That faint praise applies to models that are wildly wrong. Good idealizations can help us understand even when we know they are false. Those who think that explanations must be true may insist that what does the explaining is not the false idealization I but the true statement that I is a good idealization. Even so, instrumentalism about models does not mean that models cannot help explain.

The connection between the Akaike framework and Dennett's "mild and intermediate realism" is worth exploring further, but I will not attempt to do so here. The observation I would make in conclusion is that the framework offers something to both instrumentalists and realists. Instrumentalists can see the point of false models as predictive and explanatory devices and realists can see the point of comparing fitted models in order to judge which are closest to the truth. And both can see why parsimony matters. This last dividend may be the one most relevant to cognitive scientists who puzzle over what the principle of conservatism means and why it should be taken seriously.

CHAPTER 14

The primate mindreading controversy: a case study in simplicity and methodology in animal psychology

Simon Fitzpatrick

I. INTRODUCTION

What, if anything, do non-human primates (henceforth, "primates") understand about the minds of other agents? Can they mentally represent and reason about the mental states of others? If they can, what kinds of mental states can they represent (e.g., perceptions, goals, intentions, beliefs) and what kinds of reasoning about mental states are they capable of? These are the central questions in the field of primate "mindreading," or "theory of mind." However, some thirty years after Premack and Woodruff (1978) posed such questions, there remains very little consensus on how we should answer them.

Much of the recent debate has centred on an ongoing controversy over whether primates are capable of reasoning about basic aspects of the visual perspective and perceptual awareness of others. Several researchers claim that recent behavioral experiments provide strong evidence for such a mindreading capacity in several primate species. Other prominent researchers, however, vigorously deny that these studies provide any evidence at all for mindreading.

One issue that has played a prominent role in this controversy and throughout the history of the debate over primate mindreading concerns the relative "simplicity" or "parsimony" (these terms are typically used interchangeably) of mindreading and non-mindreading explanations of behavior. In interpreting the available data, both proponents and skeptics about primate mindreading have argued that their chosen explanation is "simpler" or "more parsimonious" than the alternatives, and hence should be preferred. In both instances, considerations of simplicity have been

Thanks to George Botterill, Stephen Laurence, Jane Suilin Lavelle, Robert Lurz, Elliott Sober, and the audience for the session on "Animal Minds" at ISHPSSB 2007 for helpful discussion and suggestions. The UK Arts Humanities Research Council provided financial support through a postdoctoral fellowship associated with the AHRC Culture and the Mind Project.

invoked to bolster the case for a particular hypothesis in the face of seemingly equivocal data.

My aim in this chapter is to look at the role that such appeals to simplicity have played in this controversy as a case study for thinking about the proper place of simplicity considerations in inferring cognitive processes in non-human animals, and in science more generally (see also Sober, chapter 13). After providing some background to the controversy and describing the appeals to simplicity that have been made, I will pose some problems for such appeals, which call into question the appropriateness of bringing in simplicity considerations when evaluating behavioral data. I will then outline a general philosophical account of simplicity, which, I will argue, makes the best sense of what is going on in the recent controversy over primate mindreading. In doing this, I hope to shed new light on the nature of the evidence for primate mindreading, and on how future work might be able to resolve this controversy.

2. PERSPECTIVE-TAKING IN PRIMATES?

2.1. Some background

Mindreading is a form of *higher-order* cognition, involving reasoning processes and mental states whose contents concern other agents' mental states. In humans, at least, such reasoning plays a key role in our ability to predict and explain the behavior of other agents. A central area of research for comparative psychologists looking for possible mindreading capacities in primates and other non-human animals concerns *visual perspective-taking*, in particular, reasoning about what others can and cannot see and how others are likely to behave in a given situation based on what they perceive. Primates often behave in ways that seem to suggest such reasoning: for example, primates will often hide contested food items from others' view (Byrne and Whiten [1988]) and follow the gaze of others to locate the object of attention (Tomasello and Call [1997]).

However, the problem is that such observations also seem to be consistent with an alternative hypothesis: instead of being *mind*readers primates could just be *behavior*-readers. In contrast to mindreading, behavior-reading involves purely first-order reasoning about non-mental phenomena, such as the regularities in others' behavior. For example, from past experience a chimpanzee might learn that a competitor will be less likely to take a food item if she places it behind certain kinds of objects. Similarly, she might learn that certain movements of a conspecific's eyes toward a location are correlated with the presence of an interesting object at that location. The key aim of experimentalists has thus been to develop behavioral tests for mindreading that can rule out purely first-order explanations for success in the relevant task. This project has, however, proved to be extremely difficult (Heyes [1998]).

Moreover, in the late 1990s there emerged experimental results that seemed to provide evidence *against* perspective-taking abilities in primates. Famously, Povinelli and Eddy (1996) presented chimpanzees with a choice of begging for food from one of two experimenters: one who could see them and another who could not (e.g., because she was blindfolded or had a bucket covering her head). Povinelli and Eddy found that even after repeated trials subjects begged just as much from unseeing as from seeing experimenters, suggesting that chimpanzees do not reason about what others can and cannot see.

However, in recent years these results have been challenged on method-ological grounds. Since the social life of chimpanzees is dominated by *competition* for food rather than *communicative-cooperative* interactions of the sort involved in Povinelli and Eddy's study, it has been argued that subjects may have failed to perform well in this and other similar tasks, not because they lack the ability to reason about others' perceptions, but because they did not properly understand the task (Hare *et al.* [2000]). This concern provided the impetus for Hare, Call, and Tomasello to develop a more naturalistic approach to investigating chimpanzees' understanding of visual perspective.

2.2. Food competition

The starting assumption for Hare, Call, and Tomasello was that if primates possess mindreading capacities, these would be more likely to show them-selves in competitive situations that closely resemble their natural social interactions. In the first of a series of studies, Hare *et al.* (2000) placed a subordinate and dominant chimpanzee in cages on opposite sides of a middle room that contained two pieces of food: one visible to both chim-panzees, the other placed behind an opaque barrier and only visible to the subordinate. They were initially prevented from entering the middle room by guillotine doors, which, when slightly raised, allowed them to see each other and the layout of the room. They were then released, with the subordinate given a slight head start. Dominant chimpanzees tend to take all the food that is available to them and punish subordinates who challenge them. So the prediction was that if subordinates are capable of reasoning about the visual perspective of others, they should preferentially target the piece of food behind the barrier, which the dominant cannot see. This is exactly what happened.

Controls were introduced for various behavior-reading hypotheses. Subordinates were given a head start to help rule out the hypothesis that they merely chose the food that the dominant *did not* go for. Also in some conditions the dominant's door was completely closed until the subordinate made a choice to go for one of the pieces. Subordinates still preferred the hidden food; so they could not have merely reacted to the dominant's behavior upon being released. In another condition the opaque barrier was replaced with a *transparent* one. Here subordinates did not show a preference, thus seeming to be aware that the dominant had visual access to both pieces of food and ruling out the hypothesis that subordinates merely prefer food behind barriers.

In a follow-up study (Hare *et al.* [2001]) the middle room contained two opaque barriers. A single piece of food was placed on the subordinate's side of one of the barriers, with the experimenters varying whether the subordinate and the dominant or just the subordinate saw this. In a control condition a dominant that witnessed the food being placed was switched with a dominant that had not, just before the subordinate was released. The result was that subordinates tended to go for the food more when the competitor had *not* witnessed the placement of the food.

Hare *et al.* have thus concluded that chimpanzees *are* in fact sensitive to what others can and cannot see and also to at least some aspects of what others *know* about a situation based on what they have and have not seen in the recent past.

Subsequent work has expanded on these initial studies in various ways. Flombaum and Santos (2005) have produced similar results with rhesus monkeys, suggesting that it is not just apes that have such capacities. Melis *et al.* (2006) gave chimpanzees the opportunity to steal food from an experimenter who was inside a booth covered by opaque glass on three sides, apart from a slit at the front. On the left and right hand sides of the booth were holes connected to tunnels through which subjects could reach into the booth. One tunnel was transparent, the other opaque. During the test condition the experimenter placed food next to the ends of both tunnels and then stared directly ahead. In a control condition the experimenter placed food next to the tunnels and walked away. From the first trial subjects had a preference for grabbing food through the opaque tunnel in the test condition but *not* in the control condition. Melis *et al.* conclude that this shows that chimpanzees engage in quite subtle mentalistic reasoning: even though the experimenter has visual access to both pieces of food, chimpanzees use the opaque tunnel to conceal their *reach* to the food, giving the experimenter less chance to take it away.

2.3. Povinelli and Vonk's critique

While Hare *et al.* and colleagues suspect that primates lack more sophisticated human mindreading capacities, such as the ability to reason about false beliefs (Call and Tomasello [2008]), these new studies are claimed to show that visual perspective-taking is at least one important mindreading capacity that is *not* uniquely human. A number of theorists, however, are extremely skeptical about these claims. Most strikingly, Povinelli and Vonk (2006) have argued that these studies are incapable *in principle* of providing any evidence at all for mindreading.

The problem, according to Povinelli and Vonk, is that since mental states are not directly observable, subordinates can only infer particular mental states in dominants based on features of the situation that they *can* observe. For example, in the Hare *et al.* (2000) study the subordinate can only infer that the dominant can or cannot see the food based on whether or not an opaque barrier stands in between the dominant's eyes and the food. Povinelli and Vonk claim that there is therefore a purely first-order explanation for the results: subjects make a direct inference from these observable cues to a behavioral prediction *without* any reasoning about others' mental states. Subordinates could, for instance, reason according to a behavioral rule (acquired by learning or known innately) which says that dominants are less likely to go for a particular food item if an opaque barrier stands in between their eyes and the food. Similarly, in the Hare *et al.* (2001) study subordinates may reason that dominants are less likely to go for food behind an opaque barrier if they were not present when the food was placed at that location.

Since these experiments do not control for this possibility they are, according to Povinelli and Vonk, completely *irrelevant* to the question of whether primates understand anything about the minds of others. If we are to have a genuine behavioral test for perspective-taking a very different kind of experimental paradigm will have to be developed – one that does not give subjects any observable cues that could be used to predict behavior.[1]

---

[1] This conclusion is meant to apply to *any* study where the relevant differences in others' mental states and behavior correlate with observable differences between conditions. Povinelli and Vonk do suggest alternative paradigms, which they claim avoid this problem, though it is far from clear why these are not open to the same criticisms leveled at the Hare *et al.* studies.

2.4. Which is simpler?

For the most part, Hare *et al.* have been prepared to concede that Povinelli and Vonk's alternative explanation for their results is not directly ruled out by their control conditions. Nonetheless, they insist that they still provide strong evidence for visual perspective-taking and that Povinelli and Vonk's alternative explanation is extremely ad hoc. But why do they claim this? It is here that considerations of simplicity/parsimony have been seen to enter the fray. For example, Tomasello and Call (2006) argue that:

> The results of each experiment may be explained by postulating some behavioral rule that individuals have learned that does not involve an understanding of seeing. But the postulated rule must be different in each case, and most of these do not explain more than one experiment. This patchiness of coverage gives this kind of explanation a very *ad hoc* feeling, especially since there is rarely any concrete evidence that animals have had the requisite experiences to learn the behavioral rule – there is just a theoretical possibility. It is thus more plausible to hypothesize that apes really do know what others do and do not see in many circumstances. (p. 371)

Tomasello and Call do not claim to be proposing a simplicity argument here, but this is primarily how their argument has been interpreted.[2] Their first claim is that though explanations of the sort proposed by Povinelli and Vonk can in principle be offered for each of their results, since the relevant observable cues and behavioral predictions are different in each experiment, skeptics will need to posit a huge number of different rules governing subordinates' reasoning across all the cases. For instance, different rules will be required in the condition where the food is already behind an opaque barrier, the condition where the dominant observes food being placed behind an opaque barrier, and the condition where the food is behind a transparent barrier. An entirely different kind of rule will also be needed in the Melis *et al.* (2006) experiment, since here the competitor has a direct line of sight towards both pieces of food: the key thing for the subject is to conceal its *reach* from the experimenter. Skeptics will also need to explain how subjects have learnt each of these specific rules (or somehow possess them innately). The claim then seems to be that we can offer a *simpler*, more unified, explanation for the results by just

---

[2] According to Povinelli and Vonk (2006, p. 394) Hare *et al.* have claimed that "although it is possible that chimpanzees form concepts solely about behavior, the case for this is unproven, and they seem to imply that parsimony should push us toward assuming that they do, in fact, represent mental states."

granting chimpanzees a psychological understanding of visual perspective that underlies their reasoning in all the various conditions.[3]

This type of simplicity argument has had a long history in the debate over primate mindreading (see, e.g., Premack and Woodruff [1978]; Whiten [1996]). The idea is that attributing higher-level mentalistic concepts (such as a concept of *visual awareness*) allows us to avoid attributing to subjects a cluster of rules that specify a one-to-one mapping between particular observable cues and predictions of how others are going to behave in specific circumstances.

Povinelli and Vonk (2006), however, are not impressed by this kind of argument:

> [R]easoning about mental states must entail observing and reasoning about behavior (in all its subtleties) and, on the basis of such observed features, generating and reasoning about representations of unobserved mental states. Thus the capacity to reason about mental states does not somehow relieve the burden of representing the massive nuances of behavior or the statistical invariances that sort them into more and less related groups. In either event, these behavioral abstractions must be represented . . . [Thus] there is no sense in which a system that makes inferences about behavioral concepts alone provides a *less* parsimonious account of behavior than a system that must make all of those same inferences *plus* generate inferences about mental states. (pp. 393–394, emphasis in original)

Since mindreading must involve reasoning about behavior and other observable features of the situation – due to the fact that mental states must be inferred indirectly – the only difference between mindreading and behavior-reading is that the latter process skips the middle step of inferring and representing others' mental states before generating a behavioral prediction. Consequently, a mindreading explanation must in fact be *less* parsimonious than a behavior-reading explanation.

Povinelli and Vonk do not explicitly claim that this greater parsimony gives us a reason to prefer a behavior-reading explanation of Hare *et al.*'s results. However, they are clearly motivated by parsimony considerations since they repeatedly claim that it is "sufficient" to explain the current data by attributing chimpanzees a capacity for behavior-reading alone. Other skeptics are more explicit: after replicating the results of Hare *et al.* (2000) with marmosets (a species of new world monkey), Burkart and Heschl (2007) claim that "at least at the present state of evidence, the more parsimonious explanation seems to be that they deal with a directed gaze

---

[3] Editor's note: See Sober (chapter 13) for an explanation of how, on model selection theory, a unified mindreading hypothesis could turn out to be simpler than a disunified behavior-reading hypothesis.

without understanding visual perspective" (p. 468). This is in spite of the fact that their results are perfectly consistent with perspective-taking.

How should this dispute be adjudicated? Should we side with proponents like Tomasello and Call, with skeptics like Povinelli and Vonk, or with neither of them? My aim in the rest of the chapter is to focus on the logic of these conflicting arguments and go some way towards answering these questions. My conclusion will be that Tomasello and Call's argument against Povinelli and Vonk does have a high degree of plausibility to it and that Povinelli and Vonk's criticisms are misguided. First, however, I want to pose some general problems for appeals to simplicity in this kind of context. Then in section 4 I will outline a philosophical account of simplicity that provides us with a productive framework for interpreting and evaluating these arguments.

3. SUBSTANCE OR PROCRASTINATION?

As we have seen, the controversy over the new food competition experiments has in part taken the form of a controversy over what is the "simplest"/"most parsimonious" explanation of subjects' behavior. In the absence of further data that might prove more decisive, both sides, it seems, explicitly or implicitly take simplicity considerations to provide an additional criterion that can be used to choose between competing hypotheses. However, they seem to have very different ideas of how such a criterion should be applied in this context.

Though the appropriateness of these kinds of simplicity arguments is normally just taken for granted, there are a number of serious worries that can be raised about the appeals to simplicity that have been made in this debate. To begin with, the notions of simplicity/parsimony involved here seem to be extremely slippery. If we look closely, the dispute between Tomasello and Call and Povinelli and Vonk highlights the fact that there are several *different* and *conflicting* respects in which hypotheses about the cognitive basis of primate social behavior could be said to be "simple" or "complex."

In their response to Tomasello and Call, Povinelli and Vonk view themselves as rebutting the claim that a mindreading explanation is more parsimonious than a behavior-reading explanation: a mindreading explanation cannot be more parsimonious because mindreading *entails* representing and reasoning about observables, but behavior-reading does not entail representing and reasoning about mental states. However, Tomasello and Call's claim is not concerned with whether or not subjects represent and reason about observable features, but rather the psychological *unity* of the explanation being offered. On their view we can unify the subjects' behavior in the different conditions by attributing to them a general concept of *visual awareness* that underlies their responses in all the conditions. Even though, as Povinelli and Vonk point out, applying this concept must involve representing and reasoning about observable features this does not undermine the claim that a behavior-reading account is less psychologically unified than a mindreading account, in the sense that no comparably general concept is activated in all the different conditions; instead there has to be a cluster of specific rules linking particular observations with predictions of others' behavior.

If this is right, it seems that we have two different kinds of simplicity here – *simplicity as psychological unity*, which seems to favor a mindreading account, and *simplicity as parsimony of mental representation*, which seems to favor a behavior-reading account. In fact, I suggest that a number of other different kinds of simplicity could equally be taken into consideration here; these also come to contrasting verdicts. For example:

- *Simplicity as (less) cognitive sophistication.* A long tradition in comparative psychology holds that the simplest explanation of animal behavior is the one that attributes to the animal the "lowest" or least sophisticated cognitive processes consistent with the available data.[4] Behavior-reading is usually regarded as a less sophisticated (and hence simpler) cognitive process than mindreading since it involves purely first-order reasoning and representation, while mindreading involves higher-order reasoning and representation. This is another, slightly different, kind of simplicity that seems to favor a behavior-reading account.

- *Simplicity as analogy.* Another common notion of simplicity in the literature is that the simplest explanation for similar behavior in different species is one that cites the operation of similar cognitive mechanisms. Thus, given that we would attribute perspective-taking abilities to a human that behaved in the same way as the Hare *et al.* subjects, it would seem that the simplest explanation of the similarity is that chimpanzees also have such capacities.

- *Simplicity as evolutionary parsimony.* De Waal (1991; see also Sober [2000]) has argued that when closely related species such as chimpanzees and humans are found to behave in similar ways it is simpler, evolutionarily

---

[4] A common symptom of this view is enthusiasm for a methodological principle known as *Morgan's Canon*, which has been widely seen as a simplicity principle: "In no case may we interpret an action as the outcome of the exercise of a higher psychical faculty, if it can be interpreted as the outcome of the exercise of one which stands lower in the psychological scale" (Morgan [1894], p. 53). See Fitzpatrick (2008) and Sober (chapter 13).

speaking, to posit *homologous* cognitive mechanisms in order to account for this similarity – shared mechanisms inherited from a common ancestor. The alternative is to posit different cognitive mechanisms that evolved independently of each other but nonetheless produce similar behavior. In this case de Waal would claim that the simplest explanation for the results is that a mechanism for visual perspective-taking was present in the common ancestor of humans and chimpanzees and is retained by both species.

Here we have several different and conflicting respects in which mindreading and behavior-reading explanations can each be seen as "simple" or "complex." This list could be extended indefinitely. For example there are many different ways in which we could assess the "amount of stuff" that psychological explanations have to posit: we could count the number of cognitive processes involved, the number of iterations of each cognitive process involved, the number of rules or principles involved in any given instance of reasoning, the number of steps involved in any reasoning process, etc.

This poses a very significant problem for an attempt to make sense of which direction simplicity considerations should take us in this context. It is not enough just to say that we should prefer "simpler" explanations of behavior – *which* aspects of the respective explanations are we to be concerned with when attempting to assess their relative simplicity? From discussions in the literature it is not at all clear why we should measure simplicity in one of these ways rather than any of the others. Nor is it clear how different kinds of simplicity should be balanced against each other – in principle there are many different ways of trading off a given amount of simplicity of kind X against a given amount of simplicity of kind Y with respect to the "overall" simplicity of the rival explanations. What we need, it seems, is a principled account of why we should value *any* of these putative simplicity properties and of what weight, if any, they should carry relative to each other.

This naturally focuses attention on another worry about these arguments. Both sides seem to assume that simplicity carries some degree of *epistemic* weight here: if one explanation is simpler than another this makes it more plausible, or somehow better supported by the data. But what *justification* is there for this? After all, there doesn't seem to be any a priori reason to think that simpler explanations are more likely to be true.

Similar sorts of worries about appeals to simplicity have been raised earlier in the literature. Heyes (1998) describes the various simplicity arguments that have been proposed in the primate mindreading debate as empty "procrastination." Here she echoes a general philosophical skepticism about simplicity. Though many scientists and philosophers have advocated principles of simplicity in theory choice, we do not have adequate answers to general versions of the worries just raised: how should the simplicity of theories be measured and what justification is there for preferring simple theories to less simple ones? Heyes takes the view that if the experimental data is open to both mindreading and behavior-reading interpretations, we should just be agnostic as to which hypothesis is correct until decisive evidence is found: "To answer Premack and Woodruff's question, we need more strong experiments, not more weak arguments" (Heyes [1998], p. 112).

Prima facie Heyes' skepticism with respect to simplicity does seem to have much to recommend it. It seems difficult to avoid the concern that all this talk of simplicity is just arcane bean-counting and of dubious relevance to the fundamental questions that these researchers are interested in – are primates capable of visual perspective-taking and do the food competition studies really provide evidence for such a capacity?

However, I want to resist dismissing all of the simplicity arguments that have featured in the primate literature as mere "procrastination." Tomasello and Call's argument in favor of a mindreading interpretation of their results *does* seem to have an important ring of plausibility to it, though the arguments of Povinelli and Vonk and Burkart and Heschl seem much less plausible. The problem then is to explain how there can be plausibility in some appeals to simplicity and not others, in a way that addresses, or somehow avoids, the worries about simplicity discussed above, and to supply a principled assessment of what bearing these considerations have on the broader debate about primate mindreading.

What I will do now is to describe my own view about the role of simplicity considerations in science, which, I will argue, can help us to resolve these issues.

4. THE DEFLATIONARY ACCOUNT OF SIMPLICITY

The general philosophical account of simplicity that I endorse is what I call the "deflationary account" (Fitzpatrick [2006]). This account represents a significant departure from the standard view that philosophers have taken on the role of simplicity in science. The standard view (among those who are not skeptics about simplicity) is that simplicity constitutes one of the central criteria that scientists do, and should, use for evaluating and choosing between rival theories: other things being equal, simple theories should be chosen over less simple ones. Simplicity is thus seen as a general *theoretical virtue*, alongside such things as empirical adequacy, consistency with established background theories, and so on.

The deflationary account departs from the standard view in that it denies that simplicity should be seen as a general theoretical virtue and criterion for theory choice *in its own right*. There is no adequate general justification for favoring simple theories over less simple ones. However, the claim is not that we are *never* justified in preferring "simple" theories to less "simple" ones. Rather the claim is that in cases where we do seem to be justified in preferring theories that are "simpler" in some particular respect, some *other* consideration is doing the real epistemic work. Typically, what is doing the real work are various background theoretical considerations, often specific to the scientific context at hand. So for instance the justification for preferring theory T_1 to T_2 comes not from the fact that T_1 is more "parsimonious," but because the specific additional entities that T_2 posits (and T_1 does not) are theoretically *implausible* – for example, they contradict or pose problems for accepted background theories in that domain. Thus on the deflationary account, we may be warranted in preferring theories that are "simpler" (in some particular respect) in some contexts but *not* in others. Moreover, the reason why we are warranted in one context may be very different from why we are warranted in another context. This is because different kinds of background consideration do the epistemic work in the different cases.

Broadly deflationary views of simplicity have been defended by philosophers such as Richard Boyd (1990), John Norton (2003), and, most notably, Elliott Sober (1990; this vol., chapter 13). Such a view, I think, has very significant advantages over more traditional accounts of simplicity. In particular it makes the problem of justification tractable, reducing it to the problem of explaining what are the other considerations that do the real work in specific cases where certain kinds of simplicity considerations seem to be epistemically motivating. This is a much less onerous problem than explaining how a completely general preference for "simplicity" can be justified across all scientific contexts. Moreover, the deflationary account provides a more accurate understanding of scientific practice. When reflecting on their methodology scientists often *misdescribe* highly context-specific preferences for theories with very specific kinds of properties as a general preference for "simple" theories. Thus the deflationary account provides us with a better understanding of the actual underlying reasons for preferring putatively "simpler" theories in real cases in science (for examples, see Fitzpatrick [2006]; Sober [1990]).

I will now argue that the deflationary account provides substantial illumination on the debate about simplicity and primate mindreading.[5] In so doing I will also illustrate the attractions of the deflationary account.

5. TOMASELLO AND CALL'S ARGUMENT REVISITED

I noted earlier that Tomasello and Call do not claim that their response to Povinelli and Vonk is a simplicity argument – indeed, they actually express similar skepticism to Heyes about such arguments (2006, pp. 380–381). However, it is no surprise that their argument has been understood in this way. They seem to be claiming that behavior-reading explanations just become too complicated when applied to a diverse range of situations in which subjects correctly anticipate others' behavior. In this respect the argument has been compared with a common simplicity argument against behaviorism: when patterns of behavior become very elaborate it is often simpler to ascribe sophisticated cognitive processes to organisms rather than having to postulate an enormous web of learnt associations between individual stimuli and responses.

Now, I think it is easy to make sense of this anti-behaviorist argument from a deflationary point of view. It is really a sort of *poverty of the stimulus* argument: as patterns of behavior become more elaborate – i.e., subjects respond adaptively to a wider range of situations, many of which are novel for them – associative learning explanations become increasingly implausible, not because the web of stimulus-response associations becomes too "complex," but because it is difficult to explain how subjects could have *acquired* the requisite associations.[6] The more subtle and specific these associations have to be and the more of them that have to be posited, the less tenable it becomes to claim that subjects will have reliably encountered all the environmental stimuli a behaviorist account would require in order for them to be acquired. Thus, more sophisticated cognitive machinery is required to adequately explain subjects' behavior.

---

[5] Sober (1998a, 2000; this vol., chapter 13) has also discussed issues surrounding simplicity and primate mindreading. My analysis of Tomasello and Call's argument in section 5 is different, but complimentary to Sober's (1998a) discussion of a similar argument from Whiten (1996). See also Sober (chapter 13) for application of a model selection framework to this debate.

[6] Poverty-of-the-stimulus arguments claim that the environmental input to a given set of cognitive mechanisms possessed by an organism underdetermines the demonstrated behavioral capacities of the organism. Thus *additional* cognitive structure – additional knowledge, concepts, or cognitive mechanisms – must be posited to explain adequately these capacities. Such arguments are most well known from Chomsky's work on human language acquisition (see Laurence and Margolis [2001]), but they have also played a significant role in arguments for sophisticated cognitive mechanisms in animals.

Tomasello and Call's argument is best understood in a similar fashion:[7] we cannot just *assume* that the Hare *et al.* subjects will have had experiences sufficient to acquire generalizations about others' behavior that would enable them to respond appropriately to the situations they are confronted with. Consider the subordinate chimpanzee that has to decide whether or not to go for food behind a transparent barrier. Suppose, as Hare *et al.* (2000) claim, that this situation is highly novel for subjects, so they "could not have had many opportunities to learn specific contingencies between [transparent] objects and the behavior of their groupmates" (p. 783). As I see it, Tomasello and Call's claim is that it is difficult to see how a behavior-reader who has no understanding of visual perception could predict that the relevant observable cue in this situation – the transparency of the barrier – is going to make a difference to the dominant's behavior without generalizing from past experience in similar situations. A mindreader, however, who possesses a concept of *visual awareness* might plausibly do without such prior experience. All it needs to do is reason about whether or not the dominant can *see* the food, and the transparency or opacity of the barrier is likely going to be a salient consideration for an agent that possesses such a higher-level concept. Plausibly, then, a mindreader could potentially respond appropriately in this situation even if it has never previously interacted with other agents in situations involving transparent barriers, or perhaps never seen a transparent barrier. But there is no reason to think that a behavior-reader could do this since it needs to have some basis for associating this observable cue with a behavioral outcome.

Mindreading is thus assumed to be more of a *generative* capacity than behavior-reading – allowing subjects to adapt to novel situations in a way that goes beyond the contingencies of their previous experience. Povinelli and Vonk object to this generative view of mindreading on the grounds that mental states can only be attributed to others based on a *prior* understanding of the correlations between particular observable features and others' behavior (recall the passage quoted in section 2.4). Discussing Hare *et al.* (2000) they claim that:

[T]he subordinate's reaction . . . can be explained either by the subject's possession of a concept about the statistical invariants that exist in head/eye/body orientation toward food, on the one hand, and future behavior, on the other, or all of that *plus* a representation of an unobservable mental state. (Povinelli and Vonk [2006], p. 396; emphasis in original)

---

[7] This is not to suggest that Povinelli and Vonk are behaviorists (they are not), only that there are commonalities in the structure of the arguments.

Here mindreading is characterized as a process of inference from observed statistical associations between observable features and others' behavior, where it is the recording of these associations that leads the mindreader to infer particular mental states in others. On this view it is easy to see how reasoning about mental states can in principle be dropped from an account of how individuals make predictions about others' behavior: the only difference between mindreading and behavior-reading is the inter-vening (and superfluous) attribution of mental states in between recording a set of token observations and computing a prediction of behavior based on statistical associations between previous observations of the same type and subsequent behaviors of a given type.

However, this is an extremely impoverished view of how mindreading must work. On any serious theoretical model of mindreading, mindreaders do not make inferences to mental states and behavioral predictions based purely on statistical associations between observables. The key function that higher-level mentalistic concepts play in behavior prediction is that they endow subjects with *inferential abilities* that are necessarily lacking in subjects possessed of only low-level concepts about correlations between observables. These are crucial for picking up on the *significance* of novel observable cues for predicting others' behavior in situations where subjects have had *no opportunity* to observe correlations between the relevant cues and others' behavior.

Different theoretical models of mindreading provide rather different accounts of the nature of these abilities (see Goldman [2006]; Nichols and Stich [2003]). For instance, on a "theory-theory" model, reasoning about visual awareness relies upon a tacit psychological theory about the basic mechanics of visual perception. This psychological knowledge drives subjects' mental state inferences from what they observe. It is assumed to be rich and general enough that, combined with other reasoning processes, it can enable subjects to work out the significance of features of novel social situations in the absence of previous experience of similar situations (indeed, explaining such flexibility is a key motivation for theory-theory accounts). For instance, it could include an abstract theory of occlusion or visibility, which specifies in general terms the sorts of conditions in which objects are occluded or visible to other agents, and which would enable a mindreader to *work out* that the dominant can *see* the food behind the transparent barrier, even if she has never previously interacted with other agents in situations involving transparent barriers. She will then reason that the dominant will likely compete for it, since she knows that dominants normally compete for food that they can *see*.

On a "simulationist" model the story would be rather different. Mind-readers don't base their inferences on a tacit theory about visual perception; rather, they imagine themselves in the situation that the other agent is in and then *mentally simulate* their own behavioral responses "off-line" to generate a prediction of what the other agent will do. Here the subordinate would utilize her own perception of being able to *see* through the transparent barrier and her own practical reasoning about what *she* would do if she were in the dominant's position and could see the food.

There is no need here to stake a position on which theoretical model is more plausible for primate perspective-taking.[8] On both of these sorts of models, by conceptualizing the situation in mentalistic terms mindreaders possess powerful *inferential abilities* – underlain by tacit theory, or simula-tion – that allow them to go beyond their previous experience. (Note the importance on both models of attributing states of *seeing* to the dominant for making an inference from the novel observation – the transparency of the barrier – to a prediction of her behavior.) The presence of such abilities in mindreaders, but not in behavior-readers, is what allows us to pose a poverty-of-the-stimulus problem for a behavior-reading account: if we cannot plausibly assume appropriate experiences – e.g., interaction with others involving transparent barriers – in order for subjects to be able to correctly associate the relevant observable cue with a prediction of how the other agent will behave, then subjects' success in this kind of task would constitute evidence for some form of mindreading mechanism that supplies this extra information.

An obvious response is to claim that knowledge of the relevant cor-relations between specific cues and behavior could be innate rather than learned. But this just pushes the explanatory burden back a level: we need to explain how evolution could have endowed subjects with specific rules that would correctly pick up on the significance of the transparent barrier. If transparent barriers were not a typical feature of the habitats of ancestral primates, then we merely replace an ontogenetic poverty-of-the-stimulus problem with a phylogenetic one.[9]

---

[8] Recent models of human mindreading combine elements of tacit theory *and* simulation, plus mechanisms not easily categorized on either view (e.g., Nichols and Stich [2003]). It is likely that if primates have any mindreading capacities theirs will also be made up of a variety of mechanisms.

[9] Could subjects have a purely behavioral analog to a concept of *visual awareness* that could do the same work? I am skeptical. The problem is spelling out such a concept so that it is (i) not just a mentalistic concept in disguise; (ii) sufficiently broad that it can account for the flexibility of subjects' responses to different types of stimuli (i.e., it can't be tied to a small set of very specific observable cues); (iii) not so broad that it becomes massively implausible that subjects could have such a concept, as a

Now, I want to emphasize that it is a further question how compelling this kind of poverty-of-the-stimulus argument should be in support of visual perspective-taking, given the data that is currently available for chimpanzees and other primates. But before discussing this, I want to make some remarks about the worries about simplicity from section 3. This deflationary interpretation of Tomasello and Call's argument provides a much better understanding of the main simplicity argument that has been proposed in support of primate mindreading. Whiten (1996), for example, puts the argument in terms of "economy of representation": reasoning about others' mental states allows agents to dispense with a body of rules that encode a one-to-one mapping between sets of observable cues and behavioral predictions. But it is not really the *amount* of mental representation that matters here. It is the fact that having higher-level mental concepts allows agents to recognize the significance of features of novel situations that cannot be picked up on by mere behavior-readers. In both the anti-behaviorist argument and the reading of Tomasello and Call's argument I am proposing, it is clear that what is doing the real epistemic work is not the "simplicity" of behaviorist versus cognitive, or behavior-reading versus mindreading explanations per se – for example, the sheer number of stimulus-response connections/behavioral rules required. Rather, it is a set of background assumptions concerning the previous experiences (or innate endowment) of subjects that cast doubt on the plausibility of the kind of story that behaviorist/behavior-reading accounts have to tell in order to account for the data. Seen in this light, the worries about simplicity raised in section 3 can be addressed reasonably straightforwardly. The justification for these arguments depends not on a general justification for preferring simple theories to less simple ones, but rather on the justification for the relevant background assumptions. If these are independently motivated, and they do in fact discriminate between the rival explanations in the right way, then it is easy to see how these arguments could have epistemic force. Heyes' general skepticism about simplicity arguments in this context can thus be resisted.

In addition, on deflationary readings of these arguments we can avoid worries about the slipperiness of notions of simplicity/parsimony, and the

product of learning or innately (i.e., it can't specify the behavioral significance of every perceptual subtlety that a subject might be confronted with). With respect to (i) it should be remembered that when behaviorists tried to offer behavioral analyses of mental concepts they often turned out to be just as mentalistic as the concepts they were trying to replace. Indeed, I suspect that there are serious problems in even making sense of apparently low-level concepts like *barrier, transparent,* or *opaque,* without implicitly relying on psychological concepts like *goal, agent,* or *visibility.*

possibility that there are conflicting respects in which behaviorist/behavior-reading accounts can be seen as "simpler" than cognitive/mindreading accounts. As it stands, Povinelli and Vonk's response to Tomasello and Call – that behavior-reading explanations must be more "parsimonious" because representing and reasoning about mental states entails representing and reasoning about observables, but not vice versa – is completely beside the point, since it is not some general notion of "simplicity"/"parsimony" that is doing the real work here. Of course it is open to skeptics to elucidate other background considerations that might ground simplicity arguments in the opposite direction. A key advantage of the deflationary account is that it reduces the problem of adjudicating between conflicting claims about "simplicity" to a problem of weighing these kinds of background considerations, where they exist. Though this can be difficult, weighing different kinds of background evidence is a standard sort of problem that scientists face. Hence, on the deflationary view, we do at least seem to stand a chance of getting at the real epistemic force of these kinds of arguments, and being able to distinguish what seem to be genuinely plausible appeals to simplicity from less plausible ones.[10]

Now for a more difficult question: should Tomasello and Call's argument, combined with the current data, persuade us that chimpanzees (and other primates, such as rhesus monkeys) *do* in fact reason about visual perspective? A problem here is that it does seem difficult to evaluate claims about the previous experiences of experimental subjects. For instance, according to Melis *et al.* (2006) "it seems highly unlikely that our subjects had had experience stealing food from a competitor whom they could only partially see and whose behavior could not be monitored during the ongoing transgression" (p. 161). But is there really good evidence for this and can we plausibly rule out the hypothesis that behavior-readers could have made appropriate generalizations from other experiences of approaching food in concealed ways?

I don't think that these issues are by any means settled as yet, and much further empirical work needs to be done to see if proponents of primate mindreading are right.[11] However, my analysis in this chapter shows how an

---

[10] An under-recognized aspect of the role of simplicity in science is that it is often employed as methodological cudgel to beat the opposition. For instance, skeptics about animal minds have often appealed to "parsimony" merely in order to pour scorn on attributions of sophisticated cognitive capacities to animals (Fitzpatrick [2008]). An attraction of the deflationary account is that it allows us to tease apart ad hoc rhetorical appeals to simplicity from those that do have some epistemic force.

[11] Here we should not forget recent work on primates' understanding of other kinds of mental states such as goals and intentions (Call and Tomasello [2008]).

argument of the sort proposed by Tomasello and Call and others, properly understood, may contribute to the resolution of this and other similar debates. We can now diagnose what is wrong with Povinelli and Vonk's blanket rejection of any study in which the relevant difference in the other agent's mental states and behavior is correlated with observable differences between the conditions. The mere fact that there *is* such a correlation does not suffice to show that a behavior-reading explanation must be at least as plausible as a mindreading explanation for subjects' success in predicting behavior. Studies like Hare *et al.*'s *can* provide evidence for mindreading, given appropriate background assumptions about subjects' previous experience (or innate endowment), which question the plausibility of a behavior-reader (but not a mindreader) being able to *discover* the relevant correlations and use the observable cue(s) in the right way.

We can also see how future empirical work might bolster a case for primate mindreading that utilizes this kind of argument. For instance, insofar as a behavior-reading account does depend on some kind of learning hypothesis, we can indirectly test this hypothesis by actually probing the learning abilities of primates. Povinelli and Vonk's claims assume that primates are very good at noticing statistical regularities between observable states of affairs. So we can actually look to see how good they are at doing this (see Call and Tomasello [2008] for some suggestive remarks). Also, if primates have no insight into others' mental states and reason purely according to observed regularities then we can expect that they will sometimes form *over-* or *under-generalized* expectations about how others will behave in various situations. Hunting for errors of over- or under-generalization has been a successful approach in developmental psychology. For instance, Baillargeon (2004) has found striking errors of under-generalization in young infants' reasoning about the physics of hidden objects, suggesting that infants may not have particularly rich understanding of some of the underlying principles until later in development. Thus one thing to do here is to continue to extend the range of perspective-taking scenarios that primates are tested in. Keeping in mind issues of ecological validity, we can see if transporting tasks to perceptually different but logically similar contexts, or perceptually similar but logically different contexts, alters subjects' performance. For example, does adding a frame, or changing the color, size, or some other arbitrary feature of a transparent barrier that has no influence on its occluding properties, affect subjects' performance? We might also try to *manipulate* the regularities that subjects actually observe. In one of their conditions Melis *et al.* (2006) rewarded subjects for responding to an entirely arbitrary cue that actually had nothing to do with the competitor's mental states, but through experimental conceit did in fact influence the competitor's behavior. They found that subjects did not learn to respond differently according to the presence or absence of this cue even though they were rewarded for doing so. Though this sort of finding is by no means conclusive evidence against learnt behavioral rules, proponents of such an account will need to explain how subjects can easily acquire *some* behavioral rules – presumably on what will have to be quite meager evidence – but not others.

There are therefore a number of avenues for research to pursue that could shed light on whether primates actually reason in the way that Povinelli and Vonk suggest. If we fail to find evidence for this type of reasoning this would not by itself be a knock-down argument for mindreading, but it would substantially strengthen Tomasello and Call's argument – particularly if we find further evidence for primates' flexibility in predicting behavior across different situations.

Glossary of key terms

Anthropomorphism The ascription of psychological or human-like characteristics to animals and other non-human beings. The term is often used pejoratively, describing the practice as epistemically and scientifically suspect.

Anti-realism about the mental A theory in the philosophy of mind that holds that our ordinary mental-state terms, such as "belief" and "desire," do not refer to any real (causally efficacious or non-reducible) states of subjects. Applied to animals, the theory holds that our ordinary mental-state terms do not refer to any real states in animals.

Argument from science The argument that we are justified in believing that animals have minds on the grounds that in various sciences of animal behavior, researchers have found it useful and (in some cases) indispensable in their explanations and predictions of animal behavior to attribute mental states to animals. The argument has a stronger version which holds that we are justified in believing that animals have minds *only if* the researchers in these various sciences find it useful and indispensable in their explanations and predictions to attribute mental states to animals.

Cognitive ethology The scientific discipline that studies the evolutionary, adaptive, causal, and developmental aspects of consciousness and thought in animals. Special emphasis is placed on observing and testing animals in their natural habitats (or in experimental settings designed to simulate such natural conditions) as opposed to the laboratory.

Cognitive maps Internal mental representations whose content, structure, and functionality are significantly map-like (as opposed to linguistic or digital), which subjects use to navigate through and locate items within their environments. The term is originally due to psychologist Edward Tolman, who used it to explain (among other things) various latent learning abilities in rats.

Common-sense functionalism A theory about the nature and possession conditions of folk-psychological states. The theory consists of two general ideas. The first is that our ordinary mental-state concepts, such as our concepts *belief*, *desire*, and *perceiving*, are theoretical concepts whose identity and existence are determined by a common-sense theory or **folk psychology** (see glossary). The second important idea of the theory is its *realist* and *functionalist* interpretation of folk psychology. On this interpretation, for a subject to have mental states is for the subject to have in his brain a variety of discrete internal states that play the causal/functional roles and have the internal structures that our folk-psychological concepts describe.

Concepts The components of thought. The thought *that birds fly*, for example, is composed of the concepts *bird* and *fly*. In this sense, concepts are abstract entities. However, on the representational theory of mind, to think or grasp a thought involves bringing together various concrete representations in one's brain. To think that birds fly, for example, involves bringing together the representation in one's head that stands for *bird* and another that stands for the action *fly*. These individual concrete representations are called concepts as well. A central question concerning concepts in this latter sense is whether they are word-like or iconic, and whether animals, in lacking a public language, can possess them.

Concern-based construal theory of emotion A theory of emotions due to Robert C. Roberts according to which emotions are a kind of perception (not thought) whose content is both evaluative and factual. The theory is contrasted with the neo-stoic theory of emotions that holds that emotions are (or essentially involve) judgments or the assent to propositions.

Consciousness The property that mental states possess in virtue of which they are conscious. There is no general agreement about what this property is or whether there are various kinds of consciousness. **First-order representational (FOR) theories** (see glossary) hold that a mental state is conscious in virtue of making the subject aware of various external items in the environment. **Higher-order representational (HOR) theories** (see glossary) hold that a mental state is conscious in virtue of the subject being higher-order aware of having the mental state. Both representational accounts aim to define "consciousness" in terms of a kind of awareness (either outer or inner awareness) and are thus labeled as theories of access consciousness. In contrast, there is a tradition in philosophy and psychology that defines "consciousness" in terms of experience or the "what it's like" aspect of having a mental state. On this view, a mental state is conscious (or phenomenally conscious) just in case there is something that it's like for the subject to undergo the mental state.

Deflationary model of simplicity According to this theory, simplicity per se is not and should not be used as a criterion for theory choice; rather, appeals to simplicity (e.g., Lloyd Morgan's canon, the principle of conservatism, or Ockham's razor) in theory choice are and should be understood as appeals to other considerations concerning background theoretical matters. Thus, it is not the fact that theory T1 is simpler than theory T2 that makes it epistemically preferable, but the fact that the additional items that T2 posits are implausible given certain relevant theoretical assumptions in play.

***De re/de dicto* belief ascriptions** A *de re* belief ascription aims to pick out the object of a subject's belief without aiming to describe how the subject thinks or represents the object. A *de dicto* belief ascription, on the other hand, aims to describe how the subject thinks or represents the object of his belief.

Episodic memory The recollection of having done or experienced something. Thus, what one recalls is a past event involving oneself (e.g., one's seeing

Mt. Rushmore) as opposed to some impersonal, time-independent fact (e.g., that Mt. Rushmore is in South Dakota). Episodic memory is thereby contrasted with semantic memory, which is remembering or knowing facts (even facts about the past) without necessarily recalling (or "mentally reliving") the events in which one first encountered the facts. Episodic memory is also distinguished from semantic memory in necessarily involving a special type of awareness called *autonoetic consciousness* in which the subject is aware not only of recollecting an event but of "reliving" the event which he is recollecting.

Feature-placing Features are general kinds of stuff (e.g., rain, snow, gold) that are neither sortals (e.g., drops of rain, snowflakes, etc.) nor properties (e.g., being made of water, being made of snow, etc.). Feature-placing sentences or thoughts (e.g., it is raining) place a feature at a location and time but do not predicate a property to an individual. Hence, a creature that can think only feature-placing thought lacks a conception of individual particulars (e.g., this cat, this tree, etc.). There is a question of whether animals are mere feature-placers or whether they understand the world as consisting of particulars and properties as well.

First-order representational (FOR) theories of consciousness According to FOR theories, a mental state (e.g., a state of perception) is conscious in virtue of it making the subject aware of items or facts in the environment, *not* in virtue of the subject being higher-order aware of his having the mental state. This last part is what distinguishes FOR theories from **higher-order representational (HOR) theories** (see glossary). Not all mental states, of course, make their subject aware of items or facts in the environment; those that do, according to FOR theories, are states that are poised to make an impact on the subject's belief-forming system.

Folk psychology Our ordinary, every-day notions of the mind and the principles and laws that organize and govern them. Concepts such as *belief, desire, see, know, intend,* and *conscious* belong to our folk psychology, as do a number of law-like principles, such as that subjects tend to do what they think will get them what they want, all things being equal. Folk psychology is contrasted with scientific psychology (e.g., behaviorism, learning theory, psychoanalysis, etc.), many of whose concepts, laws, and methodological principles are not part of folk psychology.

Generality constraint A general requirement on concept possession and thought due to Gareth Evans. The constraint holds that any creature capable of thinking thoughts of the form *a is F* and *b is G* must be capable of thinking thoughts of the form *b is F* and *a is G* (and possibly *Fs are Gs* and *Gs are Fs*, if these are well-formed thoughts). An important assumption behind the constraint is that thinking involves bringing together individual **concepts** (see glossary), which can then be recombined in various ways to think different thoughts.

Higher-order representational (HOR) theories of consciousness According to HOR theories, a mental state is conscious just in case the subject is higher-order aware of the mental state. Higher-order theories divide over the question of the nature of the higher-order awareness involved. *Higher-order thought (HOT) theories* take the higher-order awareness involved to be a form of thought. On the HOT theory, a mental state is conscious just in case the subject has (or is disposed to have) a suitably formed higher-order thought that he has the mental state. *Higher-order perception (HOP) theories*, however, take the higher-order awareness involved to be significantly perception-like. According to the HOP theory, a mental state is conscious just in case the subject has a suitably formed higher-order perception of the mental state.

Instrumentalism A theory in the philosophy of mind that holds that whether attributions of mentality are true or justified depends on their instrumental value, such as their predictability and control of behavior. Dennett's **intentional stance theory** is a well-known instrumentalist theory.

Intentional stance theory A theory about the nature and possession conditions of folk-psychological states, especially intentional states (see **intentionality**), due to Daniel Dennett. The theory consists of two general ideas. The first is that our ordinary mental-state concepts are theoretical concepts whose identity and existence are determined by a common-sense theory or **folk psychology** (see glossary). The second important idea of the intentional stance theory is its *instrumentalist* interpretation of folk psychology. On the instrumentalist interpretation, what it is for a creature to have mental states is simply for its behaviors to be richly and voluminously predicted by the principles of folk psychology.

Intentionality The feature that an object or state has in virtue of which it is about or represents something. Conventional words and symbols have intentionality, since they represent items; however, their intentionality is derived from the intentionality of the thoughts that we express in using the words and symbols. The intentionality of thought and other mental states is not derivative in this way but is considered original or basic. Mental states that have intentionality, such as beliefs, thoughts, desires, perceptions, mental images, and concepts, are called *intentional states*.

Interpretivism A theory in the philosophy of mind that holds that whether attributions of mentality are true or justified is a matter of interpretation and is not solely determined by the (mind-independent) objective facts. Dennett's **intentional stance theory** (see glossary) is often taken as a kind of interpretivism.

Lloyd Morgan's canon A methodological principle of parsimony due to the nineteenth-century psychologist Conwy Lloyd Morgan that recommends that scientists should not interpret animal behavior in terms of higher psychological processes if the behavior can be adequately interpreted in terms of processes that are lower on the scale of psychological evolution and development.

Metacognition The ability to form cognitive states about (the presence, absence, or degree of) one's own cognitive states. The ability to know or judge that one does (or does not) to some degree remember or know something are cases of metacognition. On this definition, metacognition involves *metarepresentation*, the ability to form higher-order representations about one's lower-order mental states (see also **orders of intentionality** in glossary). However, there are uses of the term that do not entail metarepresentation.

Mindreading (or **theory of mind**) The ability to predict, explain, or understand the behavior of other subjects by means of attributing mental states to them. Historically, mindreading was taken to involve a type of analogical inference based on perceived similarities between one's own behavior and that of another, and on what one knew introspectively about one's own mind in relation to these types of behaviors. However, the two dominant contemporary theories of mindreading in cognitive science do not appeal to analogical inferences of this sort. The *theory-theory* account holds that mindreading involves theoretical inferences from law-like principles about the mind and facts about the target's observable behavior and environment. The *simulation* account holds that mindreading involves the subject imaginatively placing herself in the target's situation and projecting onto the target the pretend mental states that she introspectively finds herself having (in this imaginative mode).

Neo-expressivism A theory in the philosophy of language about the nature of avowals and ethical claims due to Dorit Bar-On. According to the theory, avowals (e.g., "I'm hungry") and ethical claims (e.g., "abortion is wrong") not only express emotive or cognitive states of the speaker but produce linguistic items (e.g., utterances or written words) that express truth-evaluable propositions. The theory is contrasted with *traditional expressivism* which denies that avowals and ethical claims express truth-evaluable propositions.

Non-conceptual content The content of a mental state is (roughly) what the state represents or is about. Thus, if a mental state represents something without employing concepts, its content is non-conceptual. Perceptual experiences are often taken as paradigm examples, since (it is argued) a subject can perceive (say) a particular shade of color or a distinct smell or taste for which he does not possess a concept.

Orders of intentionality Intentional states (see glossary) can be classified in a hierarchical order. First-order intentional states are states that are about non-mental items (e.g., the desire for *water*); second-order intentional states are states about mental states (e.g., the belief that Fred *desires* water); third-order intentional states are states about second-order intentional states (e.g., the thought that one *believes* that Fred *desires* water); and so on. Higher orders of intentionality play an important role in some accounts of **mindreading**, **metacognition**, **self-awareness**, and **consciousness** (see glossary).

Principle of conservatism A methodological principle of parsimony similar to **Lloyd Morgan's canon** (see glossary), according to which hypotheses that explain animal behavior in terms of lower-order intentionality are preferable to those that explain the behavior in terms of higher-order intentionality, all things being equal (see **orders of intentionality** in glossary).

Propositional attitudes Psychological states that have whole propositions as contents. Paradigm examples are beliefs, desires, knowledge, and intentions.

Realism about the mental A theory in the philosophy of mind that holds that our ordinary mental-state terms, such as "belief" and "desire," refer to real (causally efficacious or non-reducible) states of subjects. Applied to animals, the theory holds that our ordinary mental-state terms refer to real states in animals.

Self-awareness Often used to describe the kind of awareness that one has of oneself when one is introspectively aware of being in a current, conscious mental state. On this definition, self-awareness involves higher-order awareness of one's own mental states. However, there are uses of the term that do not entail such higher-order awareness.

Systematicity A property of thought that enables a thinker to think all structural permutations of the thought. If a subject thinks that Bill loves Mary, for example, and his thoughts are systematic, he is thereby capable of thinking the thought that Mary loves Bill. As with the **generality constraint** (see glossary), the important assumption behind systematicity is that thinking involves bringing together individual token representations (e.g., concepts) which can then be recombined in various ways to think new thoughts that are structural permutations of the original thought.

References

Ackers, S. H. and Slobodchikoff, C. N. (1999). Communication of stimulus size and shape in alarm calls of Gunnison's prairie dogs, *Cynomys gunnisoni*. *Ethology*, 105, 149–162.

Aizawa, K. (1997). Explaining systematicity. *Mind & Language*, 12, 115–136.

Akaike, H. (1973). Information theory as an extension of the maximum likelihood principle. In B. Petrov and F. Csaki (eds.), *Second International Symposium on Information Theory*. Budapest: Akademiai Kiado.

Allen, C. (1992). Mental content. *British Journal for the Philosophy of Science*, 43, 537–553.

(1999). Animal concepts revisited: the use of self-monitoring as an empirical approach. *Erkenntnis*, 51, 33–40.

(2006). Transitive inference in animals: reasoning or conditioned associations? In S. Hurley and M. Nudds (eds.), *Rational Animals?* Oxford: Oxford University Press.

Allen, C. and Bekoff, M. (1997). *Species of Mind: The Philosophy and Biology of Cognitive Ethology*. Cambridge, MA: MIT Press.

(2005). Animal play and the evolution of morality: an ethological approach. *Topoi*, 24, 125–135.

Allen, C. and Hauser, M. (1991). Concept attribution in nonhuman animals: theoretical and methodological problems in ascribing complex mental processes. *Philosophy of Science*, 58, 221–240.

Allen, C. and Saidel, E. (1998). The evolution of reference. In D. Cummins and C. Allen (eds.), *Evolution of Mind*. Oxford: Oxford University Press.

Alp, R. (1997). "Stepping-sticks" and "seat-sticks": new types of tools used by wild chimpanzees (*Pan troglodytes*) in Sierra Leone. *American Journal of Primatology*, 41, 45–52.

Ambrose (1961). *Hexameron*. In J. Savage (trans.), *The Fathers of the Church: A New Translation*, vol. 42. New York: Fathers of the Church, Inc.

Anderson, A. and Kacelnik, A. (2004). Don't call me bird-brain. *New Scientist*, 12 June, 46–47.

Anderson, J. R. (1978). Arguments concerning representations for mental imagery. *Psychological Review*, 85, 249–277.

Aristotle (1941). *De Anima*. In R. McKeon (ed.), *The Basic Works of Aristotle*. New York: Random House.

Aristotle (1980). *Nicomachean Ethics.* Translated by W. D. Ross, revised by J. Akrill and J. Urmson. Oxford: Oxford University Press.

Armstrong, D. (1973). *Belief, Truth and Knowledge.* Cambridge: Cambridge University Press.

(1997). What is consciousness? In N. Block, O. Flanagan, and G. Güzeldere (eds.), *The Nature of Consciousness.* Cambridge, MA: MIT Press.

Arnold, K. and Zuberbühler, K. (2006). Language evolution: semantic combinations in primate calls. *Nature,* 441, 303.

(2008). Meaningful call combinations in a non-human primate. *Current Biology,* 18, 202–203.

Babb, S. and Crystal, J. (2005). Discrimination of what, when, and where: implications for episodic-like memory in rats. *Learning and Motivation,* 36, 177–189.

Baillargeon, R. (2004). Infants' reasoning about hidden objects: evidence for event-general and event-specific expectations. *Developmental Science,* 7, 391–424.

Balakrishnan, K., Bousquet, O., and Honavar, V. (1999). Spatial learning and localization in rodents: a computational model of the hippocampus and its implications for mobile robots. *Adaptive Behavior,* 7, 173–216.

Bar-On, D. (2004). *Speaking My Mind: Expression and Self-Knowledge.* Oxford: Oxford University Press.

Bar-On, D. and Chrisman, M. (in press). Ethical neo-expressivism. *Oxford Studies in Metaethics,* Volume IV.

Bastian, J. R. (1965). Primate signalling systems and human languages. In I. Devore (ed.), *Primate Behavior: Field Studies in Monkeys and Apes.* New York: Holt, Rinehart, and Winston.

Bekoff, M. (1995). Play signals as punctuation: the structure of social play in canids. *Behavior,* 132, 419–429.

Bekoff, M. and Allen, C. (1992). Intentional icons: towards an evolutionary cognitive ethology. *Ethology,* 91, 1–16.

Bekoff, M. and Jamieson, D. (1991). Reflective ethology, applied philosophy, and the moral status of animals. In P. Bateson and P. Klopfer (eds.), *Perspectives in Ethology.* New York: Plenum Publishing Corporation.

Beninger, R., Kendall, S., and Vanderwolf, C. H. (1974). The ability of rats to discriminate their own behaviours. *Canadian Journal of Psychology,* 28, 79–91.

Bennett, J. (1988). Thoughtful brutes. *Proceedings and Addresses of the American Philosophical Association,* 62, 197–210.

Bermúdez, J. L. (1994). Peacocke's argument against the autonomy of nonconceptual representational content. *Mind & Language,* 9, 402–418.

(1998). *The Paradox of Self-Consciousness.* Cambridge, MA: MIT Press.

(2003a). *Thinking Without Words.* Oxford: Oxford University Press.

(2003b). Nonconceptual content: from perceptual experience to subpersonal computational states. In Y. H. Gunther (ed.), *Essays in Nonconceptual Content.* Cambridge, MA: MIT Press.

(2005). *Philosophy of Psychology: A Contemporary Introduction.* London: Routledge.

(in press). *Cognitive Science: An Introduction to the Science of the Mind.* Cambridge: Cambridge University Press.

Blair, R. (1995). A cognitive developmental approach to morality: investigating the psychopath. *Cognition*, 57, 1–29.

Blaisdell, A., Sawa, K., Leising, K., and Walmann, M. (2006). Causal reasoning in rats. *Science*, 311, 1020–1022.

Boesch, C. (1991). Teaching in wild chimpanzees. *Animal Behaviour*, 41, 530–532.

Boyd, R. (1990). Observations, explanatory power and simplicity. In R. Boyd, J. Glasper, and J. D. Trout (eds.), *The Philosophy of Science*. Cambridge, MA: MIT Press.

Braddon-Mitchell, D. and Jackson, F. (1996). *Philosophy of Mind and Cognition*, 1st edn. Oxford: Blackwell.

(2007). *Philosophy of Mind and Cognition*, 2nd edn. Oxford: Blackwell.

Brandom, R. (1994). *Making it Explicit*. Cambridge: Harvard University Press.

Breland, K. and Breland, M. (1951). A field of applied animal psychology. *American Psychologist*, 6, 202–204.

(1961). The misbehavior of organisms. *American Psychologist*, 16, 681–684.

Brown, A. S. (1991). A review of the tip-of-the-tongue experience. *Psychological Bulletin*, 109, 204–223.

Browne, D. (2004). Do dolphins know their own minds? *Biology and Philosophy*, 19, 633–653.

Burge, T. (2005). *Truth, Thought, and Reason*. Oxford: Oxford University Press.

Burkart, J. and Heschl, A. (2007). Understanding visual access in common marmosets, *Callithrix jacchus*: perspective taking or behavior reading? *Animal Behaviour*, 73, 457–469.

Burnham, K. and Anderson, D. (2002). *Model Selection and Multimodel Inference – a Practical Information-Theoretic Approach*, 2nd edn. New York: Springer.

Byrne, A. (1998). Interpretivism. *European Review of Philosophy*, 3, 199–223.

Byrne, R. W. and Whiten, A. (1988). *Machiavellian Intelligence*. Oxford: Clarendon Press.

(1990). Tactical deception in primates: the 1990 database. *Primate Report*, 27, 1–101.

(1991). Computation and mindreading in primate tactical deception. In A. Whiten (ed.), *Natural Theories of Mind: Evolution, Development, and Simulation of Everyday Mindreading*. Oxford: Blackwell.

Call, J. (2004). Inferences about the location of food in the great apes. *Journal of Comparative Psychology*, 118, 232–241.

(2006). Descartes's two errors: reason and reflection in the great apes. In S. Hurley and M. Nudds (eds.), *Rational Animals?* Oxford: Oxford University Press.

(2007). Apes know that hidden objects can affect the orientation of other objects. *Cognition*, 105, 1–25.

Call, J. and Carpenter, M. (2001). Do apes and children know what they have seen? *Animal Cognition*, 4, 207–220.

Call, J. and Tomasello, M. (2008). Does the chimpanzee have a theory of mind? 30 years later. *Trends in Cognitive Sciences*, 12, 187–192.

Camp, E. (2004). The generality constraints and categorical restrictions. *Philosophical Quarterly*, 54, 209–231.

(2006). Contextualism, metaphor, and what is said. *Mind & Language*, 21, 280–309.

(2007). Thinking with maps. *Philosophical Perspectives*, 21, 145–182.

(2009). Putting thoughts to work: concepts, systematicity, and stimulus-independence. *Philosophy and Phenomenological Research*, 78.2, 275–311.

Campbell, J. (1993). The body image and self-consciousness. In J. Bermúdez, T. Marcel, and N. Eilan (eds.), *The Body and the Self*. Oxford: Oxford University Press.

Carnap, R. (1937). *The Logical Syntax of Language*. London: Routledge & Kegan Paul.

Caro, T. M. and Hauser, M. D. (1992). Is there teaching in nonhuman animals? *Quarterly Review of Biology*, 67, 151–174.

Carruthers, P. (1989). Brute experience. *The Journal of Philosophy*, 86, 258–269.

(2000). *Phenomenal Consciousness: A Naturalistic Theory*. Cambridge: Cambridge University Press.

(2002). The cognitive functions of language. *Behavioral and Brain Sciences*, 25, 657–726.

(2004). On being simple-minded. *American Philosophical Quarterly*, 41, 205–220.

(2005). *Consciousness: Essays from a Higher-Order Perspective*. Oxford: Oxford University Press.

(2006). *The Architecture of the Mind*. Oxford: Oxford University Press.

(2007a). The creative-action theory of creativity. In P. Carruthers, S. Laurence, and S. Stich (eds.), *The Innate Mind*, Volume III. Oxford: Oxford University Press.

(2007b). The illusion of conscious will. *Synthese*, 159, 197–213.

(2008). Meta-cognition in animals: a skeptical look. *Mind & Language*, 23, 58–89.

(2009a). An architecture for dual reasoning. In J. Evans and K. Frankish (eds.), *In Two Minds*. Oxford: Oxford University Press.

(2009b). Introspection: divided and partly eliminated. *Philosophy and Phenomenological Research*, 78.

Carruthers, P. and Smith, P. K. (eds.) (1996). *Theories of Theories of Mind*. Cambridge: Cambridge University Press.

Carver, S. C. and Scheier, M. F. (1998). *On the Self-regulation of Behavior*. Cambridge: Cambridge University Press.

Casati, R. and Varzi, A. (1999). *Parts and Places*. Cambridge, MA: MIT Press.

Cheney, D. and Seyfarth, R. (1990). *How Monkeys See the World*. Chicago: University of Chicago Press.

(2007). *Baboon Metaphysics*. Chicago: Chicago University Press.

Child, W. (1994). *Causality, Interpretation, and the Mind*. Oxford: Clarendon Press.

Chittka, L., Kunze, J., Shipman, C., and Buchmann, S. L. (1995). The significance of landmarks for path integration in homing honeybee foragers. *Naturwissenschaften*, 82, 341–343.

Clark, A. (2003). Connectionism and cognitive flexibility. In Y. Gunther (ed.), *Essays in Nonconceptual Content*. Cambridge, MA: MIT Press.

(2005). Intrinsic content, active memory and the extended mind. *Analysis*, 65, 1–11.

Clarke, E., Reichard, U., and K. Zuberbühler (2006). The syntax and meaning of wild gibbon songs, *PLoS One*, 1, e73, doi: 10.1371/journal.pone.0000073.

Clayton, N., Bussey, T., and Dickinson, A. (2003). Can animals recall the past and plan for the future? *Nature Reviews Neuroscience*, 4, 685–691.

Clayton, N., Emery, N., and Dickinson, A. (2006). The rationality of animal memory: complex caching strategies of western scrub jays. In S. Hurley and M. Nudds (eds.), *Rational Animals?* Oxford: Oxford University Press.

Collett, M., Harland, D., and Collett, T. S. (2002). The use of landmarks and panoramic context in the performance of local vectors by navigating honeybees. *The Journal of Experimental Biology*, 205, 807–814.

Collett, T. and Collett, M. (2002). Memory use in insect visual navigation. *Nature Reviews: Neuroscience*, 3, 542–552.

Collett, T. S., Fry, S. N., and Wehner, R. (1993). Sequence learning by honey bees. *Journal of Comparative Physiology A*, 172, 693–706.

Connor, R. and Peterson, D. (1994). *The Lives of Whales and Dolphins*. New York: Holt.

Craik, K. (1943). *The Nature of Explanation*. Cambridge: Cambridge University Press.

Crockford, C. and Boesch, C. (2005). Call combinations in wild chimpanzees. *Behavior*, 142, 397–421.

Cussins, A. (1992). Content, embodiment and objectivity: the theory of cognitive trails. *Mind*, 101, 651–688.

Dacke, M., and Srinivasan, M. V. (2007). Honeybee navigation: distance estimation in the third dimension. *The Journal of Experimental Biology*, 210, 845–853.

Dally, J. M., Emery, N. J., and Clayton, N. S. (2006). Food-caching western scrub jays keep track of who was watching when. *Science*, 312, 1662–1665.

Damasio, A. R., Everitt, B. J., and Bishop, D. (1996). The somatic marker and hypothesis and the possible functions of the prefrontal cortex. *Philosophical Transactions. Biological Sciences*, 351, 1413–1420.

Davidson, D. (1980). *Essays on Actions and Events*. Oxford: Clarendon Press.

(1980). Mental events. In *Essays on Actions and Events*. Oxford: Oxford University Press.

(1982). Rational Animals. *Dialectica*, 36, 318–327.

(1983/1986). A coherence theory of truth and knowledge. In E. LePore (ed.), *Truth and Interpretation: Perspectives on the Philosophy of Donald Davidson*. Oxford: Basil Blackwell.

(1984a). *Inquiries into Truth and Interpretation*. Oxford: Clarendon Press.

(1984b). Thought and talk. In *Inquiries into Truth and Interpretation*. Oxford: Clarendon Press.

(1985). Rational animals. In E. Lepore and B. McLaughlin (eds.), *Actions and Events: Perspectives on the Philosophy of Donald Davidson*. New York: Basil Blackwell.

(1997). The emergence of thought. *Erkenntnis*, 51, 7–17.

(2005). *Problems of Rationality*. Oxford: Clarendon Press.

Davies, M. and Stone, T. (1995). *Folk Psychology: The Theory of Mind Debate*. Oxford: Basil Blackwell.

Dawkins, M. S. (1993). *Through Our Eyes Only?* Oxford: Freeman Press.

Dawkins, R. and Krebs, J. R. (1978). Animal signals: information or manipulation? In J. R. Krebs and N. B. Davies (eds.), *Behavioural Ecology: An Evolutionary Approach*. Oxford: Blackwell Scientific Publications.

DeGrazia, D. (1996). *Taking Animals Seriously: Mental Life and Moral Status*. Cambridge: Cambridge University Press.

Deigh, J. (2004). Primitive emotions. In R. Solomon (ed.), *Thinking about Feeling*. Oxford: Oxford University Press.

Dennett, D. (1969). *Content and Consciousness*. London: Routledge Kegan Paul.

(1971). Intentional systems. *Journal of Philosophy*, 8, 87–106.

(1975). Brain writing and mind reading. In K. Gunderson (ed.), *Language, Mind, and Knowledge*. Minnesota Studies in the Philosophy of Science, 7. Minneapolis: University of Minnesota Press.

(1978). *Brainstorms*. Cambridge, MA: MIT Press.

(1983). Intentional systems in cognitive ethology: the "Panglossian paradigm" defended. *Behavioral and Brain Sciences*, 6, 343–390.

(1987). *The Intentional Stance*. Cambridge, MA: MIT Press.

(1990). The myth of original intentionality. In K. Said, W. Newton-Smith, R. Viale, and K. Wilkes (eds.), *Modeling the Mind*. Oxford: Clarendon Press.

(1991a). Mother nature vs. the walking encyclopedia. In W. Ramsey, S. Stich, and D. E. Rumelhart (eds.), *Philosophy and Connectionist Theory*. Hillsdale, NJ: Erlbaum.

(1991b). Real patterns. *Journal of Philosophy*, 88, 27–51.

(1995). Do animals have beliefs? In H. Roitblat and J.-A. Meyer (eds.), *Comparative Approaches to Cognitive Science*. Cambridge, MA: MIT Press.

(1996). *Kinds of Minds*. New York: Basic Books.

Dere, E., Kart-Teke, E., Huston, J., and Silva, D. (2006). The case for episodic memory in animals. *Neuroscience and Biobehavioral Reviews*, 30, 1206–1224.

Descartes, R. (1637/1988). Discourse on the method. In Cottingham, Stoothoff, and Murdoch (trans.), *Descartes: Selected Philosophical Writings*. Cambridge: Cambridge University Press.

(1641/1984). Fourth objections. In Cottingham, Stoothoff, and Murdoch (trans.), *The Philosophical Writings of Descartes*, Volume II. Cambridge: Cambridge University Press.

290   *References*

(1644/1988). *Principles of Philosophy.* In Cottingham, Stoothoff, and Murdoch (trans.), *Descartes: Selected Philosophical Writings.* Cambridge: Cambridge University Press.

Devitt, M. (2006). *Ignorance of Language.* Oxford: Clarendon Press.

Dretske, F. (1981). *Knowledge and the Flow of Information.* Cambridge, MA: MIT Press.

(1988). *Explaining Behavior.* Cambridge, MA: MIT Press.

(1995). *Naturalizing the Mind.* Cambridge, MA: MIT Press.

(2000). *Perception, Knowledge and Belief.* Cambridge: Cambridge University Press.

Dummett, M. (1973). *Frege: Philosophy of Language.* London: Duckworth.

(1993). *The Seas of Language.* Oxford: Clarendon Press.

(1996). *Origins of Analytical Philosophy.* Cambridge, MA: Harvard University Press.

Dyer, F. C. (1985). Nocturnal orientation by the Asian honeybee, *Apis dorsata.* *Animal Behaviour,* 33, 769–774.

(2002). The biology of the dance language. *Annual Review of Entomology,* 47, 917–949.

Dyer, F. C. and Dickinson, J. A. (1994). Development of sun compensation by honey bees: how partially experienced bees estimate the sun's course. *Proceedings of the National Academy of Sciences USA,* 91, 4471–4474.

Edelman, G. and Tononi, G. (2001). *A Universe of Consciousness: How Matter Becomes Imagination.* New York: Basic Books.

Edrich, W. (1981). Night-time sun-compass behaviour of honeybees at the equator. *Physiological Entomology,* 6, 7–13.

Eichenbaum, H., Fortin, N., Ergorul, C., Wright, S., and Agster, K. (2005). Episodic recollection in animals: "If it walks like a duck and quacks like a duck . . . ". *Learning and Motivation,* 36, 190–207.

Emery, N. and Clayton, N. (2001). Effects of experience and social context on prospective caching strategies in scrub jays. *Nature,* 414, 443–446.

Erdőhegyi, Á., Topál, J., Vrányi, Z., and Miklósi, Á. (2007). Dog-logic: inferential reasoning in a two-way choice task and its restricted use. *Animal Behavior,* 74, 725–737.

Evans, C. S. and Marler, P. (1995). Language and animal communication: parallels and contrasts. In H. L. Roitblat and J.-A. Meyer (eds.), *Comparative Approaches to Cognitive Science.* Cambridge, MA: MIT Press.

Evans, G. (1982). *The Varieties of Reference.* Oxford: Oxford University Press.

Evans, J. and Over, D. (1996). *Rationality and Reasoning.* Hove, Sussex: Psychology Press.

Fitzpatrick, S. (2006). *Simplicity, Science and Mind.* Doctoral dissertation, Department of Philosophy, University of Sheffield.

(2008). Doing away with Morgan's canon. *Mind & Language,* 23, 224–246.

Flavell, J. H. (2004). Theory-of-mind development: retrospect and prospect. *Merrill-Palmer Quarterly,* 50, 274–290.

Flombaum, J. and Santos, L. (2005). Rhesus monkeys attribute perceptions to others. *Current Biology*, 15, 447–452.

Floridi, L. (1997). Skepticism and animal rationality: the fortune of Chrysippus's dog in the history of Western thought. *Archiv für Geschichte der Philosophie*, 79, 27–57.

Fodor, J. (1975). *The Language of Thought.* Cambridge, MA: Harvard University Press.

(1981). *Representations.* Cambridge, MA: MIT Press.

(1983). *The Modularity of Mind.* Cambridge, MA: MIT Press.

(1987). *Psychosemantics.* Cambridge, MA: MIT Press.

(1991). Replies. In B. Loewer (ed.), *Meaning in Mind.* Cambridge, MA: Blackwell.

(1998). *Where Cognitive Science Went Wrong.* Oxford: Oxford University Press.

(2003). Review of Bermúdez's *Thinking Without Words. London Review of Books*, 25, 16–17.

Fodor, J. and McLaughlin, B. (1990). Connectionism and the problem of systematicity. *Cognition*, 35, 183–204.

Fodor, J. and Pylyshyn, Z. (1988). Connectionism and the cognitive architecture of mind. *Cognition*, 28, 3–71.

(1995). Connectionism and cognitive architecture: a critical analysis. In C. MacDonald and G. MacDonald (eds.), *Connectionism: Debates on Psychological Explanation.* Oxford: Blackwell.

Forster, M. and Sober, E. (1994). How to tell when simpler, more unified, or less *ad hoc* theories will provide more accurate predictions. *British Journal for the Philosophy of Science*, 45, 1–36.

Fouts, R., Fouts, D., and Shoenfeld, D. (1984). Sign language conversational interactions between chimpanzees. *Sign Language Studies*, 34, 1–12.

Frankish, K. (2004). *Mind and Supermind.* Cambridge: Cambridge University Press.

Frege, G. (1892/1951). On concept and object, trans. P. T. Geach and M. Black. *Mind*, 60, 168–180.

Frisch, K. von (1967). *The Dance Language and Orientation of Bees.* Cambridge, MA: Belknap/Harvard.

Fry, R. (2002). The engineering of cybernetic systems. *Bayesian Inference and Maximum Entropy Systems in Science and Engineering: American Institute of Physics Conference Proceedings*, 617, 497–528.

Galef, B. (1996). Tradition in animals: field observations and laboratory analyses. In M. Bekoff and D. Jamieson (eds.), *Readings in Animal Cognition.* Cambridge, MA: MIT Press.

Galen, C. (1999). Sun stalkers: flowers and sun. *Natural History*, May.

Gallistel, C. R. (1990). *The Organization of Learning.* Cambridge, MA: MIT Press.

(2003). Conditioning from an information processing perspective. *Behavioural Processes*, 62, 89–101.

Gallup, G. (1977). Self-recognition in primates: a comparative approach to the bidirectional properties of consciousness. *American Psychologist*, 32, 330–338.

Gallup, G., Anderson, J., and Shillito, D. (2002). In M. Bekoff, C. Allen, and G. Burghardt (eds.), *The Cognitive Animal*. Cambridge, MA: MIT Press.

Gardener, R. A. and Gardener, B. (1969). Teaching sign language to a chimpanzee. *Science*, 165, 664–672.

Gärdenfors, P. (2003). *How Homo Became Sapiens: On the Evolution of Thinking*. Oxford: Oxford University Press.

Gennaro, R. (1993). Brute experience and the higher-order thought theory of consciousness. *Philosophical Papers*, 22, 51–69.

(1996). *Consciousness and Self-consciousness: A Defense of the Higher-Order Thought Theory of Consciousness*. Amsterdam and Philadelphia: John Benjamins.

(2004a). *Higher-Order Theories of Consciousness*. Amsterdam and Philadelphia: John Benjamins.

(2004b). Higher-order thoughts, animal consciousness, and misrepresentation: a reply to Carruthers and Levine. In R. Gennaro (ed.), *Higher-Order Theories of Consciousness*. Amsterdam and Philadelphia: John Benjamins.

(2006). Review of Peter Carruthers' *Consciousness: Essays From a Higher-Order Perspective*. *Psyche*, 12, http://psyche.cs.monash.edu.au/book_reviews/carruthers3/Carruthers.pdf.

Gibson, J. (1966). *The Senses Considered as Perceptual Systems*. Boston: Houghton Mifflin.

(1979). *The Ecological Approach to Visual Perception*. Boston: Houghton Mifflin.

Giurfa, M. (2007). Behavioral and neural analysis of associative learning in the honeybee: a taste from the magic well. *Journal of Comparative Physiology A*, 193, 801–824.

Glock, H.-J. (1999). Animal minds: conceptual problems. *Evolution and Cognition*, 5, 174–188.

(2000). Animals, thoughts, and concepts. *Synthese*, 123, 35–64.

Glouberman, M. (1976). Prime matter, predication, and the semantics of feature-placing. In A. Kasher (ed.), *Language in Focus*. Boston: Reidel.

Goldman, A. (2006). *Simulating Minds*. Oxford: Oxford University Press.

Goodall, J. (1986). *The Chimpanzees of Gombe*. Cambridge, MA: Harvard University Press.

Gopnik, A. and Schulz, L. (2007). *Causal Learning*. Oxford: Oxford University Press.

Gould, J. (1986). The locale map of bees: do insects have cognitive maps? *Science*, 232, 861–863.

Gould, J. and Gould, C. (1988). *The Honey Bee*. New York: Science American Library.

(1994). *The Animal Mind*. New York: Scientific American Library.

Grandin, T. and Johnson, C. (2005). *Animals in Translation*. New York: Scribner.

Grau, J. W. (2002). Learning and memory without a brain. In M. Bekoff, C. Allen, and G. M. Burghardt (eds.), *The Cognitive Animal*. Cambridge, MA: MIT Press.

Grice, H. P. (1957). Meaning. *Philosophical Review*, 66, 377–388.

Griffin, D. (1976). *The Question of Animal Awareness*. New York: Rockefeller University Press.

   (2001). *Animal Minds: Beyond Cognition to Consciousness*. Chicago: Chicago University Press.

Gruber, O. and von Cramon, D. Y. (2003). The functional neuroanatomy of human working memory revisited. *NeuroImage*, 19, 797–809.

Grünwald, P. (2007). *The Minimum Description Length Principle*. Cambridge, MA: MIT Press.

Gunther, Y. H (ed.) (2003). *Essays on Nonconceptual Content*. Cambridge, MA: The MIT Press.

Güzeldere, G., Nahmias, E., and Deaner, R. (2002). Darwin's continuum and the building blocks of deception. In M. Bekoff, C. Allen, and G. Burghardt (eds.), *The Cognitive Animal*. Cambridge, MA: MIT Press.

Hadley, R. F. (2004). On the proper treatment of semantic systematicity. *Minds and Machines*, 14, 145–172.

Hampton, R. (2001). Rhesus monkeys know when they remember. *Proceedings of the National Academy of Sciences U.S.A.*, 98, 5359–5362.

   (2005). Can rhesus monkeys discriminate between remembering and forgetting? In H. Terrace and J. Metcalfe (eds.), *The Missing Link in Cognition: Origins of Self-Reflective Consciousness*. Oxford: Oxford University Press.

Hare, B., Addessi, E., Call, J., Tomasello, M., and Visalberghi, E. (2003). Do capuchin monkeys, *Cebus apella*, know what conspecifics do and do not see? *Animal Behaviour*, 65, 131–142.

Hare, B., Brown, M., Williamson, C., and Tomasello, M. (2002). The domestication of social cognition in dogs. *Science*, 298, 1634–1636.

Hare, B., Call, J., Agnetta, B., and Tomasello, M. (2000). Chimpanzees know what conspecifics do and do not see. *Animal Behaviour*, 59, 771–785.

Hare, B., Call, J., and Tomasello, M. (2001). Do chimpanzees know what conspecifics know? *Animal Behaviour*, 61, 139–151.

Hare, B. and Tomasello, M. (2004). Chimpanzees are more skilled in competitive than in cooperative cognitive tasks. *Animal Behaviour*, 68, 571–581.

Hauser, M. D. (1996). *The Evolution of Communication*. Cambridge, MA: MIT Press.

   (2000). *Wild Minds*. New York: Holt.

Hauser, M. D., Chomsky, N., and Fitch, W. (2002). The faculty of language: What is it, who has it, and how did it evolve? *Science*, 298, 1569–1579.

Herman, L. (2002). Exploring the cognitive world of the bottlenosed dolphin. In M. Bekoff, C. Allen, and G. Burghardt (eds.), *The Cognitive Animal*. Cambridge, MA: MIT Press.

Heyes, C. M. (1998). Theory of mind in nonhuman primates. *Behavioral and Brain Sciences*, 21, 101–134.

Horgan, T. and Tienson, J. (1996). *Connectionism and the Philosophy of Psychology*. Cambridge, MA: MIT Press.

Hume, D. (1739/1978). *A Treatise of Human Nature*, ed. P. H. Nidditch. Oxford: Oxford University Press.

Hurley, S. (2003). Animal action in the space of reasons. *Mind & Language*, 18, 231–315.

Hurley, S. and Nudds, M. (2006). *Rational Animals?* Oxford: Oxford University Press.

Hyatt, C. W. and Hopkins, W. D. (1994). Self-awareness in bonobos and Chimpanzees: a comparative approach. In S. Parker, R. Mitchell, and M. Boccia (eds.), *Self-Awareness in Animals and Humans*. Cambridge: Cambridge University Press.

Inman, A. and Shettleworth, S. J. (1999). Detecting metamemory in nonverbal subjects: a test with pigeons. *Journal of Experimental Psychology: Animal Behavioral Processes*, 25, 389–395.

Jackson, R. and Li, D. (2004). One-encounter search-image formation by araneophagic spiders. *Animal Cognition*, 7, 247–254.

Jacob, P. and Jeannerod, M. (2003). *Ways of Seeing: The Scope and Limits of Visual Cognition*. Oxford: Oxford University Press.

Jamieson, D. (2002). *Morality's Progress*. Oxford: Clarendon Press.

Jamieson, D. and Bekoff, M. (1993). On aims and methods of cognitive ethology. *Philosophy of Science Association*, 2, 110–124.

Jeffrey, R. (1985). Animal interpretation. In E. Lepore and B. McLaughlin (eds.), *Actions and Events: Perspectives on the Philosophy of Donald Davidson*. New York: Basil Blackwell.

Jensen, K., Hare, B., Call, J., and Tomasello, M. (2006). What's in it for me? Self-regard precludes altruism and spite in chimpanzees. *Proceedings of the Royal Society B*, 273, 1013–1021.

Johnson, K. (2004). On the systematicity of language and thought. *The Journal of Philosophy*, 101, 111–139.

Johnson-Laird, P. (1983). *Mental Models*. Cambridge: Cambridge University Press.

Jolly, A. (1999). *Lucy's Legacy*. Cambridge, MA: Harvard University Press.

Kahneman, D. (2002). Maps of bounded rationality: a perspective on intuitive judgment and choice. Nobel laureate acceptance speech, http://nobelprize.org/economics/laureates/2002/kahneman-lecture.html.

Kaye, L. (1995). The languages of thought. *Philosophy of Science*, 65, 92–110.

Kennedy, J. (1992). *The New Anthropomorphism*. Cambridge: Cambridge University Press.

Kinsbourne, M. (2005). A continuum of self-consciousness that emerges in phylogeny and ontogeny. In H. Terrace and J. Metcalfe (eds.), *The Missing Link in Cognition: Origins of Self-Reflective Consciousness*. Oxford: Oxford University Press.

Kitchin, R. (1994). Cognitive maps: what are they and why study them? *Journal of Environmental Psychology*, 14, 1–19.

Knill, D. and Richards, W. (1996). *Perception as Bayesian Inference*. Cambridge: Cambridge University Press.

Koriat, A. (2000). The feeling of knowing: some metatheoretical implications for consciousness and control. *Consciousness and Cognition*, 9, 149–171.

(2007). Metacognition and consciousness. In P. Zelazo, M. Moscovitch, and E. Thomson (eds.), *The Cambridge Handbook of Consciousness*. Cambridge: Cambridge University Press.

Koriat, A., Ma'ayan, H., and Nussinson, R. (2006). The intricate relationships between monitoring and control in metacognition: lessons for the cause-and-effect relation between subjective experience and behavior. *Journal of Experimental Psychology: General*, 135, 36–69.

Kornell, N., Son, L., and Terrace, H. (2007). Transfer of metacognitive skills and hint seeking in monkeys. *Psychological Science*, 18, 64–71.

Kort, S. de, Dickinson, A., and Clayton, N. (2005). Retrospective cognition by food-caching western scrub-jays. *Learning and Motivation*, 35, 159–176.

Kosslyn, S. M., Thompson, W. L., and Ganis, G. (2006). *The Case for Mental Imagery*. Oxford: Oxford University Press.

Krebs, J. R. and Dawkins, R. (1984). Animal signals: mind reading and manip-ulation. In J. R. Krebs and N. B. Davies (eds.), *Behavioural Ecology: An Evolutionary Approach*. Oxford: Blackwell Scientific Publications.

Kripke, S. (1982). *Wittgenstein on Rules and Private Language*. Cambridge, MA: Harvard University Press.

Kummer, H. (1982). Social knowledge in free-ranging primates. In D. Griffin (ed.), *Animal Mind – Human Mind*. Berlin: Springer-Verlag.

Laurence, S. and Margolis, E. (2001). The poverty of the stimulus argument. *British Journal for the Philosophy of Science*, 52, 217–276.

(2007). The ontology of concepts: abstract objects or mental representations? *Noûs*, 41, 561–593.

Lemon, O. and Pratt, I. (1998). On the insufficiency of linear diagrams for syllo-gisms. *Notre Dame Journal of Formal Logic*, 39, 573–580.

Levin, D. T. (2004). *Thinking and Seeing: Visual Metacognition in Adults and Children*. Cambridge, MA: MIT Press.

Liebenberg, L. (1990). *The Art of Tracking: The Origin of Science*. Cape Town: David Philip.

Lindauer, M. (1957). Sonnenorientierung der Bienen unter der Aequatorsonne und zur Nachtzeit. *Naturwissenschaften*, 44, 1–6.

(1960). Time-compensated sun orientation in bees. *Cold Spring Harbor Symposia on Quantitative Biology*, 25, 371–377.

Loewer, B. (1987). From information to intentionality. *Synthese*, 70, 287–317.

Lurz, R. (2002). Neither HOT nor COLD: An alternative account of consciousness. *Psyche*, 9, http://psyche.cs.monash.edu.au/v9/psyche-9-01-lurz.html.

(2004). Either FOR or HOR: a false dichotomy. In R. C. Gennaro (ed.), *Higher-Order Theories of Consciousness*. Amsterdam: John Benjamins.

(2006). Conscious beliefs and desires: a same-order approach. In U. Kriegel and K. Williford (eds.), *Self-Representational Approaches to Consciousness*. Cambridge, MA: MIT Press.

(2007). In defense of wordless thoughts about thoughts. *Mind & Language*, 22, 270–296.

(2008). Animal minds. *Internet Encyclopedia of Philosophy*, www.utm.edu/research/iep/.

(2009). If chimpanzees are mindreaders, could behavioral science tell? Toward a solution of the logical problem. *Philosophical Psychology*, 22, 305–328.

Lycan, W. G. (1996). *Consciousness and Experience*. Cambridge, MA: MIT Press.

(2001). A simple argument for a higher-order representation theory of consciousness. *Analysis*, 61, 3–4.

Malcolm, N. (1972). Thoughtless brutes. *Proceedings and Addresses of the American Philosophical Association*, 46, 5–20.

Mann, J., Connor, R., Tyack, P., and Whitehead, H. (2000). *Cetacean Societies*. Chicago: University of Chicago Press.

Marcus, G. (2001). *The Algebraic Mind: Integrating Connectionism and Cognitive Science*. Cambridge, MA: MIT Press.

Marler, P. (1989). Learning by instinct: birdsong. *American Speech-Language-Hearing Association* (AHSA), 31, 75–79.

(1992). Functions of arousal and emotion in primate communication: a semiotic approach. In T. Nishida, W. C. McGrew, P. Marler, M. Pickford, and F. B. de Waal (eds.), *Topics in Primatology*, Vol. 1: *Human Origins*. Tokyo: University of Tokyo Press.

Matsuzawa, T. (1994). Field experiments on use of stone tools by chimpanzees in the wild. In R. Wrangham, W. C. McGrew, F. B. M. de Waal, and P. Heltne (eds.), *Chimpanzee Cultures*. Cambridge, MA: Harvard University Press.

Matsuzawa, T. and Yamakoshi, G. (1996). Comparison of chimpanzee material culture between Bossou and Nimba, West Africa. In A. Russon, K. Bard, and S. Parker (eds.), *Reaching into Thought*. Cambridge: Cambridge University Press.

McDowell, J. (1996). *Mind and World*, 2nd edn. Cambridge, MA: Harvard University Press.

McGrew, W. C. (1992). *Chimpanzee Material Culture*. Cambridge: Cambridge University Press.

McLaughlin, B. (1998). Connectionism. In E. Craig (ed.), *Routledge Encyclopedia of Philosophy*. London: Routledge.

Melis, A., Call, J., and Tomasello, M. (2006). Chimpanzees (*Pan troglodytes*) conceal visual and auditory information from others. *Journal of Comparative Psychology*, 120, 154–162.

Menzel, C. (2005). Progress in the study of chimpanzee recall and episodic memory. In H. Terrace and J. Metcalfe (eds.), *The Missing Link in Cognition: Origins of Self-Reflective Consciousness*. Oxford: Oxford University Press.

Menzel, R., Brandt, R., Gumbert, A., Komischke, B., and Kunze, J. (2000). Two spatial memories for honeybee navigation. *Proceedings of the Royal Society: London B*, 267, 961–966.

Menzel, R., Geiger, K., Joerges, J., Müller, U., and Chittka, L. (1998). Bees travel novel homeward routes by integrating separately acquired vector memories. *Animal Behaviour*, 55, 139–152.

Menzel, R. and Giurfa, M. (2006). Dimensions of cognition in an insect, the honeybee. *Behavioral and Cognitive Neuroscience Reviews*, 5, 24–40.

Menzel, R., Greggers, U., Smith, A., Berger, S., Brandt, R., Brunke, S., Bundrock, G., Hülse, S., Plümpe, T., Schaupp, F., Schüttler, E., Stach, S., Stindt, J., Stollhoff, N., and Watzl, S. (2005). Honeybees navigate according to a map-like spatial memory. *Proceedings of the National Academy of Sciences USA*, 102, 3040–3045.

Mercado, E., Murray, R., Uyeyama, R., Pack, A., and Herman, L. (1998). Memory for recent actions in the bottlenosed dolphin (*Tursiops Truncates*): repetition of arbitrary behaviors using an abstract rule. *Animal Learning & Behavior*, 26, 210–218.

Metcalfe, J. and Shimamura, A. P. (1994). *Metacognition: Knowing about Knowing*. Cambridge, MA: MIT Press.

Miles, H. L. W. (1993). Language and the orang-utan: the old "person" of the forest. In P. Cavalieri and P. Singer (eds.), *The Great Ape Project*. New York: St. Martin's Press.

Millikan, R. G. (1984). *Language, Thought, and Other Biological Categories*. Cambridge, MA: MIT Press.

(1993). *White Queen Psychology and Other Essays for Alice*. Cambridge, MA: MIT Press.

(1995). Pushmi-Pullyu. *Philosophical Perspectives*, 9, 185–200.

Minsky, M. (1975). A framework for representing knowledge. In P. Winston (ed.), *The Psychology of Computer Vision*. New York: McGraw-Hill.

Mitchell, R. (1994). Multiplicities of Self. In S. T. Parker, R. Mitchell, and M. Bocca (eds.), *Self-Awareness in Animals and Humans*. Cambridge: Cambridge University Press.

Mithen, S. (1996). *The Prehistory of the Mind*. London: Thames and Hudson.

Morgan, C. Lloyd (1894). *An Introduction to Comparative Psychology*, 1st edn. London: Walter Scott.

(1903). *An Introduction to Comparative Psychology*, 2nd edn. London: Walter Scott.

Murphy, D. and Stich, S. (2000). Darwin in the madhouse: evolutionary psychology and the classification of mental disorders. In P. Carruthers and A. Chamberlain (eds.), *Evolution and the Human Mind*. Cambridge: Cambridge University Press.

Nagel, T. (1974). What is it like to be a bat? *Philosophical Review*, 83, 435–450.

Nebel, B. (1999). Frame-based systems. In R. A. Wilson and F. Keil (eds.), *MIT Encyclopedia of the Cognitive Sciences*. Cambridge, MA: MIT Press.

Nelson, K. (2005). Emerging levels of consciousness in early human development. In H. Terrace and J. Metcalfe (eds.), *The Missing Link in Cognition: Origins of Self-Reflective Consciousness*. Oxford: Oxford University Press.

Nelson, T. O. and Narens, L. (1992). Metamemory: a theoretical framework and new findings. In T. O. Nelson (ed.), *Metacognition: Core Readings*. New York: Allyn & Bacon.

Neu, J. (2000). *A Tear is an Intellectual Thing*. Oxford: Oxford University Press.

Nichols, S. and Stich, S. (2003). *Mindreading*. Oxford: Oxford University Press.

Nisbett, R. and Wilson, T. (1977). Telling more than we can know. *Psychological Review*, 84, 231–295.

Norton, J. (2003). A material theory of induction. *Philosophy of Science*, 70, 647–670.

Nowak, M. A., Plotkin, J., and Jansen, V. (2000). The evolution of syntactic communication. *Nature*, 404, 495–498.

Nussbaum, M. (2001). *Upheavals of Thought: The Intelligence of Emotions*. Cambridge: Cambridge University Press.

O'Keefe, J. and Nadel, L. (1978). *The Hippocampus as a Cognitive Map*. Oxford: Clarendon Press.

Panksepp, J. and Burgdorf, J. (2003). "Laughing" rats and the evolutionary antecedents of human joy? *Physiology and Behavior*, 79, 533–547.

Parker, S. T. (1994). Incipient mirror self-recognition in zoo gorillas and chimpanzees. In S. T. Parker, R. Mitchell, and M. Boccia (eds.), *Self-Awareness in Animals and Humans*. Cambridge: Cambridge University Press.

Patterson, F. and Gordon, W. (1993). The case for the personhood of gorillas. In P. Cavalieri and P. Singer (eds.), *The Great Ape Project*. New York: St. Martin's Press.

Peacocke, C. (1992). *A Study of Concepts*. Cambridge, MA: MIT Press.

(1994). Content, computation and externalism. *Mind & Language*, 9, 303–335.

(1997). Concepts without words. In R. Heck (ed.), *Language, Thought, and Logic*. Oxford: Oxford University Press.

(2001). Phenomenology and nonconceptual content. *Philosophy and Phenomenological Research*, 62, 609–615.

Pearle, J. (2000). *Causality*. Cambridge: Cambridge University Press.

Penn, D., Holyoak, K., and Povinelli, D. (in press). Darwin's mistake: explaining the discontinuity between human and non-human minds. *Behavioral and Brain Sciences*, 31, 109–178.

Penn, D. and Povinelli, D. (2007a). Causal cognition in humans and non-human animals: a comparative, critical review. *Annual Review of Psychology*, 58, 97–118.

(2007b). On the lack of evidence that non-human animals possess anything remotely resembling a "theory of mind." *Philosophical Transactions of the Royal Society B*, 362, 731–744.

Phillips, H. (2006). Known unknowns. *New Scientist*, December 16, 28–31.

Pietroski, P. and Rey, G. (1995). When other things aren't equal: saving ceteris paribus. *British Journal for the Philosophy of Science*, 46, 81–110.

Pinker, S. and Bloom, P. (1990). Natural language and natural selection. *Behavioral and Brain Sciences*, 13, 707–784.

Plotnik, J., de Waal, F., and Reiss, D. (2006). Self-recognition in an Asian elephant. *Proceedings of the National Academy of Science*, 103, 17053–17057.

Plutarch (1957). *Moralia: De Solertia Animalium*, vol. XII, trans. H. Cherniss and W. Helmbold. Cambridge, MA: Harvard University Press.

Povinelli, D. (1996). Chimpanzee theory of mind? In P. Carruthers and P. Smith (eds.), *Theories of Theories of Mind*. Cambridge: Cambridge University Press.

(2000). *Folk Physics for Apes*. Oxford: Oxford University Press.

Povinelli, D. and Eddy, T. J. (1996). What young chimpanzees know about seeing. *Monographs of the Society for Research in Child Development*, 61, 1–152.

Povinelli, D. and Vonk, J. (2006). We don't need a microscope to explore the chimpanzee's mind. In S. Hurley and M. Nudds (eds.), *Rational Animals?* Oxford: Oxford University Press.

Pratt, I. (1993). Map semantics. In A. Frank and I. Campari (eds.), *Spatial Information Theory: A Theoretical Basis for GIS*. Berlin: Springer-Verlag.

Premack, D. and Premack, A. J. (1994). Levels of causal understanding in chimpanzees and children. *Cognition*, 50, 347–362.

Premack, D. and Woodruff, G. (1978). Does the chimpanzee have a theory of mind? *Behavioral and Brain Sciences*, 1, 515–526.

Proust, J. (1997). *Comment l'Esprit Vient aux Bêtes, Essai sur la Représentation*. Paris: Gallimard.

(1999). Mind, space and objectivity in nonhuman animals. *Erkenntnis*, 51, 41–58.

(2006). Rationality and metacognition in nonhuman animals. In S. Hurley and M. Nudds (eds.), *Rational Animals?* Oxford: Oxford University Press.

(2007). Metacognition and metarepresentation: is a self-directed theory of mind a precondition for metacognition? *Synthese*, 2, 271–295.

(2009). What is a mental function? In A. Brenner and J. Gayon (eds.), *French Philosophy of Science*. Boston: Springer.

Putnam, H. (1992). *Renewing Philosophy*. Cambridge, MA: Harvard University Press.

Pylyshyn, Z. (1973). What the mind's eye tells the mind's brain: a critique of mental imagery. *Psychological Bulletin*, 80, 1–24.

(1981). The imagery debate: analogue media versus tacit knowledge. *Psychological Review*, 88, 16–45.

(1986). *Computation and Cognition*. Cambridge, MA: MIT Press.

(2003). *Seeing and Visualizing*. Cambridge, MA: MIT Press.

(2004). *Seeing and Visualizing: It's Not What You Think*. Cambridge, MA: MIT Press.

Quine, W. V. O. (1960). *Word and Object*. Cambridge, MA: MIT Press.

Raby, C., Alexis, D., Dickenson, A., and Clayton, N. (2007). Planning for the future by western scrub-jays. *Nature*, 445, 919–921.

Radick, G. (2007). *The Simian Tongue: The Long Debate on Animal Language*. Chicago: The University of Chicago Press.

Reiss, D. and Marino, L. (2001). Mirror self-recognition in the bottlenose dolphin: a case of cognitive convergence. *Proceedings of the National Academy of Sciences*, 98, 5937–5942.

Rendall, D. and Owren, M. J. (2002). Animal vocal communication: say what? In M. Bekoff, C. Allen, and G. M. Burghardt (eds.), *The Cognitive Animal:*

Empirical and Theoretical Perspectives on Animal Cognition. Cambridge, MA:
MIT Press.

Rescorla, M. (in press a). Cognitive maps and the language of thought. *British
Journal for the Philosophy of Science.*

(in press b). Predication and cartographic representation. *Synthese.*

Rescorla, R. A. and Wagner, A. R. (1972). A theory of pavlovian conditioning:
variations in the effectiveness of reinforcement and nonreinforcement. In
A. H. Black and W. F. Prokasy (eds.), *Classical Conditioning II.* New York:
Appleton-Century-Crofts.

Rey, G. (1981). What are mental images? In N. Block (ed.), *Readings in the
Philosophy of Psychology*, Vol. II. Cambridge, MA: Harvard University Press.

(1995). A not "merely empirical" argument for a language of thought. *Philosophical Perspectives*, 9, 201–222.

(2002). Physicalism and psychology: a plea for substantive philosophy of mind.
In C. Gillet and B. Loewer (eds.), *Physicalism and Its Discontents.* Cambridge:
Cambridge University Press.

(2007). Resisting normativism in psychology. In J. Cohen and B. McLaughlin
(eds.), *Blackwell Debates in Philosophy of Mind.* Oxford: Blackwell.

(2008). Externalism and inexistence in early content. In R. Schantz (ed.),
Prospects for Meaning. New York: Walter De Gruyter.

Reynolds, A. M., Smith, A. D., Reynolds, D. R., Carreck, N. L., and Osborne,
J. L. (2007). Honeybees perform optimal scale-free searching flights when
attempting to locate a food source. *The Journal of Experimental Biology*, 210,
3763–3770.

Ridge, M. (2001). Taking solipsism seriously: nonhuman animals and metacognitive theories of consciousness. *Philosophical Studies*, 103, 315–340.

Riley, J. R., Greggers, U., Smith, A. D., Reynolds, D. R., and Menzel, R. (2005).
The flight paths of honeybees recruited by the waggle dance. *Nature*, 435,
205–207.

Riley, J. R., Greggers, U., Smith, A. D., Stach, S., Reynolds, D. R., Stollhoff,
N., Brandt, R., Schaupp, F., and Menzel, R. (2003). The automatic pilot of
honeybees. *Proceedings of the Royal Society of London B*, 270, 2421–2424.

Ristau, C. (1996). Aspects of the cognitive ethology of an injury-feigning bird,
the piping plover. In M. Bekoff and D. Jamieson (eds.), *Readings in Animal
Cognition.* Cambridge, MA: MIT Press.

Roberts, R. (1988). What an emotion is: a sketch. *The Philosophical Review*, 97,
183–209.

(1996). Propositions and animal emotion. *Philosophy*, 71, 147–156.

(2003). *Emotions: An Essay in Aid of Moral Psychology.* Cambridge: Cambridge
University Press.

(2009a). Emotions and the canons of evaluation. In P. Goldie (ed.), *The Oxford
Handbook of the Philosophy of Emotion.* Oxford: Oxford University Press.

(2009b). Emotional consciousness and personal relationships. *Emotion Review.*

Roberts, W. (2002). Are animals stuck in time? *Psychological Bulletin*, 128, 473–
489.

Rosenthal, D. (1986). Two concepts of consciousness. *Philosophical Studies*, 49, 329–359.

(2005). *Consciousness and Mind*. Oxford: Oxford University Press.

Ross, J. and McKinney, B. (1995). *Dog Talk: Training Your Dog Through a Canine Point of View*. New York: St. Martin's Press.

Rowell, T. E. and Hinde, R. A. (1962). Vocal communication by the rhesus monkey (*Macaca mulatta*). *Proceedings of the Zoological Society of London*, 138, 279–294.

Russell, B. (1919). *Introduction to Mathematical Philosophy*. New York: The Macmillan Company.

Russon, A. and Galdikas, B. (1993). Imitation in free-ranging rehabilitant orangutans (*Pongo Pygmaeus*). *Journal of Comparative Psychology*, 107, 147–161.

Saidel, E. (1998). Beliefs, desires, and the ability to learn. *American Philosophical Quarterly*, 35, 21–37.

Santos, L., Nissen, A., and Ferrugia, J. (2006). Rhesus monkeys, *macaca mulatta*, know what others can and cannot hear. *Animal Behaviour*, 71, 1175–1181.

Savage-Rumbaugh, S., Toth, N., and Schick, K. (2006). Kanzi learns to knapp stone tools. In D. Washburn and D. Rumbaugh (eds.), *Primate Perspectives on Behavior and Cognition*. Washington, DC: American Psychological Association.

Schwartz, B. L. (2005). Do nonhuman primates have episodic memory? In H. Terrace and J. Metcalfe (eds.), *The Missing Link in Cognition: Origins of Self-Reflective Consciousness*. Oxford: Oxford University Press.

Schwartz, B. L., Hoffman, M., and Evans, S. (2005). Episodic-like memory in a gorilla: a review and new findings. *Learning and Motivation*, 36, 226–244.

Schwartz, B. L., Travis, D. M., Castro, A. M., and Smith, S. M. (2000). The phenomenology of real and illusory tip-of-the-tongue states. *Memory and Cognition*, 28, 18–27.

Seager, W. (2004). A cold look at HOT theory. In R. Gennaro (ed.), *Higher-Order Theories of Consciousness*. Amsterdam: John Benjamins.

Searle, J. (1983). *Intentionality*. Cambridge: Cambridge University Press.

(1994). Animal minds. *Midwest Studies in Philosophy*, 19, 206–219.

Sellars, W. (1963). Science, Perception, and Reality. London: Routledge & Kegan Paul.

Seyfarth, R. M. and Cheney, D. L. (2002). The structure of social knowledge in monkeys. In M. Bekoff, C. Allen, and G. Burghardt (eds.), *The Cognitive Animal*. Cambridge, MA: MIT Press.

(2003). Meaning and emotion in animal vocalizations. *Annals of the New York Academy of Sciences*, 1000, 32–55.

Seyfarth, R. M., Cheney, D. L., and Marler, P. (1980). Vervet monkey alarm calls: semantic communication in a free-ranging primate. *Animal Behaviour*, 28, 1070–1094.

Shin, Sun-Joo (1994). *The Logical Status of Diagrams*. Cambridge: Cambridge University Press.

Silk, J., Brosnan, S., Vonk, J., Henrich, J., Povinelli, D., Richardson, A., Lambeth, S., Mascaro, J., and Schapiro, S. (2005). Chimpanzees are indifferent to the welfare of unrelated group members. *Nature*, 437, 1357–1359.

Simmonds, M. (2006). Into the brains of whales. *Applied Animal Behavior Science*, 100, 103–116.

Skyrms, Brian (2004). *The Stag Hunt and the Evolution of Social Structure*. Cambridge: Cambridge University Press.

Slobodchikoff, C. N. (2002). Cognition and communication in prairie dogs. In M. Bekoff, C. Allen, and G. M. Burghardt (eds.), *The Cognitive Animal*. Cambridge, MA: MIT Press.

Slobodchikoff, C. N., Fischer, C., and Shapiro, J. (1986). Predator-specific alarm calls of prairie dogs. *American Zoologist*, 26, 557.

Slobodchikoff, C. N., Kiriazis, J., Fischer, C., and Creef, E. (1991). Semantic information distinguishing individual predators in the alarm calls of Gunnison's prairie dogs. *Animal Behaviour*, 42, 713–719.

Sloman, A. (1978). *The Computer Revolution in Philosophy*. Hassocks: The Harvester Press.

Sloman, S. (1996). The empirical case for two systems of reasoning. *Psychological Bulletin*, 119, 3–22.

    (2002). Two systems of reasoning. In T. Gilovich, D. Griffin, and D. Kahneman (eds.), *Heuristics and Biases*. Cambridge: Cambridge University Press.

Smith, B. C. (1996). *On the Origin of Objects*. Cambridge, MA: MIT Press.

Smith, J. D. (2005). Studies of uncertainty monitoring and metacognition in animals. In H. Terrace and J. Metcalfe (eds.), *The Missing Link in Cognition: Origins of Self-Reflective Consciousness*. New York: Oxford University Press.

Smith, J. D., Beran, M. J., Redford, J. S., and Washburn, D. A. (2006). Dissociating uncertainty responses and reinforcement signals in the comparative study of uncertainty monitoring. *Journal of Experimental Psychology: General*, 135, 282–297.

Smith, J. D. and Schull, J. (1989). A failure of uncertainty monitoring in the rat (unpublished raw data). Cited in Shields, W., Smith, J. D., Guttmannova, K., and Washburn, D. (2005). Confidence judgments by humans and rhesus monkeys. *Journal of General Psychology*, 13, 165–186.

Smith, J. D., Shields, W. E., Allendoerfer, K. R., and Washburn, D. A. (1998). Memory monitoring by animals and humans. *Journal of Experimental Psychology: General*, 127, 227–250.

Smith, J. D., Shields, W. E., and Washburn, D. A. (2003). The comparative psychology of uncertainty monitoring and metacognition. *Behavioral and Brain Sciences*, 26, 317–373.

Smith, J. D. and Washburn, D. (2005). Uncertainty monitoring and metacognition by animals. *Current Directions in Psychological Science*, 14, 19–24.

Smolensky, P. (1991). Connectionism, constituency and the language of thought. In B. Loewer and G. Rey (eds.), *Meaning in Mind: Fodor and His Critics*. Oxford: Blackwell.

(1995). Reply: constituent structure and explanation in an integrated connectionist/symbolic cognitive architecture. In C. MacDonald and G. MacDonald (eds.), *Connectionism: Debates on Psychological Explanation*. Oxford: Blackwell.

Sober, E. (1984). *The Nature of Selection*. Cambridge, MA: MIT Press.

(1988). *Reconstructing the Past: Parsimony, Evolution, and Inference*. Cambridge, MA: MIT Press.

(1990). Let's razor Ockham's razor. In D. Knowles (ed.), *Explanation and Its Limits*. Cambridge: Cambridge University Press.

(1998a). Black box inference: when should an intervening variable be postulated? *British Journal for the Philosophy of Science*, 49, 469–498.

(1998b). Morgan's canon. In C. Allen and D. Cummins (eds.), *The Evolution of Mind*. Oxford: Oxford University Press.

(2000). Evolution and the problem of other minds. *Journal of Philosophy*, 97, 365–386.

(2001). The principle of conservatism in cognitive ethology. In D. Walsh (ed.), *Naturalism, Evolution, and Mind*. Cambridge: Cambridge University Press.

(2005). Comparative psychology meets evolutionary biology: Morgan's canon and cladistic parsimony. In L. Daston and G. Mitman (eds.), *Thinking with Animals: New Perspectives on Anthropomorphism*. New York: Columbia University Press.

(2008). *Evidence and Evolution: The Logic Behind the Science*. Cambridge: Cambridge University Press.

Sober, E. and Wilson, D. (1998). *Unto Others: The Evolution and Psychology of Unselfish Behavior*. Cambridge, MA: Harvard University Press.

Solomon, R. (1995). *A Passion for Justice*. Lanham, MD: Rowman and Littlefield.

(2003). *Not Passion's Slave*. Oxford: Oxford University Press.

Son, L. K. and Kornell, N. (2005). Metaconfidence in rhesus macaques: explicit versus implicit mechanisms. In H. S. Terrace and J. Metcalfe (eds.), *The Missing Link in Cognition: Origins of Self-Reflective Consciousness*. Oxford: Oxford University Press.

Sorabji, R. (1993). *Animal Minds and Human Morals*. Ithaca: Cornell University Press.

Stalnaker, R. (1984). *Inquiry*. Cambridge, MA: MIT Press.

(1999). *Context and Content*. Oxford: Oxford University Press.

Stanford, C. (2001). *Significant Others: The Ape-Human Continuum and the Quest for Human Nature*. New York: Basic Books.

Stanovich, K. (1999). *Who is Rational? Studies of Individual Differences in Reasoning*. Hillsdale, NJ: Lawrence Erlbaum.

Stich, S. (1979). Do animals have beliefs? *Australasian Journal of Philosophy*, 57, 15–28.

(1983/1989). *From Folk Psychology to Cognitive Science: The Case Against Belief*. Cambridge, MA: MIT Press.

Stoerig, P. (1996). Varieties of vision: from blind responses to conscious recognition. *Trends in Neurosciences*, 19, 401–406.

Strawson, P. F. (1959). *Individuals*. London: Methuen.

Struhsaker, T. T. (1967). Auditory communication among vervet monkeys (*Cercopithecus aethiops*). In S. A. Altman (ed.), *Social Communication among Primates*. Chicago: University of Chicago Press.

Tautz, J., Zhang, S., Spaethe, J., Brockmann, A., Si, A., and Srinivasan, M. (2004). Honeybee odometry: performance in varying natural terrain. *Public Library of Science: Biology*, 2, 915–923.

Terrace, H. S. and Metcalfe, J. (2005). *The Missing Link in Cognition: Origins of Self-Reflective Consciousness*. Oxford: Oxford University Press.

Tetzlaff, M. J. (2006). *Bee-ing There: The Systematicity of Honeybee Navigation Supports a Classical Theory of Honeybee Cognition. Dissertation Abstracts International*, 67, no. 03A.

Thrun, S., Burgard, W., and Fox, D. (2005). *Probabilistic Robotics*. Cambridge, MA: MIT Press.

Tinkelpaugh, O. (1928). An experimental study of representative factors in monkeys. *Journal of Comparative Psychology*, 8, 197–238.

Tolman, E. (1948). Cognitive maps in rats and men. *Psychological Review*, 55, 189–208.

Tolstoy, L. (2007). *War and Peace*, trans. R. Pevear and L. Volokhonsky. New York: Knopf.

Tomasello, M. and Call, J. (1997). *Primate Cognition*. Oxford: Oxford University Press.

  (2006). Do chimpanzees know what others see – or only what they are looking at? In S. Hurley and M. Nudds (eds.), *Rational Animals?* Oxford: Oxford University Press.

Tomasello, M., Call, J., and Hare, B. (2003). Chimpanzees understand psychological states – the question is which ones and to what extent. *Trends in Cognitive Science*, 7, 153–156.

Toribio, J. (2007). Nonconceptual content. *Philosophy Compass*, 2, 445–460.

Travis, C. (1994). On constraints of generality. *Proceedings of the Aristotelian Society*, 94, 165–188.

Tschudin, A. (2001). "Mind-reading" mammals: attribution of belief tasks with dolphins. *Animal Welfare*, 10, S, 119–127.

Tulving, E. (1983). *Elements of Episodic Memory*. Oxford: Oxford University Press.

  (2005). Episodic memory and autonoesis: uniquely human? In H. S. Terrace and J. Metcalfe (eds.), *The Missing Link in Cognition: Origins of Self-Reflective Consciousness*. Oxford: Oxford University Press.

Turing, A. (1950). Computing machinery and intelligence. *Mind*, 59, 433–460.

Tye, M. (1997). The problem of simple minds: is there anything it is like to be a honey bee? *Philosophical Studies*, 88, 289–317.

  (2006). The thesis of nonconceptual content. *European Review of Philosophy: The Structure of Nonconceptual Content*, 6, 7–30.

Waal, F. de (1991). Complimentary methods and convergent evidence in the study of primate social cognition. *Behavior*, 118, 297–320.

(2004). Brains and the beast. *Natural History*, 113, 53–56.

(2005). *Our Inner Ape*. New York: Riverhead Books.

Wei, C. A., Rafalko, S. L., and Dyer, F. C. (2002). Deciding to learn: modulation of learning flights in honeybees, *Apis mellifera*. *Journal of Comparative Physiology A*, 188, 725–737.

White, T. (2007). *In Defense of Dolphins*. Oxford: Blackwell.

Whiten, A. (1996). When does smart behavior-reading become mind-reading? In P. Carruthers and P. Smith (eds.), *Theories of Theories of Mind*. Cambridge: Cambridge University Press.

Whiten, A. and Byrne, R. (1997). *Machiavellian Intelligence II: Extensions and Evaluations*. Cambridge: Cambridge University Press.

Whiten, A. and Ham, R. (1992). On the nature and evolution of imitation in the animal kingdom: reappraisal of a century of research. In P. Slater, J. Rosenblatt, C. Beer, and M. Milinski (eds.), *Advances in the Study of Behavior*, Vol. XXI. New York: Academic Press.

Wilson, B., Batty, R., and Dill, L. M. (2004). Pacific and Atlantic herring produce burst pulse sounds. *Proceedings of the Royal Society of London Series B – Biological Sciences*, 271, S95–S97.

Wilson, M. (1995). Animal ideas. *Proceedings and Addresses of the American Philosophical Association*, 69, 7–25.

Wimsatt, W. C. (1986). Developmental constraints, generative entrenchment, and the innate-acquired distinction. In W. Bechtel (ed.), *Integrating Scientific Disciplines*. Dordrecht: Martinus Nijhoff.

Wolpert, D. M. and Kawato, M. (1998). Multiple paired forward and inverse models for motor control. *Neural Networks*, 11, 1317–1329.

Wood, J., Glynn, D., Phillips, B., and Hauser, M. (2007). The perception of rational, goal-directed action in nonhuman primates. *Science*, 317, 1402–1405.

Wynne, C. D. L. (2004). *Do Animals Think?* Princeton, NJ: Princeton University Press.

Zentall, T. (2005). Animals may not be stuck in time. *Learning and Motivation*, 36, 208–225.

Zhang, S., Schwarz, S., Pahl, M., Zhu, H., and Tautz, J. (2006). Honeybee memory: a honeybee knows what to do and when. *The Journal of Experimental Biology*, 209, 4420–4428.

Zimmer, C. (2007). Time in the animal mind. *The New York Times*, April 3, F1, F6.

Zuberbühler, K. (2000). Referential labeling in Diana monkeys. *Animal Behaviour*, 59, 917–927.

Index

Printed in Great Britain
by Amazon.co.uk, Ltd.,
Marston Gate.